Christian Theology

Christian Theology

Copyright © 2014 by Apprehending Truth.
All Rights Reserved.

ISBN-13: 978-0615985800
ISBN-10: 0615985807

Cover Design by PureLight Graphics

Apprehending Truth Publishers
PO Box 249
Brookfield, Missouri 64628

Heritage of Truth Books
is an imprint of
Apprehending Truth Publishers
http://www.ATPublishers.com

AT 10 9 8 7 6 5 4 3 2 1
030814

Christian Theology

By

Adam Clarke

This edition of
Christian Theology by Adam Clarke is

A Heritage of Truth Book
Reclaiming the Wisdom of the Past

Apprehending Truth Publishers
Brookfield, Missouri

ADAM CLARKE LL D F A S

CHRISTIAN THEOLOGY:

BY

ADAM CLARKE, LL.D., F.A.S

SELECTED

FROM HIS PUBLISHED AND UNPUBLISHED WRITINGS, AND SYSTEMATICALLY ARRANGED:

WITH A LIFE OF THE AUTHOR.

BY SAMUEL DUNN.

SECOND EDITION.

THAT man is not the best Theologian who is the greatest disputant, but he who exhibits an exemplary life himself, and who teaches others to be exemplary in their lives. In things necessary to salvation, let every man become his own Theologian. – J. A. TURRETINE.

Heritage of Truth
2014

Foreword

What is needed now more than ever is a vibrant rebirth of pure Christian doctrine. The warnings and admonitions of 2 Timothy, chapter 3 have never been more appropriate than for today. These perilous times find us in the throes of dangerous doctrines perpetrated by the antinomian hordes of darkness who have redefined Christianity into a blasphemous and irreconcilable caricature. From the very texts of Scripture we can see that this assault on pure doctrine was ongoing from the very inception of the Church. Like the Apostle Paul, many men down the centuries, including John Wesley and Adam Clarke have endeavored to recapture and establish the essence of pure Biblical Doctrine. Because of the warnings of faithful men, false teachings and incessant misrepresentations that result in damnation have been and are being exposed.

Few in this hour recognize sound doctrine, fewer seek it, and yet even fewer appreciate it when it is presented. As Josiah embraced the book of the law found in the temple, the church must re-evaluate orthodoxy of our day and examine our ideas and ideologies with the sound teachings and wisdom of our forebears filtered through the purity of Scripture. That is the purpose of Heritage of Truth Books; to reclaim the wisdom of the past.

When the effects of Judeo-Christian ethics were more pronounced, indeed were even evident at all, Christians were more diligent to pursue the Truth, more compelled to reprove the works of darkness. As L. E. Maxwell once stated, "The Church never had more influence over the world as when it had nothing to do with the world." But now, instead of sound doctrine, the professing church is teaching tolerance; tolerance of everything except sound doctrine. Biblical Truth has become heresy, while the heresies of Calvinism, Gnosticism, & Marcionism have been, nearly universally, at some degree or other, accepted as orthodox.

Error and heresy intensify the death grip on the throat of the true Church, hoping to silence it forever. Sound judgment is turned away and the Biblical justice of God seems to stand continually farther off. Hence the voice of the world becomes more dominate, and the truths of yesteryear which were clearly understood are left, fallen in the streets, to blow away with the gloating winds of compromise and apathy. And woe unto them, for the promises of God are sure.

> *These things hast thou done, and I kept silence; thou thoughtest that I was altogether such an one as thyself: but I will reprove thee, and set them in order before thine eyes. Now consider this, ye that forget God, lest I tear you in pieces, and there be none to deliver. (Psalms 50:21-22)*

If the Remnant is to distinguish itself from the marred image of what Christianity has become, we must reclaim that which has been maligned and boldly pronounce with the Apostle Paul, "But this I confess unto thee, that after the way which they call heresy, so worship I the God of my fathers, believing all things which are written in the law and in the prophets."

-- JL Wallace
Brookfield, MO
March, 2014

This edition of CHRISTIAN THEOLOGY by Dr. Adam Clarke has been meticulously recreated from the 1835 edition, edited and compiled by Samuel Dunn. The entire work has been re-typeset and formatted by Heritage of Truth Books and Apprehending Truth Publishers. This is NOT a facsimile reproduction.

-- ed.

ADVERTISEMENT.

For some years before the lamented death of Dr. Clarke, he was repeatedly solicited to collect his rich and ample materials, and give to the world a Biblical Dictionary; and Theological Institutes, or a System of Christian Theology, in one or two portable and cheap volumes. He acknowledged that each of these was a great desideratum. He felt strongly inclined to prepare them, and even made a beginning. In one of his letters he writes:—"I have laid the foundation of a Biblical Dictionary." In another he says:—"I may possibly write some Institutes; but I shall put my Homer into a nutshell." On another occasion he observed: "If you were stationed in the south, and would assist me, I could do many things, but my eyes will not now bear any intense application." Such an appointment never took place; and before the worthy doctor had proceeded far, he was called hence. Had he accomplished his object, he would doubtless have produced a volume deserving a place in every Christian library. If it be inquired what induced me to attempt to supply his lack; I answer, my strong affection for the man; my high admiration of his writings; my deep conviction that such a volume would probably prove a blessing to many; and I may perhaps, in proof of the doctor's confidence and affection, be allowed to refer to the following passage in one of his letters, which to me is sufficiently affecting: "O that my strength were as in days that are past! While writing, it seems as if whispered to me, 'Your time is at hand—Samuel Dunn shall be your proxy in my work.' This is enough!" Though painfully conscious of great inability, I have "done what I could." Others will judge of the manner in which the part of selecting and systematizing has been executed.

That this manual will be found useful for the purpose of reference, to those individuals who possess the doctor's other works; and that those who possess them not will be induced, from this specimen, to procure them as soon as possible, is, perhaps, not an unreasonable expectation. The unrivalled Commentary, which is now in course of publication in an elegant and cheap form,—with "multitudinous emendations and corrections from the author's own and last hand,"—I should like to see in every family, from the Norman to the Shetland Isles.

While I indulge the hope that the short Life in this volume will be acceptable to many readers, I have great pleasure in stating that Mrs. Smith, of Stoke Newington, the amiable and accomplished "member of the family," to whom the public is so greatly indebted for the preservation of such valuable materials, is preparing a cheap edition of the life of her distinguished father.

TADCASTER,
April 9th, 1835.

SECOND EDITION.

Grateful for the favourable manner in which the FIRST edition of the "CHRISTIAN THEOLOGY" has been received by the public, I have endeavoured to render the SECOND more worthy of general approval, and of the great and good man from whose works it has been compiled.

SAMUEL DUNN

May 7 th, 1835

Contents

THE LIFE	1
I. THE SCRIPTURES	38
II. – GOD.	54
III. – ATTRIBUTES OF GOD.	58
IV. – THE TRINITY.	72
V. – MAN.	75
VI. – CHRIST.	96
VII. – REPENTANCE.	112
VIII. – FAITH.	119
IX. – JUSTIFICATION.	128
X. – REGENERATION.	137
XI. – THE HOLY SPIRIT.	140
XII. – ENTIRE SANCTIFICATION	171
XIII. – THE MORAL LAW.	197
XIV. – PUBLIC WORSHIP.	213
XV. – PRAYER.	217
XVI. – PRAISE.	229
XVII. – THE CHRISTIAN CHURCH.	236
XVIII. – BAPTISM.	240
XIX. – THE LORD'S SUPPER.	243
XX. – HUSBAND AND WIFE.	250
XXI. – PARENTS AND CHILDREN.	255
XXII. – MASTERS AND SERVANTS.	269
XXIII. – RULERS AND SUBJECTS.	271
XXIV. – RICH AND POOR.	275
XXV. – MINISTERS AND PEOPLE.	281
XXVI. – GOOD AND BAD ANGELS.	326
XXVII. – TEMPTATIONS.	334
XXVIII. – AFFLICTIONS	337
XXIX. – PROVIDENCE.	344
XXX. – APOSTASY.	348
XXXI. – DEATH.	355
XXXII. – JUDGMENT	359
XXXIII. – HELL.	361

XXXIV. – HEAVEN.	366
XXXV. – GENERAL PRINCIPLES.	370
XXXVI. – MISCELLANEOUS.	376
KNOWLEDGE	376
HAPPINESS.	381
COMMUNION OF SAINTS.	383
FASTING.	386
CONSCIENCE.	386
DANCING.	389
DRESS.	391
DREAMS.	393
GHOSTS.	393
TOBACCO.	394
WESLEY.	399
METHODISM.	400
IN PERPETUAM REI MEMORIAM.	400
SHETLAND.	403
SUNDAY-SCHOOLS.	410
SCHISM.	411
LUST OF POWER.	411
POLITICAL PARTY-SPIRIT.	412
FRIENDSHIP.	412
FLATTERY.	413
SELF-INTEREST.	413
GOING TO LAW.	413
SURETYSHIP.	414
USURY.	414
SLAVERY.	414
PARABLE.	415
MIRACLE.	415
MILLENNIUM.	415
TIME.	416
INDEX	**417**

THE LIFE

OF

ADAM CLARKE, LL.D., F.A.S.,

&c.

ADAM CLARKE, from whose voluminous writings the selections in this volume have been made, was born in the village of Moybeg, near Colerain, in the north of Ireland. He informed me, a short time before his death, that he had never been able to ascertain the year of his birth, his mother asserting that he was born in 1760, while his father contended that it was in 1763. Mr. John Clarke, Adam's father, was a person of very respectable literary attainments; he was educated with a view to the church, and studied successively at Edinburgh and Glasgow, where he took his degree of A.M., and afterward entered a sizar of Trinity College, Dublin, at a time when classical merit alone could gain such an admission. He was of English extraction, and Mrs. Clarke of Scottish. They had two sons and five daughters.

Adam was three years younger than his brother Tracy, and was by no means a spoiled child. He was always corrected when he deserved it, and was early inured to hardship. For this he was ever thankful, and used to say, "My heavenly Father saw that I was likely to meet with many rude blasts in journeying through life, and he prepared me in infancy for the lot his providence destined for me; so that, through his mercy, I have been enabled to carry a profitable childhood up to hoary hairs. He knew that I must walk *alone* through life, and therefore set me on my feet right early, that I might be prepared by long practice for the work I was appointed to perform." When about five years of age, he took the small pox in the natural way; but, though covered with pustules from head to foot, he was in the habit of stealing away from his *very warm* bed, whenever an opportunity presented itself, and running naked into the open air. By adopting this "cool regimen," he had a merciful termination of the disorder, and escaped without a single mark.

Mr. Clarke kept an English and classical school, and also held a small farm. This was cultivated by his sons, Adam and Tracy, one of whom attended to the farm, and the other at the school, alternately, during the day; and thus they shared between them the instruction which one boy in ordinary circumstances receives. They endeavoured to supply this defect by each, on leaving school, rehearsing to the other whatever he had on that day learned.

Adam was rather a dull boy, and was about eight years of age before he was capable of "putting vowels and consonants together." Having on one occasion failed again and again in his attempts to commit his task to memory, he threw down the book in despair; when the threats of his teacher, who told him he should be a beggar all his days, together with the jeers of the other scholars, roused him as from a lethargy: he felt as if something had broken within him; — his memory in a moment was all light. "What!" said he to himself, "shall I ever be a dunce, and the butt of these fellows' insults?" He resumed his book, conquered his task, speedily went up, and repeated it without missing a word, and proceeded with an ease he had never known before. He soon became passionately fond of reading. Into a wood near the school he oft retired, and there read the Eclogues and the Georgics of Virgil, with living illustrations of them before his eyes. He also amused himself with making hymns, and versifying the Psalms of David, and other portions of the sacred volume. He soon conquered the whole of the heathen mythology and biography. Of Littleton's Classical Dictionary he made himself complete master.

When but six years old, young Clarke was the subject of religious impressions. One day, as he and another little boy, with whom he was very intimate, sat upon a bank, they entered into conversation on the dreadful nature of eternal punishment. They were so affected with the thoughts that they wept bitterly; and prayed to God to forgive their sins, making mutual promises of amendment. Adam made known his feelings to his mother, and told her that he hoped in future to use no bad words, and always to obey his parents. She was deeply affected, and encouraged him and prayed for him. His parents were of different denominations; his father being a Churchman, while his mother was a Presbyterian, though not a Calvinist. To her he chiefly owed his early religions knowledge, and even his early religious impressions. It was her practice, especially on the Lord's day, to read to her children, catechize them, and to sing and pray with them.

On one occasion, Adam having disobeyed his mother, she immediately flew to the Bible and opened on Prov. xxx, 17, which she read and commented on in the most awful manner: "The eye that mocketh at his father, and despiseth to obey his mother, the ravens of the valley shall pick it out, and the young eagles shall eat it." He was cut to the heart, thinking the words were immediately sent from heaven! He went out into the field much distressed, and was musing on this terrible denunciation of the divine displeasure, when the hoarse croak of a raven sounded to his conscience an alarm more terrible than the cry of fire at midnight. He looked up, and soon perceived this most ominous bird; and actually supposing it to he the raven of which the text spoke, coming to pick out his eyes, he clapped his hands on them with the utmost speed and trepidation. and ran toward the house as fast as his state of salutary fright and perturbation would permit, that he might escape the impending vengeance!

He was sent by his parents to a singing school, where, after a while, he received instructions in dancing as well as music. Of this seductive art he soon became exceedingly fond; and says that he found it to be a perverting influence, an unmixed moral evil; and, to his death, on all proper occasions, he lifted up his voice against this branch of fashionable education.

In the year 1777, the Methodist preachers visited the parish in which the Clarke family resided. Adam went to hear them; and, under their preaching, especially under that of Mr. Thomas Barber, his mind became enlightened to see his danger, and he earnestly desired to flee from the wrath to come. His former evil courses were abandoned, his old companions forsaken, and he began to meet in class.

After a long night of sorrow, the day of deliverance drew near; and never shall I forget the feeling with which, about ten years ago, he related this part of his religious experience in a party of friends, among whom were several young persons not decidedly religious, for whose benefit, as he informed me afterward, he then entered so largely into the circumstances that attended his conversion. He described the field to which he went with a conscience heavily burdened with guilt, the spot on which he kneeled and wrestled with God in prayer till his strength was exhausted. The heavens appeared as brass; he found no access to the throne of grace. Concluding that there was no mercy for him, he at last rose in despair, intending "to cease the agonizing strife." On retiring from the place he heard, or thought he heard, a voice, which said to him, "Try Jesus!" He was not disobedient, but immediately went back to the same spot, there called upon Jesus, and his sorrow was instantly turned into joy. A glow of happiness seemed to thrill through his whole frame; all guilt and condemnation were gone. He examined his conscience, and found it no longer a register of sins against God. He looked to heaven, and all was sunshine. He searched for his distress, but could not find it. His heart was light, his physical strength and his animal spirits returned, and he could, more nimbly than ever, bound like a roe. He felt a sudden transition from darkness to light, from guilt and oppressive fear to confidence and peace. He could now draw nigh to God with more confidence than he ever could to his earthly father: he had freedom of access, and he had freedom of speech.

With this gladness of soul he also received great intellectual enlargement. He could prosecute his literary studies with much greater ease. He now learned more in one day than formerly he was able to do in one month. His mind became enlarged to take in any thing useful. He saw that religion was the gate to true learning and science; and soon began, in addition to his other pursuits, to apply himself to astronomy, natural philosophy, and the mathematics.

His parents at first designed him for the church, and afterward for the medical profession; but the narrowness of their pecuniary resources presented innumerable obstacles, which they were unable to surmount. It was then concluded that he should become a schoolmaster; but for this he had no inclination. He was at last sent to Mr. Francis Bennett, a linen merchant, of Colerain, a kinsman of his parents, who had proposed to take him on advantageous terms.

It should here be mentioned that the subject of this memoir, in his boyhood, had two very narrow escapes from sudden death: the one was a severe fall from a horse, when a sack of grain, which he had been unable to balance on the animal, came down with all its force upon him; and, his back happening to come in contact with a pointed stone, he was taken up apparently dead. In about four-and-twenty hours he was conveyed home, and in a short time completely restored. His second escape was from being drowned; he having imprudently, in riding for the purpose of washing his father's mare in an armlet of the sea, taken her out of her depth, till they were carried beyond the breakers into the swell, where they were both swamped in a moment. But that God whom "waves obey," and who designed him for matters of great and high importance, caused one wave after another to perform for him the genial service of rolling him to the shore before the vital spark was quite extinct.

The love of God was no sooner shed abroad in his heart, than he felt a yearning pity, a burning charity, for his friends and fellow creatures. He not only induced his parents to have family worship, on the morning and evening of every day in the week, as well as on the Sabbath, which they had been accustomed to have; but he also consented, though it was a heavy cross, regularly to officiate himself. He, however, had his reward: all his relatives became hearers of the Methodists, and most of them members of society. He then began to exhort his neighbours to turn to God. On the Sabbath he went regularly, in all weathers, a distance of more than six miles to meet a class, which assembled so early that, in the winter, he had to set out two hours before day. When he had met his class, he proceeded to the nearest village, and entering the first open door, said, "Peace be to this house!" If consent was given, he called in the neighbours, prayed, and gave a short exhortation. This done, he went to another village, and repeated the same plan; and so on through the day, without ever encountering a direct refusal. His youth and great seriousness made a favourable impression, which his prayers and exhortations tended to deepen. In this manner he not unfrequently visited nine or ten villages in one day.

After his removal to Colerain, he and his master went on for some time very comfortably, and Mr. Bennett was much pleased with him. To Mr. Henry Moore, who was personally acquainted with Mr. Bennett, we are indebted for the following information: "Mr. Bennett and young Clarke were one day engaged in measuring a piece of linen, preparatory to the great market in Dublin. They found *that* particular piece wanting some inches of a yard at the end. 'Come, Adam,' says Mr. Bennett, 'lay hold, and pull against me; and we shall soon make it come up to the yard.' But he little knew with whom he had to deal. Adam dropped the linen on the ground, and stood and looked like one benumbed. 'What's the matter?' said Mr. Bennett. 'Sir,' he replied, 'I can't do it: I think it is a wrong thing.' Mr. Bennett urged that it was done every day; that it would not make the linen any the worse; and that the process through which it had passed had made it shrink a little; and concluded by bidding him take hold! 'No,' says Adam, 'no!' Mr. Bennett was a very placid man, and they entered calmly into dispute. At last he was obliged to give it up; Adam would not consent to meddle with it; he thought it was not fair. It did not suit the standard of his conscience." He continued with Mr. Bennett about one year, without being bound an apprentice, and then parted with him in the most friendly manner.

Shortly after this, he received an invitation to visit Mr. Bredin, one of the preachers, then on the Londonderry side of the circuit. The day after his arrival Mr. Bredin desired him to preach, and take a text. This he had not yet attempted, and, being alive to its importance, objected; but his friend persisting strongly to urge him, he at length yielded, and preached his first sermon at New Buildings, a village five miles from Derry, June 19, 1782, from 1 John v. 19: "We know that we are of God, and the whole world lieth in wickedness." The generality of his hearers were so well pleased that they entreated him to preach to them the next morning at five. He consented, and during his short stay preached five times. Mr.

Bredin, believing that his young friend was called of God to the work of the ministry, wrote to Mr. Wesley concerning him, who immediately offered to take Adam into Kingswood School, near Bristol. When this proposal was communicated to his parents, they were quite indignant. His father would neither speak to him nor see him. His mother told him that, if he left them, he would go with her curse, and not her blessing. He had recourse to the throne of grace, and God heard him. His parents became convinced that he had other work to do, and granted him their permission to leave them. He sailed from Londonderry on the 17th of August, 1782; taking with him, as provision for the voyage, a loaf of bread and a pound of cheese, and reached Liverpool in two days. He travelled by coach to Bristol; and the next morning, August 25th, with only three halfpence in his pocket, walked to Kingswood.

The treatment he received while here, from the head master and his wife, was most unkind, and just the reverse of that which he had expected; but it lasted only one month and two days,—thirty-one days too much, if God had not been pleased to order it otherwise. Mr. Wesley, however, returned in a few weeks from Cornwall, and then sent for Adam. "I went into Bristol," says he, "saw Mr. Rankin, who carried me to Mr. Wesley's study, off the great lobby of the rooms over the chapel in Broadmead. He tapped at the door, which was opened by this truly apostolic man; Mr. Rankin retired. Mr. Wesley took me kindly by the hand, and asked me how long since I had left Ireland. Our conversation was short. He said, 'Well, brother Clarke, do you wish to devote yourself entirely to the work of God?' I answered, 'Sir, I wish to do and be what God pleases!' He then said, 'We want a preacher for Bradford; (Wilts.); hold yourself in readiness to go thither; I am going into the country, and will let you know when you shall go.' He then turned to me, laid his hands upon my head, and spent a few moments in praying to God to bless and preserve me, and to give me success in the work to which I was called."

Mr. Clarke entered on the regular work of a Methodist travelling preacher, on September 26th, 1782, having a tolerable acquaintance with the Scriptures and a heart full of zeal for the salvation of souls; and though he had the appearance of a "little boy," yet he was so prudent and deeply serious, that "no man despised his youth." Souls were awakened, and many young persons especially began earnestly to inquire the way of salvation. The circuit was very extensive, comprising no less than thirty-one towns and villages, and he had to preach and travel several miles every day, beside attending to various other duties; yet such was his thirst for learning, that he availed himself of every opportunity for cultivating his mind, by rising early, reading on horseback, and "never whiling away his time." But a circumstance took place about this period which had nearly proved ruinous to all his attainments in literature. In the preachers' room at Motcomb, near Shaftesbury, observing a Latin sentence on the wall, he wrote another from Virgil, corroborative of the first. One of his colleagues, Mr. J. A., subjoined, "Did you write the above to show us you could write Latin? For shame! Do send pride to hell, from whence it came. O young man! Improve your time! Eternity's at hand." This ridiculous effusion, probably the offspring of envy, had such an effect on the mind of Mr. Clarke, that in a moment of strong temptation he fell on his knees in the midst of the room, and solemnly promised to God that he would never more meddle with Greek or Latin as long as he lived! This hasty vow he observed for four years, when he bitterly repented of it, asked forgiveness of God, and recommenced the study of these languages.

During this year he read Mr. Wesley's "Letter on Tea," and resolved that he would drink neither tea nor coffee, till he could answer the arguments to his satisfaction. This resolution he kept to the end of his life.

At the following conference he was admitted into full connection, and then appointed to the Norwich circuit, which at that time extended over considerable portions of Norfolk and Suffolk. Religion was at an exceedingly low ebb; and scarcely a Sabbath passed without disturbances at the Methodist chapel. During a remarkably severe winter he endured many hardships, often sleeping in lofts and outhouses, and being obliged to subsist on very scanty fare.

From Norwich he went in the year 1784 to St. Austell, in Cornwall, which was also a very heavy circuit; the places were numerous, and he had to preach almost every week in the year in the open air, and at times too when the rain was pouring down, and when the snow lay deep upon the ground. "But the prosperity of Methodism made every thing pleasant." A heavenly flame broke out, and great numbers joined the society. Among these was Samuel Drew, who was then just terminating his apprenticeship to a shoemaker: "A man," says Mr. Clarke, "of primitive simplicity of manners, amiableness of disposition, piety toward God, and benevolence to men, seldom to be equalled; and for reach of thought, keenness of discrimination, purity of language, and manly eloquence, not to be surpassed in any of the common walks of life. In short, his circumstances considered, with the mode of his education, he is one of those prodigies of nature and grace which God rarely exhibits; but which serve to keep up the connecting link between those who are confined to houses of clay, whose foundations are in the dust, and beings of a superior order in those realms where infirmity cannot enter, and where the sunshine of knowledge suffers neither diminution nor eclipse." Eulogistic as this is, I can bear testimony to its correctness. I knew Mr. Drew well, received many a useful lesson from him, esteemed him while he lived, and now deeply revere his memory. I have frequently heard him and my venerable father, with other aged Methodists in my native circuit, speak of Mr. Clarke's unbounded popularity in those early days; he being sometimes obliged, when the chapel had been thronged, to enter through the window, and creep on his hands and knees over the heads and shoulders of the people, in order to reach the pulpit. The doctor's death was a severe stroke to Mr. Drew; he survived it only a few months; they were then joined

"In those Elysian seats
Where Jonathan his David meets."

In 1785 Mr. Clarke was appointed to Plymouth Dock, (now called Devonport,) where the society was doubled in the course of the year. Here Chambers' Cyclopaedia, in two volumes folio, was lent him by James Hore, Esq. He read it attentively, made nearly every subject discussed in it his own; and laid the whole under contribution to his ministerial labours. He also obtained the loan from Miss Kennicott, of her brother's (the celebrated Dr. Kennicott's) edition of the Hebrew Bible, two volumes folio, with various readings from near seven hundred MSS. and early printed editions. This book greatly increased his thirst for a better knowledge of biblical criticism.

The next three years were spent in the Norman Isles. Here he obtained much assistance from the public library of St. Heliers, where he spent most of his leisure hours in reading and collating the original texts in Walton's Polyglot Bible, particularly the Hebrew, Samaritan, Chaldee, Syriac, Vulgate, and Septuagint: and before he left, he was enabled to purchase a Polyglot for himself, with ten pounds which he had received in a letter from a person from whom he had no expectation of receiving any thing of the kind. But what was more pleasing to him, the word of the Lord had free course and was glorified. Among the converts was a soldier who had been a slave to drunkenness. One morning, having become intoxicated before five o'clock, he had strolled out to Les Torres, where Mr. Clarke was preaching, and was deeply convinced of his lost condition. At the close of the service, he took Mr. Clarke by the hand, and with the tears streaming down his cheeks, between drunkenness and distress, said, "O sir! I know you are a man possessed by the Spirit of God!" He went home; and after three days' agonies, God, in tender compassion, set his soul at liberty.

While on this station he had several very remarkable deliverances: once or twice from the hands of a furious mob; another time from the fatal effects of intense cold, while walking through deep snow; and once from a watery grave, while in a little vessel, during a tremendous storm, off Alderney.

On the 17th of April, 1788, Mr. Clarke was married to Miss Mary Cooke, the eldest daughter of Mr. John Cooke, clothier, Trowbridge. In a private communication he says, "Before I took my beloved Mary by the hand, who was most delicately brought up, I asked her, 'As I am at the disposal of Mr. Wesley and the conference, and they can send me whither they please, will you go with me whithersoever I am sent?' 'Yes; if I take you, I take you as a minister of Christ, and shall go with you to the ends of the earth.' And the first step she took was with me on my mission to the Norman Isles." As Mrs. Clarke is still living, it is only necessary to say that, for above forty-two years, during which they were united, she showed, in all the various circumstances through which they passed, she was the woman worthy of being the wife of Adam Clarke. Six sons and six daughters were the fruit of their marriage. Miss Anne Cooke, one of Mrs. Clarke's sisters, became the wife of John Butterworth, Esq., and, with her husband, was brought to God through Mr. and Mrs. Clarke's instrumentality, and for many years, in a very elevated station, adorned the doctrine of God their Saviour in all things.

In 1789 Mr. Clarke received his appointment as superintendent for the Bristol circuit. This, in consequence of family afflictions and other causes, he informed me, was one of the most painful years of his life.

The conference of 1790 appointed him to Dublin[1], where he no sooner arrived than he found himself exposed to numberless difficulties and distressing circumstances. He and his family were obliged to go into very inconvenient lodgings; and when the preacher's new house was finished, they were induced to go into it before it was dry, which nearly cost all of them their lives. He was seized with a severe rheumatic affection in the head, from which he very slowly recovered. There were also very warm disputes in the society, respecting the use of the liturgy in the Whitefriar-street Chapel, which gave him great uneasiness. While in this circuit he formed a charitable institution, called "The Strangers' Friend Society," the first of several that were organized by him in the principal towns of England, as Manchester, Liverpool, and London; and which have contributed greatly to the relief of suffering

---

[1] He had previously received the following letter from Mr. Wesley: —

"Near Dublin, June 25, 1789.

"Dear Adam,

"You send me good news with regard to the islands. Who can hurt us, if God is on our side? Trials may come, but they are all good. I have not been so tried for many years. Every week, and almost every day, I am bespattered in the public papers. Many are in tears on the occasion, many terribly frightened, and crying out, 'O, what will the end be? what will the end be?' Why, glory to God in the highest, and peace and good will among men. But, meantime, what is to be done? What will be the most effectual means to stem this furious torrent? I have just visited the classes, and find still in the society upward of a thousand members; and, among them, many as deep Christians as any I have met with in Europe. But who is able to watch over these that they may not be moved from their steadfastness? I know none more proper than Adam Clarke and his wife. Indeed, it may seem hard for them to go into a strange land again. Well, you may come to me, at Leeds, the latter end of next month; and if you can show me any that are more proper, I will send them instead, that God may be glorified in all that is designed by,

"Dear Adam,

"Your affectionate friend and brother,

"J. Wesley."

humanity.

The year 1791 is remarkable in the history of Methodism for the death of Mr. Wesley. When Mr. Clarke first heard of this solemn event, he says that he "was overwhelmed with grief; and that such were his feelings, all he could do was to read the little printed account of his last moments." His admiration of Mr. Wesley was such as I have not perceived in any other of the followers of that extraordinary individual. I have more than once heard him say, that, taking him altogether, as a man, a Christian, a divine, a philanthropist, a favoured instrument in the hands of God in winning souls, he had not been surpassed, if equalled, since the days of the apostles. It is deeply to be regretted that peculiar circumstances should have prevented the doctor from writing the Life of the Founder of Methodism,—an Apelles that could have painted an Alexander. Mr. Wesley's opinion of Mr. Clarke we have in a letter of his to Mr. King. So early as the year 1787, that correct judge of character hesitated not to affirm, " Adam Clarke is doubtless an extraordinary young man, and capable of doing much good." In his will, Mr. Wesley appointed him one of the seven trustees of all his literary property.

The first conference after the death of Mr. Wesley, as Mr. Clarke's health was in a very declining state, he was appointed to the Manchester circuit, principally with a view to his using the Buxton waters, as the likeliest means of his recovery. The remedy was tried, and his health completely restored. About this time the French revolution was the universal topic; and various political questions were agitated with considerable excitement. These were sometimes introduced into the pulpit, but never by Mr. Clarke: he informed me that, during this painful period, in almost every sermon he urged his hearers to seek entire sanctification. Of his colleagues, Messrs. Samuel Bradburn and Joseph Benson, I have heard him speak in the highest terms. He thought them the two greatest preachers of the day. It is somewhat remarkable that it fell to his lot to perform the last office of friendship to the mortal remains of both these eminent men, by delivering an address at their graves. The former died in 1810, the latter in 1821.

From Manchester Mr. Clarke went to Liverpool, where he and the venerable Mr. Pawson, with whom he acted in perfect unison, had the satisfaction of seeing the society more than doubled during their joint ministry. Mrs. Pawson then entered, in her private journal, her opinion of her husband's colleague in the following terms: — "Brother Clarke is, in my estimation, an extraordinary preacher; and his learning confers great lustre on his talents: he makes it subservient to grace. His discourses are highly evangelical: he never loses sight of Christ. In regard of pardon and holiness, he offers a present salvation. His address is lively, animated, and very encouraging to the seekers of salvation. In respect to the unawakened, it may indeed be said, that he obeys that precept, 'Cry aloud; spare not; lift up thy voice like a trumpet.' His words flow spontaneously from the heart; his views enlarge as he proceeds; and he brings to the mind a torrent of things new and old. While he is preaching, one can seldom cast an eye on the audience, without perceiving a melting unction resting upon them. His 'speech distils as the dew, and as the small rain upon the tender herb.' He generally preaches from some part of the lesson for the day; and, on the Sabbath morning, from the Gospel for the day: this method confers an abundant variety on his ministry."

While in this circuit, Mr. Clarke nearly lost his life by assassination. Returning home one evening from a country village accompanied by two friends, a stone, upward of a pound weight, struck him on the head, cut through his hat, and inflicted a deep wound. This horrid deed was proved to be the act of a Papist, who, with another of the same creed, had been to hear him preach, and waylaid him on his return; and, had he been alone, would in all probability have murdered him. He was confined for more than a month, a considerable part of which time his life was in great jeopardy. The men were brought before a magistrate; but, on their confessing their fault, and binding themselves never more to offend, both of them were discharged, — though in a few years they both came to a tragical end.

The next three years Mr. Clarke spent in London, and during that time walked upward of seven thousand miles, merely in the performance of his duty as a Methodist preacher. In the year 1797 he commenced his career of authorship by the publication of a pamphlet, entitled, "A Dissertation on the Use and Abuse of Tobacco."

From the year 1798 to 1805 the subject of our memoir was appointed successively to Bristol, Liverpool, and Manchester. His father died in November, 1798, full of faith and hope. This he laid deeply to heart, and expressed himself as if the hands of life were loosened around him, and that he wished to "go and die with him." He never afterward passed Ardwick churchyard, where his father was interred, without taking off his hat, and holding it in his hand until he had made his way beyond it, to manifest how much he honored, as well as loved, this guide of his youth.

In the year 1800, Mr. Clarke published a translation of "Sturm's Reflections on the Works of God," which had an extensive and rapid sale.

In 1802 he edited and published "A Bibliographical Dictionary," in 6 vols., 12mo., to which, in the year 1806, he added two other volumes, as a "Bibliographical Miscellany or Supplement;" and, about the same time, "A Succinct Account of Polyglot Bibles, from the publication of that by Porrus in the year 1516, to that of Reineccius in 1750: including several curious particulars relative to the London Polyglot, and Castell's Heptaglott Lexicon, not noticed by Bibliographers:" also, "A Succinct Account of the principal Editions of the Greek Testament, from the first printed at Complutum, in 1514, to that by Professor Griesbach, in 1797." These several works contain a mass of information, and will be found a useful guide to the study of Biblical literature.

While in Liverpool Mr. Clarke projected the formation of a "Philological Society;" of which he was unanimously chosen president. The same honour was conferred upon him a few years after, when a similar society was instituted in Manchester. The code of rules, and one hundred and seventy-one questions on various literary and scientific subjects came from the pen of Mr. Clarke. A copy of them now lies before me. Some of the questions are exceedingly important and curious.

In 1804 Mr. Clarke gave to the public an improved edition of "Fleury's Manners of the Ancient Israelites;" and an abridgment of "Baxter's Christian Directory," in 2 vols., 8vo. During the same year, the Eclectic Review was commenced; and Mr. Clarke was earnestly requested to lend his able assistance in reviewing some Hebrew and other oriental works. After some reluctance he consented, and furnished some reviews, which contributed not a little to the respectability of the new periodical. Of his review of Holmes' Septuagint, Professor Bentley writes, "It is more conformable to my ideas of what a review should be, than is generally to be met with in the periodical publications of the present day: it is such a complete account and analysis of the work an will enable a person to form a just opinion of it. The article contains many particulars of additional information, more than Holmes has given; and these you have so intermingled with those drawn from Holmes, that the generality of readers will not perceive to whom they are indebted for them. The opposite to this is, I believe, the usual practice of reviewers: they often display information as their own, which they owe altogether to their author, whom they perhaps are abusing; and thus make it more their object to seem *knowing* themselves than even to give a proper and just account of the author whose work they are professing to review."

He was appointed a second time to the London circuit in 1805; and, at the conference held in Leeds in 1806, he was elected president; and, in defiance of all his protestations against it, he was taken by main force, lifted out of his seat, and placed in the chair!

About this time "the British and Foreign Bible Society" nominated Mr. Clarke a member of its committee. The assistance which he rendered was most important, such as "was indispensable to the successful prosecution of the society's plans," and which cost him no ordinary sacrifice of time and labour. For it the committee requested permission to present him with fifty pounds; "an offering," says the late Rev. John Owen, "which that learned and public-spirited individual respectfully but peremptorily declined to accept."

His "Concise View of the Succession of Sacred Literature" made its appearance in 1807. For the completion of the second volume of this valuable work the doctor could never find leisure; but this, and a new and enlarged edition of the first, in 8vo., have been finished and published by the doctor's youngest son, the Rev. J. B. B. Clarke, A.M., in a manner highly creditable to his scholarship and talents.

In the same year the University of Aberdeen, at the suggestion of the celebrated Professor Porson, conferred on Mr. Clarke the degree of A.M.; and, in the following year, presented him with a diploma of LL.D. Both diplomas were sent to him in the most honourable and flattering manner, the college refusing to accept even the customary clerks' fees given on such occasions.

"Some time in February, 1808," he observes, "I learned that I had been recommended to his majesty's commissioners of the public records of the kingdom, by the Right Honourable Charles Abbot, speaker of the house of commons, and one of the commissioners, to whom I was known only by some of my writings on Bibliography, as a fit person to undertake the department of collecting and arranging those state papers which might serve to complete and continue that collection of state papers generally called *Rymer's Faedora.*" He was struck with astonishment, and endeavoured to excuse himself on the grounds of general unfitness. But being strongly urged by John Caley, Esq., secretary to the commission, and some of his friends, to try, he commenced this Herculean task. He had to examine sixty folio volumes, with numerous collateral evidence, to visit the different public offices, and to make a selection of such records as it might be expedient to print, under the authority of parliament, either as a supplement or continuation of Rymer's work. These excessive labours[2] tended greatly to impair his health, until he was obliged, on three different occasions, to send in his resignation to the "board:" it was not, however, accepted before March, 1819; when he took leave of this part of his public duties in the following language: "And here I register my thanks to God, the Fountain of wisdom and goodness, who has enabled me to conduct this most difficult and delicate work for ten years, with credit to myself, and satisfaction to his majesty's government. During that time I have been requested to solve many difficult questions, and illustrate many obscurities; in none of which have I ever failed, though the subjects were such as were by no means familiar to me, having had little of an antiquarian, and nothing of a forensic education.

In 1808, Dr. Clarke was prevailed upon to become librarian of the Surrey Institution; and when he relinquished the office, the managers, as a mark of respect, constituted him "honorary librarian;" which title he retained as long as the institution existed. In the course of the same year he published A Short Account of the last Illness and Death of the learned Porson, with a *facsimile* of an

---

[2] In a letter to myself, he says, "Lord Glenbervie, who was one of the commissioners, once wrote to me: 'Dr. Clarke, *festina lente:* you will destroy yourself by your labour. Do a little, that you may do it long.' The same advice I give you. May God bless you, my dear Sammy."

ancient Greek inscription, which formed the topic of the professor's last literary conversation.

In the year 1810, Dr. Clarke projected, in conjunction with the Rev. Josiah Pratt, a new edition of the London Polyglot Bible. The prospectus was printed and circulated, but, for want of adequate support, the important undertaking was abandoned. This he greatly regretted to the day of his death. It was in the month of July of this year that the first part of his Commentary on the Holy Scriptures was issued from the press. This monument of learning and piety we shall afterward notice.

On the 1st of December, 1814, a Wesleyan Methodist missionary meeting was held for the first time in City-Road Chapel, London. Dr. Clarke, being that year president of the conference, was called to the chair; and shortly after published the address which he delivered, under the title of "A Short Account of the Introduction of the Gospel into the British Isles; and the Obligation of Britons to make known its Salvation to every Nation of the Earth."

In 1815, Dr. Clarke removed from London, and took up his residence at Millbrook, in Lancashire. Here he was relieved from many burdens that in the metropolis had pressed heavily upon him, breathed a pure air, and engaged himself in his favourite agricultural pursuits, which had a most beneficial effect upon his constitution. In the summer of 1816, he made a tour through part of Scotland and Ireland, and visited what he calls, in a letter now before me, "the place that had every thing to recommend it to *my attention and heart.* The place is that in which I spent my boyish days; where I received the rudiments of the little education I have; where I first felt conviction of sin, righteousness, and judgment; where I first saw or heard a Methodist; where I first tasted the pardoning love of God, after having passed through a great fight of affliction; where I joined the Methodist society; where I first led a class; where I first began to preach redemption in Christ Jesus, and from which I was called to become an itinerant preacher. And these things took place in the parish, and in the compass of about three fields' breadth in that parish, which is on the edge of the sea, where there is the most beautiful shore in the world, extending above twenty miles, of as perfectly level hard sand as can be conceived;—the very place where

I was once drowned, and perhaps *miraculously* restored to life;

where I was accustomed to bathe, and from the rocks of which I used to catch many fish, and among the rocks of which I spent many an hour in catching crabs, &c. Such a place, thus circumstanced, must afford a multitude of the most impressive reminiscences. No place on the face of the earth can have so many attractions for *me*."

Dr. Clarke came to town in May, 1818, to attend the anniversary meetings of the Wesleyan Methodist Missionary Society; and, while on the platform, he received a note from Sir Alexander Johnston, who was then within sight of land, on his return from Ceylon, and who had brought with him, at their own most earnest entreaties, two high priests of Budhoo, who wished to be instructed in the principles of Christianity. Sir Alexander and the missionary committee prevailed on Dr. Clarke to take charge of them, and afford them all the instructions he could in the knowledge of divine things. Two days after their arrival in London, I had the pleasure of accompanying the doctor and these two interesting strangers, one of whom was then forty-five years of age, and the other twenty-seven, to Bristol. They travelled without hat or cap, with a splendid yellow garment thrown loosely over the left shoulder, and with not only the head, but also the neck, breast, and right arm entirely bare, to the no little astonishment of beholders. They remained with their kind and eminent instructer for about two years, were baptized into the Christian faith, and then returned to Ceylon, where they have held fast their profession. One fills an important office under government, and the other is a licensed teacher in the Church establishment.

In June, 1821, the doctor again visited Ireland, and, shortly after, his name was enrolled among the chief literati of the country. In a letter to me he writes:

"M.R.I.A. signify *Member of the Royal Irish Academy,* to which I was most honourably elected, without knowing any of the parties who brought me before the Academy; my countrymen being determined to bestow on me the highest literary honour in their gift."

In the spring of the following year an acquaintance was commenced between Dr. Clarke and his royal highness the duke of Sussex. This was most honourable to the doctor, was unsolicited on his part, and continued without any compromise of either his character or principles.

At the conference held in London in the year 1822, Dr. Clarke was, for the third time, chosen president; a circumstance as yet unique in the history of Methodism. It was determined at this conference that two preachers should be sent to the Shetland Isles. The writer of these lines, who was present on the occasion, was the first who offered his services, if his brethren thought him adequate for the arduous enterprise. He was immediately appointed; and, with the Rev. John Ruby, after spending a few days at Millbrook, proceeded to Edinburgh, there took ship, and, after four days' sail, safely arrived in Lerwick. In the name of the Lord of hosts they set up their banner; they preached a free, full, and present salvation; multitudes flocked to hear the word, and not a few felt its transforming efficacy. Other preachers followed in the same track, and were equally successful. From ten to twenty chapels have been erected, and numerous societies formed. There are now six Wesleyan Methodist preachers labouring in the islands, and one thousand three hundred and seventy members in society. What the mission to these "naked melancholy isles" is indebted to Dr. Clarke, will not be known before "that day shall break which never more shall close." He travelled, he begged, he wrote, he prayed for it; and it is my decided conviction that, without his very efficient aid, such as no other man in the kingdom could have rendered, it would have been long since abandoned. Of that assistance it is now deprived, and is dependent for its support on the Methodists' Contingent Fund, and on the contributions of an enlightened and benevolent public. I most strongly, therefore, recommend it to the attention and liberality of all who revere the memory of the venerable doctor, or who feel compassion for the sheep that are scattered over the mountains.[3]

The doctor visited the islands himself in the year 1826, and again in 1827; and on his return, when I was stationed in Newcastle-on-Tyne, wrote to me thus: "And now, Sammy, what shall I say about the *work* of which we have written and spoken so much? I cannot say that it *answered* my expectation. It *far exceeded* all that I had even hoped. I have not witnessed so much good done in so

---

[3] Subscriptions and donations will be thankfully received by the amiable relict of the Doctor, Mrs. Clarke, Stoke Newington, or by any of the Wesleyan Ministers.

short a time, with such slender means, wherever I have travelled; nor have I read of such. I saw all the preachers, and had the leaders from every isle and place of preaching, (either at Walls or Lerwick,) and I inquired closely into the work everywhere; and I believe I pretty well know the whole; I have seen the grace of God which is among them, and am sovereignly glad. The half of the good I witnessed had not been told me. Indeed, the preachers themselves do not fully know it. When I reflected on *your first entering in* among this people, the difficulties which you had to encounter, the soil wholly unprepared, &c., &c., I stand astonished at the work. I see fully that of the great harvest in the principal parts of Shetland, *you* sowed the seed. God has put great honour upon you, and multitudes remember you even with tears of affection."

It was in the year 1824 that Dr. Clarke sold his house and land in Lancashire, quitted Millbrook, and purchased, and then removed to Haydon Hall, a lovely spot, near Pinner, and about sixteen miles from London.

In 1830, the doctor, on his visit to Ireland, established several schools in the extensive and populous districts around Colerain, where many were perishing for lack of knowledge. These schools were inspected by him in 1831.

In January, 1830, he gave the following account of the death of Robert Scott, Esq., of Pensford, near Bristol, in a letter to Mrs. Clarke: "At half past ten this evening, Mr. Scott changed mortality for life. Such a death I never witnessed. We had prayed to God to give him an easy passage; and we did not pray in vain: for he had one of the most placid and easiest I have ever heard or seen. His wife, and several of the relatives, and myself were kneeling around his bed. I offered the departing prayer; and, after it, had just time to rise from my knees, to go to him, lay my hands on his head, and pronounce the blessing of Aaron on the Israelites:

'The Lord bless thee, and keep thee! The Lord make his face shine upon thee, and be gracious unto thee! The Lord lift up his countenance upon thee, and give thee peace,' when his last breath went forth! Thus, in the eighty-fifth year of his age, died this undeviating friend of Shetland[4] I would not have missed this sight

---

[4] The following letter I received in 1825:—
"MY DEAR SAMMY,

for a great deal. I seem to have come hither in order to learn to die."

On his return to Haydon-Hall, he found a letter containing an invitation from the board of managers of the Missionary Society of the Methodist Episcopal Church of New-York, to go over to America, and assist them in their missionary labours, and in their church assembly. After stating the reasons why he could not accept the invitation, and expressing his regret, he proceeds thus: "Yet I am far from supposing that there may not be a providential interference in the way. I am an old man, having gone beyond threescore years and ten, and, consequently, not able to perform the labour of youth. You would naturally expect me to preach much; and this I could not do . . . . I would say to all, Keep your doctrines and your discipline, not only in your church books, and in your society rules, but preach the former without refining upon them, observe the latter without

---

"When I had but one sovereign in the world for Shetland, I prayed, called earnestly upon God, and sat down and wept—and wept till I could scarcely see to write or read. Well, I once more thought, I must lay the whole before our best earthly friend. With a full heart, I stated the matter in a letter to Mr. Scott, which letter was watered with fast falling tears. He wrote me word that he and Mrs. Scott would be up in a fortnight and see me. They came; and I set off in very bad health to London to meet them:—and O, what a meeting!—their hearts were nearly as full as mine. Says Mr. Scott, 'Come, let me have a check, I will give orders on my bank for £100.' Says Mrs. Scott, 'And I will, out of my private purse, give £5?' 'And I am desired,' says Mr. Scott, 'by my sister-in-law, Miss Grainger, to give £5; and lest any chapel begun should be impeded, here is £10 more, and thus I will give the check for £120. And this is not all that I will do; I tell you again, I will give £10 to every chapel or house begun under your direction in Shetland.' O, my Sammy! you can hardly tell how much I rejoiced—I thanked God, I thanked them, and could have kissed the ground on which they trod. I said in my heart, 'O my poor Shetlanders! (whom I have never seen, and now never shall see, but God has laid you upon my heart) God has not forgotten you.' I sent my check to the bankers, got the cash, £120, and immediately wrote to you, and told you what God had done, to take courage and go forward. Mr. Scott has written to me, two or three days ago, stating that he is very poorly, and wishes to make a 'trust deed' in behalf of Shetland, and to do this immediately; and wishes me to give him the names with which I wish it to be filled. Old as I am, I must be one, Mr. Butterworth will be another, and you shall be the third.

"Yours, my dear Sammy, affectionately,
"ADAM CLARKE"

Mr. Butterworth, Mr. Scott, and the dear doctor, have all since been called to give an account of their stewardship. Mr. Scott left three thousand pounds to the Shetland mission, in the three-and-half per cents.

bending it to circumstances, or impairing its rigour by frivolous exceptions and partialities. As I believe your nation to be destined to be the mightiest and happiest nation on the globe, so I believe that your church is likely to become the most extensive and pure in the universe. As a church, abide in the apostles' doctrine and fellowship. As a nation, be firmly united; entertain no petty differences; totally abolish the slave trade; abhor all offensive wars; never provoke even the puniest state; and never strike the first blow. Encourage agriculture and friendly traffic. Cultivate the sciences and arts; let learning have its proper place, space, and adequate share of esteem and honour. If possible, live in peace with all nations; retain your holy zeal for God's cause and your country's weal; and that you may ever retain yore' liberty, avoid, as its bane and ruin, a national debt."

In May, 1832, he visited Ireland for the last time; and in a private communication gives the following account of his voyage:—"On Tuesday, I left Bruerton in the mail for Liverpool, where I arrived at six in the evening; immediately crossed the Mersey, and got to Oakfield, to my old friend, Mr. Forshaw, where I rested myself till Friday, and then put myself on board the 'Corsair' at half past twelve; and although we had the wind right ahead, we had a very calm sea, and one of the best passages, for the distance, I ever had, either in these or any other seas. In fifteen hours I was completely across the channel; and, having dined in the one kingdom, I was long before breakfast time in the other. It was indeed a mercy that the passage was so short, for a worse set of passengers I never met with. They passed for, and affected to be, Irish gentlemen; and by their conduct seemed to be in league with hell and death, and with the devil to hold agreement—drinking, vociferating, arguing politics, in the most ferocious manner; talking high treason; abusing the king, the queen, the duke of Wellington, and many others, in the most unmeasured manner; swearing, cursing, vowing the death of all the tithe proctors; one stated that he had engaged a man at half a crown a head to cut the throats, and take off the heads, of all and every of the tithe proctors that might show themselves on his estate. And to all this was added the vilest brothel obscenity. My heart was often obliged to say, 'Gather not my soul with sinners, nor my life with the blood thirsty;' and could say with one of old, 'O Lord, thou knowest I have not loved the company of the unrighteous in this world, let me not be condemned to have it eternally in the world to come.' To avoid these infernals, I walked the deck to a late hour, and then came down among them to lie upon a sofa, for I had no other bed. O what a hell to be condemned to keep company with such workers of iniquity! After such a companionship, what a blessing, on the following Sabbath morning, I felt the communion of saints to be! We had a lovely congregation at the chapel in this place, (Donaghadee,) and all appeared cordially to hear, and deeply to feel."

The conference of 1832 was held in Liverpool, at the time that the cholera was raging to an alarming degree. Though the doctor was in a very poor state of health, and was affectionately expostulated with by Mrs. Clarke not to go, he answered: "I know you never grudged me in my duty and work; and I think with you that I am scarcely fit to go. But I have duties to perform in reference to Shetland and the Irish schools: and, besides, I earnestly wish to leave my testimony for God and Methodism once more in the midst of my brethren." He attended; but, while there, wrote to a friend thus: "I have been variously afflicted, and, indeed, have been brought down almost to the sides of the pit, and, though much better, my health is in a great measure prostrated; and though I am here at conference, I am far from being in a state either to do or to attend to much business. I went to Ireland to work much, but I was called to suffer, not to labour. Indeed, I was overworked before I crossed the channel, and had little strength to lose when I got to the scene of my labours. Striving to do what I was not able to perform, I had four relapses. Well, in all these I was preserved from every murmuring thought. I knew I was in the hand of the Lord, and therefore was safe, and my expectation has not been disappointed; I feel that God alone is my portion. I write in conference, and have such a troublesome cough that I can scarcely write intelligibly, and must give it up." He, however, at the earnest request of his brethren, preached twice. His sermons will not soon be forgotten by those who heard them. After the conference he went to Frome, where his son Joseph was curate, to assist in the formation of a "Society for the Melioration of the Condition of the Poor" in that extensive parish. On the 19th of August he preached his last sermon at Westbury, near Bristol, from 1 Tim. i, 15: "This is a faithful saying, and worthy of all acceptation, that Christ Jesus came into the world to save sinners." On the 23d he safely arrived at home. At family worship he offered up his supplications in reference to the cholera, that "each and all might be saved from its influence, or prepared for sudden death." On Saturday, the 25th, it was observed by the family that he commenced his prayer with these words: "We thank thee, O heavenly Father! that we have a blessed hope through Christ of entering into thy glory." On rising from his knees, he remarked to Mrs. Clarke that he thought he must not kneel down much longer, as it was with pain and difficulty he could rise up again. In the evening he rode into Bayswater, at which place he was engaged to preach the following day. He appeared fatigued with the journey; and when application was made to him to fix the time for preaching a charity sermon, he replied, "I am not well; I cannot fix a time; I must first see what God is about to do with me." The next morning he was seized with cholera morbus, had just time and strength to declare that his trust was in Christ, and, about eleven o'clock the same evening, August 26th, 1832, he fell asleep in Jesus. On Wednesday, the 29th, his remains were interred in the burying ground adjoining the Methodist chapel City-Road. His grave is the next to that of Mr. Wesley. "Them which sleep in Jesus will God bring with him."

From the leading incidents in Dr. Clarke's life, as narrated in the preceding pages, the reader may obtain a tolerably correct view of his character, and cannot fail to perceive that the doctor was no ordinary man. We shall now briefly notice his peculiar characteristics. In his personal appearance there was nothing very remarkable. He was about five feet ten inches in height, and had rather a tendency, as he advanced in age, to a free habit of body. His frame was well compacted together, his limbs symmetrical, and his whole person remarkably erect. His eyes were small and brilliant, and of a light gray. His countenance was exceedingly rubicund; and his hair, when young, was of a reddish kind of yellow, but very soon assumed a silvery hue. His very walk was expressive of the buoyancy of his mind, and the whole of his features characteristic of the benevolence of his heart.

His understanding was clear, active, searching, and vigorous; formed for investigation, capable of grappling with any difficulty, remarkable for its patient application, and possessed a singular ability for arranging and generalizing subjects; perhaps more adapted for analysis than for synthesis. His powers of invention were fruitful, and his imagination vivid; but this faculty he neglected, rather than cultivated. His memory was surprisingly retentive, he states, indeed, that of the thousands of sermons which he delivered he never knew beforehand one single sentence that he should utter, and that this was owing to the verbal imperfection of his memory. But those who have been much in his company have been frequently struck with his powerful recollection, not only of a subject in the mass, but also in its minutest details. The multitude of books which he read, the manuscripts which he examined, the sermons that he preached, the sick whom he visited, the journeys that he performed, the committees which he attended, the public business in which he assisted, the private interviews that he granted, the many volumes which he composed and published, the thousands of letters which he wrote,—in addition to all his other duties as a Methodist preacher,—are proofs that his industry must have been unintermitted, and pursued with unexampled energy. At the commencement of his public life he wrote: "I am determined, by the grace of God, to conquer and die; and I have taken the subsequent motto, and have placed it before me on the mantelpiece: 'Stand thou as a beaten anvil to the stroke; for it is the property of a good warrior to be flayed alive, and yet to conquer.'" But, like Mr. Wesley, though he "was always in haste, he was never in a hurry." His dress, library, garden, farm, all showed him to be a man of order. What his hand found to do he did it with all his might, and he did it at once. To nearly every letter he replied by return of post. To idleness he seems to have had no propensity: in whatever company or situation he was found, even in his relaxations, his mind was occupied. While others slept or banqueted, or idled out their despicable days in gossiping and folly, he kept the glorious harvest of this issue full in view, and ploughed with all his heifers, reckless of the sun and rain. To a young man he says, "As a travelling preacher I learned more in one year than I learned before in many at school. The grand secret is to save time. Spend none needlessly; keep from all unnecessary company; never be without a praying heart; and have, as often as possible, a book in your hand. Make yourself master of Mr. Wesley's Works, and those of Mr. Fletcher and Mr. Sellon. Read over the Lives of the first Methodist preachers,—they are in the former Magazines;—and read the Journal of David Brainerd, Missionary to the North American Indians; and 'the Saints' Everlasting Rest,' as abridged by Mr. Wesley. Do not lie long in bed, nor sit up late at night."

Doctor Clarke cultivated the useful rather than the ornamental arts. Of all the liberal arts he ever considered music as the least useful. The few first-rate poets he read with high relish. On those of a second or third order he seldom cast his eye. He possessed, in a high degree, the rare ability to use knowledge. He himself observed that the learning that is got from books, or the study of languages, is of little use to any man, and is of no estimation, unless practically applied to the purposes of life; and it is said by one who knew him well, that "there never was an individual who could use to such purpose all the stores which he accumulated. He possessed an astonishing power of gathering together rays of light from the whole circuit of his knowledge, and pouring them, in one bright beam, upon any point which he wished to illustrate or explain. And the treasures of knowledge which his unwearied industry had drawn together, were all made subservient to the more effective execution of his ministerial office."

His conversion, as we have seen, was clear, sound, and decided: of this, a life of uniform, practical, growing piety, covering over the space of more than half a century, is the delightful witness. But the following testimony of the venerable Henry Moore, who knew the doctor longer than any man who survived him, must not be withheld: "Our connection, I believe, never knew a more blameless life than that of Dr. Clarke. He had his opponents; he had those that differed from him, sometimes in doctrine, sometimes in other things; but these opponents, whatever they imputed to him, never dared to fix a stain either upon his moral or religious character. He was, as Mr. Wesley used to say a preacher of the Gospel should be, 'without stain;' or, as a greater than he had said, Dr. Clarke could have said, 'Which of you convinceth me of sin?'" Like the patriarch, he said, "Till I die, I will not remove my integrity from me. My righteousness I hold fast, and will not let it go. My heart shall not reproach me as long as I live." Such was his unbending integrity that it may be said of him, as truly as it ever was affirmed of any statesman or patriot, "He would lay down his life for his country, and would not do a base thing to save it; one who would neither tread upon an insect, nor crouch to an emperor."

His attachment to Methodism continued to the last, and was then shown by a bequest for the relief of its chapels. He has been heard to say more than once, "I belong to the Methodists,—body and soul, blood and sinews. This coat" (seizing hold of his own sleeve) "is theirs." In a letter to me he remarks: "For nearly fifty years I have lived only for the support and credit of Methodism: myself and my interests, the Searcher of hearts knows, were never objects of my attention: I came into the connection with a single eye and an upright heart; and by the mercy of God I have been able to retain both." From censoriousness he was perfectly free. His judgment of his brethren was never harsh or severe. He was always ready to speak in their praise, and to put the best construction on their sayings and doings. His humility was deep and unaffected; with all his learning there was no parade. However familiar he might be among his friends, yet among the great and the learned he was modest to an excess. He shunned the gaze of the public, and preferred preaching in small chapels to large ones. He had a high sense of honour, but without pride and ambition. He would submit, with all cheerfulness, and without the least affectation, to perform the meanest offices for himself, his friends, or the poor. In a letter, dated Feb. 4, 1823, he writes: "Visit the people from house to house; and speak in the most affectionate manner to them. Take notice of the children; treat them lovingly: this will do the children good, and the parents will like it. Cheerfully partake of the meanest fare, when the people invite you. About two years ago, when travelling among the cottages in Ireland, I went into a most wretched hovel, and they had just poured out the potatoes into a basket, which, with a little salt, were to serve for their dinner. I said, 'Good people, will you let me take one of your potatoes?' 'O yes, sir! and a thousand welcomes, were they covered with gold!' The people were delighted to see me eat one, and another, and a third; and thought that I had laid them under endless obligation. But they thought me an angel when for every potato I had eaten I gave them a shilling. But they had no expectation of this kind when I first asked liberty to taste with them. Other clergy carry themselves *aloft* from their people, and thus assume and maintain a sort of anti-scriptural consequence. Methodist preachers have another kind of consequence—their humility, their heavenly unction, and the sound of their Master's feet behind them. Too much familiarity breeds contempt, but humility and condescension are other qualities."

His disinterestedness was beyond all praise. He never once used the influence which he possessed with some of high rank in behalf of himself or family. When he had the opportunity of reaping considerable emolument for his labours under government, and he was asked what they could do for him, he replied, "O, nothing; I dwell among my own people." He had also a kind heart: the various forms of human woe excited his softest sympathy. The distressed never left his door unrelieved. He has several times been known, when near his own gate, to give away his shoes in order to cover the feet of another. In the commencement of the year 1816, which was unusually severe, many hundreds of sailors were thrown upon the benevolence and compassion of the inhabitants of Liverpool: Dr. Clarke had some cottages untenanted, into which he put a quantity of straw and blankets, and then sent for twenty of the poor fellows. In the day time, they were employed in making the road to his house; and at set hours they assembled in his kitchen to their meals, one of the party having remained in-doors to cook for the rest. As a master he was, if possible, over indulgent. As a father, though he very seldom directly praised any of his children, he was notwithstanding passionately fond of them: and they, in return, were as fond of their father. When he heard his son Joseph preach the first time, he wrote to me in language which, perhaps, it would hardly be prudent to publish; but which fully exemplified the saying: "A wise son maketh a *glad* father." As a husband, he was just what a husband ought to be: he loved his wife, as Christ loved the church. As a friend, he was accessible, affable, communicative, obliging, faithful, and affectionate. It was, however, a maxim with him, that "proffered sympathy, in the time of deep sorrow and privation, whether it come personally or by letter, tends to exacerbate the evil which it wishes to remove." When I was deprived, by death, of a lovely son, he wrote to me thus: "I know well what it is to bury a child; for I have buried six: a *sympathizing* friend may say, 'Well! it is the Lord's will, and they are better provided for!' Thus I have learned that it is a mighty easy thing to bury *other folks'* children!" In every private relation of life he was an example worthy the imitation of all; nor was he less so in his *public character* as a minister of Christ.

Before I make any remarks on the doctor's preaching or

writing, I will gratify my readers with a valuable letter of his to a young preacher, who had written to him for advice on the subjects of which it speaks:—

"MY DEAR BROTHER,

"I have given many general and particular advices to my younger brethren in 'A Letter to a Preacher on his first Entrance into the Work of the Ministry.' If you have not read this little tract, you should get it without delay. I would lay down two maxims for your conduct: 1. Never *forget* any thing you have learned, especially in language, science, history, chronology, antiquities, and theology. 2. *Improve* in every thing you have learned, and *acquire* what you never had, especially whatever may be useful to you in the work of the ministry. As to your *making* or *composing* sermons, I have no good opinion of it. Get a thorough knowledge of your subject: understand your text in all its connection and bearings, and then go into the pulpit depending on the Spirit of God to give you power to explain and illustrate to the people those general and particular views which you have already taken of your subject, and which you conscientiously believe to be correct and according to the word of God. But get nothing by heart to speak there, else even your *memory* will contribute to keep you in perpetual bondage. No man was ever a successful preacher who did not discuss his subject from his own *judgment* and *experience*. The *reciters* of sermons may be *popular;* but God scarcely ever employs them to convert sinners, or build up saints in their most holy faith. I do not recommend in this case a blind reliance upon God; taking a text which you do not know how to handle, and depending upon God to give you *something to say.* He will not be thus employed. Go into the pulpit with your understanding full of light, and your heart full of God; and his Spirit will help you, and then you will find a wonderful *assemblage of ideas* coming in to your assistance; and you will feel the benefit of the doctrine of *association,* of which the *reciters* and *memory men* can make no use. The finest, the best, and the most impressive thoughts are obtained in the pulpit when the preacher enters it with the preparation mentioned above.

"As to Hebrew, I advise you to learn it with the points. Dr. C. Bayley's Hebrew Grammar is one of the best; as it has several analyzed portions of the Hebrew text in it, which are a great help to learners. And Parkhurst's Hebrew Lexicon exceeds all that ever went before it. It gives the *ideal* meaning of the roots without which who can understand the Hebrew language? Get your verbs and nouns so well fixed in your memory that you shall be able to tell the conjugation, mood, tense, person, and number of every word; and thus you will feel that you tread on sure ground as you proceed. Genesis is the simplest book to begin with; and although the Psalms are highly poetic, and it is not well for a man to begin to acquire a knowledge of any language by beginning with the highest poetic production in it; yet the short hemistich form of the verses, and the powerful experimental religion which the Psalms inculcate, render them comparatively easy to him who has the life of God in his soul. Bythner's *Lyra-Prophetica,* in which all the Psalms are analyzed, is a great help; but the roots should be sought for in Parkhurst. Mr. Bell has published a good Greek grammar in English; so have several others. The Greek, like the Hebrew, depends so much on its verbs, their formation and power, that, to make any thing successfully out, you must thoroughly acquaint yourself with them in all their conjugations, &c. It is no mean labour to acquire these; for, in the above, even one regular verb will occur up ward of eight hundred different times! Mr. Dawson has published a lexicon for the Greek Testament, in which you may find any word that occurs, with the mood, tense, &c. Any of the later editions of Schrevelius will answer your end. Read carefully Prideaux's History. The editions prior to 1725 are good for little; none since that period has been much improved, if any thing. Acquaint yourself with British history. Read few sermons, they will do you little good; those of Mr. Wesley excepted. The Lives of holy men will be profitable to you. Live in the divine life; walk in the divine life, Live for the salvation of men."

In this letter the doctor has given his own method of preparing for the pulpit, and of announcing the words of eternal life. In the year 1825 I had the pleasure to travel, in company with my venerable friend, from London to Liverpool, for the purpose of preaching in behalf of the Wesleyan Methodist Sunday schools. We lodged under the hospitable roof of W. Comer, Esq. On Sunday morning the doctor called me into his room, and, with his wonted affection, said, "Sammy, tell me what subject I shall take this forenoon." "Why, doctor, what sermons or skeletons have you brought with you?" "Skeletons!" said he, "I never write skeletons, nor have I one line of any kind with me." At this I expressed my surprise, knowing that he had to preach in Liverpool on the Sunday and Monday; at the opening of Brunswick chapel, Leeds, and another new chapel in Bradford, in the following week; and a missionary sermon in Lincoln, in his way homeward. He then said, "Read me a chapter." I took the Bible and read.—When I had got partly through the chapter, he interrupted me by saying, "Read that verse again; I think it will do." This was done, and in a short time we went down to breakfast. At half past ten I proceeded to Mount Pleasant chapel, and he to Leeds-street, where he delivered, from the text I had read to him, a sermon, as no mean judge informed me, of the highest order. Now this will help to put the matter on its proper basis; and unless the doctor's preaching be judged by the circumstances under which he appeared in the pulpit, justice is not done to him. The question is not, whether some preachers, by bending the whole of their strength for weeks or months to get up a sermon, and then preaching it again and again for many years, have not produced as finished a discourse as what the doctor in general gave; but it is, whether we have known any preachers, who, without having written a word, could go into the pulpit on the shortest notice, and pour forth such a torrent of important matter, and all flowing out of the text, as Dr. Clarke frequently did? I trow not. He might not in every instance please the admirers of "elaborate, artificial eloquence, of studied grace and euphony, of methodical exactness and imaginative brilliancy;" yet he possessed, beyond all doubt,—even if the unbounded popularity and success of fifty years, from the Norman Isles in the south, to the Shetlands in the north, were the only proof—the essentials of a great preacher. His matter was rich and various; his heart was fervid; and he excelled in the power of selecting from his stores, almost at once, the suitable materials for the instant occasion, which he poured forth with energy and freedom. His plan was to prepare his *mind,* rather than his *paper* of particular arrangements; to keep the fountain full, and he knew that at his bidding it would flow; and by his commanding genius he gave the proper measure and direction of the streams; while God accompanied his word with an extraordinary unction of the Holy Spirit. Dr. Clarke's preaching was chiefly expository. He endeavoured to explain the terms in his text; to ascertain the precise meaning of the Holy Ghost; and then to apply to the understandings and consciences of his hearers the hallowing truths thus discovered. His preaching, though argumentative, was decidedly evangelical. No minister ever lived, who gave a greater prominence in his discourses to the vital truths of Christianity, or who contended for them with more consistency and zeal. In all his ministrations, there was a constant reference to the divinity and atonement of Christ, to the doctrines of justification through faith in his blood, and sanctification through the all-pervading and all-purifying energy of the Spirit. The "illimitable mercy of Heaven," the universal redemption of mankind, and especially the witness of the Spirit to the fact of the believer's adoption into the family of God, and Christian perfection, were his favourite topics, those on which he laid the greatest stress; and he frequently said, that, if the Methodists gave up these doctrines, they would soon lose their glory. He had also a peculiarly happy method of describing the simple, adapted, expeditions terms of salvation; and was the honoured instrument of leading many a penitent sinner immediately to the Saviour. The religion which he recommended to his hearers was eminently of an experimental, practical, and happy kind; such as is felt in the heart, exemplified in the life, and causes its possessor to "rejoice in the Lord alway, and again to rejoice." And all his subjects he applied with peculiar faithfulness, point, and expressiveness. He was once preaching on the love of God to man, and toward the conclusion of his discourse he gave a sweep to his arm, drawing it toward himself, and grasping his hand, as though he had collected in it several objects of value, and then, throwing them, like alms, in the full bounty of his soul, among the people. "Here," he said, "take the arguments among you — make the best of them for your salvation — I will vouch for their solidity — I will stake my credit for intellect upon them. Yes, if it were possible to collect them into one, and suspend them, as you would suspend a weight, on a single hair of this gray head, that very hair would be found to be so firmly fastened to the throne of the all-merciful and ever loving God, that all the devils in hell might be defied to cut it in two." Nor was he ever "hard to be understood." A poor woman in Shetland unintentionally paid the following compliment to him. She had heard of his celebrity, and went to hear him at Lerwick. On her return home, she remarked, with great simplicity: "They say that Dr. Clarke is a learned man, and I expected to find him such; but he is only like another man; for I could understand every word he said."

In prayer Dr. Clarke was simple, spiritual, and sometimes singularly ardent. He approached the throne of grace with a holy and reverential boldness, as if he were speaking to One with whom he was familiar, to One of whom he had an inexpressible estimation. His prayers "were literally collects, in which the whole collected meaning and ardour of his soul, for the time being, were darted forth at once."

Nor did the fervour of his love to Christ, and to the souls of perishing sinners, cool in the least, "as days and months increased." When he had passed his threescore years, he wrote: "O Sammy! how highly has God favoured you, to employ you in this work! How glad I should be to be your companion! *When I could,* I was a missionary; and many hardships have I suffered: and I feel the same spirit still. Chasms, and bogs, and voes, and men, and devils would be nothing to me: I have met *all such* in the name of Jesus, and have suffered, and have conquered."

And in another letter:—"Were God to restore me to youth again, I would glory to be your companion,—to go through your thick and thin,—to lie on the ground, herd with the oxen, or lie down on a bottle of straw, as I have been obliged to do in former times. I do envy you. Where duty is concerned, winds, waves, and hyperborean regions are nothing to me. I can eat even the meanest things—I can dine heartily on a few potatoes, and some salt, or half a pint of milk. I can wear a sack, if necessary; for fine clothing I never affected. The S. P. are all gentlemen. I thank God I bore the yoke in my youth. You do not take too much upon you. Somebody must work; the burthen is laid on you. If God spare life, I will stand by you: and he will, should he be pleased to take me."

The writings of Dr. Clarke are very voluminous; and for simplicity, perspicuity, and energy of style,—for various, extensive, and important information,—are, perhaps, not surpassed in this or in any other language. Few writers have more successfully conveyed "thoughts that breathe in words that burn." The measure of syllables, and the dance of periods, were beneath his notice. He never sacrificed sense to sound; but communicated, and that without laborious effort, the treasures of his mind to others, in words best adapted to convey his meaning and most likely to be understood. The same great truths on which he laid such stress in his preaching, are equally prominent in his writings. On the "five points," all his readers know that his views were similar to those of the celebrated Arminius, of whom he entertained a high opinion, and once said to me that "the British public was greatly indebted to Mr. Nichols for his excellent translation of the Works of that eminent divine," which he warmly recommended to his friends, at every convenient opportunity. On the leading subjects of revelation, the doctor spoke and wrote as one having authority. "For comprehension of thought, clear and forcible argumentation, and profound views of divine truth, some of his sermons," says an able reviewer, "are equal to the best of Farindon, Barrow, or South; but, on the subject of personal godliness, incomparably superior.

We know of no sermons in which so much learning is brought to bear upon the all- important subject of experimental religion." His "Bibliographical Dictionary," and "The Succession of Sacred Literature," display most extraordinary research and application, and form a cyclopaedia on bibliographical subjects, worthy the attention of every student in divinity. An uninteresting or unimportant volume, or even pamphlet, Dr. Clarke never wrote. But his chief work, that on which he spent a laborious life, and on which his name will descend to posterity with greatest lustre, is his "COMMENTARY ON THE HOLY SCRIPTURES." It is undoubtedly the most critical and literary, and at the same time the most spiritual and practical, of any work of the kind, that was ever published in any living language. The author had an indescribable method of simplifying his learning; and hence it is difficult to say whether the Commentary is most read and valued by the learned or by the unlearned, by the prince or by the peasant. It is a river in which an elephant may swim and a lamb may wade. He has not, like too many commentators, "each dark passage shunned;" but has routed the enemies of revelation from every text in which they had endeavoured to trench themselves, and fairly met and satisfactorily answered their strongest objections. The late Rev. John Newton, calling one day upon the Rev. Eli Bates, and seeing the first part of Dr. Clarke's Commentary lying upon the table, happened to open it in the place where the doctor makes several calculations in reference to the size of Noah's ark. When Mr. N. had finished reading the criticism, he closed the book, exclaiming, "Thank God! I never found these difficulties in the sacred record:" to which Mr.

Bates replied, "Yes, sir, you have found them as well as Dr. Clarke; but the difference is, you always *leap over them,* while he *goes through them."*

Dr. Clarke ever gave his opinion on what he conscientiously believed to be the mind of the Spirit, with "unflinching, uncompromising, unprevaricating honesty and faithfulness;" and when he has differed from commonly received notions, he has done it in the most modest, candid, and Christian manner. The following are the terms in which he speaks of himself: "Though perfectly satisfied of the purity of my motives and the simplicity of my intention, I am far from being pleased with the work itself. Whatever errors may be observed, must be attributed to my scantiness of knowledge. I do not pretend to write for the learned; I look up to them myself for instruction. All the pretensions of my work are included in the sentence that stands in the title: it is '*designed as a help to a better understanding of the sacred Writings.'*" To the numerous pamphleteering and magazine writers that took up pen against him while his Commentary was in course of publication, his constant reply was: "I am doing a great work, so that I cannot come down: why should the work cease, while I leave it, and come down to you?" In a letter to the late Rev. Joseph Hughes he says, "I never wrote a controversial tract in my life; I have seen with great grief the provokings of many, and a thousand times has my heart said,

Semper ego auditor TANTUM, *nunauamque reponam,*
Vexatus toties?

But my love of peace, and detestation of religious disputes, induced me to keep within my shell, and never to cross the waters of strife. I had hoped, as I was living at least an inoffensive life, not without the most cordial and strenuous endeavours, in my little way, to do all the public and private good in my power, I might be permitted to drop quietly into the grave. But this is denied me"

To some remarks of mine in 1825, he replied: "You say my notes on Isaiah are too short—I do not think so: on my plan they are as long as they should be. It would have been easy to have made them much longer. Jeremiah and Lamentations are just finishing at press. Ezekiel and Daniel are ready to go in, as soon as the others come out. And, if God spare life and health, the twelve minor prophets will be finished before next Christmas: so I see land at last in this long and dangerous voyage."

At the conclusion of the Commentary in 1820, he says, "In this arduous labour I have had no assistants; not even a single week's help from an *amanuensis;* no person to look for common places, or refer to an ancient author; to find out the place and transcribe a passage of Greek, Latin, or any other language, which my memory had generally recalled, or to verify a quotation; — the help excepted which I received, in the chronological department, from my own nephew. I have laboured alone for nearly twenty-five years previously to the work being sent to the press; and fifteen years have been employed in bringing it through the press to the public: and thus about forty years of my life have been consumed." The following observations which he made in a letter to a young friend, should be more publicly known: "Mr. Wesley's Notes on the New Testament are excellent and useful; and, were I not fully convinced in the fear of God of what I am about to say, I would not say it. I then say, Carefully read over my comment on the Scriptures. I wrote every page of it in reference to the ministers of the word of God, and especially those among the Methodists; and I know of no work, be it what it may, in which the doctrines of the Methodists are so clearly stated, illustrated, and proved." In this I heartily concur.

At an early age Dr. Clarke took for his motto: "Through desire a man having separated himself, seeketh and intermeddleth with all wisdom;" and I remember asking him, some years ago, if he would advise me to apply myself to the study of geology and mineralogy, when he promptly replied, "Yes; a Methodist preacher should know every thing." He not only possessed one of the most select and valuable libraries in the kingdom, but he made such use of his opportunities as but few persons have done. The stores of useful knowledge which he amassed were prodigious. The late Rev. Robert Hall pronounced him to be "an ocean of learning;" while another eminent Baptist minister says he was "unquestionably the most universal scholar of his age." He never sought, but rather shunned, literary honours; thinking himself to be undeserving of them: but learned and literary societies thought otherwise. He received, as we have seen, his diplomas of A.M. and LL. D. from the University and King's College, Aberdeen; and was successively elected president of the Liverpool and Manchester Philological Society,—member of the Oriental Sub-Committee of the British and Foreign Bible Society,—sub- commissioner of Public Records,—librarian of the Surrey Institution,—fellow of the Antiquarian Society,—member of the Royal Irish Academy,—member of the American Antiquarian Society,—member of the Geological Society of London,—member of the Royal Asiatic Society, and member of the Eclectic Society of London. But, in a letter to his friend Mr. Drew, he piously observes: "Learning I love,—learned men I prize,—with the company of the great and the good I am often delighted: but, infinitely above all these and all other possible enjoyments, I glory in Christ,—in me living and reigning, and fitting me for his heaven."

To slavery Dr. Clarke was a most determined foe, considering "it and all its appendages the first brood of hell." In politics he was a whig; but he very seldom looked over the pages of a newspaper. I was with him when be read the "Voice from St. Helena;" and shall not soon forget the terms in which he spoke of the treatment of the exiled emperor, and of the manner in which the last war was conducted. On several subjects both civil and ecclesiastical, which of late years have created no small stir, he wrote to me with the utmost freedom. These letters, for reasons which need not be mentioned, are not published in this memoir of my dear and venerable friend, whose face I shall see no more. To say that I esteemed, admired, and loved him, is saying but little: for my esteem, and admiration, and affection were such as I never felt for any other man; and I am constrained to add, "Take him for all in all, I ne'er shall look upon his like again."

He was a burning and a shining light; and thousands for a season rejoiced in his light. He suffered, from the shadow of death, a momentary obscuration, and now appears in that region where "they that be wise shall shine as the brightness of the firmament; and they that turn many to righteousness as the stars for ever and ever."

END OF THE LIFE.

CHRISTIAN THEOLOGY,

&c.

I. THE SCRIPTURES.[5]

THE NECESSITY OF REVELATION. — The absolute necessity of a divine revelation is sufficiently established. If God be the sole Fountain of light and truth, all knowledge must be derived from him. "The spirit of a man may know the things of a man; but the Spirit of God can alone know and teach the things of God." That is, the human intellect, in its ordinary power and operation, is sufficient to comprehend the various earthly things that concern man's sustenance and welfare in social life; but this intellect cannot fathom the things of God; it cannot find out the mind of the Most High; it knows not his will; it has no just idea of the end for which man was made; of that in which his best interests lie; of its own nature; of the nature of moral good and evil; how to avoid the latter, and how to attain the former, in which true happiness, or the supreme good, consists: and these things it is the province of divine revelation to teach, for they have never been taught or conceived by man.

How unspeakably we are indebted to God for giving us a revelation of his WILL and of his WORKS! Is it possible to know the

---

[5] For a brief account of the subjects, the author, and the date of every book in the Holy Scriptures, see the preface to each in Dr. Clarke's Commentary; and also his " *Clavis Biblica,*" a work that contains a fund of most important information in a very small compass. — S.D.

mind of God but from himself? It is impossible. Can those things and services which are worthy of, and pleasing to, an infinitely pure, perfect, and holy Spirit, be ever found out by reasoning and conjecture? Never; for the Spirit of God alone can know the mind of God; and by this Spirit he has revealed himself to man, and in this revelation has taught him, not only to know the glories and perfections of the Creator, but also his own origin, duty, and interest. Thus far it was essentially necessary that God should reveal his WILL; but if he had not given a revelation of his WORKS, the origin, constitution, and nature of the universe could never have been adequately known. *The world by wisdom knew not God.* This is demonstrated by the writings of the most learned and intelligent heathens. They had no just, no rational notion of the origin and design of the universe. Moses alone, of all ancient writers, gives a consistent and rational account of the creation; an account which has been confirmed by the investigations of the most accurate philosophers.

THE SCRIPTURES ARE REVELATIONS FROM GOD. — The Scriptures of the Old and New Testament are, generally, through all Christian countries, and in almost all languages, termed, THE BIBLE, from a Greek word, Βιβλος, A BOOK, as being the only book that teaches the knowledge of the true God; the origin of the universe; the creation and fall of man; the commencement of the different nations of the earth; the confusion of languages; the foundation of the church of God; the abominable and destructive nature of idolatry and false worship; the divine scheme of redemption; the immortality of the soul; the doctrine of the invisible and spiritual world; a future judgment; and the final retribution of the wicked in the pains of eternal perdition, and of the good in the blessedness of an endless glory. These Scriptures we know to be revelations from heaven: —

1. By the sublimity of the doctrines they contain; all descriptions of God, of heaven, of the spiritual and eternal worlds, being in every respect worthy of their subjects; and, on this account, widely differing from the childish conceits, absurd representations, and ridiculous accounts given of such subjects in the writings of idolaters and superstitious religionists, in all nations of the earth.

2. By the reasonableness and holiness of its precepts; all its

commands, exhortations, and promises, having the most direct tendency to make men wise, holy, and happy in themselves, and useful to one another.

3. By the miracles which they record; miracles of the most astonishing nature, which could be performed only by the almighty power of God; miracles which were wrought in the sight of thousands, were denied by none, and attested through successive ages by writers of the first respectability, as well enemies as friends of the Christian religion.

4. By the truth of its prophecies, or predictions of future occurrences, which have been fulfilled exactly in the way, and in those times, which the predictions, delivered many hundreds of years before, had pointed out.

5. By the promises which they contain; promises of pardon and peace to the penitent, of divine assistance and support to true believers, and of holiness and happiness to the godly, which are ever exactly fulfilled to all those who by faith plead them before God.

6. By the effects which those Scriptures produce in the hearts and in the lives of those who piously read them; it being always found that such persons become wiser, better, and happier in themselves, and more useful to others; better husbands and wives; better parents and children; better governors and subjects; and better friends and neighbours. While those who neglect them are generally a curse to themselves, a curse to society, and a reproach to the name of man.

7. To these proofs may be added the poverty, and illiterate and defenceless state of our Lord's disciples and the primitive preachers of his Gospel. The Jewish rulers and priesthood were, as one man, opposed to them; they sought by every means in their power to prevent the preaching of Christianity in Judea; the disciples were persecuted everywhere, and had not one man in power or authority to support them, or espouse their cause: yet a glorious Christian church was founded even at Jerusalem; thousands received and professed the faith of Christ crucified, and many of them gladly sealed the truth with their blood. When they had preached the Gospel throughout Judea, they went to the heathen, preached the Gospel in different parts of the Lesser Asia, Greece, and Italy. In all these places they had to contend with the

whole power and influence of the Roman empire, then entirely heathen, and the mistress of all the known world! Christian churches notwithstanding, were founded everywhere; and even in Rome itself, the throne of the Roman emperor! Here they were as defenceless as in Judea itself. They had to contend with all the idolatrous priests, with all the Greek philosophers, with the secular government, and with many millions of the deluded and superstitious populace, who, instigated by furious zeal, endeavoured by the most barbarous acts of persecution to support their false gods, idols, temples, and false worship. Yet before the preaching of these poor, comparatively unlearned, and totally defenceless men, idolatry fell prostrate; the heathen oracles were struck dumb; the philosophers were confounded; and the people were converted by thousands; till at last all Asia Minor and Greece, with Italy, and the various parts of the Roman Empire, received the Gospel, and abolished idolatry! Had not this doctrine been from God, and had not he by his almighty power aided these holy men, such effects could never have been produced. The success, therefore, of the unarmed and defenceless apostles and primitive preachers of Christianity is an incontrovertible proof that the Gospel is a revelation from God; that it is the means of conveying light and life to the souls of men; and that no power, whether earthly or diabolic, shall ever be able to overthrow it. It has prevailed, and must prevail till the whole earth shall be subdued, and the universe filled with the glory of God. Amen.

This revelation is now complete. God will add nothing more to it, because it contains every thing necessary for men, both in reference to this world and that which is to come; and he has denounced the heaviest judgments against those who shall add to it, or diminish any thing from it.

The oldest records among both Jews and Christians mention the books, both by number and name, which constitute the Old Testament Scriptures, and these are the identical books, both in number and name, that remain in the Hebrew canon to the present day. Not one has been added; not one has been taken away. Nor have we the slightest evidence that even one chapter or paragraph, in any one of the books come down to us, has been either added or omitted. And it is the same with the New Testament: we have not lost or received a single book or chapter which the genuine church of God has ever accounted divinely inspired and canonical. I have diligently examined this question in all the accounts we have from antiquity; and in all the collections of Hebrew and Greek MSS., both of the Old and New Testament, and their various readings, which the ablest critics have produced to public view, and some of the chief of those MSS. I have collated myself, and most, if not all, of the ancient versions, and I can conscientiously say that we have the sacred oracles, at least in essential sum and substance, as they were delivered by God to Moses and the prophets; and to the church of Christ by Jesus, his evangelists and apostles; and that nothing in the various readings of the Hebrew and Greek MSS. can be found to strengthen any error in doctrine, or obliquity in moral practice. All is safe and sound,—all pure and holy: it is the perfect law of the Lord, that converts the soul; the testimony of the Lord, that abideth for ever; and the unadulterated Gospel of Jesus Christ, which is able to make men wise unto salvation, through faith in him. This is the testimony of one who has examined this subject from the beginning to the end. And may I not ask, Is not such a testimony infinitely superior to the rash and bold assumptions of such men as are slaves to their passions, who find from the unholiness of their own hearts, and the irregularity of their lives, that it is their interest to find that called the word of God to be false or spurious, because they have too much reason to dread the perdition of ungodly men, of which the Scriptures so amply treat? I might add, too, the superiority of such a testimony to that of those bold and presumptuous men who have never examined the question, and who were as incapable of examining the streams which have proceeded from the fountain, as they were of tracing those streams to the fountain itself! Of what worth is the testimony of such men against the testimony of God, and of the whole church of Christ, through all ages; and of the best, wisest, and most learned men that ever existed? Well may it be said here, and said with triumph, "What is the chaff to the wheat? saith the Lord."

Who then are they who cry out, "The Bible is a fable?" Those who have never read it, or read it only with the fixed purpose to gainsay it. I once met with a person who professed to disbelieve every tittle of the New Testament, a chapter of which, he acknowledged, he had never read. I asked him, had he ever read the Old? He answered, No! And yet this man had the assurance to reject the whole as an imposture! God has mercy on those whose ignorance leads them to form prejudices against the truth; but he confounds those who take them up through envy and malice, and endeavour to communicate them to others.

The men who can despise and ridicule this sacred book are those who are too blind to discover the objects presented to them by this brilliant light, and are too sensual to feel and relish spiritual things.

The book of GENESIS is the most ancient record in the world; including the history of two grand subjects, CREATION and PROVIDENCE; of each of which it gives a summary, but astonishingly minute and detailed account. From this book almost all the ancient philosophers, astronomers, chronologists, and historians have taken their respective *data;* and all the modern improvements and accurate discoveries in different arts and sciences have only served to confirm the facts detailed by Moses; and to show that all the ancient writers on these subjects have approached to or receded from TRUTH and the phenomena of nature, in proportion as they have followed the Mosaic history.

The works of Moses, we may justly say, have been a kind of text book to almost every writer on geology, geography, chronology, astronomy, natural history, ethics, jurisprudence, political economy, theology, poetry, and criticism, from his time to the present day; books to which the choicest writers and philosophers in pagan antiquity have been deeply indebted, and which were the text books to all the prophets; books from which the flimsy writers against divine revelation have derived their natural religion and all their moral excellence; books written in all the energy and purity of the incomparable language in which they are composed; and finally, books which, for importance of matter, variety of information, dignity of sentiment, accuracy of facts, impartiality, simplicity, and sublimity of narration, tending to improve and ennoble the intellect, and meliorate the physical and moral condition of man, have never been equalled, and can only be paralleled by the GOSPEL of the Son of God! Fountain of endless mercy, justice, truth, and beneficence! how much are thy gifts and bounties neglected by those who do not read this law; and by those who, having read it, are not morally improved by it, and made wise unto salvation!

Had not the history of Joseph formed a part of the sacred

Scriptures, it would have been published in all the living languages of man, and read throughout the universe! But it contains "the things of God," and to all such the "carnal mind is enmity."

Numerous prophecies, long previously delivered, and in the keeping of those who in the days of Christ's flesh were his most inveterate enemies, had announced his approach, described his person, detailed his sufferings, showed forth his death and resurrection, and foretold the propagation and influence of his religion over the earth. From this fountain of light and salvation a new race of inspired authors proceeded, who shone with that clear and steady light which they received from Him, and reflected his brightness throughout the universe. It is worthy of remark that, notwithstanding the most numerous and the most eminent writers that ever adorned the republic of letters sprang from this light of life and truth, yet He himself was never known to write but once, John viii, 8, and that in the dust, in reference to a sinner who was brought to be condemned by him; — and what he then wrote no man knows, as he did not think proper to hand it down to posterity.

The facts which St. Luke mentions, chap. iii, 1, 2, tend much to confirm the truth of the evangelical history. Christianity differs widely from philosophic system; it is founded in the goodness and authority of God; and attested by historic facts. It differs also from popular tradition, which either has had no pure origin, or which is lost in unknown or fabulous antiquity. It differs also from pagan and Mohammedan revelations, which were fabricated in a corner, and had no witnesses. In the above verses we find the persons, the places, and the times marked with the utmost exactness. It was under the first Caesars that the preaching of the Gospel took place; and in their time the facts on which the whole of Christianity is founded made their appearance: an age the most enlightened and best known from the multitude of its historic records. It was in Judea, where every thing that professed to come from God was scrutinized with the most exact and unmerciful criticism. In writing the history of Christianity, the evangelists appeal to certain facts which were publicly transacted in such places, under the government and inspection of such and such persons, and in such particular times. A thousand persons could have confronted the falsehood, had it been one. These appeals are made — a challenge is offered to the Roman government, and to the Jewish rulers and people—a new religion has been introduced in such a place, at such a time—this has been accompanied with such and such facts and miracles! Who can disprove this? All are silent. None appears to offer even an objection. The cause of infidelity and irreligion is at stake! If these facts cannot be disproved, the religion of Christ must triumph. None appears, because none could appear. Now, let it be observed that the persons of *that time,* only, could confute these things had they been false; they never attempted it; therefore these facts are absolute and incontrovertible truths: this conclusion is necessary. Shall a man, then, give up his faith in such attested facts as these, because, more than a thousand years after, an infidel creeps out, and ventures publicly to sneer at what his iniquitous soul hopes is not true?

How impartial is the history that God writes! We may see, from several commentators, what man would have done, had he had the same facts to relate. The history given by God details as well the vices as the virtues of those who are its subjects. How widely different from that in the Bible is the biography of the present day! Virtuous acts that were never performed, voluntary privations which were never borne, piety which was never felt, and, in a word, lives which were never lived, are the principal subjects of *our* biographical relation. These may be well termed the *Lives of the Saints,* for to these are attributed all the virtues which can adorn the human character, with scarcely a failing or a blemish; while, on the other hand, those in general mentioned in the sacred writings stand marked with deep shades. What is the inference which a reflecting mind, acquainted with human nature, draws from a comparison of the biography of the Scriptures with that of uninspired writers? The inference is this—the Scripture history is natural, is probable, bears all the characteristics of veracity, narrates circumstances which seem to make against its own honour, yet dwells on them, and often seeks occasion to REPEAT them. It is true! infallibly true! In this conclusion common sense, reason, and criticism join. On the other hand, of biography in general, we must say that it is often unnatural, improbable; is destitute of many of the essential characteristics of truth; studiously avoids mentioning those circumstances which are dishonourable to its subject; ardently endeavours either to cast those which it cannot wholly hide into deep shades, or sublime them into virtues. This is notorious, and we need not go far for numerous examples. From these facts a reflecting mind will draw this general conclusion—an impartial history, in every respect true, can be expected only from God himself.

The Sacred Writings contain such proofs of a Divine origin that, though all the dead were to rise to convince an unbeliever of the truths therein declared, the conviction could not be greater, nor the proofs more evident, of the divinity and truth of those sacred records, than that which themselves afford.

HOW REVELATION HAS BEEN GIVEN.—God communicated the Scripture in ancient times to holy men, by the inspiration of his own Spirit, who carefully wrote it down, and delivered it to those to whom it was at first more immediately sent; and they have handed it down from generation to generation, without addition, defalcation, or wilful corruption of any kind.

In many cases the silence of Scripture is not less instructive than its most pointed communications.

There is sufficient evidence from the Scriptures themselves, that the Revelation of the Divine Will was given to men in the five following ways:—

1. By the personal appearance of Him who is termed "the Angel of the Covenant," and "the Angel in whom was the name of Jehovah;" who was afterward revealed as the Saviour of mankind.

2. By an audible voice, sometimes accompanied by emblematical appearances.

3. By the ministry of angels, often working miracles.

4. By dreams and visions of the night, or in trances by day.

5. But the most common way was by direct inspiration by the powerful agency of God on the mind, giving it a strong conception and supernatural persuasion of the truth of the things which he revealed to the understanding.

Why is it that God has observed so slow a climax in bringing the necessary knowledge of his will and their interest to mankind? For instance, giving a little under the patriarchal, an increase under the Mosaic, and the fulness of the blessing under the Gospel dispensation? It is true, he could have given the whole in the beginning to Adam, to Noah, to Abraham, or any other of the *ante* or *post-diluvian* fathers; but that this would not have as effectually answered the divine purpose, may be safely asserted.

God, like his instrument nature, delights in progression; and although the works of both, *in semine*, were finished from the beginning, nevertheless they are not brought forward to actual and complete existence, but by various accretions. And this appears to be done that the blessings resulting from both may be properly valued, as, in their approach, men have time to discover their necessities; and, when relieved, after a thorough consciousness of their urgency, they see and feel the propriety of being grateful to their kind Benefactor.

Were God to bestow his blessings before the want of them were truly felt, men could not be properly grateful for the reception of blessings the value of which they had not known by previously feeling the want of them. God gives his blessings that they may be duly esteemed, and he himself become the sole object of our dependence: and this end he secures by a gradual communication of his bounties as they are felt to be necessary. To give them all at once would defeat his own intention, and leave us unconscious of our dependence on and debt to his grace. He, therefore, brings forward his various dispensations of mercy and love, as he sees men prepared to receive and value them; and as the receipt of the grace of one dispensation makes way for another, and the soul is thereby rendered capable of more extended views and communications, so the divine Being causes every succeeding dispensation to exceed that which preceded it: on this ground we find a climax of dispensations, and in each a progressive, graduated scale of light, life, power, and holiness.

THE USE OF REVELATION.—The word *torah* or LAW comes from the root *yarah,* which signifies to "aim at, teach, point out, direct, lead, guide, make straight or even;" and from these significations of the word (and in all these senses it is used in the Bible) we may see at once the nature, properties, and design of the law of God. It is a system of INSTRUCTION in righteousness; it teaches the difference between moral good and evil; ascertains what is right and fit to be done, and what should be left undone, because improper to be performed. It continually aims at the glory of God, and the happiness of his creatures; teaches the true knowledge of the true God, and the destructive nature of sin; points out the absolute necessity of an atonement as the only means by which God can be reconciled to transgressors; and in its very significant rites and ceremonies points out the Son of God, till he should come to put away iniquity by the sacrifice of himself. It is a revelation of God's wisdom and goodness, wonderfully well calculated to direct the hearts of men into the truth, to guide their feet into the path of life, and to make straight, even, and plain, that way which leads to God, and in which the soul must walk in order to arrive at eternal life. It is the fountain whence every correct notion relative to God — his perfections, providence, grace, justice, holiness, omniscience, and omnipotence — has been derived. And it has been the origin whence all the true principles of law and justice have been derived. The pious study of it was the grand means of producing the greatest kings, the most enlightened statesmen, the most accomplished poets, and the most holy and useful men that ever adorned the world. It is exceeded only by the Gospel of Jesus Christ, which is at once the accomplishment of its rites and predictions, and the fulfilment of its grand plan and outline. As a system of teaching or instruction, it is the most sovereign and most effectual; as by it is the knowledge of sin; and it alone is the schoolmaster that leads men to Christ, that they may be justified through faith, Gal. iii, 24. Who can absolutely ascertain the exact quantum of obliquity in a crooked line, without the application of a straight one? And could sin, in all its twistings, windings, and varied involutions, have ever been truly ascertained, had not God given to man this perfect rule to judge by? The nations who acknowledge this revelation of God have, as far as they attend to its dictates, the wisest, purest, most equal, and most beneficial laws. The nations that do not receive it have laws at once extravagantly severe and extravagantly indulgent. The proper distinctions between moral good and evil, in such states, are not known: hence the penal sanctions are not founded on the principles of justice, weighing the exact proportion of moral turpitude; but on the most arbitrary caprices, which in many cases show the utmost indulgence to first-rate crimes, while they punish minor offences with rigour and cruelty. What is the consequence? Just what might be reasonably expected: the will and caprice of man being put in the place of the wisdom of God, the government is oppressive, and the people, frequently goaded to distraction, rise up in a mass and overturn it; so that the monarch, however powerful for a time, seldom lives out half his days. This *was* the case in Greece, in Rome, in the major part of the Asiatic governments, and *is* the case in all nations of the world to the present day, where the government is despotic, and the laws not formed according to the revelation of God.

The word *lex*, "law," among the Romans, has been derived from *lego*, "I read," because when a law or statute was made, it was hung up in the most public places, that it might be *seen, read*, and *known* by all men; that those who were to obey the laws might not break them through ignorance, and thus incur the penalty. This was called *promulgatio legis, quasi provulgatio,* "the promulgation of the law," that is, the laying it before the common people. Or from *ligo,* "I bind," because the law binds men to the strict observance of its precepts. The Greeks call a law νομος *nomos,* from νεμο "to divide, distribute, minister to, or serve," because the law divides to all their just rights, appoints or distributes to each his proper duty, and thus serves or ministers to the welfare of the individual, and the support of society. Hence, where there are either no laws, or unequal and unjust ones, all is distraction, violence, rapine, oppression, anarchy, and ruin.

"The sword of the Spirit, which is the word of God," cuts every way; it convinces of sin, righteousness, and judgment; pierces between the joints and the marrow, divides between the soul and the spirit, dissects the whole mind, and exhibits a regular anatomy of the soul. It not only reproves and exposes sin, but it slays the ungodly, pointing out and determining the punishment they shall endure.

"It is a critic of the propensities and suggestions of the heart." How many have felt this property of God's word where it has been faithfully preached! How often has it happened that a man has seen the whole of his own character, and some of the most private transactions of his life, held up as it were to public view by the preacher; and yet the parties absolutely unknown to each other! Some, thus exhibited, have even supposed that their neighbours must have privately informed the preacher of their character and conduct; but it was the word of God, which, by the direction and energy of the divine Spirit, thus searched them out, was "a critical examiner of the propensities and suggestions of their hearts," and had pursued them through all their public haunts and private ways.

Every genuine minister of the Gospel has witnessed such effects as these under his ministry in repeated instances.

The law of God is a code of instruction, in which God makes himself known in the holiness and justice of his nature, his displacence at sin, and his love of righteousness; — as also to manifest himself in the magnitude of his mercy, and readiness to save. In a word, it is God's system of instruction by which men are taught the knowledge of their Creator and of themselves — directed how to walk so as to please God — redeemed from crooked paths — and guided in the way that leads to everlasting life. This is the Bible — The Book, by way of eminence — the Book made by God — the only book that is without blemish or error — the book that contains the TRUTH, the *whole* TRUTH, and nothing but the TRUTH: that without which we should have known *little* about God, less concerning ourselves, and *nothing* about heaven, the resurrection, or a future state: the book that contains the greatest mass of learning ever put together — the book from which all the sages of antiquity have, directly or indirectly, derived their knowledge: by means of which, the nations who have studied it most, and known it best, have formed the wisest code of laws, and have become the wisest and the most powerful nations of the earth.

The revelation which God has given of himself is a perfect system of instruction. It reveals no more than we ought to know; it keeps nothing back that would be profitable. It gives us a proper view of the nature and authority of the Lawgiver. It shows the right he has to govern us.

All well constituted and wisely enacted laws are for the benefit of the subjects. This is emphatically the case with the law of God. He needs not our allegiance — He wants not our tribute. He is infinitely perfect, and needs nothing that we can bring. There was the utmost necessity for this law: — He that is without law is without reason and rule. He has no line to walk by — nothing to teach, restrain, or correct him. He is led astray by his passions; and lives to his own ruin and destruction. God in his mercy has given him a law to bind, to instruct, and to lead him. In this law he has shown man at once his duty and his interest.

The revelation of God is the mind of God made known to man; and the mind is not truer to itself, than the inspired writings are to the mind and purpose of God.

All God's commandments lead to purity, enjoin purity, and point out that sacrificial offering by which cleansing and purification are acquired.

How true is that word, "The law of the Lord is PERFECT!" In a small compass, and in a most minute detail it comprises every thing that is calculated to instruct, direct, convince, correct, and fortify the mind of man. Whatever has a tendency to corrupt or injure man, that it forbids; whatever is calculated to comfort him, promote and secure his best interests, that it commands. It takes him in all possible states, views him in all connections, and provides for his present and eternal happiness.

As the human soul is polluted and tends to pollution, the great doctrine of the law is "holiness to the Lord." This it keeps invariably in view in all its commands, precepts, ordinances, rites, and ceremonies. And how forcibly in all these does it say, "Thou shalt love the Lord thy God with all thy heart, and with all thy soul, and with all thy mind, and with all thy strength; and thy neighbour as thyself!" This is the prominent doctrine of the Bible; and this shall be fulfilled in all them who believe, for "Christ is the end of the law for righteousness to them that believe." Reader, magnify God for his law, for by it is the knowledge of sin; and magnify him for his Gospel, for by this is the cure of sin. Let the law be thy schoolmaster to bring thee to Christ, that thou mayest be justified by faith; and that the righteousness of the law may be fulfilled in thee, and that thou mayest walk, not after the flesh, but after the Spirit.

The law is not to be considered as a system of external rites and ceremonies; nor even as a rule of moral action. It is a spiritual system; it reaches to the most hidden purposes, thoughts, dispositions, and desires of the heart and soul; and it reproves and condemns every thing, without hope of reprieve or pardon, that is contrary to eternal truth and rectitude.

The law could not pardon; the law could not sanctify; the law could not dispense with its own requisitions; it is the rule of righteousness, and therefore must condemn unrighteousness. This is its unalterable nature. Had there been perfect obedience to its dictates, instead of condemning, it would have applauded and rewarded; but as the flesh, the carnal and rebellious principle, had prevailed, and transgression had taken place, it was rendered weak, inefficient to undo this work of the flesh, and bring the sinner into a state of pardon and acceptance with God.

Where the law ends, Christ begins. The law ends with representative sacrifices; Christ begins with the real offering. The law is our schoolmaster to lead us to Christ; it cannot save, but it leaves us at his door, where alone salvation is to be found. Christ, as an arguing sacrifice for sin, was the grand object of the whole sacrificial code of Moses; his passion and death were the fulfilment of its great object and design. Separate this sacrificial death of Christ from the law, and the law has no meaning, for it is impossible that the blood of bulls and goats should take away sins.

Take Jesus, his grace, Spirit, and religion out of the Bible, and it has neither scope, design, object, nor end.

The Gospel is God's method of saving a lost world, in a way which that world could never have imagined. There is nothing human in it; it is all truly and gloriously divine, essentially necessary to the salvation of man, and fully adequate to the purposes of its institution.

Every language is confounded, less or more, but that of eternal truth. This is ever the same; in all countries, climates, and ages, the language of truth, like that God from whom it sprang, is unchangeable. It speaks in all tongues, to all nations, and in all hearts: "There is one GOD, the Fountain of goodness, justice, and truth. MAN, thou art his creature, ignorant, weak, and dependent; but he is all- sufficient—hates nothing that he has made— loves *thee* — is able and willing to save *thee;* return to and depend on him, take his revealed will for thy law, submit to his authority, and accept eternal life on the terms proposed in his word, and thou shalt never perish nor be wretched." This language of truth all the ancient and modern Babel-builders have not been able to confound, notwithstanding their repeated attempts. How have men toiled to make this language clothe their own ideas; and thus cause God to speak according to the pride, prejudice, and worst passions of men! But through a just judgment of God, the language of all those who have attempted to do this has been confounded, and the word of the Lord abideth for ever.

ALL SHOULD KNOW THE SCRIPTURES. — The Holy Scriptures are plain enough; but the heart of man is darkened by sin. The Bible does not so much need a comment, as the soul does the light of the

Holy Spirit. Were it not for the darkness of the human intellect, the things relative to salvation would be easily apprehended.

Nothing can be more preposterous and monstrous than to call people to embrace the doctrines of Christianity, and refuse them the opportunity of consulting the book in which they are contained. Persons who are denied the use of the sacred writings may be manufactured into different forms and modes; and be mechanically led to believe certain dogmas, and perform certain religious acts; but without the use of the Scriptures they never can be intelligent Christians; they do not search the Scriptures, and therefore they cannot know Him of whom these Scriptures testify.

II. – GOD.

MANY attempts have been made to define the term God:[6] As to the word itself, it is pure Anglo-Saxon, and among our ancestors signified, not only the divine Being, now commonly designated by the word, but also *good;* as in their apprehensions it appeared that *God* and *good* were correlative terms; and when they thought or spoke of him they were doubtless led from the word itself to consider him as THE GOOD BEING, a Fountain of infinite benevolence and beneficence toward his creatures.

A general definition of this great First Cause, as far as human words dare attempt one, may be thus given: The eternal, independent, and self- existent Being: the Being whose purposes and actions spring from himself, without foreign motive or influence: he who is absolute in dominion; the most pure, the most simple, and most spiritual of all essences; infinitely benevolent, beneficent, true, and holy: the cause of all being, the upholder of all things; infinitely happy, because infinitely perfect; and eternally self-sufficient, needing nothing that he has made; illimitable in his immensity, inconceivable in his mode of existence, and indescribable in his essence; known fully only to himself, because an infinite mind can be fully apprehended only by itself – in a word,

---

[6] Those who wish to see an attempt to demonstrate, by arguments *a priori* and *a posteriori*, the necessary existence of a supreme and eternal Being, are referred to the doctor's Commentary, Heb. xi, at the end. – S.D.

a Being who, from his infinite wisdom, can not err or be deceived; and who, from his infinite goodness, can do nothing but what is eternally just, right, and kind. Reader, such is the God of the Bible; but how widely different from the God of most human creeds and apprehensions!

The Being called "GOD" is allowed by all who think rightly on the subject to be a living, rational Essence.

A. He is an *Essence;* that is, something that exists, and exists distinctly from every thing: and is an independent Essence or Being; it exists of or by itself; is not connected with any other to be preserved in existence; so that were all other essences destroyed this would still subsist; and this must imply that this Essence must be underived, else it could not be independent: and the destruction of its principle must necessarily involve its destruction also; for all effects must cease with their producing causes.

As therefore this Essence is independent and underived, existing of and by itself, it must also be eternal: for as it is the First Cause, and independent of all other kinds of being, so it cannot be affected by any other; and cannot destroy itself, for this would suppose it to possess a power superior to itself, which is absurd; and as nothing else can destroy it, and it cannot destroy itself, it must therefore be eternal.

If all other beings be derived beings, (that is, cannot be the cause of their own existence,) and this is the only first and unoriginated Cause, therefore all others must owe their being to it, and be dependent on it. This Being then is the Creator and Preserver of all things: and this is the general notion entertained of GOD.

B. I have said above that this Being is considered as a *living* Essence. — This distinguishes him from matter, from all chaos, or first seeds, or principles of things; and from all *inertiae* or *vis inertiae* — that disposition of matter by which it resists all endeavours to alter its state of rest: and as life implies an active, operative existence, so it is properly applied to GOD, from whose life comes the living; principle of all things; and by whose activity or energy comes all life, and all the operations of animate and inanimate beings.

C. He is called a *rational* Essence. — As reason implies that faculty whereby we discern good from evil, right from wrong, so in the divine Essence it implies a boundless knowledge or sagacity, by which it comprehends all ideas of all things that do or can exist, with all their relations, connections, combinations, uses, and ends. Such a rational essence is GOD; and as he is the cause of all being, so all reason, sagacity, knowledge and understanding, come from him.

Thus we find that he is *the most excellent,* and most perfect, of all living and rational essences; and whatever excellence or perfection is found in any being must be derived from himself.

D. This Essence is the most excellent. — Excellence signifies *a surpassing or going beyond others in grand or useful qualities.* Whatever of this sort we see in any being, — whatever we hear has been possessed by any, — and whatever we can conceive possible to be possessed by any, — God excels all this, and infinitely more than this; and therefore he is the most excellent of all essences.

E. This Essence is *the most perfect.* — Perfection signifies *any thing complete, consummate;* in every respect made and finished; so that nothing is wanting, nothing redundant; and, in a moral sense, which is entirely pure, unblamable and immaculate; or that which in every moral and spiritual respect has consummate excellence: so GOD, as being the cause of all that is great, good, immaculate and excellent, is himself the most perfect of all essences; for we can conceive of nothing that can be added to his excellence, to make it greater or more perfect than it is; and we can conceive of no perfection that he does not possess in an absolute and unlimited manner.

Adonai is the word which the Jews in reading always substitute for Jehovah, as they count it impious to pronounce this name. Adonai signifies *my director, basis, supporter, prop,* or *stay;* and scarcely a more appropriate name can be given to that God who is the framer and director of every righteous word and action; the basis or foundation on which every rational hope rests; the supporter of the souls and bodies of men, as well as of the universe in general; the prop and stay of the weak and fainting; and the buttress that shores up the building which otherwise must necessarily fall. This word often occurs in the Hebrew Bible, and is rendered in our translation "Lord;" the same term by which the word "Jehovah" is expressed: but to distinguish between the two, and to show the reader when the original is Jehovah, and when Adonai, the first is always put in capitals, LORD, the latter in plain

Roman characters, Lord.

Lord and *God* are frequently interchanged; but every *Lord* is not *God*. It is the dominion of a spiritual Being or Lord, that constitutes GOD; true dominion, true GOD; supreme dominion, the supreme GOD; feigned dominion, the false god. He governs all things that exist, and knows all things that are to be known, He is not eternity, nor infinity: but he is eternal and infinite. He is not duration, nor space; but he endures always, is present everywhere; and by existing always and everywhere, he constitutes the very things *duration* and *space, eternity* and *infinity*.

The nature of God is illimitable, and all the attributes of that nature infinitely glorious: they cannot be lessened by the transgressions of his creatures, nor can they be increased by the uninterrupted, eternal obedience, and increasing hallelujahs, of all the intelligent creatures that people the whole vortex of nature.

III. – ATTRIBUTES OF GOD.

This Jehovah is a Being of such infinite perfections, that no defect in him can be imagined; nor can we conceive any thing that might raise, improve, or exalt his nature. Because he is an infinite fulness, nothing can be added: and because he fills all space – the heavens and the earth, and inhabits eternity – nothing can be taken away from him. Whatever exists must necessarily be his creature, or an effect produced by him, the supreme First Cause. As he is independent and self- sufficient, he needs nothing that he has made. From eternity he existed without any other kind of being; and when he chose to create innumerable beings of endlessly varied natures, and possessing various degrees of relative perfection, he still continued to be the same independent being; all others deriving their existence and support from him.

UNITY . – There is ONE GOD, who is self-existing, uncreated, infinitely wise, powerful, and good; who is present in every place; and fills the heavens, and earth, and all things. Now, as THIS ONE God is eternal, that is, without beginning or end, and is present everywhere, and fills all space, there can be only ONE such Being; for there cannot be two or more eternals, or two or more who are present everywhere, and fill all things. To suppose more than one supreme source of infinite wisdom, power, and all perfections, is to assert that there is no Supreme Being in existence. A plurality of eternal beings would resemble a plurality of universes, eternities, and infinite spaces; all which would be contradictory and absurd.

SPIRITUALITY.—We must not attempt to form conceptions of the supreme Being as if confined to *form,* to any kind of *limits,* to any particular *space* or *place.* As JEHOVAH, he is in every respect inconceivable;—no mind can grasp him;—he is an infinite Spirit;—equally in every place, and in all points of duration;—he cannot be more present in one place than in another, because he fills the heavens and the earth, though the manifestations of his presence may be more in particular places and especial times. His working shows that he is here and present; though he would be no less present, were there no apparent working. He is not like man, though, in condescension to our weakness, he represents himself often as possessing human members and human affections. When a thing is said to be done by the finger, the hand, or the arm of God,—this only points out degrees of power manifested in performing certain works of mercy, providence, deliverance, &c. And these degrees of power are always in proportion to the work that is to be effected. The *finger* may indicate a comparatively slight interference, where a miracle is wrought; but not one that is stupendous: the *hand,* one where great power is necessary, accompanied by evident skill and design: and the *arm,* one in which the mighty power of God comes forward with sovereign, overwhelming, irresistible effect. When the *shoulder* is attributed to him, it points out his almighty sustaining power,—maintaining his government of the world, and of his church; supporting whatever he has made;—so his *heart* represents his concern for his own honour, for the welfare of his followers, and for the afflicted and distressed.

This one infinite and eternal Being is a Spirit: that is, he is not compounded, nor made up of parts; for then he would be nothing different from matter, which is totally void of intelligence and power. And hence he must be invisible; for a spirit cannot be seen by the eye of man: nor is there any thing in this principle contradictory to reason or experience. We all know there is such a thing as the air we breathe, as the wind that whistles through the trees, fans and cools our bodies, and sometimes tears up mighty trees from their roots, overturns the strongest buildings, and agitates the vast ocean: but no man has ever seen this air or wind; though every one is sensible of its effects, and knows that it exists.

Now, it would be as absurd to deny the existence of God because we cannot see him, as it would be to deny the existence of the air or wind because we cannot see *it*.

God is a Spirit: he is nothing like man, nothing like matter, nothing like any of the creatures that he has made. For, although he be a Spirit, and he have created innumerable spirits, yet he has nothing in common with them. He is a SPIRIT, an impalpable substance of a widely different kind. As far as his nature transcends all created nature; so far does his spirituality transcend the spirituality of all created spirits.

Spirit is defined, "an uncompounded, immaterial substance." Let us not be alarmed at the word *substance,* which many compound with *matter.* Substance is *subsistence,* whether material or immaterial; but spirit is *immaterial substance,* and consequently uncompounded and indivisible. And from the ineffable spirituality of the divine Nature, we can at once conceive that he has no parts: he is unlimited, infinite, and eternal. He cannot be seen by the eye; but he may be perceived by the mind. He is not palpable to the hand; but he may be felt by the soul. By his mighty working, the most powerful and salutary changes may be wrought in the mind, which it at once perceives to be supernatural, and which, from the holiness of the effects, it knows to be the work of God.

ETERNITY.—What is most interesting is the *name by* which God was pleased to make himself known to Moses and the Israelites, a name by which the supreme Being was afterward known among the wisest inhabitants of the earth; he who IS and who WILL BE what he IS. This is a proper characteristic of the divine Being, who is, properly speaking, the only BEING, because he is independent and eternal; whereas, all other beings, in whatsoever forms they may appear, are derived, finite, changeable, and liable to destruction, decay, and even to annihilation. When God, therefore, announced himself to Moses by this name, he proclaimed his own eternity and immateriality; and the very name itself precluded the possibility of idolatry, because it was impossible for the mind, in considering it, to represent the divine Being in an assignable shape; for who could represent BEING or existence by any limited form? And who can have any idea of a form that is unlimited? Thus, then, we find that the first discovery which God made of himself was intended to show the people the simplicity and spirituality of his nature; that while they considered him as BEING, and the cause of all BEING, they might be preserved from all idolatry for ever. The very name itself is a proof of a divine revelation; for it is not possible that such an idea could have entered into the mind of man, unless it had been communicated from above. It could not have been produced by reasoning, for there were no premises on which it could be built, nor any analogies by which it could have been formed. We can as easily comprehend eternity as we can being, simply considered in and of itself, when nothing of assignable forms, colours, or qualities existed, beside its infinite and illimitable self.

All time is as nothing before him, because in the presence as in the nature of God all is eternity; therefore nothing is long, nothing short, before him; no lapse of ages impairs his purposes, nor need he wait to find convenience to execute those purposes. And when the longest period of time has passed by, it is but as a moment or indivisible point in comparison of eternity.

OMNIPOTENCE.—Every attribute of God is equal. Each is infinite, eternal, unoriginated, and without bound or limit. Such is the potency of God, it can do all things that do not imply absurdity or contradiction; it can do any thing in any way it pleases; and it can do any thing when it pleases; and it will do any thing, that is necessary to be done, and should be done, when it ought to be done, and when the doing of it will most manifest his own glory: and his glory is chiefly manifested in promoting the happiness, and saving the souls of men.

What is nature but an instrument in God's hands? What we call "natural effects" are all performed by supernatural agency; for nature, that is, the whole system of inanimate things, is as inert as any of the particles of matter of the aggregate of which it is composed, and can be a cause to no effect but as it is excited by a sovereign power. This is a doctrine of sound philosophy, and should be carefully considered by all, that men may see that, without an overruling and universally energetic providence, no effect whatever can be brought about. But beside these general influences of God in nature, which are all exhibited by what men call *general laws,* he chooses often to act supernaturally; that is, independently of, or against, these general laws, that we may see that there is a God who does not confine himself to one way of working, but with means, without means, and even against natural means, accomplishes the gracious purposes of his mercy in the behalf of man. Where God has promised, let him be implicitly credited, because he cannot lie; and let not hasty nature intermeddle with his work.

If there be laws which God has imposed on the universe, whether they be general or particular, they must have their action and efficiency from HIMSELF; and whatever be the mode according to which he governs, he himself must be the energy by which the government is administered; and therefore it is not general not particular laws which govern the world, but the great, wise, and holy God, governing according to a particular mode of his own devising; and according to which he is disposed to work. Properly speaking, he governs, not by either general or particular laws, but by his own infinite wisdom, adapting his operations to all those circumstances and occurrences which are ever before him, and ever under his direction and control; "from seeming evil still educing good—and better still in infinite progression." As all matter and spirit were created by him, and all that he has created he upholds, so all matter and spirit are governed by him. Every thing, therefore, is under his continual superintendence or governance: and as that governance is wise, holy, and good, so whatever is governed by it is governed in the best manner, and conducted to the best end.

It is granted that sin has a mighty power; and that Satan, who arms himself with the vile affections of man, and rules in the uncleanness of the heart, has a mighty power also. But what is power, however great, however malevolent, however well circumstanced to accomplish the purposes of its malevolence, when opposed by infinite Potency! All power must originally emanate from God. Power, in the above sense, must be lodged in, and must be exercised by, some intelligent being. Now, all such things, as well as others, must be dependent on Him who is the Fountain whence they were derived. Hence, they can neither exist nor act, but as he wills or permits: and hence it is evident he can at any time counteract, or suspend, or destroy all exertions of all finite beings. Therefore, be the power of sin and Satan what it may, this can be no objection against the destruction of sin in the heart of man. He is

ABLE to do THIS.

It is the prerogative of God alone to save the human soul. Nothing less than unlimited power, exerted under the direction and impulse of unbounded mercy, can save a sinner.

The resurrection of the dead is a stupendous work of God; it requires his might in sovereign action: and when we consider that all mankind are to be raised and changed in a moment, in the twinkling of an eye, then the *momentum,* or velocity, with which the power is to be applied, must be inconceivably great. All motion is in proportion to the quantity of matter in the mover, and the velocity with which it is applied. The effect here is in proportion to the cause and the energy he puts forth in order to produce it. But such is the nature of God's power in action, that it is perfectly inconceivable to us.

Every thing is equally easy to that Power which is unlimited. A universe can be as easily produced by a single act of the divine Will as the smallest elementary part of matter.

I have no doubt that the power or strength of the Divine Nature was the attribute principally contemplated by our rude ancestors, and indeed by all the primitive inhabitants of the earth, Hence colossal statues, immense rocks, and massive temples were dedicated to this power or strength, which at last the licentious imagination of man personified and adored, in a monstrous human form, under the name of *Hercules,* among the Greeks and Romans; *Baal,* among the Canaanites; *Bramah,* among the ancient Hindoos, &c.; and *Tuisco,* &c., among our Teutonic and Celtic ancestors; and hence every strong man was supposed to be the principal favourite of the Deity, and to be under the peculiar direction of this strength or power. It was this which gave rise to the histories of Hercules, Theseus, Bellerophon, and the giants of different countries.

OMNIPRESENCE.—Darkness and light, ignorance and knowledge, are things that stand in relation to us: God sees equally in darkness as in light; and knows as perfectly, however man is enveloped in ignorance, as if all were intellectual brightness. What is to us hidden by darkness, or unknown through ignorance, is perfectly seen and known by God; because he is all sight, all hearing, all feeling, all soul, all spirit— *all* in ALL, and infinite in himself. He lends to every thing; receives nothing from any thing. Though his essence be not impartible, yet his influence is diffusible through time and through eternity. Thus God makes himself known, seen, heard, felt; yet, in the infinity of his essence, neither angel, nor spirit, nor man, can see him; nor can any creature comprehend him, or form any idea of the *mode* of his existence. And yet vain man would be wise, and ascertain his foreknowledge, eternal purposes, infinite decrees, with all operations of infinite love and infinite hatred, and their objects specifically and nominally, from all eternity, as if himself had possessed a being and powers co-extensive with the Deity! O ye wise fools!—Jehovah, the Fountain of eternal perfection and love, is unlike your *creeds*, as he is unlike *yourselves*, forgers of doctrines to prove that the Source of infinite benevolence is a *streamlet of capricious love* to thousands, while he is an overflowing, eternal, and irresistible *tide of hatred* to millions of millions, both of angels and men! The antiproof of such doctrine is this:—He bears with such blasphemies, and does not consume their abettors. "But nobody holds these doctrines." Then I have written against *nobody;* and have only to add the prayer, May no such doctrines ever disgrace the page of history; or farther dishonour, as they have done, the annals of the church!

It is strange that the doctrine of real, absolute, and external space, should have induced some philosophers to conclude it was a part or attribute of God, or that God himself was space; inasmuch as incommunicable attributes of the Deity appeared to agree to this; such as infinity, immutability, indivisibility, and incorporeity; it being also uncreated, impassive, without beginning or ending:—not considering that all these negative properties belong to NOTHING. For *nothing* has no limits; cannot be moved, nor changed, nor divided: nor is it created, nor can it be destroyed.

It is, therefore, his presence that constitutes this space, without which it could not exist: and since every particle of space is always, and, in every indivisible moment, *everywhere*, the Creator and Lord of all things cannot be *never* or *nowhere*.

He is omnipresent, not only virtually, but substantially; for POWER without SUBSTANCE cannot exist.

All things are contained and move in or by him, but without any mutual passion: he suffers nothing from the motions of bodies; nor do they undergo any resistance from his omnipresence.

OMNISCIENCE.—God is infinitely wise. He knows himself, and what he has formed, and what he can do. He well knew how to construct his word so as to suit it to the state of all hearts; and he has given it that infinite fulness of meaning so as to suit it to all cases. And so infinite is he in his knowledge, and so omnipresent is he, that the whole creation is constantly exposed to his view; nor is there a creature of the affections, mind, or imagination, that is not constantly under his eye. He marks every rising thought, every budding desire.

"The manifold wisdom of God;" that multifarious and greatly diversified wisdom of God; laying great and infinite plans, and accomplishing them by endless means, through the whole lapse of ages; making every occurrence subservient to the purposes of his infinite mercy and goodness. God's gracious design to save a lost world by Jesus Christ could not be defeated by any cunning, skill, or malice of men or devils. Whatever hinderances are thrown in the way his wisdom and power can remove; and his infinite wisdom can never want ways or means to effect its gracious designs.

BENEVOLENCE.—Entertain just notions of God; of his nature, power, will, justice, goodness, and truth. Do not conceive of him as being actuated by such passions as men; separate him in your hearts from every thing earthly, human, fickle, rigidly severe, or capriciously merciful. Consider that he can neither be like man, feel like man, nor act like man. Ascribe no human passions to him; for this would desecrate, not sanctify him. Do not confine him in your conceptions to place, space, vacuity, heaven, or earth; endeavour to think worthily of the immensity and eternity of his nature, of his omniscience, omnipresence, and omnipotence. Avoid the error of the heathens, who bound even their *Dii Majores,* their greatest gods, by fate, as many well meaning Christians do the true God by decrees. Conceive of him as infinitely free to act or not act, as he pleases. Consider the goodness of his nature; for goodness, in every possible state of perfection and infinitude, belongs to him. Ascribe no malevolence to him; nor any work, purpose, or decree that implies it: this is not only a human passion, but a passion of fallen man. Do not suppose that he can do evil, or that he can destroy when he might save; that he ever did or ever can hate any of those whom he made in his own image, and in his own likeness, so as by a positive decree to doom them, unborn, to everlasting perdition; or, what is of the same import, pass them by without affording them the means of salvation, and consequently rendering it impossible for them to be saved. Thus endeavour to conceive of him; and by so doing you separate him from all that is imperfect, human, evil, capricious, changeable, and unkind. Ever remember that he has wisdom without error, power without limits, truth without falsity, love without hatred, holiness without evil, and justice without rigour or severity on the one hand, or capricious tenderness on the other: in a word, that he neither can be, say, purpose, or do any thing that is not infinitely just, holy, wise, true, and gracious; that he hates nothing that he has made; and has so loved the world, the whole human race, as to give his only begotten Son to die for them, that they might not perish, but have everlasting life. The system of humanizing God, and making him, by our unjust conceptions of him, to act as ourselves would in certain circumstances, has been the bane both of religion and piety; and on this ground infidels have laughed us to scorn. It is high time that we should no longer, "know God after the flesh;" for even if we have known Jesus Christ after the flesh, we are to know him so no more.

"God is love:" and in this an infinity of breadth, length, depth, and height is included; or rather all breadth, length, depth, and height are lost in this immensity. It comprehends all that is above, all that is below, all that is present, all that is past, and all that is to come. In reference to human beings, the love of God in its breadth is a girdle that encompasses the globe, or a mantle in which it is wrapped up. Its length reaches from the eternal purpose of the mission of Christ, to the eternity of blessedness which is to be enjoyed by the pure in heart in his ineffable glories. Its depth reaches to the lowest-fallen of the sons of Adam, and to the deepest depravity of the human heart; and its height to the infinite dignities of the throne of Christ.

Whatever is good is from God; whatever is evil is from man himself. As from the sun, which is the father or fountain of light, all light comes; so from GOD, who is the infinite Fountain, Father, and Source of good, all good comes. And whatever can be called good, or pure, or light, or excellence of any kind, must necessarily spring from him, as he is the only source of all goodness and perfection.

God dispenses his benefits when, where, and to whom he pleases. No person can complain of his conduct in these respects, because no person deserves any good from his hand. God never punishes any but those who deserve it; but he blesses incessantly those who deserve it not. The reason is evident: justice depends on certain rules; but beneficence is free. Beneficence can bless both the good and the evil; justice can punish the latter only. Those who do not make this distinction must have a very confused notion of the conduct of divine Providence among men.

Philanthropy is a character which God gives to himself: while human nature exists, this must be a character of the divine nature. God loves man: he delighted in the idea when formed in his own infinite mind; he formed man according to that idea, and rejoiced in the work of his hands.

When man fell, the same love induced him to devise his redemption, and God the Saviour flows from God the Philanthropist.

It cannot appear strange that God should will all men to be saved; for this necessarily follows from his willing the salvation of any. For that nature has not been divided, and every portion of it falls equally under the merciful regards of the Father of the spirits of all flesh.

As God is "not willing that any should perish," and as he is "willing that all should come to repentance," consequently he has never devised nor decreed the damnation of any man, nor has he rendered it impossible for any soul to be saved, either by necessitating him to do evil, that he might die for it, or refusing him the means of recovery, without which he could not be saved.

The will of God is infinitely good, wise, and holy. To have it fulfilled in and among men, is to have infinite goodness, wisdom, and holiness diffused throughout the universe; and earth made the counterpart of heaven.

Will in GOD is that which he chooses or determines to do or leave undone. Now, as an excellent, perfect, and wise Being cannot will, or wish, or desire any thing that is not good, wise, useful, and proper to be done, so the will of God is ever influenced by his goodness; therefore he can never make a bad or improper choice, nor determine any thing that is not good in itself; and good or proper to all those who may be the objects of its operation. As will implies desire, and God's nature is good, so his will or desire must be good,—good in itself, and good to all those whom it affects: hence he must be good in all his actions, and good to all his creatures, in all his determinations and providential dispensations toward them.

"God is love;" an infinite Fountain of benevolence and beneficence to every human being. He hates nothing that he has made. He cannot *hate,* because he is *love.* He causes his sun to rise on the evil and the good, and sends his rain on the just and the unjust. He has made no human being for perdition, nor ever rendered it impossible, by any necessitating decree, for any fallen soul to find mercy. He has given the fullest proof of his love to the whole human race by the incarnation of his Son, who tasted death for every man. How can a decree of absolute, unconditional reprobation of the greater part, or any part of the human race, stand in the presence of such a text as this? It has been well observed that, although God is holy, just, righteous, &c., he is never called Holiness, Justice, &c., in the abstract, as he is here called LOVE. This seems to be the essence of the divine nature, and all other attributes to be only modifications of this.

It has ever been a matter of astonishment to me that any soul of man, partaking at all of the divine nature, or knowing any thing of the ineffable love and goodness of God, should have ever indulged the sentiment, or have laboured to prove, that the God whose name is Mercy, and whose nature is Love, and "who hateth nothing that he hath made," should, notwithstanding, have a sovereign, irrespective, eternal love to a few of the fallen human race; together with a sovereign, irrevocable, and eternal hatred to the great mass of mankind; according to which the salvation of the former, and the perdition of the latter, have been, from all eternity, absolutely and irrevocably fixed, preordained, and decreed!

JUSTICE.—All the divine perfections are in perfect unity and harmony among themselves: God never acts from one of his attributes exclusively, but in the infinite unity of all his attributes. He never acts from benevolence to the exclusion of justice; nor from justice to the exclusion of mercy. Though the effect of his operations may appear to us to be in one case the offspring of power alone; in another, of justice alone; in a third, of mercy alone; yet, in respect to the divine nature itself, all these effects are the joint produce of all his perfections, neither of which is exerted more or less than another.

God's justice can have no demands but what are perfectly equitable: his justice is infinite righteousness, as totally distant from rigour, on the one hand, as from laxity or partiality on the other. Should it be said that "the wretched state of the sinner pleads aloud in the ear of God's mercy, and this is a sufficient reason why his mercy should be exercised;" I answer, that his wicked state calls as loudly in the ears of God's justice, that it might be exclusively exercised; and thus the hope from mercy is cut off. Besides, to make the culprit's MISERY, which is the effect of his sin, the reason why God should show him mercy, is to make sin and its fruits the reason why God should thus act. And thus, that which is in eternal hostility to the nature and government of God must be the motive why he should, in a most strange and contradictory way, exercise his benevolence to the total exclusion of his justice, righteousness, and truth.

All those who have read the Scriptures with care and attention know well that God is frequently represented in them as doing what he only permits to be done. So, because man has grieved his Spirit, and resisted his grace, he withdraws that Spirit and grace from him, and thus he becomes bold and presumptuous in sin. Pharaoh made his own heart stubborn against God, Exodus ix, 34, and God gave him up to judicial blindness, so that he rushed on stubbornly to his own destruction. But let it be observed that there is nothing spoken here of the eternal state of the Egyptian king; nor does any thing in the whole of the account authorize us to believe that God hardened his heart against the influence of his own grace, that he might occasion him so to sin that his justice might consign him to hell. This would be such an act of flagrant injustice as we could scarcely attribute to the worst of men. He who leads another into an offence that he may have a fairer pretence to punish him for it, or brings him into such circumstances that he cannot avoid committing a capital crime, and then hangs him for it, is surely the most execrable of mortals. What then should we make of the God of justice and mercy, should we attribute to him a decree, the date of which is lost in eternity, by which he has determined to cut off from the possibility of salvation millions of millions of unborn souls, and leave them under a necessity of sinning, by actually hardening their hearts against the influences of his own grace and Spirit, that he may, on the pretence of justice, assign them to endless perdition? Whatever may be pretended on behalf of such unqualified opinions, it must be evident to all who are not deeply prejudiced, that neither the justice nor sovereignty of God can be magnified by them.

Even justice itself, on the ground of its holy and eternal nature, gives salvation to the vilest who take refuge in Christ's atonement; for justice has nothing to grant, or Heaven to give, which the blood of the Son of God has not merited.

HOLINESS. — "God is light;" the source of wisdom, knowledge, holiness, and happiness; "and in him is no darkness at all;" no ignorance, no imperfection, no sinfulness, no misery, And from him wisdom, knowledge, holiness, and happiness are received by every believing soul. This is the grand message of the Gospel, the great principle on which the happiness of man depends. Light implies every essential excellence, especially wisdom, holiness, and happiness. Darkness implies all imperfection, and principally ignorance, sinfulness, and misery. Light is the purest, the most subtile, the most useful, and the most diffusive of all God's creatures; it is, therefore, a very proper emblem of the purity, perfection, and goodness of the divine nature. God is to human souls what light is to the world. Without the latter, it would be dismal and uncomfortable, and terror and death would universally prevail; and without an indwelling God, what is religion? Without his all-penetrating and diffusive light, what is the soul of man? Religion would be an empty science, a dead letter, a system unauthoritated and uninfluencing; and the soul a trackless wilderness, a howling waste, full of evil, of terror and dismay, and ever racked with realizing anticipations of future, successive, permanent, substantial, and endless misery.

Nothing can humble a pious mind so much as scriptural apprehensions of the majesty of God. It is easy to contemplate his goodness, loving kindness, and mercy: in all these we have an interest, and from them we expect the greatest good. But to consider his holiness and justice, the infinite righteousness of his nature, under the conviction that we have sinned, and broken the laws prescribed by his sovereign Majesty, and feel ourselves brought as into the presence of his judgment seat: who can bear the thought. If cherubim and seraphim veil their faces before his throne, and the holiest soul cries out,—

> "I loathe myself when God I see,
> And into nothing fall;"

what must a sinner feel whose conscience is not yet purged from dead works, and who feels the wrath of God abiding on him? And how, without such a Mediator and Sacrifice as Jesus Christ is, can any human spirit come into the presence of its Judge? Those who can approach him without terror know little of his justice, and nothing of their sins. When we approach him in prayer, or in any ordinance, should we not feel more reverence than we generally do?

Though all earth and hell should join together to hinder the accomplishment of the great designs of the Most High, yet it shall all be in vain—even the sense of a single letter shall not be lost.

The words of God, which point out his designs, are as unchangeable as his nature itself.

IV. – THE TRINITY.

In Genesis i, 1, the original word *Elohim,* "God," is certainly the plural form of *El,* or *Eloah,* and has long been supposed, by the most eminently learned and pious men, to imply a plurality of persons in the divine nature. As this plurality appears in so many parts of the sacred writings to be confined to three persons, hence the doctrine of the TRINITY, which has formed a part of the creed of all those who have been deemed sound in the faith, from the earliest ages of Christianity. Nor are the Christians singular in receiving this doctrine, and in deriving it from the first words of divine revelation. An eminent Jewish rabbin, Simeon ben Joachi, has these remarkable words: "Come and see the mystery of the word *Elohim;* there are three degrees, and each degree by itself alone, and yet, notwithstanding, they are all one, and joined together in one, and are not divided from each other." In the ever blessed Trinity, from the infinite and indivisible unity of the persons, there can be but one will, one purpose, and one infinite and uncontrollable energy.

In God there are found three persons, not separately existing, but in one infinite unity; who are termed Father, Son, and Spirit; or GOD the FATHER, GOD the SON, and GOD the HOLY GHOST, all existing in the one infinite and eternal GODHEAD ; neither being before or after the other, none being greater or less than the other. These three divine persons are frequently termed among Christians THE TRINITY.

This passage, Matt. iii, 16, 17 affords no mean proof of the doctrine of the Trinity. That three distinct persons are here represented, there can be no dispute: 1. The person of Jesus Christ baptized by John in Jordan. 2. The person of the Holy Ghost in a bodily shape, like a dove. 3. The person of the Father; a voice came out of heaven, saying, "This is my beloved Son," &c. The voice is here represented as proceeding from a different place to that in which the persons of the Son and the Holy Spirit were manifested; and merely, I think, more forcibly to mark this divine personality.

The apostles were commissioned to teach and proselyte all the nations, and baptize them in the name of the holy Trinity, Matt. xxviii, 19. Baptism, properly speaking, whether administered by dipping, or sprinkling, signifies a full and eternal consecration of the person to the service and honour of that Being in whose name it is administered; but this consecration can never be made to a creature; therefore the Father, and the Son, and the Holy Spirit are not creatures. Again: baptism is not made in the name of a quality or attribute of the divine nature; therefore the Father, and the Son, and the Holy Spirit are not qualities or attributes of the divine nature. The orthodox, as they are termed, have generally considered this text a decisive proof of the doctrine of the holy Trinity: and what else can they draw from it? Is it possible for words to convey a plainer sense than these do? And do they not direct every reader to consider the Father, the Son, and the Holy Spirit, as three distinct persons? "But this I can never believe." I cannot help that. You shall not be persecuted by me for differing from my opinion. I cannot go over to you; I must abide by what I believe to be the meaning of the Scriptures.

Eph. ii, 18: "For through him," Christ Jesus, "we both," Jews and Gentiles, "have access by one Spirit," through the influence of the Holy Ghost, "unto the Father," God Almighty. This text is a plain proof of the holy Trinity. Jews and Gentiles are to be presented to God the Father; and the Spirit of God works in their hearts, and prepares them for this presentation: and Jesus Christ himself introduces them. No one can have access to God but by Jesus Christ, and he introduces none but such as receive his Holy Spirit.

Even the doctrine of the eternal *Trinity* in *unity* may be collected from numberless appearances in nature. A consideration of the herb *trefoil* is said to have been the means of fully convincing the learned Erasmus of the truth of the assertion, "These three are one;" and yet three distinct. He saw the same root, the same fibres, the same pulpy substance, the same membraneous covering, the same colour, the same taste, the same smell, in every part; and yet the three leaves distinct; but each and all a continuation of the stem, and proceeding from the same root. Such a fact as this may at least illustrate the doctrine. An intelligent shepherd, whom he met upon the mountains, is said to have exhibited the herb and the illustration, while discoursing on certain difficulties in the Christian faith. When a child I heard a learned man relate this fact.

May God the Father adopt me fully for his child! May God the Son dwell in my heart by faith! May God the Holy Spirit purge my conscience from dead works, and purify my soul from all unrighteousness! May the holy, blessed, and glorious TRINITY take me and mine, and seal us for his own in time and in eternity!

O thou incomprehensible Jehovah, thou eternal Word, thou ever during and all- pervading Spirit;—Father! Son! and Holy Ghost! in the plenitude of thy eternal Godhead, in thy light, I, in a measure see thee; and in thy condescending nearness to my nature I can love thee, for thou hast loved me. In thy strength may I begin, continue, and end every design and every work, so as to glorify thee by showing how much thou lovest man, and how much man may be ennobled and beatified by loving thee! Here am I fixed, here am I lost, and here I find my GOD, and here I find myself!

V. – MAN.

THE CREATION OF MAN. — Let us figure to ourselves, for we may innocently do it, the state of the divine nature previously to the formation of the human being. Infinitely happy, because infinitely perfect and self- sufficient, the supreme Being could feel no wants; — to him nothing was wanting, nothing needful. As the "good man is satisfied from himself," from the contemplation of his conscious rectitude; so, comparing infinitely great with small things, the divine mind was supremely satisfied with the possession and contemplation of its own unlimited excellences. From unmixed, unsullied goodness sprang all the endlessly varied attributes, perfections, and excellences of the divine nature; or rather, in this principle all are founded, and of this each is an especial modification. Benevolence is, however, an affection inseparable from goodness. God, the All-sufficient, knew that he could, in a certain way, communicate influences from his own perfections: but the being must resemble himself to whom the communication could be made. His benevolence, therefore, to communicate and diffuse his own infinite happiness, we may naturally suppose, led him to form the purpose of creating intelligent beings, to whom such communication could be made. He, therefore, in the exuberance of his eternal goodness, projected the creation of man, whom he formed in his own image, that he might be capable of those communications. Here, then, was a motive worthy of eternal goodness, the desire to communicate its own blessedness; and here was an object worthy of the divine wisdom and power, the making an intelligent creature a transcript of his own eternity, Psalm viii, 5, just less than God; and endowing him with powers and faculties of the most extraordinary and comprehensive nature.

I do not found these observations on the supposition of certain excellences possessed by man previously to his fall: I found them on what he is now. I found them on his vast and comprehensive understanding; on his astonishing powers of ratiocination; on the extent and endless variety of his imagination or inventive faculty: and I see the proof and exercise of these in his invention of arts and sciences. Though fallen from God, naturally degraded and depraved, he has not lost his natural powers; he is yet capable of the most exalted degrees of knowledge in all natural things; and his "knowledge is power."

Let us take a cursory view of what he has done, and of what he is capable: he has numbered the stars of heaven; he has demonstrated the planetary revolutions and the laws by which they are governed; he has accounted for every apparent anomaly in the various affections of the heavenly bodies, he has measured their distances, determined their solid contents, and weighed the sun!

His researches into the three kingdoms of nature, the animal, vegetable, and mineral, are, for their variety, correctness, and importance, of the highest consideration. The laws of matter, of organized and unorganized beings, and those chymical principles by which all the operations of nature are conducted, have been investigated by him with the utmost success. He has shown the father of the rain, and who has begotten the drops of dew; he has accounted for the formation of the snow, the hailstones, and the ice; and demonstrated the laws by which the tempest and tornado are governed; he has taken the thunder from the clouds; and he plays with the lightnings of heaven!

He has invented those grand subsidiaries of life, the lever, the screw, the wedge, the inclined plane, and the pulley: and by those means multiplied his power beyond conception; he has invented the telescope, and by this instrument has brought the hosts of heaven almost into contact with the earth. By his engines he has acquired a sort of omnipotency over inert matter; and produced effects which, to the uninstructed mind, present all the appearance of supernatural agency. By his mental energy he has sprung up into illimitable space; and has seen and described those worlds which an infinite skill has planned, and an infinite benevolence sustains. He has proceeded to all describable and assignable limits, and has conceived the most astonishing relations and affections of space, place, and vacuity; and yet, at all those limits, he has felt himself unlimited; and still can imagine the possibility of worlds and beings, natural and intellectual, in endless variety, beyond the whole. Here is a most extraordinary power; describe all known or conjectured beings, and he can imagine more; point out all the good that even God has promised, and he can desire still greater enjoyments!

Of no creature but man is it said, that it was made in the image and likeness of God. Neither the thrones, dominions, principalities, powers, cherubim, seraphim, archangels nor angels, have shared this honour. It is possible that only one order of created beings could be thus formed.

"God made man in his own image, and in his own likeness." Now this must have been what is termed "the moral image of God;" for it cannot be expounded of any formal image or likeness of that infinite Spirit: and from St. Paul, Col. iii, 10, and Eph. iv, 24, we learn that this image consisted in knowledge, righteousness, and true holiness. 1. Man had an intellect which God filled with his own wisdom, therefore he was wise; and he had from that wisdom a knowledge of himself, of God, and of his works, far beyond what we can now comprehend. His giving names to the different creatures was one proof of the extent of that knowledge, and of its special power to take in particular, as well as general views. He gave each creature its name; and, as it appears, this name was expressive of some essential characteristic or quality of the creature to which it was applied. The only thing to which this knowledge did not apply, was the knowledge of good and evil; of good, as contradistinguished from evil; and of evil, an implying the opposite of good. This distinction could not have been known but by experience; and such an experience could not comport with the perfection of his state, as it would be the consequence of his transgression of his Maker's command. When he ate of the forbidden tree of the knowledge of good and evil, he then received a knowledge which God never designed him to have. He knew good lost, and evil got; but, previously, his knowledge was pure, holy, good, clear, and perfective of his being. 2. Righteousness. This word among our ancestors signified the same as "right-wise-ness," thorough wisdom; that which gave a man to distinguish between right and wrong: this is the wisdom which comes from above; and that man is the right-wise man who acts by its dictates. Right is straight; and wrong is crooked. Hence the righteous man is one who goes straight on or forward; acts and walks by line and rule: and the unrighteous is he who walks in crooked paths, does what is wrong, and is never guided by true wisdom. This power, and, with it, the propensity to act aright, was one of the characteristics of the human soul as it came out of the hand of God. It was created in knowledge and righteousness. 3. Holiness, piety toward God; heart worship, pure from hypocrisy and superstition; steady, uniform piety; worshipping God in spirit and in truth. This was another constituent of the image of God in which man was made. And he walked in truth. It was the holiness of truth, unsophisticated piety. Every feeling was a feeling of true piety; and every act of worship flowed from that feeling. This was a state of perfection. He knew every thing that belonged to his being and his duty perfectly; he acted perfectly; he walked in the right way; he went straight forward; he ever did what was lawful and right in the sight of God his Maker; he reverenced him in the highest degree; offered the purest worship from a pure and holy heart; and all was according to truth; there were no semblances, no outsides of piety; all was sterling, all substantial; all such as God could require; and with every act and feeling was the Lord pleased.

It is not enough to say that God made all his works to show forth his glory. He had no need to contemplate his own works to be satisfied with the exertion of his power and wisdom. This would suppose that his gratification depended on his own work. He needs not the exertions of his eternal power and Godhead to minister to, or augment his happiness; for, although he can not but be pleased with every work of his hand, as all that he has created is very good, yet it was not for this end, but it was in reference to a great design, that they were created and still subsist. This design was the formation and eternal beatification of intelligent beings. He therefore made MAN in his own image and in his own likeness: he made him immortal, rational, and holy. He endowed him with intellectual powers of the most astonishing compass. He made him capable of knowing the Author of his being in the glory of his perfections, and of deriving unutterable happiness from this knowledge. But he made him immortal, a transcript of his own eternity; he cannot wholly die—cannot be annihilated, but must exist, and exist intellectually, to all eternity. He has made him holy, that he might be for ever capable of union with HIM who is the Source and Fountain of all purity; and his eternal happiness is to consist in his eternal union with this Being; seeing him as he is, knowing him in his own light, and endlessly receiving additional degrees of knowledge and happiness out of his fulness.

The soul of man was made in the image and likeness of God. Now, as the divine Being is infinite, he is neither limited by parts, nor definable by passions; therefore he can have no corporeal image after which he made the body of man. The image and likeness must necessarily be intellectual; his mind, his soul, must have been formed after the nature and perfections of his God. The human mind is still endowed with most extraordinary capacities; it was more so when issuing out of the hands of its Creator. God was now producing spirit, and a spirit too formed after the perfections of his own nature. God is the Fountain whence this spirit issued: hence the stream must resemble the spring which produced it. God is holy, just, wise, good, and perfect; so must the soul be that sprang from him; there could be in it nothing impure, unjust, ignorant, evil, low, base, mean, or vile. It was created after the image of God; and that image, St. Paul tells us, consisted in righteousness, true holiness, and knowledge. Hence man was wise in his mind, holy in his heart, and righteous in his actions. Were even the word of God silent on this subject, we could not infer less from the lights held out to us by reason and common sense. The text, Gen. i, 26, tells us he was the work of ELOHIM, the divine plurality, marked here more distinctly by the plural pronouns, US and OUR; and, to show that he was the masterpiece of God's creation, all the persons in the Godhead are represented as united in counsel and effort to produce this astonishing creature.

Both his body and soul are adapted with astonishing wisdom to their residence and occupations; and also the place of their residence, as well as the surrounding objects, in their diversity, colour, and mutual relations, to the mind and body of this lord of the creation. The contrivance, arrangement, action, and reaction of the different parts of the body show the admirable skill of the wondrous Creator; while the various powers and faculties of the mind, acting on and by the different organs of this body, proclaim the soul's divine origin, and demonstrate that he who was made in the image and likeness of God was a transcript of his own excellence, destined to know, love, and dwell with his Maker throughout eternity.

That God made man conditionally immortal cannot, I think, be reasonably doubted. Though formed out of the dust of the earth, his Maker breathed into his nostrils the breath of life, and he became a living soul; and as there was then nothing violent, nothing out of its place, no agent too weak or too slow on the one hand, or too powerful or too active on the other; so all the operations of nature were only performed in time, in quantity, and in power, according to the exigencies of the ends to be accomplished. So that in number, weight, and measure, every thing existed and acted according to the unerring wisdom and skill of the omnipotent Creator. There could, therefore, be no corruption or decay; no disorderly induration, nor preternatural solution or solubility of any portions of matter; no disorders in the earth; nothing noxious or unhealthy in the atmosphere. The vast mass was all perfect: the parts of which it was composed equally so. As he created, so he upheld all things by the word of his power: and as he created all things, so by him did all things consist; and among these MAN. Every solid had its due consistency; every fluid its proper channel; some for support and strength, others for activity and energy; and the various fluids to conduct to every part the necessary supplies, and to furnish those spirits by whose natural and regular agency life, under God, is sustained.

It would be absurd to suppose that God formed any intelligent beings without a law or rule of life, when we know that he formed them to show forth his glory: which they can do no otherwise than by exhibiting, in actions, those virtues derived from the perfections of God. And those actions must be founded on some prescription or rule. What our blessed Lord calls the "first and greatest commandment," must be the law in question; namely, "Thou shalt love the Lord thy God with all thy heart, with all thy soul, with all thy mind, and with all thy strength." The very nature of man's creation must show that this was the law or rule of life by which he was called to act. This law is suited to the nature of an intelligent being; and as man was made in the image and likeness of God, this law was suitable to his nature; and the principles of it must have been impressed on that nature.

God gave man a law; the spirit of which was, "Thou shalt love the Lord thy God with all thy heart, soul," &c. This was plain, simple, holy, just, and good. 1. It was plain,—so that it could not be mistaken. 2. Simple,—so that it could not perplex nor confound by distinctions and subtleties. 3. Holy,—totally free either from sin or imperfection. 4. Just,—as requiring no obedience but what the creature owed to its Creator. And, 5. Good,—as it led to the continual perfection of the creature, and secured its increasing felicity.

The first positive precept God gave to man was given as a test of obedience, and a proof of his being in a dependent, probationary state. It was necessary that, while constituted lord of this lower world, he should know that he was only God's vicegerent, and must be accountable to him for the use of his mental and corporeal powers, and for the use he made of the different creatures put under his care. The man from whose mind the strong impression of this dependence and responsibility is erased, necessarily loses sight of his origin and end, and is capable of any species of wickedness. As God is sovereign, he has a right to give to his creatures what commands he thinks proper. An intelligent creature without a law to regulate his conduct is an absurdity; this would destroy at once the idea of his dependence and accountableness. Man must ever feel God as his sovereign, and act under his authority, which he cannot do unless he have a rule of conduct. This rule God gives; and it is no matter of what kind it is, as long as obedience to it is not beyond the powers of the creature who is to obey. God says, "There is a certain fruit-bearing tree; thou shalt not eat of its fruit; but of all the other fruits, and they are all that are necessary for thee, thou mayest freely, liberally eat." Had he not an absolute right to say so: And was not man bound to obey?

Let it be observed that such a law to such a being cannot admit of deviations; it requires a full, perfect, and universal obedience; and an obedience performed with all the powers and energies of body and soul.

But does it follow that man, in this pure and perfect state, fulfilling at all times the sublime duty required by this law, could merit an eternal glory by his obedience? No. For he is the creature of God; his powers belong to his Maker: he owes him all the services he can perform; and, when he has acted up to the utmost limits of his exalted nature, in obedience to this most pure and holy law, it will appear that he can make no demand on divine justice for remuneration; he is, as it respects God, an "unprofitable servant;" he has only done his duty, and he has nothing to claim. In these circumstances was not only man in paradise, but also every angel and archangel of God. Throughout eternity, no created being, however pure, holy, submissive, and obedient, can have any demand on its Creator. From him its being was originally derived, and by him that being is sustained; to him, therefore, by right it belongs; and whatever he has made it capable of he has a right to demand. As well might the cause be supposed to be a debtor to the effect produced by it, as the Creator, in any circumstances, to be a debtor to the creature.

THE FALL OF MAN.—Let us review the whole of this melancholy business, the fall and its effects.

1. From the New Testament we learn that Satan associated himself with the creature which we term the serpent, and the original, the *nachash,* in order to seduce and ruin mankind; 2 Cor. xi, 3; Rev. xii, 9; xx, 2. 2. That this creature was the most suitable to his purpose, as being the most subtle, the most intelligent and cunning of all beasts of the field, endued with the gift of speech and reason, and consequently one in which he could best conceal himself. 3. As he knew that while they depended on God they could not be ruined, he therefore endeavoured to seduce them from this dependence. 4. He does this by working on that propensity of the mind to desire an increase of knowledge with which God, for the most gracious purposes, had endued it. 5. In order to succeed, he insinuates that God through motives of envy had given the prohibition: "God doth know that in the day you eat of it ye shall be like himself," &c. 6. As their present state of blessedness must be inexpressibly dear to them, he endeavours to persuade them that they could not fall from this state: "Ye shall not surely die:"—"Ye shall not only retain your present blessedness, but it shall be greatly increased;" a temptation by which he has ever since fatally succeeded in the ruin of multitudes of souls, whom he persuaded

that, being once right, they could never finally go wrong. 7. As he has kept the unlawfulness of the means proposed out of sight, persuaded them that they could not fall from their steadfastness, assured them that they should resemble God himself, and consequently be self-sufficient, and totally independent of him; they listened, and, fixing their eye only on the promised good, neglected the positive command, and, determining to become wise and independent at all events, "they took of the fruit, and did eat."

Let us now examine the effects.

1. "Their eyes were opened, and they saw they were naked." They saw what they never saw before,—that they were stripped of their excellence; that they had lost their innocence; and that they had fallen into a state of indigence and danger. 2. Though their eyes were opened to see their nakedness, yet their mind was clouded, and their judgment confused. They seem to have lost all just notions of honour and dishonour, of what was shameful and what was praiseworthy. It was dishonourable and shameful to break the commandment of God; but it was neither to go naked when clothing was not necessary. 3. They seem, in a moment, not only to have lost sound judgment, but also reflection; a short time before Adam was so wise that he could name all the creatures brought before him according to their respective natures and qualities; now he does not know the first principle concerning the divine nature,— that it knows all things, and that it is omnipresent; therefore he endeavours to hide himself among the trees from the eye of the all-seeing God! How astonishing is this! When the creatures were brought to him he could name them because he could discern their respective natures and properties; when Eve was brought to him he could immediately tell what she was, who she was, and for what end made, though he was in a deep sleep when God formed her; and this seems to be particularly noted, merely to show the depth of his wisdom, and the perfection of his discernment. But, alas! how are the mighty fallen! Compare his present with his past state, his state before the transgression with his state after it; and say, Is this the same creature? the creature of whom God said, as he said of all his works, "He is very good;" just what he should be, a living image of the living God; but now lower than the beasts of the field? 4. This account could never have been credited had not the indisputable proofs and evidences of it been continued by uninterrupted

succession to the present time. All the descendants of this first guilty pair resemble their degenerate ancestors, and copy their conduct. The original mode of transgression is still continued, and the original sin in consequence. Here are the proofs:—1. Every human being is endeavouring to obtain knowledge by unlawful means, even while the lawful means and every available help are at hand. 2. They are endeavouring to be independent, and to live without God in the world; hence prayer, the language of dependence on God's providence and grace, is neglected, I might say detested, by the great majority of men. Had I no other proof than this that man is a fallen creature, my soul would bow to this evidence. 3. Being destitute of the true knowledge of God, they seek privacy for their crimes, not considering that the eye of God is upon them, being only solicitous to hide them from the eye of man.

The simple, plain, easy condition on which depended his immortality, man broke; and thus forfeited his life to the blessing with which he was naturally endowed; and thus corruption and decay, and a disorderly course of nature, were superinduced. The air that he breathed became unfriendly to the continual support of life; the seeds of dissolution were engendered in his constitution; and out of these various diseases sprang, which, by their repeated attacks, sapped the foundation of life, till at last the fruit of his dissolution verified the judgment of his Creator; for, after living a dying life, it was at last terminated by death.

There was not only no death before sin, but also no predisposing cause of death: nothing that in the course of nature could bring it about. The ground was fertile, and it seems there were neither noxious nor troublesome productions from the soil; and the benediction of the Most High rested upon the earth, mountains, hills, plains, and valleys. But when sin entered, what a change! The glebe becomes stubborn and intractable noxious and troublesome weeds have their full growth; though the husbandman exerts all his muscular force in painful and exhausting labour, his toil is ill repaid; thorns and thistles—every genus, family, and order of injurious plants spring up with rapid speed into destructive perfection; and often, when the labourer is about to fill his arms with the productions of a painfully earned harvest, a blight vitiates the grain;—tornadoes and tempests shake it out of its husk, and give it to the fowls of the air, or tear up the stalks from the root and scatter them to the winds of heaven;—or land floods carry off the shocks which stood nearly ready to be housed;—and thus the hope of the husbandman perishes. By these, and by various other means, does the righteous God fulfil the purposes of his justice, and accomplish his declaration, "In sorrow shalt thou eat of it;" for on thy account the earth itself is cursed. Thou shalt return to the ground whence thou wert taken. Thou hast forfeited thy natural happiness and immortality; death spiritual has already entered thy soul, and the death of thy body shall soon succeed—THOU SHALT DIE.

Man is not what God made him. Were the Scriptures silent on the subject, all reason and common sense would at once declare that it is impossible that the infinitely perfect God could make a morally imperfect, much less a corrupt and sinful being. Yet God is the maker of man, and he tells us that he made him in his own image, and in his own likeness; it follows, then, that man has fallen from that state of holiness and perfection in which he was created. And that his fall took place in the head and root of human nature, before any of the generations of men were propagated on the earth, is evident, not only from the declaration of God himself in his word, but also from this strong commanding fact, that there never was yet discovered a nation or tribe of holy or righteous men in any part of the world; nor is there a record that any such people was ever known. This is a truly surprising circumstance, and a most absolute proof that not only all mankind are now fallen and sinful, but have ever been in the same state: and this fall must have taken place previously to the propagation of mankind; for, had it not taken place in our first parents before they began to propagate and people the earth, the heads of families and their successors who might have been born previously to such fall, could not have partaken of the contagion; and consequently must have been the progenitors of nations doing righteousness, loving God with all their heart, soul, mind, and strength; and their neighbour as themselves. But no such nation exists; no such nation ever did exist. Thus we find that universal experience and knowledge agree with and confirm the account given in the book of Genesis of the fall of man. The root being corrupted, the fruit also must be corrupt; the fountain being poisoned, the streams must be impure. All men coming into the world in the way of natural generation must be precisely the same with him from whom they derive their being. The body, soul, and spirit of all the descendants of Adam must partake of his moral imperfections; for it is an inflexible and invariable law in nature that "like shall produce its like." We, therefore, seeing this total corruption of human nature, no longer hope to gather grapes off thorns or figs off thistles.

Experience not only confirms the great but tremendous truth, that all mankind are fallen from the image of God, but it shows us that man has naturally a propensity to do evil, and none to do good; yea, to do evil, when it is most demonstrably to his own hurt; that the great principles of self-love and self-interest weigh nothing against the sinful propensities of his mind; that he is continually and confessedly running to his own ruin; and has of himself no power or influence by which he can correct, restrain, or destroy the viciousness of his own nature; in short, that he "lieth in the wicked one," with an unavailing wish, yet without any efficient power, to rise. Understanding, judgment, and reason, those so much boasted, strong and commanding powers of the soul, which should regulate all the inferior faculties, are themselves so fallen, enfeebled, darkened, and corrupted, as to spiritual good, that they see not how to command, and feel not how to perform: there is, therefore, no hope that the man can raise himself from the fall, and replace himself in a state of moral rectitude; for the very principles by which he should rise are themselves equally fallen with all the rest. Wishing and willing are all that he can exercise; but those, through want of moral energy, are totally inefficient: God has inspired him with the desire to be saved; and this alone places him in a salvable state. There is, therefore, in the human soul no self-reviviscent power, no innate principle which may develope itself, expand, and arise; all is infirm; all is wretched, diseased, and helpless. This view of the wretched state of mankind led one of the primitive fathers to consider the whole human race as one great diseased man, lying helpless, stretched out over the whole inhabited globe, from east to west, from north to south; to heal whom the omnipotent Physician descended from heaven.

From all the accounts we have of the most eminent, ancient, and celebrated nations, such as the Egyptians, Chaldeans, Assyrians, Persians, Greeks, and Romans, we find them, from their own relations, to have been destitute of the knowledge of the true

God, and although cultivating the various arts and sciences, yet fierce, barbarous, and cruel. Their history is a tissue of frauds, aggressions, broken truces, assassinations, revolts, insurrections, general disorder, and insecurity. Their laws despotic and oppressive; their kings and governors tyrants; their statesmen time-servers and oppressors of the common people; their soldiers licensed plunderers, their heroes human butchers; their conquests the blast of desolation and death on empires and nations; their religion superstitious, gross, brutal, and unclean; and their gods, and general objects of their worship, worse in their character and acknowledged practices than the most villanous and execrable of men. And what must be the imitations in their votaries when they had such originals to copy? This was their general state and character.

"But were not the highly cultivated Greeks and the learned and polite Romans illustrious exceptions?" I except none of them from this general censure. Read their own histories: those of the republics of Greece; and what do you find? Treasons, insurrections, crimes, and carnage of all descriptions. Consult also the Roman writers on their republican, consular tribunal, regal and imperial states; and see the portraits which those master painters have sketched; and what do you behold? No caricatures, but likenesses from life—features fell and distorted, scowling through the deep and murky shades which serve to relieve and make them prominent.

Nor has the lapse of time mended the moral condition and character of the heathen nations. Our extensive commercial connections, not only with the nations of Europe and America, but also with the principal heathen kingdoms and states in most parts of the world, have brought us to an intimate acquaintance with the dark places of the earth which are filled with the habitations of cruelty; and what have we seen? Darkness covering every land, and gross darkness the hearts of the people; idolatry the most disgusting, and superstition the most foolish and degrading, closely associated with ridiculous ceremonies and cruel rites; religious suicide; abandonment of the aged to starvation when past labour, or left in the woods to be devoured by wild beasts when in hopeless disease; exposure of infants; burning of widows with the bodies of their deceased husbands, their own children lighting the funeral pyre; the most painful, unmeaning, and lengthened- out pilgrimages; religious fasts, by which health and strength are exhausted; and feasts where the man sinks into the beast: — all these, and more of a similar kind, equally degrading and destructive, prevail among the millions of Asia, and especially among what are called the civilized, mild, and pacific inhabitants of Hindostan.

What a gradation is here! 1. In our fall from God, our first apparent state is, that we are without strength; have lost our principle of spiritual power, by having lost the image of God, righteousness and true holiness, in which we were created. 2. We are ungodly; having lost our strength to do good, we have also lost all power to worship God aright. The mind which was made for God is no longer his residence. 3. We are sinners; feeling we have lost our centre of rest, and our happiness, we go about seeking rest, but find none. What we have lost in losing God we seek in earthly things; and thus are continually missing the mark, and multiplying transgressions against our Maker. 4. We are enemies; sin indulged increases in strength; evil acts engender fixed and rooted habits; the mind, everywhere poisoned with sin, increases in averseness from good; and mere aversion produces enmity, and enmity acts of hostility, fell cruelty, &c. So that the enemy of God hates his Maker and his service; is cruel to his fellow creatures; "a foe to God was ne'er true friend to man;" and even torments his own soul! Though every man brings into the world the seeds of all these evils, yet it is only by growing up in him that they acquire their perfection: *Nemo repente fuit turpissimus,* "no man becomes a profligate at once;" he arrives at it by slow degrees; and the speed he makes is proportioned to his circumstances, means of gratifying sinful passions, evil education, bad company, &c., &c. These make a great diversity in the moral states of men. All have the same seeds of evil: *Nemo sine vitiis nascitur,* "all come defiled into the world;" but all have not the same opportunities of cultivating these seeds. Besides, as God's Spirit is continually convincing the world of sin, righteousness, and judgment, and the ministers of God are seconding its influence with their pious exhortations, — as the Bible is in almost every house, and is less or more heard or read by almost every person, — these evil seeds are receiving continual blasts and cheeks, so that, in many cases, they have not a vigorous growth. These causes make the principal moral difference that we find among men; though in evil propensities they are all radically the same.

This completes their bad character; they are downright atheists, at least practically such. They fear not God's judgments, although his eye is upon them in their evil ways. There is not one article of what is charged against the Jews and Gentiles here that may not be found justified by the histories of both, in the most ample manner. And what was true of them in those primitive times is true of them still. With very little variation, these are the evils in which the vast mass of mankind delight and live. Look especially at men in a state of warfare; look at the nations of Europe, who enjoy most of the light of God; see what has taken place among them from 1792 to 1814; see what destruction of millions, and what misery of hundreds of millions, have been the consequence of Satanic excitement in fallen, ferocious passions! O SIN, what hast thou done! How many myriads of souls hast thou hurried unprepared into the eternal world! Who, among men or angels, can estimate the greatness of this calamity! this butchery of souls! What widows, what orphans are left to deplore their sacrificed husbands and parents, and their own consequent wretchedness! And whence sprang all this? From that, whence come all wars and fightings — the evil desires of men; the lust of dominion; the insatiable thirst for money; and the desire to be sole and independent. This is the sin that ruined our first parents, expelled them from paradise, and which has descended to all their posterity; and proves fully, incontestably proves that we are their legitimate offspring, the fallen progeny of fallen parents, children in whose ways are destruction and misery, in whose heart there is no faith, and before whose eyes there is nothing of the fear of God.

What an awful character does God give of the inhabitants of the antediluvian world! 1. They were fleshly, wholly sensual, the desires of the mind overwhelmed and lost in the desires of the flesh; their souls no longer discerning their high destiny, but ever minding earthly things, so that they were sensualized, brutalized, and become flesh; incarnated so as not to retain God in their knowledge, and they lived seeking their portion in this life. 2. They were in a state of wickedness. All was corrupt within, and all unrighteous without; neither the science nor practice of religion existed. Piety was gone, and every form of sound words had disappeared. 3. This wickedness was great, "was multiplied;" it was continually increasing, and multiplying increase by increase, so that the whole earth was corrupt before God, and was filled with violence; profligacy among the lower, and cruelty and oppression among the higher classes being only predominant. 4. All "the imaginations of their thoughts were evil"—the very first embryo of every idea, the figment of every thought, the very materials out of which perception, conception, and ideas were formed, were all evil; the fountain which produced them, with every thought, purpose, wish, desire, and motive was incurably poisoned. 5. All these were evil "without any mixture of good;" the Spirit of God which strove with them was continually resisted, so that evil had its sovereign sway. 6. They were evil continually; there was no interval of good, no moment allowed for serious reflection, no holy purpose, no righteous act. What a finished picture of a fallen soul! Such a picture as God alone, who searches the heart and tries the spirit, could possibly give. 7. To complete the whole, God represents himself as repenting because he had made them, and as grieving at the heart because of their iniquities! Had not these been voluntary transgressions, crimes which they might have avoided, had they not grieved and quenched the Spirit of God, could he speak of them in the manner he does here? 8. So incensed is the most holy and the most merciful God, that he is determined to destroy the work of his hands: "And the Lord said, I will destroy man whom I have created." How great must the evil have been, and how provoking the transgressions which obliged the most compassionate God, for the vindication of his own glory, to form this awful purpose! "Fools make a mock at sin," but none except fools.

The whole world lieth in wickedness—lieth in the wicked one—is embraced in the arms of the devil, where it lies fast asleep and carnally secure, deriving its heat and power from its infernal fosterer. What a truly awful state! And do not the actions, tempers, propensities, opinions, and maxims of all worldly men prove and illustrate this? "In this short expression," says Mr. Wesley, "the horrible state of the world is painted in the most lively colours; a comment on which we have in the actions, conversations, contracts, quarrels, and friendships of worldly men." Yes, their actions are opposed to the law of God; their conversations shallow, simulous, and false; their contracts forced, interested, and deceitful; their quarrels puerile, ridiculous, and ferocious; and their friendships hollow, insincere, capricious, and fickle;—all, all the effect of their lying in the arms of the wicked one; for thus they become instinct with his own spirit; and because they are of their father, the devil, therefore his lusts will they do.

Even the most unconcerned about spiritual things have understanding, judgment, reason, and will. And by means of these we have seen even scoffers at divine revelation become very eminent in arts and sciences; some of our best metaphysicians, physicians, mathematicians, astronomers, chemists, &c., have been known—to their reproach be it spoken and published—to be without religion; nay, some of them have blasphemed it, by leaving God out of his own work, and ascribing to an idol of their own, whom they call "nature," the operations of the wisdom, power, and goodness of the Most High. It is true that many of the most eminent in all the above branches of knowledge have been conscientious believers in divine revelation; but the case of the other proves that, fallen as man is, he yet possesses extraordinary powers, which are capable of very high cultivation and improvement. In short, the soul seems capable of any thing but knowing, fearing, loving, and serving God. And it is not only incapable, of itself, for any truly religions acts; but what shows its fall in the most indisputable manner is its enmity to sacred things. Let an unregenerate man pretend what he pleases, his conscience knows that he hates religion; his soul revolts against it; his "carnal mind is not subject to the law of God, neither indeed can it be." There is no reducing this fell principle to subjection; it is sin, and sin is rebellion against God; therefore sin must be destroyed, not subjected; if subjected, it would cease to be sin, because sin is in opposition to God: hence the apostle says, most conclusively, it cannot be subjected; that is, it must be destroyed, or it will destroy the soul for ever.

There is a contagion in human nature, an evil principle, that is opposed to the truth and holiness of God. This is the grand hidden cause of all transgression. It is a contagion from which no soul of man is free: it is propagated with the human species; no human being was ever born without it: it is the infection of our nature; is commonly called original sin,—sin, because it is without conformity to the nature, will, and law of God; and is constantly in opposition to all three. The doctrine of original sin has been denied by many, while its opposers, as well as those who allow it, give the most unequivocal proofs that they are subjects of its working. I have seen its opposers and supporters impugn and defend it with an asperity of temper and coarseness of diction, that gave sufficient evidence of a fallen nature; both, Jonah-like, thinking they did well to be angry! A late writer on the subject has excelled in this way; and by his bad tempers spoiled his works. Evil tempers are leprous spots, which sufficiently indicate the deeply radicated contagion in the hearts of those in whose lives they are evident.

The original infection or corruption of nature is the grand hidden cause, source, and spring of all transgression. Iniquity is a seed that has its growth, gradual increase, and perfection. As the various powers of the mind are developed, so it diffuses itself, infecting every passion and appetite through their whole extent and operation.

As a sinner is infected, so is he infectious; by his precept and example he spreads the infernal contagion wherever he goes; joining with the multitude to do evil, strengthening and being strengthened in the ways of sin and death, and becoming especially a snare and a curse to his own household.

That a sinner is abominable in the sight of God and of all good men; that he is unfit for the society of the righteous; and that he cannot, as such, be admitted into the kingdom of God, needs no proof. It is owing to the universality of the evil that sinners are not expelled from society as the most dangerous of all monsters, and obliged to live without having any commerce with their fellow creatures. Ten lepers could associate together, because partaking of the same infection; and civil society is generally maintained, because composed of a leprous community.

All are born with a sinful nature; and the seeds of this evil soon vegetate, and bring forth corresponding fruits. There has never been one instance of an immaculate human soul since the fall of Adam. Every man sins, and sins too after the similitude of Adam's transgression. Adam endeavoured to be independent of God; all his offspring act in the same way: hence prayer is little used, because prayer is the language of dependence; and this is inconsistent with every motion of original sin. When these degenerate children of degenerate parents are detected in their sins, they act just as their parents did; each excuses himself, and lays the blame on another.

"What hast thou done?" "The woman whom thou gavest me, — SHE gave me, and I did eat." "What hast THOU done?" "The serpent beguiled me, and I did eat." Thus, it is extremely difficult to find a person who ingenuously acknowledges his own transgression.

Sin is represented as a king, ruler, or tyrant, who has the desires of the mind and the members of the body under his control; so that by influencing the passions he governs the body. Do not let sin reign, do not let him work; that is, let him have no place, no being in your souls; because wherever he is he governs, less or more: and indeed sin is not sin without this. How is sin known? By evil influences in the mind, and evil acts in the life. But do not these influences and these acts prove his dominion? Certainly, the very existence of an evil thought to which passion or appetite attaches itself, is a proof that there sin has dominion; for without dominion such passions could not be excited. Where-ever sin is felt, there sin has dominion; for sin is sin only as it works in action or passion against God. Sin cannot be a quiescent thing: if it do not work, it does not exist.

After all the proofs of man's natural excellence, we have ten thousand others of his internal moral depravity, and alienation from the divine life. The general tenor of his moral conduct is an infraction of the laws of his Creator. While lord of the lower world, he is a slave to the vilest and most degrading passions; he loves not his Maker; and is hostile and oppressive to his fellows. In a word, he is as fearfully and wonderfully vile, as he was "fearfully and wonderfully made;" and all this shows most forcibly that he stands guilty before God, and is in danger of perishing everlastingly.

Men may amuse themselves by arguing against the doctrine of original sin, or the total depravity of the soul of man; but while there is religious persecution in the world, there is the most absolute disproof of all their arguments. Nothing but a heart wholly alienated from God could ever devise the persecution or maltreatment of a man, for no other cause than that he has given himself up to glorify God with his body and spirit, which are his.

Another proof of the fall and degeneracy of men is their general enmity to the doctrine of holiness; they cannot bear the thought of being sanctified through body, soul, and spirit, so as to "perfect holiness in the fear of God." A spurious kind of Christianity is gaining ground in the world. Weakness, doubtfulness, littleness of faith, consciousness of inward corruptions, and sinful infirmities of different kinds, are by some considered the highest proofs of a gracious state; whereas in the primitive church they would have been considered as evidences that the persons in question had received just light enough to show them their wretchedness and danger, but not the healing virtue of the blood of Christ.

The human heart, left to its own workings, either sinks in the mire, or falls over precipices. What aid has man ever found from what is called natural religion? In comparison with revelation it is a rush light against the sun, however modelled by the inventions of man.

Had man been left just as he was when he fell from God, he, in all probability, had been utterly unsalvable; as he appears to have lost all his spiritual light and understanding, and even his moral feeling. We have no mean proof of this, in his endeavouring to "hide himself, among the trees of the garden," from the presence and eye of Him whom, previously to his transgression, he knew to be everywhere present; to whose eye the darkness and the light are both alike; and who discerns the most secret thoughts of the heart of man. Add to this, it appears as if he had neither self-abasement nor contrition; and therefore he charged his crime upon the woman, and indirectly upon God; while the woman, on her side, charged her delinquency upon the serpent. As they were, so would have been all their posterity, had not some gracious principle been supernaturally restored to enlighten their minds, to give them some knowledge of good and evil, of right and wrong, of virtue and vice, and thus bring them into a salvable state.

The besetting sin – "the well circumstanced sin;" that which has every thing in its favour, – time, and place and opportunity, the heart and the object; and a sin in which all these frequently occur, and consequently the transgression is frequently committed. What we term the "easily besetting sin" is the sin of our constitution, the sin of our trade, that in which our worldly honour, secular profit, and sensual gratification are most frequently felt and consulted. Some understand it of original sin, as that by which we are enveloped in body, soul, and spirit. Whatever it may be, the word gives us to understand that it is what meets us at every turn; that it is always presenting itself to us; that as a pair of compasses describe a circle by the revolution of one leg, while the other is at rest in the centre, so this, springing from that point of corruption within, called "the carnal mind," surrounds us in every place; we are bounded by it, and often hemmed in on every side; it is a circular, well fortified wall, over which we must leap, or through which we must break. The man who is addicted to a particular species of sin (for every sinner has his way) is represented as a prisoner in this strong fortress.

"The unpardonable sin," as some term it, is neither less nor more than ascribing the miracles of Christ, wrought by the power of God, to the spirit of the devil. Many sincere people have been grievously troubled with apprehensions that they had committed the unpardonable sin; but let it be observed that no man who believes the divine mission of Jesus Christ ever can commit this sin; therefore let no man's heart fail because of it from henceforth and for ever. Amen.

If we look on sin in itself, our minds get soon bounded in their views, by particular acts (if transgression, of which we can scarcely perceive the turpitude and demerit, as we neither consider the principle whence they have proceeded, "the carnal mind, which is enmity against God," nor the nature and dignity of that God against whom they are committed. But when we consider the infinite dignity of Jesus, whose passion and death were required to make atonement for sin, then we shall see it as exceeding sinful, that its vitiosity and turpitude are beyond all comparisons and description.

VI. – CHRIST.

THE DIVINITY OF CHRIST. Four things are asserted in Col. i, 16, 17: —

1. That Jesus Christ is the Creator of the universe; of all things visible and invisible; of all things that had a beginning, whether they exist in time or in eternity.

2. That whatsoever was created was created for himself; that he was the sole end of his own work.

3. That he was prior to all creation; to all beings, whether in the visible or invisible world.

4. That he is the Preserver and Governor of all things; "for by him all things consist."

Now, allowing St. Paul to have understood the terms which he used, he must have considered Jesus Christ as being truly and properly God: —

1. Creation is the proper work of an infinite, unlimited, and unoriginated Being, possessed of all perfections in their highest degrees, capable of knowing willing, and working infinitely, unlimitedly, and without control: and as creation signifies the production of being where all was absolute nonentity; so it necessarily implies that the Creator acted of and from himself: for as previously to this creation there was no being, consequently he could not be actuated by any motive, reason, or impulse, without himself; which would argue that there was some being to produce the motive or impulse, or to give the reason. Creation, therefore, is

the work of Him who is unoriginated, infinite, unlimited, and eternal; but Jesus Christ is the Creator of all things; therefore Jesus Christ must be, according to the plain construction of the apostle's words, truly and properly God.

2. As previously to creation there was no being but God, consequently the great First Cause must, in the exertion of his creative energy, have respect to himself alone; for he could no more have respect to that which had no existence, than he could be moved by nonexistence to produce existence or creation. The Creator, therefore, must make every thing for himself. Should it be objected that Christ created officially, or by delegation, I answer, This is impossible; for as creation requires absolute and unlimited power or omnipotence, there can be but one Creator, because it is impossible that there can be two or more omnipotent, infinite, or eternal beings. It is therefore evident that creation cannot be effected officially, or by delegation; for this would imply a being conferring the office, and delegating such power; and that the being to which it was delegated was a dependent being,—consequently not unoriginated or eternal. But this the nature of creation proves to be absurd: 1. The thing being impossible in itself, because no limited being could produce a work that necessarily requires omnipotence. 2. It is impossible, because, if omnipotence be delegated, he to whom it is delegated had it not before; and he who delegates it ceases to have it, and consequently ceases to be God; and the other to whom it is delegated becomes God; because such attributes as those with which he is supposed to be invested are essential to the nature of God. On this supposition God ceases to exist, though infinite and eternal; and another not naturally infinite and eternal becomes such; and thus an infinite and eternal being is produced in time, and has a beginning, which is absurd. Therefore, as Christ is the Creator, he did not create by delegation, or in any official way. Again, if he had created by delegation, or officially, it would have been for that Being who gave him that office, and delegated to him the requisite power; but the text says that "all things were created by him, and for him," which is a demonstration that the apostle understood Jesus Christ to be the end of his own work, and truly and essentially God.

3. As all creation necessarily exists in time, and had a commencement; and there was an infinite duration in which it did

not exist; whatever was before or prior to that must be no part of creation; and the Being who existed prior to creation, and "before all things," — all existence of every kind — must be the unoriginated and eternal God: but St. Paul says, Jesus Christ "was before all things;" *ergo,* the apostle conceived Jesus Christ to be truly and essentially God.

4. As every effect depends upon its cause, and cannot exist without it, so creation, which is an effect of the power and skill of the Creator, can only exist and he preserved by a continuance of that energy that first gave it being; hence God, as the Preserver, is as necessary to the continuance of all things, as God, as the Creator, was to their original production: but this preserving or continuing power is here attributed to Christ; for the apostle says, "And by him do all things consist;" for, as all being was derived from him as its cause, so all being must subsist by him, as the effect subsists by and through its cause. This is another proof that the apostle considered Jesus Christ to be truly and properly God, as he attributes to him the preservation of all created things, which property of preserving belongs to God alone; *ergo,* Jesus Christ is, according to the plain obvious meaning of every expression in this text, truly, properly, independently, and essentially God.

"In the beginning was the Word;" – That is, before any thing was formed, ere God began the great work of creation. This phrase fully proves, in the mouth of an inspired writer, that Jesus Christ was no part of the creation, as he existed when no part of that existed; and that consequently he is no creature, as all created nature was formed by him. Now, as what was before creation must be eternal, and as what gave being to all things could not have borrowed or derived its being from any thing, therefore Jesus, who was before all things, and who made all things, must necessarily be the ETERNAL GOD .

In Genesis i, 1, God is said to have created all things. In John i, 3, Christ is said to have created all things; the same unerring Spirit spoke in Moses and in the evangelists; therefore Christ and the Father are one. To say that Christ made all things by a delegated power from God is absurd; because the thing is impossible. Creation means causing that to exist that had no previous being: this is evidently a work which can be effected only by Omnipotence. Now, God cannot delegate his omnipotence to another; were this possible, he to whom this omnipotence was delegated would, in consequence, become God; and he from whom it was delegated would cease to be such; for it is impossible that there should be two omnipotent beings.

From the first impression made by the reported miracles of Christ, Nicodemus could say, "No man can do the miracles which thou doest, except God be with him." And every reasonable man, on the same evidence, would draw the same inference. But we certainly can go much farther, when we find him, by his own authority and power, without the invocation of any foreign help, with a word, or a touch, and in a moment restoring sight to the blind, speech to the dumb, hearing to the deaf, and health to the diseased; cleansing the lepers, and raising the dead. These are works which could only be effected by the omnipotence of God. This is incontestable. Therefore, while the cleansing of the lepers, and the feeding to the full so many thousands of men and women with five barley loaves and two small fishes, stand upon such irrefragable testimony as that contained in the four evangelists, Jesus Christ must appear, in the eye of unbiased reason, as the Author of nature, the true and only Potentate, the Almighty and everlasting God.

"I will, be thou clean." The most sovereign authority is assumed in this speech of our blessed Lord. I WILL. There is here no supplication of any power superior to his own; and the event proved to the fullest conviction, and by the clearest demonstration, that his authority was absolute, and his power unlimited.

What an astonishing manifestation of omnific and creative energy must the reproduction of a hand, foot, &c., be at the word or touch of Jesus! As this was a mere act of creative power, like that of multiplying the bread, those who allow that the above is the meaning of the word will hardly attempt to doubt the proper divinity of Christ.

How much must this person be superior to men! They are brought into subjection by unclean spirits; this person subjects unclean spirits to himself.

If Jesus Christ were not equal with the Father, could he have claimed this equality of power without being guilty of impiety and blasphemy? Surely not. And does he not in the fullest manner assert his Godhead, and his equality with the Father, by claiming and possessing all the authority in heaven and earth?

"There am I in the midst." None but God could say these words, to say them with truth; because God alone is everywhere present, and these words refer to his omnipresence. *Wherever* — suppose millions of assemblies were collected in the same moment in different places of the creation, (which is a very possible case,) this promise states that Jesus is in each of them. Can any, therefore, say these words except that God who fills both heaven and earth? But Jesus says these words: *Ergo* – Jesus is God.

How correct is the foreknowledge of Jesus Christ! Even the minutest circumstances are comprehended by it!

To worship any creature is idolatry: Christ is to be honoured even as the Father is honoured; therefore Christ is not a creature; and if not a creature, consequently the Creator.

Jesus Christ can be no creature, else the angels who worship him must be guilty of idolatry, and God the author of that idolatry, who commanded those angels to worship Christ. Take Deity away from any redeeming act of Christ, and redemption is ruined.

THE INCARNATION OF CHRIST. — We must carefully distinguish the two natures in Christ, the divine and human. As MAN, he laboured, fainted, hungered, was thirsty; ate, drank, slept, suffered, and died. As GOD, he created all things, governs all, worked the most stupendous miracles; is omniscient, omnipresent, and is the Judge, as well as the Maker, of the whole human race. As God and man, combined in one person, he suffered for man, died for man, rose again for man; causes repentance and remission of sins to be preached in the world in his name; forgives iniquity; dispenses the gifts and graces of the Holy Ghost; is Mediator between God and man; and the sole Head and Governor of his church.

It was necessary that the fullest evidence should be given, not only of our Lord's divinity, but also of his humanity: his miracles sufficiently attested the former; his hunger, weariness, and agony in the garden, as well as his death and burial, were proofs of the latter.

He was a man, that he might suffer and die for the offences of man; for justice and reason both required that the nature that sinned should suffer for the sin. But he was God, that the suffering might be stamped with an infinite value.

That God manifested in the flesh is a great mystery none can doubt; but it is what God himself has most positively asserted, John i, 1-14, and is the grand subject of the New Testament. How this could be we cannot tell; indeed the union of the soul with its body is not less mysterious; we can just as easily comprehend the former as the latter: and how believers can become "habitations of God through the Spirit," is equally inscrutable to us. Yet all these are facts sufficiently and unequivocally attested; and on which scarcely any rational believer, or sound Christian philosopher entertains a doubt. These things are so; but how they are so belongs to God alone to comprehend; and, as the manner is not explained in any part of divine revelation, though the facts themselves are plain, yet the proofs and evidences of the reasons of these facts, and the manner of their operation, lie beyond the sphere of human knowledge.

Reason, in reference to the incarnation, can at least proceed thus: "I have an immortal spirit; it dwells in and actuates my mortal body; as, then, my soul can dwell in my body, so could the Deity dwell in the man Christ Jesus."

He who can believe that Isaiah, or any of the prophets spoke by inspiration, that is, "as they were moved by the Holy Ghost," must believe in the possibility of the incarnation of Christ. And he who can believe it possible that Christ can dwell in the hearts of his followers, can as easily believe that the Messiah or Logos, which was in the beginning with God, and was God, "was made flesh, and dwelt among us full of grace and truth," John i, 14. Reason says, If the one were possible, so is the other; and as one is fact, so may the other be also. The possibility of the thing is evident: God says the fact has taken place: that, therefore, which faith saw before to be possible and probable, it sees now to be certain; for God's testimony added puts all doubts to flight. The Lord Jesus, the Almighty's Fellow, was incarnated of the Holy Ghost, and was made man; and by being God and man was every way qualified to be Mediator between God and man.

But while we distinguish the two natures in Jesus Christ, we must not suppose that the sacred writers always express these two natures by distinct and appropriate names: the names given to our blessed Lord are used indifferently to express his whole nature:

Jesus Christ, Jesus the Christ, the Messiah, Son of man, Son of God, beloved Son, only begotten Son, our Lord Jesus Christ, our Saviour, &c., &c., are all repeatedly and indiscriminately used to designate his whole person as God and man, in reference to the great work of human salvation, which, from its nature, could not be accomplished but by such a union.

THE OFFICES OF CHRIST. — No person ever born could boast, in a direct line, a more illustrious ancestry than Jesus Christ. Among his progenitors, the regal, sacerdotal, and prophetic offices existed in all their glory and splendour.

Christ alone was Prophet, Priest, and King; and possessed and executed these offices in such a supereminent degree as no human being ever did, or ever could do.

Jesus is a Prophet to reveal the will of God, and instruct men in it. He is a Priest, to offer up sacrifice, and make atonement for the sin of the world. He is Lord, to rule over and rule in the souls of the children of men; in a word, he is Jesus the Saviour, to deliver from the power, guilt, and pollution of sin; to enlarge and vivify, by the influence of his Spirit; to preserve in the possession of the salvation which he has communicated; to seal those who believe heirs of glory; and at last to receive them into the fulness of beatitude in his eternal glory.

Jesus was ever acting the part of the philosopher, moralist, and divine, as well as that of the Saviour of sinners. In his hand every providential occurrence and every object of nature became a means of instruction; the stones of the desert, the lilies of the field, the fowls of heaven, the beasts of the forests, fruitful and unfruitful trees, with every ordinary occurrence, were so many grand texts from which he preached the most illuminating and impressive sermons, for the instruction and salvation of his audience. This wisdom and condescension cannot be sufficiently admired.

It is worthy of remark that on the fourth day of the creation the sun was formed, and then "first tried his beams athwart the gloom profound;" and at the conclusion of the fourth millenary from the creation, according to the Hebrew, the Sun of Righteousness shone upon the world, as deeply sunk in that mental darkness produced by sin as the ancient world was while teeming darkness held the dominion, till the sun was created as the dispenser of light. What would the natural world be without the sun? A howling waste in which neither animal nor vegetable life could possibly be sustained. And what would the moral world be without Jesus Christ, and the light of his word and Spirit? Just what those parts now are where his light has not yet shone: "Dark places of the earth, filled with the habitations of cruelty," where error prevails without end, and superstition, engendering false hopes and false fears, degrades and debases the mind of man.

Christ is called the Prince of peace, because by his incarnation, sacrifice, and mediation he procures and establishes peace between God and man; heals the breaches and dissensions between heaven and earth, reconciling both; and produces glory to God in the highest, and on earth peace and good will among men. His residence is peace, and quietness, and assurance for ever, in every believing and upright heart.

In all his miracles Jesus showed the tenderest mercy and kindness. Not only the cure, but the manner in which he performed it, endeared him to those who were objects of his compassionate regards.

Reader, take him for thy King as well as thy Priest. He saves those only who submit to his authority, and take his Spirit for the regulator of their heart, and his word for the director of their conduct. How many do we find among those who would be sorry to be rated so low as to rank only with nominal Christians, talking of Christ as their Prophet, Priest, and King, who are not taught by his word and Spirit, who apply not for redemption in his blood, and who submit not to his authority! Reader, learn this deep and important truth: "Where I am, there also shall my servant be; and he that serveth me, him shall my Father honour."

The kingdom of Christ is truly spiritual and divine; having for its objects the present holiness and future happiness of mankind. Worldly pomp as well as worldly maxims were to be excluded from it. Christianity forbids all worldly expectations, and promises blessedness to those alone who hear the cross, leading a life of mortification and self- denial.

The name of this kingdom should put you in mind of its nature: 1. The King is heavenly. 2. His subjects are heavenly minded. 3. Their country is heavenly, for they are strangers and pilgrims on earth. 4. The government of his kingdom is wholly spiritual and divine.

Christ will never accommodate his morality to the times, nor to the inclinations of men.

Every thing that our blessed Lord did he performed either as our pattern or as our sacrifice.

The incarnation of Christ might have been supposed sufficient to answer all the purposes of reconciling men to God. Could it be supposed that the good and benevolent God would look on those with indifference who were represented by so august a person; one who shared their nature, who assumed it for the very purpose of recommending them to God, and who, while he felt the sympathies and charities of humanity, was equally concerned for the honour and justice of God; and who, from the perfection of his nature, could feel no partialities, nor maintain nor advocate the interests of one against the honour of the other! I believe the reason of man could not have gone farther than this; and had revelation stopped here, reason would have thought that the incarnation was sufficient, and that even divine Justice could not have withheld any favour from such an Intercessor. Even this would have appeared a noble expedient, worthy of the benevolence of God; and a sufficient reason why he should receive into his favour the beings who were, by this incarnation, united to Him who from eternity lay in the Father's bosom, and in whom he ever delighted. But God's "ways are not as our ways, nor his thoughts as our thoughts." Had man never sinned, and was only to be recommended to the divine notice, in order to receive favours, or even to obtain eternal life, this might have been sufficient; but, when he had sinned, and become a rebel and traitor against his Maker and Sovereign, the case was widely different. Atonement for the offence was indispensably requisite; in default of which the penalty, fully known to him previously to the offence, must be exacted: "In the day thou eatest thereof thou shalt surely die;" "for the soul that sinneth it shall die." On this account the incarnation alone could not be sufficient, nor did it take place in reference to this, but in reference to his bearing the penalty due to man for his transgression; for without being incarnated he could not have suffered nor died.

It does appear to me that it is absolutely necessary to believe the proper and essential Godhead of Christ, in order to be convinced that the sacrifice which has been offered is a sufficient sacrifice. Nothing less than a sacrifice of infinite merit can atone for the offences of the whole world, and purchase for mankind an eternal glory: and if Jesus be not properly, essentially, and eternally God, he has not offered, he could not offer such a sacrifice. The sacred writers are nervous and pointed on this subject; nor can I see that any sinner, deeply convinced of his fallen, guilty state, can rely on the merit of his sacrifice for salvation, unless they have a plenary conviction of this most glorious and momentous truth. As eternal glory must be of infinite value, if it be purchased by Christ, or be given as the consequence of his meritorious death, then that death must be of infinite merit, or else it could not procure what is of infinite value. So that, could we even suppose the possibility of the pardon of sin without such a merit, we could not possibly believe that eternal glory could be procured without it. It must be granted, if Christ be but a mere man, as some think, or the highest and first of all the creatures of God, as others suppose, let his actions and sufferings be whatever they may, they are only the obedience and sufferings of an originated and limited being, and cannot possess infinite and eternal merit.

God destroys opposites by opposites. Through pride and self-confidence man fell; and it required the humiliation of Christ to destroy that pride and self-confidence, and to raise him from his fall. There must be an indescribable malignity in sin, when it required the deepest abasement of the highest Being to remove and destroy it. The humiliation and passion of Christ were not accidental, they were absolutely necessary; and had they not been necessary, they had not taken place. Sinner, behold what it cost the Son of God to save thee! And wilt thou, after considering this, imagine that sin is a small thing? Without the humiliation and sacrifice of Christ, even thy soul could not be saved. Slight not, therefore, the mercies of thy God, by underrating the guilt of thy transgressions and the malignity of thy sin.

Christ's agony and distress can receive no consistent explication but on this ground: "He suffered, the just for the unjust, that he might bring, us to God." O glorious truth! O infinitely meritorious suffering! And O, above all, the eternal love that caused him to undergo such sufferings for the sake of sinners!

There are many things in the person, death, and sacrifice of Christ, which we can neither explain nor comprehend. All we should say here is, "It is by this means that the world was redeemed; through this sacrifice men are saved: it has pleased God that it should be so, and not otherwise."

The death of Christ was ordered so as to be witnessed by thousands; and if his resurrection take place, it must be demonstrated; and it cannot take place without being incontestable: such are the precautions used here to prevent all imposture.

The more the circumstances of the death of Christ are examined, the more astonishing the whole will appear. The death is uncommon, the person uncommon, and the object uncommon; and the whole is grand, majestic, and awful. Nature itself is thrown into unusual action, and by means and causes wholly supernatural. In every part the finger of God most evidently appears.

How glorious does Christ appear in his death! Were it not for his thirst, his exclamation on the cross, and the piercing of his side, we should have found it difficult to believe that such a person could ever have entered the empire of death; but the divinity and the manhood equally appear, and thus the certainty of the atonement is indubitably established.

Fear of death was in Christ a widely different thing from what it is in men; they fear death because of what lies beyond the grave; they have sinned, and they are afraid to meet their Judge. Jesus could have no fear on these grounds: he was now suffering for man, and he felt as their expiatory victim; and God only can tell, and perhaps neither men nor angels can conceive, how great the suffering and agony must be which, in the sight of infinite Justice, was requisite to make this atonement. Death, temporal and eternal, was the portion of man; and now Christ is to destroy death by agonizing and dying! The tortures and torments necessary to effect this destruction Jesus Christ alone could feel, Jesus Christ alone could sustain, Jesus Christ alone can comprehend.

He died for every human soul, for all who are partakers of the same nature which he has assumed; the merit and benefits of his death must necessarily extend to all mankind, because he has assumed that nature which is common to all. Nor could the merit of his death be limited to any particular part, nation, tribe, or individuals of the vast human family. It is not the nature of a particular nation, tribe, family, or individual, which he has assumed, but the nature of the whole human race: and "God has made of one blood all the nations, for to dwell on all the face of the earth," that all those might be redeemed with "one blood;" for he is the kinsman of the whole. The merit of his death must, therefore, extend to every man, unless we can find individuals or families that have not sprung from that stock of which he became incarnated. His death must be infinitely meritorious, and extend in its benefits to all who are partakers of the same nature, because he was God manifested in the flesh; and to contract or limit that merit, that it should apply only to a few, or even to any multitudes short of the whole human race, is one of those things which is impossible to God himself, because it involves a moral contradiction. He could no more limit the merit of that death, than he could limit his own eternity, or contract that love which induced him to undertake the redemption of a lost world.

If the many, that is, all mankind, have died through the offence of one; certainly, the gift by grace, which abounds unto the many, by Christ Jesus, must have reference to every human being. If the consequences of Christ's incarnation and death extend only to a few, or a select number of mankind, which, though they may be considered many in themselves, are few in comparison of the whole human race, then the consequences of Adam's sin have extended only to a few, or to the same select number: and if only *many* and not *all* have fallen, only that *many* had need of a Redeemer. For it is most evident that the same persons are referred to in both clauses of the verse. If the apostle had believed that the benefits of the death of Christ had extended only to a select number of mankind, he never could have used the language he has done here; though, in the first clause, he might have said, without any qualification of the term, "Through the offence of one, *many* are dead;" in the second clause, to be consistent with the doctrine of particular redemption, he must have said, "The grace of God, and the gift by grace, hath abounded unto *some*. As, by the offence of one, judgment came upon *all* men to condemnation; so, by the righteousness of one, the free gift came upon *some* to justification. As, by one man's disobedience, *many* were made sinners; so, by the obedience of one, shall *some* be made righteous. As in Adam *all* die; so in Christ shall *some* be made alive." But neither the doctrine nor the thing ever entered the soul of this divinely inspired man.

As the light and heat of the sun are denied to no nation nor individual, so the grace of the Lord Jesus—this also shines out upon all; and God designs that all mankind shall be as equally benefited by it in reference to their souls, as they are in respect to their bodies by the sun that shines in the firmament of heaven. But as all the parts of the earth are not immediately illuminated, but come into the solar light successively, not only in consequence of the earth's diurnal revolution around its own axis, but in consequence of its annual revolution around its whole orbit; so this Sun of righteousness, who has shined out, is bringing every part of the habitable globe into his divine light; that light is shining more and more to the perfect day, so that gradually and successively he is enlightening every nation and every man; and when his great year is filled up, every nation of the earth shall be brought into the light and heat of this unspotted, uneclipsed, and eternal Sun of righteousness and truth. Wherever the Gospel comes, it brings salvation, it offers deliverance from all sin to every soul that hears or reads it. As freely as the sun dispenses his genial influences to every inhabitant of the earth, so freely does Jesus Christ dispense the merits and blessings of his passion and death to every soul of man. From the influence of this spiritual Sun no soul is reprobated, any more than from the influences of the natural sun. In both cases, only those who wilfully shut their eyes, and hide themselves in darkness, are deprived of the gracious benefit. It is no objection to this view of the subject, that all nations have not yet received this divine light. When the earth and the sun were created, every part of the globe did not come immediately into the light; to effect this purpose fully there must be a complete revolution, as has been marked above, and this could not be effected till the earth had not only revolved on its own axis, but passed successively through all the signs of the zodiac. When its year was completed, and not till then, every part had its due proportion of light and heat. God may, in his infinite wisdom, have determined the times and the seasons for the full manifestation of the Gospel to the nations of the world, as he has done in reference to the solar light; and when the Jews are brought in with the fulness of the Gentiles, then, and not till then, can we say that the grand revolution of the important year of the Sun of righteousness is completed: But, in the meantime, the unenlightened parts of the earth are not left in total darkness; as there was light

> " — — ere the infant sun
> Was roll'd together, or had tried his beams
> Athwart the gloom profound."

Light being created, and in a certain measure dispersed, at least three whole days before the sun was formed; (for his creation was a part of the fourth day's work;) so, previously to the incarnation of Christ, there was spiritual light in the world; for he diffused his beams while his orb was yet unseen. And even now, where, by the preaching of his Gospel, he is not yet manifested, he is that true Light which enlightens every man coming into the world; so that the moral world is no more left in absolute darkness where the Gospel is not yet preached, than the earth was the four days which preceded the creation of the sun, or those parts of the world are where the Gospel has not yet been preached. The great year is rolling on, and all the parts of the earth are coming successively, and now rapidly, into the light. The vast revolution seems to be nearly completed, and the whole world is about to be filled with the light and glory of God. Hasten the time, thou God of ages! Even so. Amen. Come, Lord Jesus.

"His disciples came by night." This was as absurd as it was false. On the one hand, the terror of the disciples, the smallness of their number, (only eleven,) and their almost total want of faith; on the other, the great danger of such a bold enterprise, the number of armed men who guarded the tomb, the authority of Pilate and of the Sanhedrim, must render such an imposture as this utterly devoid of credit. "Stole him away while we slept." Here is a whole heap of absurdities. 1. Is it likely that so many men would all fall asleep, in the open air, at once? 2. Is it at all probable that a Roman guard should be found off their watch, much less asleep, when it was instant death, according to the Roman military laws, to be found in this state? 3. Could they be so sound asleep as not to awake with all the noise which must be necessarily made by removing the great stone, and taking away the body? 4. Is it at all likely that these disciples could have had time sufficient to do all this, and to come and return without being perceived by any person? And, 5. If they were asleep, how could they possibly know that it was the disciples that stole him, or indeed that any person or persons stole him?—for, being asleep, they could see no person. From their own testimony, therefore, the resurrection may be as fully proved as the theft.

The resurrection of Christ is a subject of terror to the servants of sin, and a subject of consolation to the sons of God; because it is a proof of the resurrection of both, the one to shame and everlasting contempt, the other to eternal glory and joy.

Christ, having made an atonement for the sin of the world, has ascended to the right hand of the Father, and there he appears in the presence of God for us. In approaching the throne of grace, we keep Jesus, as our sacrificial victim, continually in view; our prayers should be directed through him to the Father; and under the conviction that his passion and death have purchased every possible blessing for us, we should, with humble confidence, ask the blessings we need; and, as in him the Father is ever well pleased, we should most confidently expect the blessings he has purchased. We may consider, also, this his appearance before the throne, in his sacrificial character, constitutes the great principle of mediation or intercession. He has taken our nature into heaven; in that he appears before the throne; this, without a voice, speaks loudly for the sinful race of Adam, for whom it was assumed, and on whose account it was sacrificed. On these grounds every penitent and every believing soul may ask and receive, and their joy be complete. By the sacrifice of Christ, we approach God; through the mediation of Christ, God comes down to man.

So important is the sacrificial offering of Christ in the sight of God, that he is still represented as being in the very act of pouring out his blood for the offences of man. This gives great advantages to faith; when any soul comes to the throne of grace, he finds a sacrifice there provided for him to offer to God. Thus all succeeding generations find they have the continual sacrifice ready, and the newly shed blood to offer.

We are not only indebted to our Lord Jesus Christ for the free and full pardon which we have received, but our continuance in a justified state depends upon his gracious influence in our hearts, and his intercession before the throne of God.

As we cannot contemplate the humiliation and death of Christ without considering it a sufficient sacrifice, oblation, and atonement for sin, and for the sin of the whole world; so we cannot contemplate his unlimited power and glory, in his state of exaltation, without being convinced that he is able to save them to the uttermost that come unto God through him. What can withstand the merit of his blood? What can resist the energy of his omnipotence? Can the power of sin? — its infection? — its malignity? No! he can as easily say to an impure heart, "Be thou clean," and it shall be clean; as he could to the leper, "Be thou clean," and immediately his leprosy was cleansed. Reader, have faith in him; for all things are possible to him that believeth.

JESUS! be thou the centre to which my soul shall incessantly gravitate! Yea, more, — let it come more particularly into contact, and rest in thee for ever and ever! Amen

VII. – REPENTANCE.

REPENTANCE implies that a measure of divine wisdom is communicated to the sinner, and that he thereby becomes wise to salvation; that his mind, purposes, opinions, and inclinations are changed; and that, in consequence, there is a total change in his conduct. It need scarcely be remarked that, in this state, a man feels deep anguish of soul, because he has sinned against God, unfitted himself for heaven, and exposed his soul to hell. Hence a true penitent has that sorrow whereby he forsakes sin, not only because it has been ruinous to his own soul, but because it has been offensive to God.

Though many have, no doubt, repeatedly felt smart twingings in their conscience, they have endeavoured to quiet them with a few such aspirations as these, "Lord, have mercy upon me! Lord, forgive me, and lay not this sin to my charge, for Christ's sake!" Thus of the work of repentance they know little; they have not suffered their pangs of conscience to form themselves into true repentance – a deep conviction of their lost and ruined state both by nature and practice; conviction of sin, and contrition for sin, have only had a superficial influence upon their hearts. Their repentance is not a deep and radical work; they have not suffered themselves to be led into the various chambers of the house of imagery to detect the hidden abominations that have everywhere been set up against the honour of God, and the safety of their own souls. When they have felt a little smarting from a wound of sin they have got it slightly healed; and their repentance is that of which they may repent,—it was partial and inefficient: and its end proves this. They have not, through the excess of sorrow for sin, fled to lay hold on the hope set before them; and refused to be comforted till they felt that word powerfully spoken into their hearts, "Son! daughter!—be of good cheer, thy sins are forgiven thee." No man should consider his repentance as having answered a saving end to his soul, till he feels that "God for Christ's sake has forgiven him his sins," and the Spirit of God testifies with his spirit that he is a child of God. How few ingenuously confess their own sin! They see not their guilt. They are continually making excuses for their crimes. The strength and subtlety of the tempter, the natural weakness of their own minds, the unfavourable circumstances in which they were placed, &c., &c., are all pleaded as excuses for their sins, and thus the possibility of repentance is precluded; for till a man take his sin to himself, till he acknowledge that he alone is guilty, he cannot be humbled, and consequently cannot be saved. Reader, till thou accuse thyself, and thyself only, and feel that thou alone art responsible for all thy iniquities, there is no hope of thy salvation.

Reader, learn that true repentance is a work,—and not the work of an hour: it is not passing regret, but a deep and alarming conviction, that thou art a fallen spirit,—hast broken God's laws,—art under his curse,—and in danger of hell fire.

Deep and overwhelming sorrow does not depend merely on the degree of actual guilt, but rather on the degree of heavenly light transfused through the soul. Man is a fallen spirit; his inward parts are very wickedness; in his fall he has lost the image of God. Let God shine into such a heart; let him visit every chamber in this house of imagery; let him draw every thing to the light of his own holiness and justice,—and, put the case that there had not been one act of transgression, what must be his feelings who thus saw, in the only light that could make it manifest, the deep depravity of his heart! sin becoming indescribably sinful, the commandment ascertaining its obliquity, and illustrating all its vileness! He who sees his inward parts in God's light will not need superadded transgression to produce compunction and penitence.

Confession of sin is essential to true repentance; and till a man take the whole blame on himself he cannot feel the absolute need he has of casting his soul on the mercy of God that he may be saved.

A genuine penitent will hide nothing of his state; he sees and bewails not only the acts of sin which he has committed, but the disposition that led to these acts. He deplores not only the transgression, but "the carnal mind, which is enmity against God." The light that shines into his soul shows him the very source whence transgression proceeds; he sees his fallen nature, as well as his sinful life; he asks pardon for his transgressions,—and he asks washing and cleansing for his inward defilement.

If every penitent were as ready to throw aside his self-righteousness and sinful incumbrances as the blind man was to throw aside his garment, we should have fewer delays in conversions than we now have; and all that have been convinced of sin would have been brought to the knowledge of the truth.

Every true penitent admires the moral law, longs most earnestly for a conformity to it, and feels that he can never be satisfied till he awakes up after this divine likeness; and he hates himself, because he feels that he has broken it, and that his evil passions are still in a state of hostility to it.

There is one doctrine relative to the economy of divine providence little heeded among men; I mean the doctrine of restitution. When a man has done wrong to his neighbour, though on his repentance and faith in our Lord Jesus Christ, God forgives him his sin, yet he requires him to make restitution to the person injured, if it lie in the compass of his power. If he do not, God will take care to exact it in the course of his providence. Such respect has he for the dictates of infinite justice that nothing of this kind shall pass unnoticed. Several instances of this have already occurred in this history, and we shall see several more.

No man should expect mercy at the hand of God who, having wronged his neighbour, refuses, when he has it in his power, to make restitution. Were he to weep tears of blood, both the justice and mercy of God would shut out his prayer, if he made not his neighbour amends for the injury he may have done him. The mercy of God, through the blood of the cross, can alone pardon his guilt: but no dishonest man can expect this; and he is a dishonest man who illegally holds the property of another in his hand. To man should defer his salvation to any future time. If God speaks to-day, it is to-day that he should be heard and obeyed. To defer reconciliation to God to any future period is the most reprehensible and destructive presumption. It supposes that God will indulge us in our sensual propensities, and cause his mercy to tarry for us till we have consummated our iniquitous purposes. It shows that we prefer, at least for the present, the devil to Christ, sin to holiness, and earth to heaven. And can we suppose that God will be thus mocked? Can we suppose that it can at all consist with his mercy to extend forgiveness to such abominable provocation? What a man sows that shall he reap. If he sows to the flesh, he shall of the flesh reap corruption. Reader, it is a dreadful thing to fall into the hands of the living God.

As all had sinned against God, so all should humble themselves before Him against whom they have sinned. But humiliation is no atonement for sin; therefore repentance is insufficient, unless faith in our Lord Jesus Christ accompany it. Repentance disposes and prepares the soul for pardoning mercy, but can never be considered as making compensation for past acts of transgression. This repentance and faith were necessary to the salvation both of Jews and Gentiles; for all had sinned and come short of God's glory. The Jews must repent who had sinned so much, and so long, against light and knowledge. The Gentiles must repent, whose scandalous lives were a reproach to man. Faith in Jesus Christ was also indispensably necessary; for a Jew might repent, be sorry for his sin, and suppose that, by a proper discharge of his religious duty, and bringing proper sacrifices, he could conciliate the favour of God. No, this will not do; nothing but faith in Jesus Christ, as the end of the law, and the great and only vicarious sacrifice, will do; hence he testified to them the necessity of faith in this Messiah. The Gentiles might repent of their profligate lives, turn to the true God, and renounce all idolatry; this is well, but it is not sufficient: they also have sinned, and their present amendment and faith can make no atonement for what is past; therefore they also must believe on the Lord Jesus, who died for their sins, and rose again for their justification.

Penitent sinner! thou hast sinned against God, and against thy own life! The avenger of blood is at thy heels. Jesus hath shed his blood for thee; he is thy Intercessor before the throne; flee to him! Lay hold on the hope of eternal life which is offered to thee in the Gospel! Delay not one moment! Thou art never safe till thou hast redemption in his blood! God invites thee! Jesus spreads his hands to receive thee! God hath sworn that he willeth not the death of a sinner; then he cannot will thy death; take God's oath, take his promise, credit what he hath spoken and sworn! Take encouragement! Believe on the Son of God, and thou shalt not perish, but have everlasting life!

If sin have produced suffering, is it possible that suffering can destroy sin? It is essential, in the nature of all effects, to depend on their own causes; they have neither being nor operation but what they derive from these causes; and in respect to their causes, they are absolutely passive. The cause may exist without the effect; but the effect cannot subsist without the cause. To act against its cause is impossible, because it has no independent being nor operation; by it, therefore, the being or state of the cause can never be affected. Just so sufferings, whether voluntary or involuntary, cannot affect the being or nature of sin, from which they proceed. And could we for a moment entertain the absurdity, that they could atone for, correct, or destroy the cause that gave them being, then we must conceive an effect wholly dependent on its cause for its being, to rise up against that cause, destroy it, and yet still continue to be an effect when its cause is no more! The sun, at a particular angle, by shining against a pyramid, projects a shadow according to that angle, and the height of the pyramid. The shadow, therefore, is the effect of the interception of the sun's rays by the mass of the pyramid. Can any man suppose that this shadow would continue well defined and discernible though the pyramid were annihilated, and the sun extinct? No. For the effect would necessarily perish with its cause. So sin and suffering; the latter springs from the former: sin cannot destroy suffering, which is its necessary effect; and suffering cannot destroy sin, which is its producing cause. *Ergo,* salvation by suffering is absurd, contradictory, and impossible.

"Wherefore then serveth the law?" Of what real use can it be in the economy of salvation? I answer, it serves the most important purposes: 1. Its purity and strictness show us its origin: — it came from God. All religious institutions, merely human, though pretended from heaven, show their origin by extravagant demands in some cases, and by sinful concessions in others. In the law of God nothing of this appears, and therefore we see it a transcript of the divine nature. 2. It shows us the perfection of the original state of man; for as that law was suited to his state, and the law is holy, and the commandment holy, just, and good, so was his nature: it is, therefore, a comment on those words, "God made man in his own image, and in his own likeness." 3. It serves to show the nature of sin: the real obliquity of a crooked line can only be ascertained by laying a straight one to it. Thus, the fall of man, and the depth of that fall, are ascertained by the law. 4. It serves to convict man of sin, righteousness, and judgment: it shows him the deplorable state into which he is fallen, and the great danger to which he is exposed. 5. It serves as a schoolmaster, (or leader of children to school,) to convince us of the absolute necessity and value of the Gospel; for that pure and moral law must be written upon the hearts of believers; and its precepts, both in letter and spirit, become the rule of their lives.

By the law is the knowledge of sin; for how can the finer deviations from a straight line be ascertained without the application of a known straight edge? Without this rule of right, sin can only be known in a sort of general way; the innumerable deviations from positive rectitude can only be known by the application of the righteous statutes of which the law is composed. And it was necessary that this law should be given, that the true nature of sin might be seen, and that men might be the better prepared to receive the Gospel; finding that this law worketh only wrath, that is, denounces punishment, forasmuch as all have sinned. Now, it is wisely ordered of God, that wherever the Gospel goes, there the law goes also; entering everywhere, that sin may be seen to abound, and that men may be led to despair of salvation in any other way, or on any other terms, than those proposed in the Gospel of Christ. Thus the sinner becomes a true penitent, and is glad, seeing the curse of the law hanging over his soul, to flee for refuge to the hope set before him in the Gospel.

Law is only the means of disclosing this sinful propensity, not of producing it; as a bright beam of the sun introduced into a room shows millions of motes which appear to be dancing in it in all directions. But these were not introduced by the light, they were there before, only there was not light enough to make them manifest; so the evil propensity was there before, but there was not light sufficient to discover it.

It was one design of the law to show the abominable and destructive nature of sin, as well as to be a rule of life. It would be almost impossible for a man to have that just notion of the demerit of sin, so as to produce repentance, or to see the nature and necessity of the death of Christ, if the law were not applied to his conscience by the light of the Holy Spirit; it is then alone that he sees himself to be carnal and sold under sin; and that the law and the commandment are holy, just, and good. And let it be observed that the law did not answer this end merely among the Jews in the days of the apostle; it is just as necessary to the Gentiles to the present hour. Nor do we find that true repentance takes place where the moral law is not preached and enforced. Those who preach only the Gospel to sinners, at best, only heal the hurt of the daughter of my people slightly. The law, therefore, is the grand instrument in the hands of a faithful minister to alarm and awaken sinners; and he may safely show that every sinner is under the law, and consequently under the curse, who has not fled for refuge to the hope held out by the Gospel: for in this sense also "Jesus Christ is the end of the law for justification to them that believe."

VIII. – FAITH.

"FAITH is the substance of things hoped for:"—Faith is the subsistence of things hoped for; the demonstration of things not seen. The word which we translate "substance," signifies "subsistence," "that which becomes a foundation for another thing to stand on." And ελεγχος signifies such a conviction as is produced in the mind by the demonstration of a problem, after which demonstration no doubt can remain, because we see from it that the thing is; that it cannot but be; and that it cannot be otherwise than as it is, and is proved to be. Such is the faith by which the soul is justified; or, rather, such are the effects of justifying faith: on it subsists the peace of God, which passeth all understanding; and the love of God is shed abroad in the heart where it lives, by the Holy Ghost. At the same time the spirit of God witnesses with their spirits who have this faith that their sins are blotted out; and this is as fully manifest to their judgment and conscience, as the axioms, "A whole is greater than any of its parts:" "Equal lines and angles, being placed on one another, do not exceed each other."

To provide a Saviour, and the means of salvation, is God's part; to accept this Saviour, laying hold on the hope set before us, is ours. Those who refuse the way and means of salvation must perish; those who accept of the great covenant sacrifice cannot perish, but shall have eternal life.

It is one of the least evils attending unbelief, that it acts not only in opposition to God, but it also acts inconsistently with itself.

It receives the Scriptures in bulk, and acknowledges them to have come through divine inspiration; and yet believes no part separately. With it the whole is true, but no part is true. The very unreasonableness of this conduct shows the principle to have come from beneath, were there no other evidences against it.

"He that believeth on my son Jesus shall be saved; and he that believeth not shall be damned." This is God's ultimate design; this purpose he will never change; and this he has fully declared in the everlasting Gospel. This is the grand decree of reprobation and election.

He who will not believe till he receives what he calls a reason for it, is never likely to get his soul saved. The highest, the most sovereign reason that can be given for believing, is, that God has commanded it.

God has a right to be believed on his own word alone; and it is impious, when we are convinced that it is his word, to demand a sign or pledge for its fulfilment.

Is not faith the gift of God? Yes, as to the grace by which it is produced; but the grace or power to believe, and the act of believing, are two different things. Without the grace or power to believe no man ever did or can believe; but with that power the act of faith is a man's own. God never believes for any man, no more than he repents for him; the penitent, through this grace enabling him, believes for himself: nor does he believe necessarily or impulsively when he has that power; the power to believe may be present long before it is exercised, else, why the solemn warnings with which we meet everywhere in the word of God, and threatenings against those who do not believe? Is not this a proof that such persons have the power, but do not use it? They believe not, and therefore are not established. This, therefore, is the true state of the case; God gives the power; man uses the power thus given, and brings glory to God: without the power no man can believe; with it, any man may.

Christ never says, "Believe now for a salvation which thou now needest, and I will give it to thee in some future time." That salvation which is expected through works or sufferings must of necessity be future, as there must be time to work or suffer in; but the salvation which is by faith must be for the present moment; for this simple reason, it is by faith, that God may be manifested and honoured; and not by works or by sufferings, lest any man should boast. To say that, though it is of faith, yet it may, and must, in many cases, be delayed (though the person is coming in the most genuine humility, deepest contrition, and with the liveliest faith in the blood of the Lamb,) is to say that there is still something necessary to be done, either on the part of the person, or on the part of God, in order to procure it; neither of which positions has any truth in it.

With Christ, God is ever well pleased; with all that he has done, with all that he has suffered; and with the end and object in reference to which he has lived, suffered, and died, he is well pleased: consequently he is well pleased to dispense the benefits of his priesthood, and sacrificial offering, to man. God requires no entreaty to induce him to pardon and save: he is infinitely disposed to do so; and he has an infinite reason for this disposition. This is a grand principle in theology; and a strong encourager of faith. He that believes that God is thus disposed to save his soul, and for the reasons above mentioned, can neither feel backwardness nor difficulty in coming to the throne of grace in order to obtain mercy. All the difficulties on the doctrine of faith have arisen from not considering this principle: and it is both painful and shameful to see to what magnitude and number these difficulties have been carried. Cases of conscience, cases of doubt, motives to faith, encouragement to weak believers, &c, have been multiplied by systematic preachers, and dealers in "Bodies of Divinity," to the great distraction of the church of God, and confusion of simple souls. And this is occasioned either by their not knowing or not attending to the principle laid down above. Nothing is plainer than the way of salvation by faith in Christ, had it not been puzzled and blockaded, or broken up by the thriftless systems of men.

Is it not strange when man's circumstances and danger are considered, that faith should be so little in action, that it is not one of the most popular, so to speak, of all the Christian graces? And is it not one of the wiles of the devil that persuades him that the exercise of this grace is the most difficult of all, and, in short, almost impossible without a miraculous power? Hence the saying, "We can no more believe than we can make a world." It is readily granted that without God we can do nothing; but as he gives us power to discern, to repent, to hope, to love, and to obey; so does he give us power to believe; and to us the use or exercise of the power belongs. He does not discern, repent, hope, love, or obey for us, no more than he believes for us. By using the grace he gives, we discern, repent, hope, believe, love, and obey. Without the grace we can do nothing; without the careful use of the grace, the grace profits us nothing. To every prescribed duty, God furnishes the requisite grace. The help is ever at hand, but we are not workers together with him; hence we are, in general, receiving the grace of God in vain; and, to excuse our negligence, indolence, and infidelity, we cry out, "We can do nothing!" "We have no strength!" "We can no more believe than we can make a world!" Our adversary knows well how to take advantage of such sayings, and, indeed, they are issues of his own temptations; therefore it is his business to persuade us that these are all incontrovertible truths! How strange, how disgraceful is it, that the words of the devil, and the wicked words of a lying world, and the antinomian maxims of fallen churches or fallen Christians should be implicitly believed, while the words of the living God are not credited! He commands us to believe; reproaches us for our unbelief; tells us that if we believe not, we shall not be established; asserts that he who believes not, has made God a liar; proclaims salvation by faith; and finishes the confutation of our infidel speeches with, "He that believeth not shall be damned." Now, all this supposes, that he gives us the strength, and that we do not use it. Whose word so credible as the word of God? and whose word has less credence? Many are volunteers in faith, where there is no promise, — for they can believe that we cannot be saved from all sin in this life, — that we shall be saved in the article of death, and that there is a purgatorial middle state, where we may be cleansed, by penal fire, from vices that the blood of Jesus either could not or did not purge, and that the almighty Spirit of judgment and burning did not, or could not consume: and where there are exceeding great and precious promises, which in God are yea, and in Christ amen, they can scarcely credit any thing! How abominable is this conduct! How insulting to God! How destructive to the soul! No wonder that many of our old and best writers have declaimed so much against this, calling unbelief "the damning sin," by way of eminence; and that which binds all other sins upon the soul. Men may treat the word of God as they list, but these truths of God shall endure for ever: "He that believeth shall be saved, and he that believeth not shall be damned;" and, "He is a shield unto all them that put their trust in him."

Many touch Jesus who are not healed by him; the reason is, they do it not by faith, through a sense of their wants, and a conviction of his ability and willingness to save them. Faith conveys the virtue of Christ into the soul, and spiritual health is the immediate consequence of this received virtue.

Christ does not reveal himself to incredulous and disobedient souls.

Without faith Jesus does nothing to men's souls now, no more than he did to their bodies in the days of his flesh.

Faith disregards apparent impossibilities where there is a command and promise of God. The effort to believe is often that faith by which the soul is healed.

Faith seems to put the almighty power of God into the hands of men; whereas unbelief appears to tie up even the hands of the Almighty.

Many are looking for more faith without using that which they have. It is as possible to hide this talent as any other.

The great sacrifice offered by Christ is an infinite reason why a penitent sinner should expect to find the mercy for which he pleads.

A weak faith is always wishing for signs and miracles. To take Christ at his word argues not only the perfection of faith, but also the highest exercise of sound reason, He is to be credited on his own word, because he is the "truth," and, therefore, can neither lie nor deceive.

There are degrees in faith as well as in the other graces of the Spirit. Little faith may be the seed of great faith, and therefore is not to be despised. But many who should be strong in faith have but a small measure of it, because they either give way to sin, or are not careful to improve what God has already given.

To get an increase of faith is to get an increase of every grace which constitutes the mind which was in Jesus, and prepares fully for the enjoyment of the kingdom of God.

He that has faith will get through every difficulty and perplexity; mountains shall become mole hills, or plains, before him.

Unbelief and disobedience are so intimately connected, that

the same word in the sacred writings often serves for both.

Why are not our souls completely healed? Why is not every demon cast out? Why are not pride, self-will, love of the world, lust, anger, peevishness, with all the other bad tempers and dispositions which constitute the mind of Satan, entirely destroyed? Alas! it is because we do not believe; Jesus is able; more, Jesus is willing; but we are not willing to give up our idols; we give not credence to his word; therefore sin hath a being in us, and dominion over us.

Many, by giving way to the language of unbelief, have lost the language of praise and thanksgiving for months, if not years.

There would be more miracles, at least of spiritual healing, were there more faith among those who are called believers.

How is it that faith is so rarely exercised in the power and goodness of God? We have not, because we ask not: our experience of his goodness is contracted, because we pray little, and believe less. To holy men of old the object of faith was more obscurely revealed than to us, and they had fewer helps to their faith; yet they believed more, and witnessed greater displays of the power and mercy of their Maker. Reader, have faith in God; and know that to excite, exercise, and crown this, he has given thee his word and his Spirit; and learn to know that without him you can do nothing.

Christ dwells in the heart only by faith, and faith lives only by love, and love continues only by obedience; he who believes loves, and he who loves obeys. He who obeys loves; he who loves believes; he who believes has the witness in himself; he who has this witness has Christ in his heart, the hope of glory; and he who believes, loves, and obeys, has Christ in his heart, and is a man of prayer.

We shall never find a series of disinterested, godly living without true faith. And we shall never find true faith without such a life. We may see works of apparent benevolence without faith; their principle is ostentation; and, as long as they can have the reward (human applause) which they seek, they may be continued. And yet the experience of all mankind shows how short-lived such works are; they want both principle and spring; they endure for a time, but soon wither away. Where true faith is there is God; his Spirit gives life, and his love affords motives to righteous actions. The use of any divine principle leads to its increase. The more a man exercises faith in Christ, the more he is enabled to believe; the more he believes, the more he receives; and the more he receives, the more able he is to work for God. Obedience is his delight, because love to God and man is the element in which his soul lives. Reader, thou professest to believe; show thy faith, both to God and man, by a life conformed to the royal law, which ever gives liberty and confers dignity.

Faith and hope will as necessarily enter into eternal glory as love will. The perfections of God are absolute in their nature, infinite in number, and eternal in their duration. However high, glorious, or sublime the soul may be in that eternal state, it will ever, in respect to God, be limited in its powers, and must be improved and expanded by the communications of the supreme Being. Hence it will have infinite glories in the nature of God, to apprehend by faith, to anticipate by hope, and enjoy by love.

From the nature of the divine perfections, there must be infinite glories in them, which must be objects of faith to disembodied spirits; because it is impossible that they should be experimentally or possessively known by any creature. Even in the heaven of heavens we shall, in reference to the infinite and eternal excellences of God, walk by faith, and not by sight. We shall credit the existence of infinite and illimitable glories in him, which, from their absolute and infinite nature, must be incommunicable. And as the very nature of the soul shows it to be capable of eternal growth and improvement; so the communications from the Deity, which are to produce this growth, and effect this improvement, must be objects of faith to the pure spirit; and, if objects of faith, consequently objects of hope; for as hope is "the expectation of future good," it is inseparable from the nature of the soul, to know of the existence of any attainable good without making it immediately the object of desire or hope, And is it not this that shall constitute the eternal and progressive happiness of the immortal spirit—namely, knowing, from what it has received, that there is infinitely more to be received; and desiring to be put in possession of every communicable good which it knows to exist?

As faith goes forward to view, so hope goes forward to desire; and God continues to communicate; every communication making way for another, by preparing the soul for greater enjoyment, and this enjoyment must produce love. To say that the soul can have neither faith nor hope in a future state, is to say that as soon as it enters heaven it is as happy as it can possibly be; and this goes to exclude all growth in the eternal state, and all progressive manifestations and communications of God; and consequently to fix a spirit, which is a composition of infinite desires, in a state of eternal sameness, in which it must be greatly changed in its constitution to find endless gratification.

To sum up the reasoning on this subject, I think it necessary to observe, 1. That the term "faith" is here to be taken, in the general sense of the word, for that belief which a soul has of the infinite sufficiency and goodness of God, in consequence of the discoveries he has made of himself and of his designs, either by revelation, or immediately by his Spirit. Now we know that God has revealed himself, not only in reference to this world, but in reference to eternity; and much of our faith is employed in things pertaining to the eternal world, and the enjoyments in that state. 2. That hope is to be taken in its common acceptation, the expectation of future good; which expectation is necessarily founded on faith, as faith is founded on knowledge. God gives a revelation which concerns both worlds, containing exceeding great and precious promises relative to both. We believe what he has said on his own veracity; and we hope to enjoy the promised blessings in both worlds, because He is faithful who has promised. 3. As the promises stand in reference to both worlds, so also must the faith and hope to which these promises stand as objects. 4. The enjoyments in the eternal world are all spiritual, and must proceed immediately from God himself. 5. God, in the plenitude of his excellences, is as incomprehensible to a glorified spirit, as he is to a spirit resident in flesh and blood. 6. Every created intellectual nature is capable of eternal improvement. 7. If seeing God as he is be essential to the eternal happiness of beatified spirits, then the discoveries which he makes of himself must be gradual; forasmuch as it is impossible that an infinite, eternal nature can be manifested to a created and limited nature in any other way. 8. As the perfections of God are infinite, they are capable of being eternally manifested, and, after all manifestations, there must be an infinitude of perfections still to be brought to view. 9. As every soul that has any just notion of God must know that he is possessed of all possible perfections, so these perfections, being objects of knowledge, must be objects of faith. 10. Every holy spirit feels itself possessed of unlimited desires for the enjoyment of spiritual good; and faith in the infinite goodness of God necessarily implies that he will satisfy every desire he has excited. 11. The power to gratify, in the divine Being, and the capacity to be gratified, in the immortal spirit, will necessarily excite continual desires, which desires, on the evidence of faith, will as necessarily produce hope, which is the expectation of future good. 12. All possible perfections in God are the objects of faith; and the communication of all possible blessedness the object of hope. 13. Faith goes forward to apprehend, and hope to anticipate, as God continues to discover his unbounded glories and perfections. 14. Thus discovered and desired, their influences become communicated, love possesses them, and is excited and increased by the communication. 15. With respect to those which are communicated, faith and hope cease, and go forward to new apprehensions and anticipations, while love continues to retain and enjoy the whole. 16. Thus an eternal interest is kept up; and infinite blessings, in endless succession, apprehended, anticipated, and enjoyed.

The man who professes that it is his duty to worship God must, if he act rationally, do it on the conviction that there is such a Being, infinite, eternal, unoriginated, and self-existent; the cause of all other being; on whom all being depends; and by whose energy, bounty, and providence, all other beings exist, live, and are supplied with the means of continued existence and life. He must believe, also, that he rewards them that diligently seek him; that he is not indifferent about his own worship; that he requires adoration and religious service from men; and that he blesses and especially protects and saves those who in simplicity and uprightness of heart seek and serve him. This requires faith; such a faith as is mentioned above; a faith by which we can "please God;" and, now that we have an abundant revelation, a faith according to that revelation; a faith in God through Christ, the great sin-offering, without which a man can no more please him, or be accepted of him, than Cain was.

IX. – JUSTIFICATION.

THE following are a few of the leading acceptations of the verb, which we translate "to justify:" —

1. It signifies to declare or pronounce one just or righteous; or, in other words, to declare him to be what he really is: "He was justified in the Spirit," 1 Tim. iii, 16. 2. To esteem a thing properly, Matt. xi, 19. 3. It signifies to approve, praise, and commend, Luke vii, 29; xvi, 15. 4. To clear from all sin, 1 Cor. iv, 4. 5. A judge is said to justify, not only when he condemns and punishes, but also when he defends the cause of the innocent. Hence it is taken in a forensic sense, and signifies to be found or declared righteous, innocent, &c., Matt. xii, 37. 6. It signifies to set free, or escape from, Acts xiii, 39. 7. It signifies, also, to receive one into favour, to pardon sin, Rom. viii, 30; Luke xviii, 14; Rom. iii, 20; iv, 2; 1 Cor. vi, 11, &c. In all these texts the word "justify" is taken in the sense of remission of sins through faith in Christ Jesus; and does not mean making the person just or righteous, but treating him as if he were so, having already forgiven him his sins.

Justification, or the pardon of sin, must precede sanctification; the conscience must be purged or purified from guilt, from all guilt, and from all guilt at once; for in no part of the Scripture are we directed to seek remission of sins *seriatim;* one now, another then, and so on.

The doctrine of justification by faith is one of the grandest displays of the mercy of God to mankind. It is so very plain that all may comprehend it; and so free that all may attain it. What more simple than this—Thou art a sinner, in consequence condemned to perdition, and utterly unable to save thy own soul. All are in the same state with thyself, and no man can give a ransom for the soul of his neighbour. God, in his mercy, has provided a Saviour for thee. As thy life was forfeited to death because of thy transgressions, Jesus Christ has redeemed thy life by giving up his own; he died in thy stead, and has made atonement to God for thy transgression; and offers thee the pardon he has thus purchased, on the simple condition that thou believe that his death is a sufficient sacrifice, ransom, and oblation for thy sin; and that thou bring it, as such, by confident faith to the throne of God, and plead it in thy own behalf there. When thou dost so, thy faith in that sacrifice shall be imputed to thee for righteousness; that is, it shall be the means of receiving that salvation which Christ has bought by his blood.

The doctrine of the imputed righteousness of Christ, as held by many, will not be readily found in Rom. iv, where it has been supposed to exist in all its proofs. It is repeatedly said that faith is imputed for righteousness; but in no place here that Christ's obedience to the moral law is imputed to any man. The truth is, the moral law was broken, and did not now require obedience; it required this before it was broken; but, after it was broken, it required death. Either the sinner must die, or some one in his stead; but there was none, whose death could have been an equivalent for the transgressions of the world, but Jesus Christ. Jesus, therefore, died for man; and it is through his blood, the merit of his passion and death, that we have redemption; and not by his obedience to the moral law in our stead: our salvation was obtained at a much higher price. Jesus could not but be righteous and obedient; this is consequent on the immaculate purity of his nature; but his death was not a necessary consequent. As the law of God can claim only the death of a transgressor—for such only forfeit their right to life—it is the greatest miracle of all that Christ could die, whose life was never forfeited. Here we see the indescribable demerit of sin, that it required such a death; and here we see the stupendous mercy of God, in providing the sacrifice required. It is therefore by Jesus Christ's death, or obedience unto death, that we are saved, and not by his fulfilling any moral law. That he fulfilled the moral law, we know; without which he could not have been qualified to be our

Mediator; but we must take heed lest we attribute that to obedience (which was the necessary consequence of his immaculate nature) which belongs to his passion and death. These were free-will offerings of eternal goodness, and not even a necessary consequence of his incarnation.

This doctrine of the imputed righteousness of Christ is capable of great abuse. To say that Christ's personal righteousness is imputed to every true believer, is not Scriptural: to say that he has fulfilled all righteousness for us, in our stead, if by this is meant his fulfilment of all moral duties, is neither Scriptural nor true; that he has died in our stead, is a great, glorious, and Scriptural truth; that there is no redemption but through his blood is asserted beyond all contradiction in the oracles of God. But there are a multitude of duties which the moral law requires, which Christ never fulfilled in our stead, and never could. We have various duties of a domestic kind which belong solely to ourselves, in the relation of parents, husbands, wives, servants, &c., in which relations Christ never stood. He has fulfilled none of these duties for us, but he furnishes grace to every true believer to fulfil them to God's glory, the edification of his neighbour, and his own eternal profit. The salvation which we receive from God's free mercy, through Christ, binds us to live in a strict conformity to the moral law; that law which prescribes our manners, and the spirit by which they should be regulated, and in which they should be performed. He who lives not in the due performance of every Christian duty, whatever faith he may profess, is either a vile hypocrite or a scandalous Antinomian.

God is said to be "no respecter of persons" for this reason, among many others, that, being infinitely righteous, he must be infinitely impartial. He cannot prefer one to another, because he has nothing to hope or fear from any of his creatures. All partialities among men spring from one or other of these two principles, hope or fear; God can feel neither of them, and therefore God can be no respecter of persons. He approves or disapproves of men according to their moral character. He pities all, and provides salvation for all, but he loves those who resemble him in his holiness; and he loves them in proportion to that resemblance, that is, the more of his image he sees in any the more he loves him, and *Econtra*. And every man's work will be the evidence of his conformity or nonconformity to God; and according to this evidence will God judge him. Here, then, is no respect of persons. God's judgment will be according to a man's work, and a man's work or conduct will be according to the moral state of his mind. No favouritism can prevail in the day of judgment; nothing will pass there but holiness of heart and life. A righteousness imputed, and not possessed and practised, will not avail where God judgeth according to every man's work. It would be well if those sinners and spurious believers, who fancy themselves safe and complete in the righteousness of Christ, while impure and unholy in themselves, would think of this testimony of the apostle.[7]

---

[7] The sentiments contained in the following letter are worthy the attention of the reader:—

"*Millbrook, Prescot, Jan. 21 st, 1823.*

"MY DEAR BROTHER DUNN,

"Last evening I received your letter of the 19th ult., and was not a little glad to hear from you: and still more rejoiced to hear such good news. I plainly see that every thing is going on as God usually conducts his work. I do not regret your being shut out of the churches; to such God never yet gave us a call: nor are we to build on other men's foundations. We have a work to do peculiar to ourselves. We know our own sorrows in the operation; and no stranger intermeddles with our joy. I should not wonder to hear next that you are denounced from the pulpits as deceivers and heretics. Boldly proclaim all the truth. Preach it with all its proofs and evidences; and leave that villanous stuff that is in concert with the Eleven Letters as perfectly unnoticed as if it never had existed. I am quite of Mr. Wesley's mind, that once 'we leaned too much toward Calvinism,' and especially in admitting, in any sense, the unscriptural doctrine of the imputed righteousness of Christ. I never use the distinction of righteousness imputed, righteousness imparted, righteousness practised. In no part of the book of God is Christ's righteousness ever said to be imputed to us for our justification; and I greatly doubt whether the doctrine of Christ's active obedience in our justification does not take away from the infinite merit of his sacrificial death: and whether by fair construction, and legitimate deduction, it will not go to prove, if admitted as above, that no absolute necessity of Christ's death did exist. For if the acts of his life justify in part, or conjunctly, they might, in so glorious a personage, have justified separately and wholly; and consequently his agony and bloody sweat, his cross and passion, and his death, burial, and ascension would have been utterly useless, considered as acts and consequences of acts, called atoning. Our grand doctrine is, 'We have redemption in his blood.' Nor can we ever successfully comfort the distressed but by proclaiming Christ crucified. having been 'delivered for our offences, and raised again for our justification.' He is not represented in heaven as performing acts of righteousness for our justification; but as the Lamb newly slain before the throne. I have long thought that the doctrine of imputed righteousness, as held by certain people, is equally compounded of Pharisaism and Antinomianism; and, most

As eternal life is given IN the Son of God, it follows it cannot be enjoyed WITHOUT him. No man can have it without having Christ; therefore "he that hath the Son hath life," and "he that hath not the Son hath not life." It is in vain to expect eternal glory if we have not Christ in our heart. The indwelling Christ gives both a title to it and a meetness for it. This is God's record. Let no man deceive himself here. An indwelling Christ and glory; no indwelling Christ, no glory. God's record must stand.

Who are Christ's flock? All real penitents; all true believers; all who obediently follow his example, abstaining from every appearance of evil, and in a holy life and conversation show forth the virtue of Him who called them from darkness into his marvellous light. "My sheep hear my voice and follow me." But who are not his flock? Neither the backslider in heart, nor the vile Antinomian, who thinks the more he sins the more the grace of God shall be magnified in saving him; nor those who fondly suppose they are covered with the righteousness of Christ while living in sin; nor the crowd of the indifferent and the careless; nor the immense herd of Laodicean loiterers; nor the fiery bigots who would exclude all from heaven but themselves, and the party who believe as they do. These the Scripture resembles to swine, dogs, goats, wandering stars, foxes, lions, wells without water, &c., &c. Let not any of these come forward to eat of this pasture, or take of the children's bread. Jesus Christ is the good Shepherd; the Shepherd who, to save his flock, laid down his own life.

To forsake all, without following Christ, is the virtue of a philosopher. To follow Christ in profession, without forsaking all, is the state of the generality of Christians. But to follow Christ, and forsake all, is the perfection of a Christian.

Talking about Christ, his righteousness, merits, and

---

certainly, should find very little trouble, by analysis or synthesis, to demonstrate the facts, little as its abettors think of the subject. But go on your way, preaching all our doctrines, but not in a controversial way: and if at any time you may be obliged to repel invective, do it in the meekness of Christ. Our grand doctrines of the witness of the Spirit, and Christian perfection, are opposed to all bad tempers, as well as bad words and works.

"The peace of God be with you. Write often to
"Your affectionate brother and friend,
"A. CLARKE."

atonement, while the person is not conformed to his word and Spirit, is no other than solemn deception.

The white robes of the saints cannot mean the righteousness of Christ, for this cannot be washed and made white in his own blood. This white linen is said to be the righteousness of the saints, Rev. xix, 8; and this is the righteousness in which they stand before the throne; therefore it is not Christ's righteousness, but it is a righteousness wrought in them by the merits of his blood and the power of his Spirit.

We must beware of Antinomianism, that is, of supposing that, because Christ has been obedient unto death, there is no necessity for our obedience to his righteous commandments. If this were so, the grace of Christ would tend to the destruction of the law, and not to its establishment. He only is saved from his sins who has the law of God written in his heart, who lives an innocent, holy, and useful life. Wherever Christ lives he works; and his work of righteousness will appear to his servants, and its effect will be quietness and assurance for ever. The life of God in the soul of man is the principle which saves and preserves eternally.

ADOPTION.[8] — Adoption signifies the act of receiving a stranger into a family, and conveying to him all the rights, privileges, and benefits belonging to a natural or legitimate child; the receiving a child of a stranger into a family where there was none.

This did not exist in the Jewish law; it was properly a Roman custom, and among them was regulated by law: and it is to adoption, as practiced among the Romans, that the apostle alludes in this place, Gal. iv, 5, as well as in various others in his epistles.
Among the ancient Romans every house had its altar, its religious rites; and its household gods. All these, being considered the most sacred, were ever to be continued in that family; and, on this account, if the family were in danger of becoming extinct, through want of children, adoption was admitted, that the family and its sacred rites and gods might be preserved. This was one of the laws of the very ancient "twelve tables," so celebrated in the history of

---

[8] As adoption is not so much a distinct act of God, but is involved in our justification, I have not thought it necessary to give to it a separate chapter. — S.D.

ancient Rome.

When, then, a child was to be adopted into a strange family, his father took him, and presenting himself and his son before the magistrate, and five witnesses, who were Romans, he said, "I emancipate to thee this my son." Then the adopting father, holding a piece of money in his hand, and at the same time taking hold of his son, said, "I declare this man to be my son according to the Roman law, and he is bought with this money;" and then gave it to the father as the price of his son, &c.

Every Roman had the right of life and death over his children, even as they had over slaves. In the case of adoption this right was surrendered by the natural father to the adopting father; and the person adopted entered into this new family as if it were his own naturally. He took his adopting father's name, and a legal right, not only to food, raiment, and all the comforts of life, but also to the inheritance. All the relatives of the new family bore the same relation to the adopted, as if they had been naturally his own; and in all privileges, rights, and legal transactions he was the same as if he had been born in that family.

But he was still amenable to the laws, and must be in every respect obedient, attentive to the family honour, and to its interest. In case of rebellion against the parent, he might be put to death; for the adopting father had the same authority over the adopted son as his own natural father had.

As a father might disinherit his son, so might the adopting father disinherit the adopted. For it must be considered that the adopted son, while he stood in the state and privileges of a natural child, had no privilege beyond such.

Without extending the parallel farther than is strictly necessary, we may observe,—

1. That as a man had lost all the privileges of his natural filiation, to regain them he must be received into the family by way of adoption. This was the only mode.

2. This adoption supposes that he is entirely cut off from the old family, having no longer any legal relation to or connection with it.

3. That he is received into the new family, to be entirely under the rule and government of his adopter; to be employed as he shall choose to employ him; and to be entirely at his disposal, in

body, soul, and spirit.

4. That as by this transaction he becomes an heir in the new family, so he is to enjoy those privileges while he acts according to the law in that case provided; and to the rules and constitution of the father's house.

5. That his old consanguinity is now changed: that he is considered of the same blood with the new family, standing no longer in any filial relationship to any other.

6. That he takes the very name of his adopting father, and is to be in every respect conformed to that; family.

To apply these more particularly: —

1. Man, having sinned against God, ceased to be his son; for, in order to constitute filiation, it is essential that the child share the same nature with the father. As God's nature is holy, pure, and perfect, when man sinned he lost his conformity to this nature; he lost the image of God in which he was created, and became unholy, impure, and imperfect.

2. To restore him, the way of adoption only was left; and that could not have taken place had not a previous adoption taken place, namely, the adoption of human nature by Jesus Christ.

3. This adoption, therefore, supposes, and absolutely requires, that he be cut off from the old stock, and grafted into the new; leaving behind him all his sins, sinful habits, sinful companions, and sinful dispositions; being no longer of his old father the devil, nor in any respect doing his lusts, performing his will, or associating with his followers; and that, as the old consanguinity is changed, he now stands in relation only to God, holy angels, and holy men; and that he is bound to maintain, in every respect, the honour, dignity, and respect of the divine family into which he is adopted.

4. In being adopted by God he is no longer his own, he is God's right; body, soul, and spirit belong to his heavenly Father. He is ever to feel himself absolutely at the disposal of God; and is bound, if he would enjoy the privileges of the family, to take God's word for the rule of his life, and God's Spirit for the regulator of his heart and affections.

5. And this obedience to the will of the Father, and conformity to the Ruler of the family, are founded on the state of salvation into which he is brought, and the ineffable privileges to

which he has now a right—he is an heir of God, and a joint heir with Christ Jesus.

6. That, as by this adoption he acquires a new nature, so he has a new name—he is called after God; a son of God, a child of God, an heir of God. But, properly, the family name is saint, all the adopted children are called to be saints; for holiness becomes God's house and family for ever. Where there is no saintship, there is no adoption, and consequently no heirship, and no inheritance.

X. – REGENERATION.

THE soul must be regenerated, all guilt must be purged away, and the heart must be cleansed. "But we have been regenerated, for we have been duly baptized." Baptism is the sign of regeneration, but it is not the thing; it is the "outward and visible sign of an inward and spiritual grace." You must be born of water and of the Spirit. Water is the emblem of the spiritual washing, but it is not the washing itself; "that which is born of the flesh is flesh; and that which is born of the Spirit is spirit," is holy, pure, and heavenly. If your water baptism had been spiritual regeneration, you would have a heart cleansed from all unrighteousness, free from pride, wrath, evil desires, bad tempers, &c. But you who depend upon this circumcision of the flesh, have not this; and you know you never had it. Therefore you want the blood that atones and purifies from all unrighteousness. Your having the reformers for your fathers,—baptism for the seal of your covenant,—your attendance on church and sacrament for the foundation of your hope of glory, can raise you no higher than Abraham as their father, circumcision as the seal of their covenant, sacrifices and ceremonies, carefully offered and performed, as the foundation of their hope of the continuance of the divine favour, did the ancient Jews. On these things they depended; on such things you depend.

So deep is the stain, so radicated the habits of sinning, so strong the propensity to do what is evil; that nothing less than the power by which the soul was created, can conquer these habits, eradicate these vices, and cause such a leper to change his spots, and such an Ethiop his hue. The whole change which the soul undergoes in its conversion, is the effect of a divine energy within. This the Gospel promises, when it promises to send forth the Holy Spirit. This mighty Spirit is given to enlighten, convince, strengthen, quicken, and save; and the change which is effected in the sinner's soul, in his habits, and in his life, is such as no natural cause can produce; such as no art of man can effect; and such as no religious institutions, connected with the most serious and pointed moral advices, can ever bring about. It is wholly God's work; and he performs it neither by might nor power, but by his own Spirit.

The soul of man has been perverted—turned from God to sin and death. It is to be converted—turned from sin and death to God and life eternal. It has fallen into sin, misery, and ruin; and is to be restored to holiness, happiness, and endless salvation. The law, received as coming from himself, and under the influence of his own Spirit, turns the soul back (shows the method of reconciliation) to God; and how it is to be restored from its ruined state, built up as at the beginning, and made a habitation of God through the Spirit.

Conversion is the turning or total change of a sinner from his sins to God. Conversion is often confounded with regeneration and holiness, but it properly means the effect produced by the first influence of the grace and light of God upon the heart, by which an idolater embraces the true God, a Jew the doctrine of Christ, and a sinner turns from his sins, and seeks the salvation of his soul in every means of grace.

Unless a man be born again – born from above; born not only of water, but of the Holy Ghost,– *he cannot see the kingdom of God*. These may appear hard sayings, and those who are little in the habit of considering spiritual things may exclaim, "It is enthusiasm! Who can bear it? Such things cannot possibly be." To such persons I can only say, "God hath spoken." This is sufficient for those who credit his being and his Bible. He, by whose almighty power Sarah had strength to conceive and bear a son in her old age, and by whose miraculous interference a virgin conceived, and the man Christ Jesus was born of her, can, by the same power, transform the sinful soul, and cause it to bear the image of the heavenly as it has borne the image of the earthly.

The order of the great work of salvation is—1. Conviction of sin: 2. Contrition for sin: 3. Faith in the Lord Jesus Christ as having been delivered for our offences, and risen for our justification: 4. Justification or pardon of all past sin, through faith in his blood, accompanied, ordinarily, with the testimony of his Spirit in our hearts, that our sins are forgiven us: 5. Sanctification or holiness, which is progressive, as a growing up into Jesus Christ, our living Head, in all things; and may be instantaneous, as God can, and often does, empty the soul of all sin in a moment, in the twinkling of an eye; and then, having sowed in the seeds of righteousness, they have a free and unmolested vegetation. 6. Perseverance in the state of sanctification; believing, hoping, watching, working, in order to stand in this state of salvation, receiving hourly a deeper impression of the seal of God: 7. Glorification is the result; for he who lives faithful unto death, shall obtain the crown of life. Without conviction of sin, no contrition; without contrition, no faith that justifies; without faith, no justification, no sanctification; without sanctification, no glorification.

There is every reason to believe, and genuine experience in divine things confirms it, that in the act of justification, when the Spirit of God, the Spirit of holiness, is given to bear witness with our spirits that we are the children of God; all the outlines of the divine image are drawn upon the soul: and it is the work of the Holy Spirit, in our sanctification, to touch off, and fill up, all those outlines, till every feature of the divine likeness is filled up and perfected.

XI. – THE HOLY SPIRIT.

THE WITNESS OF THE SPIRIT.—As every pious soul that believed in the coming Messiah, through the medium of the sacrifices offered up under the law, was made a partaker of the merit of his death, so every pious soul that believes in Christ crucified is made a partaker of the Holy Spirit. It is by this Spirit that sin is made known, and by it the blood of the covenant is applied; and, indeed, without this the want of salvation cannot be discovered, nor the value of the blood of the covenant duly estimated.

From the foundation of the church of God it was ever believed by his followers that there were certain infallible tokens by which he discovered to genuine believers his acceptance of them and of their services. This was sometimes done by a fire from heaven consuming the sacrifice; sometimes by an oracular communication to the priest or prophet; and at other times, according to the Jewish account, by changing the fillet or cloth on the head of the scapegoat from scarlet to white: but most commonly, and especially under the Gospel dispensation, he gives this assurance to true believers by the testimony of his Spirit in their consciences that he has forgiven their iniquities, transgressions, and sins for His sake who has carried their griefs and borne their sorrows.

"The Spirit itself"—that same Spirit, the Spirit of adoption; that is, the Spirit who witnesses this adoption; which can be no other than the Holy Ghost himself, and certainly cannot mean any disposition or affection of mind which the adopted person may feel; for such a disposition must arise from a knowledge of this adoption, and the knowledge of this adoption cannot be known by any human or earthly means; it must come from God himself. "With our spirit"—in our understanding, the place or recipient of light and information; and the place or faculty to which such information can properly be brought. This is done that we may have the highest possible evidence of the work which God has wrought. As the window is the proper medium to let the light of the sun into our apartments, so the understanding is the proper medium of conveying the Spirit's influence to the soul. We therefore have the utmost evidence of the fact of our adoption which we can possibly have: we have the word and Spirit of God, and the word sealed on our spirit by the Spirit of God. And this is not a momentary influx: if we take care to walk with God, and not grieve the Holy Spirit, we shall have an abiding testimony; and while we continue faithful to our adopting Father, the Spirit that witnesses that adoption will continue to witness it; and hereby we shall know that we are of God by the Spirit which he giveth us.

"The same Spirit," viz., the Spirit that witnesses of our adoption and sonship, makes intercession for us. Surely, if the apostle had designed to teach us that he meant our own sense and understanding by the Spirit, he never could have spoken in a manner in which plain common sense was never likely to comprehend his meaning. Besides, how can it be said that our own spirit, our filial disposition, bears witness with our own spirit; that our own spirit helps the infirmities of our own spirit; that our own spirit teaches our own spirit that of which it is ignorant; and that our own spirit maketh intercession for our spirit, with groanings unutterable? This would have been both incongrouous and absurd. We must, therefore, understand these places of that help and influence which the followers of God receive from the Holy Ghost; and consequently of the fulfilment of the various promises relative to this point which our Lord made to his disciples.

This Holy Spirit is sent forth to witness with their spirit. He is to bear his testimony where it is absolutely necessary,—where it can be properly discovered,—where it can be fully understood, and where it cannot be mistaken:—viz., in their hearts; or, as St. Paul says, "the Spirit itself beareth witness with our spirit:" the Spirit of God with the spirit of man—spirit with spirit—intelligence with intelligence; the testimony given and received by the same kind of agency: a spiritual agent in a spiritual substance.

This witness is not borne in their passions, nor in impressions made upon their imagination; for this must be from its very nature doubtful and evanescent; but it is borne in their understanding, not by a transitory manifestation, but continually—unless a man by sins of omission or commission grieve that divine Spirit, and cause him to withdraw his testimony—which is the same thing as the divine approbation. And God cannot continue to the soul a sense of his approbation when it has departed from the holy commandment that was given to it: but, even in this case, the man may return by repentance and faith to God, through Christ, when pardon will be granted and the witness restored.

Wherever this Spirit comes, it bears a testimony to itself. It shows that it is the divine Spirit by its own light; and he who receives it is perfectly satisfied of this. It brings a light, a power, and conviction, more full, more clear, and more convincing to the understanding and judgment, than they ever had, or ever can have, of any circumstance or fact brought before the intellect. The man knows that it is the divine Spirit, and he knows and feels that it bears testimony to the state of grace in which he stands.

So convincing and satisfactory is this testimony, that a man receiving it is enabled to call God his Father with the utmost filial confidence. Surprised and convinced he cries out at once, "Abba, Father! my Father! my Father!" having as full a consciousness that he is a child of God, as the most tenderly beloved child has of his filiation to his natural parent. He has the full assurance of faith; the meridian evidence that puts all doubts to flight.

And this, as was observed above, continues; for it is the very voice of the indwelling Spirit: for "crying" is not the only participle of the present tense denoting the continuation of the action; but, being neuter, it agrees with the Spirit of his Son; so it is the divine Spirit which continues to cry, "Abba, Father!" in the heart of the true believer. And it is ever worthy to be remarked that when a man has been unfaithful to the grace given, or has fallen into any kind of sin, he has no power to utter this cry. The Spirit is grieved and has departed, and the cry is lost! No power of the man's reason, fancy, or imagination, can restore this cry. Were he to utter the words with his lips his heart would disown them. But, on the other hand, while he continues faithful the witness is continued; the light and conviction, and the cry, are maintained. It is the glory of this grace that no man can command this cry; and none can assume it. Where it is, it is the faithful and true witness: where it is not, all is uncertainty and doubt.

The persons mentioned, Rom. viii, 15, 16, had the strongest evidence of the excellence of the state in which they stood; they knew that they were thus adopted; and they knew this by the Spirit of God, which was given them on their adoption; and, let me say, they could know it by no other means. The Father who had adopted them could be seen by no mortal eye; and the transaction, being of a purely spiritual nature, and transacted in heaven, can be known only by God's supernatural testimony of it upon earth. It is a matter of such solemn importance to every Christian soul, that God in his mercy has been pleased not to leave it to conjecture, assumption, or inductive reasoning; but attests it by his own Spirit in the soul of the person whom he adopts through Christ Jesus. It is the grand and most observable case in which the intercourse is kept up between heaven and earth; and the genuine believer in Christ Jesus is not left to the quibbles or casuistry of polemic divines or critics, but receives the thing and the testimony of it immediately from God himself. And were not the testimony of the state thus given, no man could possibly have any assurance of his salvation which could beget confidence and love. If to any man his acceptance with God be hypothetical, then his confidence most be so too. His love to God must be hypothetical, his gratitude hypothetical, and his obedience also. If God had forgiven me my sins then I should love him, and I should be grateful, and I should testify this gratitude by obedience. But who does not see that these must necessarily depend on the "if" in the first case? All this uncertainty, and the perplexities necessarily resulting from it, God has precluded by sending the Spirit of his Son into our hearts, by which we cry, "Abba, Father;" and thus our adoption into the heavenly family is testified and ascertained to us in the only way in which it can possibly be done, by the direct influence of the Spirit of God. Remove this from Christianity, and it is a dead letter.

The fact to be witnessed is beyond the knowledge of man: no

human power or cunning can acquire it: if obtained at all, it must come from above. In this, human wit and ingenuity can do nothing. It is to tell us that we are reconciled to God; that our sins are blotted out; that we are adopted into the family of heaven. The apostle tells us that this is witnessed by the Spirit of God. God alone can tell whom he has accepted; whose sins he has blotted out; whom he has put among his children: this he makes known by his Spirit in our spirit; so that we have (not by induction or inference) a thorough conviction and mental feeling, that we are his children.

There is as great a difference between this and knowledge gained by logical argument, as there is between hypothesis and experiment. Hypothesis states that a thing may be so: experience alone proves the hypothesis to be true or false. By the first, we think the thing to be possible or likely; by the latter we know, experience, or prove, by practical trial, that the matter is true, or is false, as the case may be.

I should never have looked for the "witness of the Spirit," had I not found numerous scriptures which most positively assert it, or hold it out by necessary induction; and had I not found that all the truly godly of every sect and party possessed the blessing—a blessing which is the common birthright of all the sons and daughters of God. Wherever I went among deeply religious people, I found this blessing. All who had turned from unrighteousness to the living God, and sought redemption by faith in the blood of the cross, exulted in this grace. It was never looked on by them as a privilege with which some peculiarly favoured souls were blessed: it was known from Scripture and experience to be the common lot of the people of God. It was not persons of a peculiar temperament who possessed it; all the truly religious had it, whether in their natural dispositions sanguine, melancholy, or mixed. I met with it everywhere, and met with it among the most simple and illiterate, as well as among those who had every advantage which high cultivation and deep learning could bestow. Perhaps I might, with the strictest truth, say that during the forty years I have been in the ministry, I have met with at least forty thousand who have had a clear and full evidence that God, for Christ's sake, had forgiven their sins, the Spirit himself bearing witness with their spirit that they were the sons and daughters of God.

We never confound the knowledge of salvation by the

remission of sins with final perseverance. This doctrine has nothing to do with a future possession; the truly believing soul has now the witness in himself; and his retaining it depends on his faithfulness to the light and grace received. If he give way to any known sin, he loses this witness, and must come to God through Christ as he came at first, in order to get the guilt of the transgression pardoned, and the light of God's countenance restored. For the justification which any soul receives is not in reference to his future pardon of sin, since God declares his righteousness "for the remission of sins which are past." And no man can retain his evidence of his acceptance with God longer than he has that faith which worketh by love. The present is a state of probation: in such a state a man may rise, fall, or recover; with this, the doctrine of the "witness of the Spirit" has nothing to do. When a man is justified all his past sins are forgiven him; but this grace reaches not on to any sin that may be committed in any following moment.

But it may be objected: "The human mind easily gets under the dominion of superstition and imagination; and then a variety of feelings, apparently divine, may be accounted for on natural principles." To this I answer, 1. Superstition is never known to produce settled peace and happiness; it is generally the parent of gloomy apprehensions and irrational fears: but surely the man who has broken the laws of his Maker, and lived in open rebellion against him, cannot be supposed to be under the influence of superstition, when he is apprehensive of the wrath of God, and fears to fall into the bitter pains of an eternal death. Such fears are as rational as they are Scriptural; and the broken and contrite heart is ever considered, through the whole oracles of God, as essentially necessary to the finding redemption in Christ. Therefore such fears, feelings, and apprehensions are not the offspring of a gloomy superstition; but the fruit and evidence of a genuine Scriptural repentance. 2. Imagination cannot long support a mental imposture. To persuade the soul that it is passed from darkness to light; that it is in the favour of God; that it is an heir of glory, &c., will require strong excitement indeed; and the stronger the exciting cause, or stimulus, the sooner the excitability and its effects will be exhausted. A person may imagine himself for a moment to be a king, or to be a child of God; but that revery, where there is no radical derangement of mind, must be transient. The person must soon awake, and come to himself. 3. But it is impossible that imagination can have any thing to do in this case, any farther than any other faculty of the mind, in natural operation; for the person must walk as he is directed by the word of God, abhorring evil, and cleaving to that which is good: and the sense of God's approbation in his conscience lasts no longer than he acts under the spirit of obedience; God continuing the evidence of his approbation to his conscience while he walks in newness of life. Has imagination ever produced a life of piety? Now multitudes are found who have had this testimony uninterruptedly for many years together. Could imagination produce this? If so, it is a unique case; for there is none other in which an excitement of the imagination has sustained the impression with any such permanence. And all the operations of this faculty prove that to an effect of this kind it is wholly inadequate. If, then, it can sustain impressions in spiritual matters for years together, this must he totally preternatural, and the effect of a miraculous operation; and this miracle must he resorted to, to explain away a doctrine which some men, because they themselves do not experience it, deny that any others can.

But might I, without offence, speak a word concerning myself? Those that know me know that I am no enthusiast; that I have given no evidence of a strong imagination; that I am far from being the subject of sudden hopes or fears; that it requires strong reasons and clear argumentation to convince me of the truth of any proposition not previously known. Now I do profess to have received, through God's eternal mercy, a clear evidence of my acceptance with God; and it was given me after a sore night of spiritual affliction, and precisely in that way in which the Scriptures promise this blessing. It has also been accompanied with power over sin; and I hold it through the same mercy, as explicitly, as clearly, and as satisfactorily, as ever. No work of imagination could have ever produced or maintained any feeling like this. I am, therefore, safe in affirming, for all these reasons, that we have neither misunderstood nor misapplied the scriptures in question.

As to the doctrine of assurance, (or the knowledge of our salvation by the remission of sins; or, in other words, that a man who is justified by faith in Christ Jesus knows that he is so, the Spirit hearing witness with his spirit that he is a child of God,) against which such a terrible outcry has been made, I would beg leave to ask, What is Christianity without it? A mere system of ethics; an authentic history; a dead letter. It is by the operations of the Holy Spirit in the souls of believers, that the connection is kept up between heaven and earth. The grand principle of the Christian religion is to reconcile men to God by Christ Jesus; to bring them from a state of wrath to reconciliation and favour with God; to break the power, cancel the guilt, and destroy the very being of sin; for Christ was manifested that he might destroy the works of the devil. And can this be done in any human soul, and it know nothing about it, except by inference and conjecture? Miserable state of Christianity indeed, where no man knows that he is born of God! This assurance of God's love is the birthright and common privilege of all his children. It is a general experience among truly religions people: they take rest, rise up, work, and live under its influence. By it they are carried comfortably through all the ills of life, bring forth the fruits of the Spirit, triumph in redeeming grace, and die exulting in Him whom they know and feel to be the God of their salvation. Nor is this confined to superannuated women, as Mr. Southey charitably hopes Mrs. Wesley was, when she professed to receive the knowledge of salvation by the remission of sins. Men also as learned as Mr. Badcock, as philosophical as Mr. Southey, as deeply read in men and things as Bishop Lavington, and as sound divines at least as the rector of Manaccan, have exulted in the same testimony, walked in all good conscience before God, illustrated the doctrine by a suitable deportment, and died full of joyful anticipation of eternal glory! Alas, what a dismal tale do these men tell, who not only strive to argue against the doctrine, but endeavour to turn it into ridicule! They tell us that they are not reconciled to God!

No salvation by induction or inference can satisfy a guilty conscience, which feels the wrath of God abiding on it; nothing but the witness of God's Spirit in our own spirit, that we are the children of God, can appease the terrors of an awakened sinner, give rest to a troubled heart, or be a foundation on which the soul can build a rational and Scriptural hope of eternal life.

The Holy Spirit in the soul of a believer is God's seal, set on his heart to testify that he is God's property, and that he should be wholly employed in God's service.

As Christ is represented as the ambassador of the Father, so the Holy Spirit is represented as the ambassador of the Son, coming vested with his authority, as the interpreter and executor of his will.

We know by the Spirit which he hath given us that we dwell in God, and God in us. It was not by conjecture or inference that Christians of old knew they were in the favour of God; it was by the testimony of God's own Spirit in their hearts; and this Spirit was not given in a transient manner, but was constant and abiding, while they continued under the influence of that faith which worketh by love. Every good man is a temple of the Holy Ghost; and wherever He is, He is both light and power. By his power he works; by his light he makes both himself and his work known. Peace of conscience and joy in the Holy Ghost must proceed from the indwelling of that Holy Spirit; and those who have these blessings must know that they have them, for we cannot have heavenly peace and heavenly joy without knowing that we have them. But this Spirit in the soul of a believer is not only manifest by its effects, but it bears its own witness to its own indwelling. So that a man not only knows that he has the Spirit from the fruits of the Spirit, but he knows that he has it from its own direct witness. It may be said, "How can these things be?" And it may be answered, "By the power, light, and mercy of God." But that such things are, the Scriptures uniformly attest; and the experience of the whole genuine church of Christ, and of every truly converted soul, sufficiently proves.

"As the wind bloweth where it listeth," and we "cannot tell whence it cometh and whither it goeth, so is every one that is born of the Spirit:" the thing is certain, and fully known by its effects; but how this testimony is given and confirmed is inexplicable. Every good man feels it, and knows he is of God by the Spirit God has given him.

We may witness in the experience of multitudes of simple people, who have been by the preaching of the Gospel converted from the error of their ways, such a strength of testimony in favour of the work of God in the heart, and his effectual teaching in the mind, as is calculated to still, or reduce to silence, every thing but bigotry and prejudice, neither of which has either eyes or ears. This teaching and these changing or converting influences come from God. They are not acquired by human learning: and those who put this in the place of the divine teaching never grow wise to salvation. To enter into the kingdom of heaven a man must become as a little child.

There is nothing more usual among even the best educated and enlightened of the members of the Methodist society, than a distinct knowledge of the time, place, and circumstances, when and where, and in which way, they were deeply convinced of sin, and afterward had a clear sense of God's mercy to their souls, in forgiving their sins, and giving them the witness in themselves that they were born of God.

The Methodists, in proof of the doctrine of the witness of the Spirit, refer to no man, not to Mr. John Wesley himself: they appeal to none—they appeal to the Bible, where this doctrine stands as inexpugnable as the pillars of heaven. Nor do they need solitary instances as facts, to prove that on this point they have not mistaken the Bible, while they, by the mercy of God, have thousands of testimonies every year of its truth; and they know it to be the common birthright of all the sons and daughters of God. Without it the whole life of faith would be hypothetical. And if a man have not the consolations of the Holy Spirit, and a Scriptural and satisfactory evidence of his own interest in Christ, and of his title through him to the kingdom of heaven, the Koran, for aught he knows, may be as true as the Bible. No man can inherit unless he be a son: "For if sons, then heirs;" and to them that are sons "God sends the Spirit of his Son into their hearts, crying, Abba, Father." These are the true sayings of God, and all his people know them.

Those who feel little or none of the work of God in their own hearts are not willing to allow that he works in others. Many deny the influences of God's Spirit, merely because they never felt them. This is to make any man's experience the rule by which the whole word of God is to be interpreted; and, consequently, to leave no more divinity in the Bible than is found in the heart of him who professes to explain it.

When moral effects, the purest, the most distinguished, and the most beneficial to society are attributed to natural causes, human passions, and the inquietudes of vanity, and not to the Author of all good, the Father of lights, then we may safely assert that the person who so views him is one of those unwise men of whom the psalmist speaks. He excludes God from his own peculiar work; gives to nature what belongs to grace; to human passions what belongs to the divine Spirit; and to secondary causes what must necessarily spring from the First Cause of all things.

Were not the subject too grave, it would be sufficient to excite something more than a smile, to see men both of abilities and learning, in their discussion of spiritual subjects which they have never thoroughly examined, because they have never experimentally felt them, labour to account for all the phenomena of repentance, faith, and holiness, by excluding the Spirit of God from his own proper work; and to the discredit of their understanding, and the dishonour of religion and sound philosophy, search for the principle that produces love to God and all mankind, with all the fruits of a holy life, in some of the worst passions of the human heart.

The Holy Ghost so satisfies the souls that receive it, that they thirst no more for earthly good: it purifies also from all spiritual defilement, on which account it is emphatically styled the *Holy* Spirit; and it makes those who receive it fruitful in every good word and work.

To produce inward spirituality is the province of the Spirit of God, and of him alone; therefore he is represented under the similitude of fire, because he is to illuminate and invigorate the soul, penetrate every part, and assimilate the whole to the image of the God of glory.

As truly as the living God dwelt in the Mosaic tabernacle and in the temple of Solomon, so truly does the Holy Ghost dwell in the souls of genuine Christians.

No man who has not divine assistance can either find the way to heaven, or walk in it when found. As Christ, by his sacrificial offering, has opened the kingdom of God to all believers; and, as Mediator, transacts the concerns of their kingdom before the throne, so the Spirit of God is the great Agent here below, to enlighten, quicken, strengthen, and guide the true disciples of Christ; and all that are born of this Spirit are led and guided by it; and none can pretend to be the children of God who are not thus guided.

To purify the soul, to refine and sublime all the passions and appetites, the operation of the Holy Spirit is promised. Spirit only can act successfully on spirit; and this Spirit is called the Holy Spirit, not only because it is holy in itself, but because it is the Author of holiness to them who receive it. Hence it is represented under the notion of fire, because it enlightens, warms, refines, and purifies. It is the property of fire either to consume and destroy, or assimilate every thing to itself with which it is brought into contact. It pervades all things, transfuses itself through every part, destroys or decomposes whatever cannot withstand its action; and communicates its own essential properties to whatever abides its test. Thus the Holy Spirit, the "Spirit of burning," destroys the pollution of the heart, and makes pure and divine all its powers and faculties.

"The communion of the Holy Ghost be with you all." May that Holy Spirit, that divine and eternal energy which proceeds from the Father and the Son; that heavenly fire that gives light and life, that purifies and refines, sublimes and exalts, comforts and invigorates, make you all partakers with himself. This points out the astonishing privileges of true believers: they have communion with God's Spirit; share in all his gifts and graces; walk in his light; through him they have the fullest confidence that they are of God, that he is their Father and Friend, and has blotted out all their iniquities: this they know by the Spirit which he has given them. And is it possible that a man shall be a partaker with the Holy Ghost, and not know it! that he shall be full of light and love, and not know it! that he shall have the Spirit of adoption by which he can cry, "Abba, Father!" and yet know nothing of his relationship to God but by inference from indirect proofs? in a word, that he shall have the grace of our Lord Jesus Christ, the love of God, and the communion of the Holy Ghost with him, and all the while know nothing certain of the grace, as to his portion in it; feel nothing warming from the love, as to its part in him; and nothing energetic from the communion, as to his participation in the gifts and graces of this divine energy? This is all as absurd as it is impossible. Every genuine Christian, who maintains a close walk with God, may have as full an evidence of his acceptance with God as he has of his own existence. And the doctrine that explains away this privilege, or softens it down to nothing, by making the most gracious and safe state consistent with innumerable doubts and fears, and general uncertainty, is not of God. It is a spurious Gospel, which, under the show of a voluntary humility, not only lowers, but almost annihilates the standard of Christianity.

One communication of this Spirit always makes way and

disposes for another. Neither apostle nor private Christian can subsist in the divine life without frequent influences from on high.

When reconciled to God, and thus brought nigh by the blood of Christ, we receive the gift of the Holy Spirit, which is the fruit of the death, resurrection, and ascension of our Lord. And this Spirit, which is emphatically called the *Holy* Spirit, because he is not only infinitely holy in his own nature, but his grand office is to make the children of men holy, is given to true believers, not only to "testify with their spirits that they are the children of God," but also to purify their hearts; and thus he transfuses through their souls his own holiness and purity; so that the image of God in which they were created, and which by transgression they had lost, is now restored; and they are, by this holiness, prepared for the enjoyment of eternal blessedness, in perfect union with Him who is the Father and God of glory, and the Fountain of holiness.

God promises his Holy Spirit to sanctify and cleanse the heart, so as utterly to destroy all pride, anger, self-will, peevishness, hatred, malice, and every thing contrary to his own holiness.

The very Spirit which is given them, on their believing in Christ Jesus, is the Spirit of holiness; and they can retain this spirit no longer than they live in the spirit of obedience.

It is the office of the Holy Spirit to witness to the conscience of man the covenant and its conditions, to apply the blood of sprinkling, and to take the things that are Christ's and show them to men; and it is his province to witness to the heart of the believing penitent, that by this shed blood his "conscience is purged from dead works to serve the living God." He is also the sanctifying Spirit; the Spirit of judgment, and the Spirit of burning; and, as such, he condemns to utter destruction the whole of the carnal mind, and purifies the very thoughts of the heart by his inspiration, enabling the true believer perfectly to love God and worthily to magnify his holy name. And this same Spirit dwelling in the soul of a believer seals him an heir of eternal glory.

The Holy Spirit is called an advocate, because he transacts the cause of God and Christ with us, explains to us the nature and importance of the great atonement, shows the necessity of it, counsels us to receive it, instructs us how to lay hold on it, vindicates our claim to it, and makes intercessions in us with unutterable groanings.

Our Lord makes intercession for us by negotiating and managing, as our friend and agent, all the affairs pertaining to our salvation. And the Spirit of God maketh intercession for the saints, not by supplication to God in their behalf, but by directing and qualifying their supplications in a proper manner, by his agency and influence upon their hearts; which, according to the Gospel scheme, is the peculiar work and office of the Holy Spirit. So that God, whose is the Spirit, and who is acquainted with the mind of the Spirit, knows what he means when he leads the saints to express themselves in words, desires, groans, sighs, or tears; in each God reads the language of the Holy Ghost, and prepares the answer according to the request.

This Spirit is not sent to stocks, stones, or machines, but to human beings endued with rational souls; therefore, it is not to work on them with that irresistible energy which it must exert on inert matter, in order to conquer the *vis inertiae,* or disposition to abide eternally in a motionless state, which is the state of all inanimate beings; but it works upon understanding, will, judgment, conscience, &c., in order to enlighten, convince, and persuade. If, after all, the understanding, the eye of the mind, refuses to behold the light; the will determines to remain obstinate; the judgment purposes to draw false inferences; and the conscience hardens itself against every check and remonstrance; (and all this is possible to a rational soul, which must be dealt with in a rational way;)then the Spirit of God, being thus resisted, is grieved, and the sinner is left to reap the fruit of his doings. To force the man to see, feel, repent, believe, and be saved, would be to alter the essential principles of his creation and the nature of mind, and reduce him into the state of a machine, the *vis inertiae* of which was to be overcome and conducted by a certain quantum of physical force, superior to that resistance which would be the natural effect of the certain quantum of the *vis inertiae* possessed by the subject on and by which this agent was to operate. Now man cannot be operated on in this way, because it is contrary to the laws of his creation and nature; nor can the Holy Ghost work on that as a machine which himself has made a free agent. Man, therefore, may, and generally does, resist the Holy Ghost; and the whole revelation of God bears unequivocal testimony to this most dreadful possibility and most awful truth. It is trifling with the sacred text to say that resisting the Holy Ghost here means "resisting the laws of Moses, the exhortations, threatenings, and promises of the prophets," &c. These, it is true, the uncircumcised ear may resist; but the uncircumcised heart is that alone to which the Spirit that gave the laws, exhortations, promises, &c., speaks; and, as matter resists matter, so spirit resists spirit. These were not only uncircumcised in ear, but uncircumcised also in heart; and, therefore, they resisted the Holy Ghost, not only in his declarations and institutions, but also in his actual energetic operations upon their minds.

"Grieve not the Holy Spirit of God," by giving way to any wrong temper, unholy word, or unrighteous action. Even those who have already a measure of the light and life of God, both of which are not only brought in by the Holy Spirit, but maintained by his constant indwelling, may give way to sin, and so grieve this Holy Spirit that it shall withdraw both its light and presence; and, in proportion as it withdraws, then hardness and darkness take place, and, what is still worse, a state of insensibility is the consequence; for the darkness prevents the fallen state from being seen, and hardness prevents it from being felt.

LOVE.—Love is a sovereign preference given to one above all others, present or absent; a concentration of all the thoughts and desires in a single object, which is preferred to all others. Now, apply this definition to the love which God requires of his creatures, and you will have the most correct view of the subject. Hence, it appears that by this love the soul cleaves to, affectionately admires, and consequently rests in, God, supremely pleased and satisfied with him as its portion; that it acts from him, as its Author; for him, as its Master; and to him, as its end; and that by it all the powers and faculties of the mind are concentrated in the Lord of the universe; that by it the whole man is willingly surrendered to the Most High; and that, through it, an identity or sameness of spirit with the Lord is acquired, the person being made a partaker of the divine nature; having the mind in him that was in Christ; and thus dwelling in God, and God in him.

He loves God with all his heart who loves nothing in comparison of him, and nothing but in reference to him; who is ready to give up, do, or suffer, any thing, in order to please and glorify him; who has in his heart neither love nor hatred, hope nor fear, inclination nor aversion, desire nor delight, but as they relate to God, and are regulated by him. Such a love that Being who is infinitely perfect, good, wise, powerful, beneficent, and merciful, merits and requires from his intelligent creatures; and in fulfilling this duty the soul finds its perfection and felicity; for it rests in the Source of goodness, and is penetrated with incessant influences from Him who is the essence and centre of all that is amiable; for he is the God of all grace.

He loves God with all his soul, with all his life, who is ready to give up his life for His sake; who is ready to endure all sorts of torments, and to be deprived of all kinds of comforts, rather than dishonour God; he who employs life, with all its comforts and conveniences, to glorify Him in, by, and through all; to whom life and death are nothing, but as they come from, and lead to God; who labours to promote the cause of God and truth in the world, denying himself, taking up his cross daily; neither eating, drinking, sleeping, resting, labouring, toiling, but in reference to the glory of God, his own salvation, and that of the lost world.

He loves God with all his mind, with all his intellect, or understanding, who applies himself only to know God and his holy will; who receives with submission, gratitude, and pleasure, the sacred truths which he has revealed to mankind; who studies neither art nor science, but as far as it is necessary for the service of God, and uses it at all times to promote his glory; who forms no projects nor designs but in reference to God, and to the interests of mankind; who banishes, as much as possible, from his understanding and memory, every useless, foolish, and dangerous thought; together with every idea which has any tendency to defile his soul, or turn it for a moment from the centre of eternal repose; who uses all his abilities, both natural and acquired, to grow in the grace of God, and to perform his will in the most acceptable manner: in a word, he who sees God in all things, thinks of him at all times, having his mind continually fixed upon God; acknowledges him in all his ways; who begins, continues, and ends all his thoughts, words, and works to the glory of his name; continually planning, scheming, and devising how he may serve God and his generation more effectually; his head, his intellect, going before; his heart, his affections, and desires, coming after.

He loves God with all his strength who exerts all the powers and faculties of his body and soul in the service of God; who, for the glory of his Maker, spares neither labour nor cost; who sacrifices his body, his health, his time, his ease, for the honour of his divine Master; who employs in his service all his goods, his talents, his power, his credit, authority, and influence; doing what he does with a single eye, a loving heart, and with all his might; in whose conduct is ever seen the work of faith, patience of hope, and labour of love.

O glorious state of him who has given God his whole heart, and in which God ever lives and rules! Glorious state of blessedness upon earth, triumph of the grace of God over sin and Satan! state of holiness and happiness far beyond this description, which comprises an ineffable union and communion between the ever blessed Trinity and the soul of man! O God! let thy work appear unto thy servants, and the work of our hands establish upon us! The work of our hands establish thou it! Amen. Amen.

This love is the spring of all our actions; it is the motive of our obedience; the principle through which we love God; "we love him because he first loved us;" and we love him with a love worthy of himself, because it springs from him: it is his own; and every flame that rises from this pure and vigorous fire must be pleasing in his sight: it consumes what is unholy; refines every passion and appetite; sublimes the whole, and assimilates all to itself. And we know that this is the love of God: it differs widely from all that is earthly and sensual. The Holy Ghost comes with it; by his energy it is diffused and pervades every part; and by his light we discover what it is, and know the state of grace in which we stand. Thus we are furnished to every good word and work; have produced in us the mind that was in Christ; are enabled to obey the pure law of our God in its spiritual sense, by loving him with all our heart, soul, mind, and strength, and our neighbour, every son of man, as ourselves. This is, or ought to be, the common experience of every believer.

The love of Christ is opposed to our enmity, and by it our hatred to God and goodness is overcome. Love counteracts the whole carnal mind, draws out the heart in affectionate attachment to God, and is the incentive to all obedience, as being the fulfilling of the law. Such a person is not obliged to derive the principle of his obedience from any thing outward: the moral law is before his eyes;

but the love of God, shed abroad in his heart, is the principle by which he obeys it. He performs nothing merely as a duty; he has the law of God written in his heart, and this ever disposes him to do what is right in the sight of his Judge. If it were not even infallibly true that a life of sin must terminate in endless misery, yet he would abhor the way of the wicked. He has tried the path of disobedience, and found it the road to ruin: he now knows the way of righteousness, and finds it the path of peace and happiness. Satan, the enslaver of the world, he found to be a hard task master, during the long period in which he laboured under chains, in the house of his bondage. God, the Saviour of the world, he finds to be a beneficent Father, and his service perfect freedom. He delights in obedience; it is the element in which his soul lives, prospers, and is happy.

Love is properly the image of God in the soul; for "God is love." By faith we receive from our Maker; by hope we expect a future and eternal good; but by love we resemble God; and by it alone are we qualified to enjoy heaven, and be one with him throughout eternity. Faith and hope respect ourselves alone; love takes in both God and man. Faith helps, and hope sustains us; but love to God and man makes us obedient and useful.

Love is the means of preserving all other graces; indeed, properly speaking, it includes them all; and all receive their perfection from it. Love to God and man can never be dispensed with. It is essential to social and religious life; without it no communion can be kept up with God; nor can any man have a preparation for eternal glory whose heart and soul are not deeply imbued with it. Without it there never was true religion, nor ever can be; and it not only is necessary through life, but will exist throughout eternity. What were a state of blessedness if it did not comprehend love to God and to human spirits in the most exquisite, refined, and perfect degrees?

That man is no Christian who is solicitous for his own happiness alone, and who cares not how the world goes, so that himself be comfortable. How much good is omitted, how many evils caused, how many duties neglected, how many innocent persons deserted, how many good works destroyed, how many truths suppressed, and how many acts of injustice authorized, by those timorous forecasts of what may happen, and those faithless apprehensions concerning the future!

Where is our zeal for God? Where the sounding of our bowels over the perishing nations who have not yet come under the yoke of the Gospel? multitudes of whom are not under the yoke, because they have never heard of it;—and they have not heard of it, because they who enjoy the blessings of the Gospel of Jesus have not felt (or have not obeyed the feeling) the imperious duty of dividing their heavenly bread with those who are famishing with hunger, and giving the water of life to those who are dying of thirst! How shall they appear in that great day when the conquests of the Lion of the tribe of Judah are ended; when the mediatorial kingdom is delivered up unto the Father; and the Judge of quick and dead sits on the great white throne, and to those on his left says, "I was hungry, and ye gave me no meat; I was thirsty, and ye gave me no drink?" I say, how shall they appear who have made no exertions to tell the lost nations of the earth the necessity for preparing to meet their God; and showing them the means of doing it, by affording them the blessings of the Gospel of the grace of God? Let us beware lest the stone that struck the motley image, and dashed it to pieces, fall on us, and grind us to powder!

A religion, the very essence of which is love, cannot suffer at its altars a heart that is revengeful and uncharitable, or which does not use its utmost endeavours to revive love in the heart of another.

Union among the followers of Christ is strongly recommended. How can spiritual brethren fall out by the way! Have they not all one Father, all one Head? Do they not form one body, and are they not all members of each other? Would it not be monstrous to see the nails pulling out the eyes, the hands tearing off the flesh from the body, the teeth biting out the tongue? &c., &c. And is it less so to see the members of a Christian society bite and devour each other till they are consumed one of another?

God has many imitators of his power, independence, justice, &c., but few of his love, condescension, and kindness.

God is merciful; he will have man to resemble him: as far as he is merciful, feels a compassionate heart, and uses a benevolent hand, he resembles his Maker; and the mercy he shows to others God will show to him. But it is not a sudden impression at the sight of a person in distress, which obliges a man to give something for the relief of the sufferer, that constitutes the merciful character. It is he who considers the poor; who endeavours to find them out; who looks into their circumstances; who is in the habit of doing so; and actually, according to his power and means, goes about to do good; that is the merciful man of whom God speaks with such high approbation, and to whom he promises a rich reward.

The apostle, 1 Cor. xvi, 2, prescribeth the most convenient and proper method of making contribution for the relief of the poor. 1. Every man was to feel it his duty to succour his brethren in distress. 2. He was to do this according to the ability which God gave him. 3. He was to do this at the conclusion of the week, when he had cast up his weekly earnings, and had seen how much God had prospered his labour. 4. He was then to bring it on the first day of the week, as is most likely, to the church or assembly, that it might be put into the common treasury. 5. We learn from this that the weekly contribution could not be always the same, as each man was to lay by as God had prospered him. Now, some weeks he would gain more; others, less. 6. It appears from the whole that the first day of the week, which is the Christian Sabbath, was the day on which their principal religious meetings were held in Corinth and the churches of Galatia; and, consequently, in all other places where Christianity had prevailed. This is a strong argument for the keeping of the Christian Sabbath. 7. We may observe that the apostle follows here the rule of the synagogue; it was a regular custom among the Jews to make their collections for the poor on the Sabbath day, that they might not be without the necessaries of life, and might not be prevented from coming to the synagogue. 8. For the purpose of making this provision, they had a purse, which was called "the purse of the alms," or, what we would term, "the poor's box." This is what the apostle seems to mean when he says, "Let him lay by him in store"—Let him put it in the alms purse, or in the poor's box. 9. It was a maxim also with them that, if they found any money, they were not to put it in their private purse, but in that which belonged to the poor. 10. The pious Jews believed that as salt seasoned food, so did alms riches; and that he who did not give alms of what he had, his riches should be dispersed. The moth would corrupt the bags, and the canker corrode the money, unless the mass was sanctified by giving a part to the poor.

Whatever love we may pretend to mankind, if we are not charitable and benevolent, we give the lie to our profession. If we have not bowels of compassion we have not the love of God in us; if we shut up our bowels against the poor, we shut Christ out of our hearts, and ourselves out of heaven.

Let the person who is called to perform any act of compassion or mercy to the wretched, do it, not grudgingly nor of necessity, but from a spirit of pure benevolence and sympathy. The poor are often both wicked and worthless; and if those who are called to minister to them as stewards, overseers, &c., do not take care, they will get their hearts hardened with the frequent proofs they will have of deception, lying, idleness, &c. And on this account it is that so many of those who have been called to minister to the poor in parishes, workhouses, and religious societies, when they come to relinquish their employment, find that many of their moral feelings have been considerably blunted, and perhaps the only reward they get for their services is the character of being hard-hearted. If whatever is done in this way be not done unto the Lord, it can never be done with cheerfulness.

Works of charity and mercy should be done as much in private as is consistent with the advancement of the glory of God, and the effectual relief of the poor.

He whom God has employed in a work of mercy has need to return, by prayer, as speedily to his Maker as he can, lest he should be tempted to value himself on account of that in which he has no merit; for the good that is done upon earth the Lord doeth it alone.

Love heightens the smallest actions, and gives a worth to them, which they cannot possess without it.

Love never supposes that a good action may have a bad motive; gives every man credit for his profession of religion, uprightness, godly zeal, &c., while nothing is seen in his conduct or in his spirit inconsistent with this profession.

Labour after a compassionate or sympathizing mind. Let your heart feel for the distressed; enter into their sorrows, and bear a part of their burdens. It is a fact, attested by universal experience, that by sympathy a man may receive into his own affectionate feelings a measure of the distress of his friend, and that his friend does find himself relieved in the same proportion as the other has entered into his griefs. "But how do you account for this?" I do not account for it at all: it depends upon certain laws of nature, the principles of which have not been as yet duly developed.

Do not withhold from any man the offices of mercy and kindness; you have been God's enemy, and yet God fed, clothed, and preserved you alive; do to your enemy as God has done to you. If your enemy be hungry, feed him; if he be thirsty, give him drink; so has God dealt with you. And has not a sense of his goodness and long suffering toward you been the means of melting down your heart into penitential compunction, gratitude, and love toward him? How know you that a similar conduct toward your enemy may not have the same gracious influence on him toward you? Your kindness may be the means of begetting in him a sense of his guilt; and, from being your fell enemy, he may become your real friend.

He who loves only his friends does nothing for God's sake. He who loves for the sake of pleasure, or interest, pays himself.

A moral enemy is more easily overcome by kindness than by hostility. Against the latter he arms himself; and all the evil passions of his heart concentrate themselves in opposition to him who is striving to retaliate by violence the injurious acts which he has received from him. But where the injured man is labouring to do him good for his evil; to repay his curses with blessings and prayers, his evil passions have no longer any motive, any incentive; his mind relaxes; the turbulence of his passions is calmed; reason and conscience are permitted to speak; he is disarmed, or, in other words, he finds that he has no use for his weapons; he beholds in the injured man a magnanimous friend, whose mind is superior to all the insults and injuries which he has received, and who is determined never to permit the heavenly principle that influences his soul to bow itself before the miserable, mean, and wretched spirit of revenge. This amiable man views in his enemy a spirit which he beholds with horror, and he cannot consent to receive into his own bosom a disposition which he sees to be destructive to another; and he knows that as soon as he begins to avenge himself, he places himself on a par with the unprincipled man whose conduct he has so much reason to blame, and whose spirit he has so much cause to abominate. He who avenges himself receives into his own heart all the evil and disgraceful passions by which his enemy is rendered both wretched and contemptible. There is the voice of eternal reason in, "Avenge not yourselves: overcome evil with good;" as well as the high authority and command of the living God.

Wicked words and sinful actions may be considered as the overflowings of a heart that is more than full of the spirit of wickedness; and holy words and righteous deeds may be considered as the overflowings of a heart that is filled with the Holy Spirit, and running over with love to God and man.

"Love ye your enemies." — This is the most sublime precept ever delivered to man: a false religion durst not give a precept of this nature, because, without supernatural influence, it must be for ever impracticable. In these words of our blessed Lord we see the tenderness, sincerity, extent, disinterestedness, pattern, and issue of the love of God, dwelling in man; a religion which has for its foundation the union of God and man in the same person, and the death of this august Being for his enemies; which consists on earth in a reconciliation of the Creator with his creatures, and which is to subsist in heaven only in the union of the members with the Head: could such a religion as this ever tolerate hatred in the soul of man, even to his most inveterate foes?

We are not to suppose that the love of God casts out every kind of fear from the soul; it only casts out that which has torment. A filial fear is consistent with the highest degrees of love; and even necessary to the preservation of that grace. This is properly its guardian; and without this, love would soon degenerate into listlessness or presumptive boldness.

Nor does it cast out that fear which is so necessary to the preservation of life; that fear which leads a man to flee from danger lest his life should be destroyed.

Nor does it cast out that fear which may be engendered by sudden alarm. All these are necessary to our well being. But it destroys, 1. The fear of want; 2. The fear of death; and, 3. The fear or terror of judgment. All these fears bring torment, and are inconsistent with this perfect love.

PEACE. — Christ keeps that heart in peace in which he dwells and rules. This peace passeth all understanding; it is of a very different nature from all that call arise from human occurrences; it is a peace which Christ has purchased, and which God dispenses; it is felt by all the truly godly, but can be explained by none; it is communion with the Father, and his Son Jesus Christ, by the power and influence of the Holy Ghost.

To live in a state of peace with one's neighbours, friends, and even family, is often very difficult. But the man who loves God must labour after this, for it is indispensably necessary even for his own sake. A man cannot have broils and misunderstandings with others, without having his own peace very materially disturbed; he must, to be happy, be at peace with all men, whether they will be at peace with him or not. The apostle knew that it would be difficult to get into and maintain such a state of peace; and this his own words amply prove: "And if it be possible, as much as lieth in you, live peaceably." Though it be but barely possible, labour after it.

In civil society men must, in order to taste tranquillity, resolve to bear something from their neighbours, they must suffer, pardon, and give up many things; without doing which, they must live in such a state of continual agitation as will render life itself insupportable. Without this giving and forgiving spirit there will be nothing in civil society, and even in Christian congregations, but divisions, evil surmisings, injurious discourses, outrages, anger, vengeance, and, in a word, a total dissolution of the mystical body of Christ. Thus our interest in both worlds calls loudly upon us to give and forgive.

Most of the disputes among Christians have been concerning nonessential points. Rites and ceremonies, even in the simple religion of Christ, have contributed their part in promoting those animosities by which Christians have been divided. Forms in worship and sacerdotal garments have not been without their influence in this general disturbance.

Such is the natural bigotry and narrowness of the human heart that we can scarcely allow that any beside ourselves possess the true religion. To indulge a disposition of this kind is highly blamable. The true religion is neither confined to one spot nor to one people; it is spread in various forms over the whole earth. He who fills immensity has left a record of himself in every nation and among every people under heaven. Beware of the spirit of intolerance; for bigotry produces uncharitableness; and uncharitableness harsh judging; and in such a spirit a man may think he does God service when he tortures or makes a burnt-offering of the person whom his narrow mind and hard heart have dishonoured with the name of "heretic." Such a spirit is not confined to any one community, though it has predominated in some more than in others. But these things are highly displeasing in the sight of God. He, as the Father of the spirits of all flesh, loves every branch of his vastly extended family; and, as far as we love one another, no matter of what sect or party, so far we resemble him.

It is astonishing that any who profess the Christian name should indulge bitterness of spirit. Those who are censorious, who are unmerciful to the failings of others, who have fixed a certain standard by which they measure all persons in all circumstances, and unchristianize every one that does not come up to this standard, they have the bitterness against which the apostle speaks. In the last century there was a compound medicine, made up from a variety of drastic acid drugs and ardent spirits, which was called, *Hiera Picra,* the *holy bitter;* this medicine was administered in a multitude of cases, where it did immense evil, and perhaps in scarcely any case did it do good. It has ever appeared to furnish a proper epithet for the disposition mentioned above, the *holy bitter,* for the religiously censorious act under the pretence of superior sanctity. I have known such persons do much evil in a Christian society, but never knew an instance of their doing any good.

Beware of contentions in religion; if you dispute concerning any of its doctrines, let it be to find out truth; not to support a preconceived and pre- established opinion. Avoid all polemical heat and rancour; these prove the absence of the religion of Christ. Whatever does not lead you to love God and man more is most assuredly from beneath. The God of peace is the Author of Christianity, and the Prince of peace the Priest and Sacrifice of it; therefore love one another, and leave off contention before it be meddled with.

JOY.—Religious joy, properly tempered with continual dependence on the help of God, meekness of mind, and self-diffidence, is a powerful means of strengthening the soul. In such a state every duty is practicable, and every duty delightful. In such a frame of mind no man ever fell.

Every one flies from sorrow, and seeks after joy; and yet true joy must necessarily be the fruit of sorrow.

Is it not common for interested persons to rejoice in the successes of an unjust and sanguinary war, in the sackage and burning of cities and towns? and is not the joy always in proportion to the slaughter that has been made of the enemy? And do these call themselves Christians? Then we may expect that Moloch and his subdevils are not so far behind this description of Christians as to render their case utterly desperate. If such Christians can be saved, demons need not despair.

HOPE.—Hope is a sort of universal blessing, and one of the greatest which God has granted to man. To mankind in general life would be intolerable without it; and it is as necessary as faith is, even to the followers of God.

Every man hopes for happiness; and it is this hope that bears him up through all the ills of life. He sees and he feels evil, but he hopes for good. Despair is the opposite to hope; where this takes place, a total derangement of all the mental faculties ensues; and generally, if not soon relieved, the wretched subject dies, or puts an end to life.

What is the proper definition of hope? The following is the most common, and probably the best:—"The expectation of future good;" an expectation, too, that arises from desire. It must be good, else it could not be desired; it must be future, or it would not be an object of expectation: good in possession precludes hope. "Hope that is seen (possessed) is not hope; for what a man seeth, why doth he yet hope for? But if we hope for that we see not, then do we with patience wait for it." A thing that was once an object of hope may have been attained; and if so, hope, in reference to that, is at an end. Hope is never exercised but where there is a conviction, less or more deep, of the possibility of attaining its object. As hope implies desire, it must be a natural or moral good that is its object, for nothing can be desired that is known to be evil. That which is good can alone gratify the heart; and to gratify is to please, satisfy, and content. When Milton puts in the mouth of Satan the following speech:--

> "So farewell hope, and with hope, farewell fear,
> Farewell remorse: all good to me is lost;
> Evil, be thou my good:"

The poet does not mean that the nature or operation of evil can be changed; but that the diabolic heart might be pleased, satisfied, for the time, and contented with it, as a means of gratifying revenge and malice; as all good was then to him beyond the reach and sphere of hope. None but the devil could have uttered such a speech; as none but that archangel ruined could bring the fellest malice and revenge into successful action, so as to desire gratification from the result. Could Satan have taken evil in the place of good, so as to have rested satisfied with it, in that moment the nature of evil must have been changed to him, and hell cease to be a place of torment. But it is a diabolical boast, and has neither truth nor reason in it.

In examining this grand subject farther, I would observe that hope may be considered in a threefold sense: 1. Simple hope. 2. Dead hope. 3. Living hope.

1. HOPE, simply considered in itself, according to its definition above, the expectation of future good; this shows the existence of the thing, without activity in itself, or operation in reference to its object. It exists, but in a state of carelessness and unconcern. This sort is nearly common to all men; is not only without profit to them, because not used, but is generally, in its flutterings in the breast, like the *ignus fatuus*, that, instead of leading aright, leads astray, causing its possessor to rest in mere expectation, inoperative and indefinite; without any time to commence, or place to act in; a principle which, from its misuse, rather deceives than helps the soul. In consequence of this, it has been called delusive hope, false hope, vain hope, &c.; but hope in itself, which is a gift from God, is neither deceptive, false, nor vain. It is the misuse, or abuse of it, that deceives, leads astray, fills with vanity, &c. If properly used and applied, it may become even the anchor of the soul; and is that power or principle on which the grace of God works in order to bring forth, in the end, that faith by which even mountains are removed. A wicked man may have this simple hope, and so may a hypocrite, and neither receive benefit from it; yea, they may abuse it to their eternal damage; and thus every power of the soul, and every gift of God, may be abused; and in reference to this we may apply the homely but expressive lines of old Francis Quarles: —

"Thus God's best gifts, usurp'd by wicked ones,
To poison turn by their con-ta-gi- ons."

2. DEAD HOPE.—I do not mean, by this, hope that is extinct; for then it would cease to be hope, or any thing else. Nor do I mean hope that is entirely *inactive,* and which may, on this account, be considered *morally dead;* but I mean that hope which has for its objects good things to come, after life is ended; a hope that expects fruition of the objects of its attention when the present state of things closes for ever on its possessor. Nor do I mean the hope that has for its object the glories of the invisible world; but the hope which misplaces its objects, that refers things which belong to the present state of being to a future state; as it does the things which should be received here, in order to prepare for glory hereafter. This is a species of religious hope, it has to do with religious matters; such as pardon of sin, sanctification of the soul, and the acquisition of those graces which constitute "the mind that was in Christ:"—in a word, that holiness without which none shall ever see the Lord. It expects none of these in this life; and that no consciousness of having received pardon can take place before death, if even then; nor can any person, according to this hope, be saved from his sins till his body and soul are separated. Hence, all its operations are in reference to death, and the separate state immediately succeeding. This hope, or this perversion of simple hope, paralyzes the Christian spirit, and in effect grieves the Spirit of God. No man ever receives good from it: it serves indeed to amuse the mind, and, in the proper sense of the word, divert the soul:—it turns it away from seeking present blessings, because its owner has made up his mind that none of these blessings can be received before death, and therefore he neither seeks nor expects them. It has the form, but it is the bane, of every good. In many, this species of hope, or this abuse of hope, is associated with much uncertainty, and sometimes with a degree of despair, even in reference to the things which it professes to have for its object, till at last the man doubts the immortality of the soul, and the resurrection of the body; and in fine, the joys of heaven become problematical! This is "dead hope"—the hope that is looking for no spiritual good before death; and generally appears to be inactive, and unconcerned even about them. It is the inhabitant of a dead soul; of a lifeless, careless, Christless professor of

Christianity; — one who, though he have a name to live, yet is dead; and who will find, when he comes to that bourne where his hope is expected to act, and be realized, that it is like regiving up of the ghost: — he gives up his ghost and his hope together. It is also the hope of the wicked; they expect to find God's mercy when they come to die: but the hope of the wicked, in death, perisheth. Of such persons, none can entertain hope but themselves.

3. LIVING HOPE. — The hope that lives and flourishes by hoping! This is simple hope, in its greatest activity and operation: — Hope with all the range of possible good in its eye, its expectation, and its desire. Its objects are necessarily future; but all is future that is in the least degree removed from the present; hence, the future, properly speaking, verges on the time that now is. The blessings that are necessary now it sees at hand; desires the possession; believes the possibility of immediate attainment; claims the grace from God through Christ; and thus realizes its object. Having received this blessing, it is strengthened to go out after more; sees, desires, and claims the next in course; receives this, and thus realizes another good that a short time before was future; and continues to be future still to all others who do not act in this way.

This hope is ever living by receiving. Pardon and holiness, the forgiveness of all sin, and purification from all unrighteousness, must be attained here. This it sees; of this it is convinced; and these blessings are the first objects of its attention. It claims them by a living energy, through faith; for hope cannot exist nor act without faith; and by faith is its work made perfect. Thus it is ever receiving. All future blessings, belonging to the human state of probation, which extends from the cradle to the grave, in the whole series of their approximations, becoming present, are realized in their order; and the innate power of the last received serves to support that which was received before, and thus on all the increasing glory there is a defence.

This hope takes up all God's blessings in their places and proper series. There are some of its objects, as stated above, which necessarily belong to this life; others that as necessarily belong to the world to come. It will not refer the blessings to be obtained here to the state after death; nor will it attempt to anticipate those blessings which belong to eternity, in the present state. It is a discriminating grace, for it is ever supported by knowledge and faith. It walks uprightly, and therefore surely.

> "Grace is in all its steps, heaven in its eye:
> In every gesture dignity and love."

The hope of eternal life is represented as the soul's anchor; the world is the boisterous, dangerous sea; the Christian course the voyage; the port everlasting felicity; and the veil, or inner road, the royal dock in which that anchor was cast. The storms of life continue but a short time; the anchor, hope, if fixed by faith in the eternal world, will infallibly prevent all shipwreck; the soul may be variously tossed by various temptations, but will not drive, because the anchor is in sure ground, and itself is steadfast; it does not drag, and it does not break; faith, like the cable, is the connecting medium between the ship and the anchor, or the soul and its hope of heaven; faith sees the haven, hope desires and anticipates the rest; faith works, and hope holds fast; and shortly the soul enters into the haven of eternal repose.

A hope that is not rationally founded will have its expectations cut off; and then shame and confusion will be the portion of its possessor. But our hope is of a different kind; it is founded on the goodness and truth of God; and our religious experience shows us that we have not misapplied it, nor exercised it on wrong or improper objects.

MEEKNESS.—That man walks most safely who has the least confidence in himself. True magnanimity keeps God continually in view. He appoints it its work, and furnishes discretion and power; and its chief excellence consists in being a resolute worker together with him. Pride ever sinks where humility swims, for that man who abases himself God will exalt. To know that we are dependent creatures is well; to feel it, and to act suitably, is still better.

A proud man is peculiarly odious in the sight of God; and in the sight of reason how absurd! A sinner, a fallen spirit—an heir of wretchedness and corruption, proud! Proud of what? Of an indwelling devil! Well;—such persons shall be plentifully rewarded. They shall get their due, their whole due, and nothing but their due.

The presumptuous person imagines he can do every thing,

and can do nothing; thinks he can excel all, and excels in nothing; promises every thing, and performs nothing. The humble man acts quite a contrary part.

The wise and just God often, in the course of his providence, permits great defects to be associated with great eminence, that he may hide pride from man, and cause him to think soberly of himself and his acquirements. "Let him that most assuredly standeth take heed lest he fall!" and let him who is in honour bear himself meekly, lest God defile his horn in the dust; for God grants his gifts, not that the creature, but that himself, may be magnified.

XII. – ENTIRE SANCTIFICATION.

THE word "sanctify" has two meanings. 1. It signifies to consecrate, to separate from earth and common use, and to devote or dedicate to God and his service. 2. It signifies to make holy or pure.

Many talk much, and indeed well, of what Christ has done for us: but how little is spoken of what he is to do in us! and yet all that he has done for us is in reference to what he is to do in us. He was incarnated, suffered, died, and rose again from the dead; ascended to heaven, and there appears in the presence of God for us. These were all saving, atoning, and mediating acts for us; that he might reconcile us to God; that he might blot out our sin; that he might purge our consciences from dead works; that he might bind the strong man armed — take away the armour in which he trusted, wash the polluted heart, destroy every foul and abominable desire, all tormenting and unholy tempers; that he might make the heart his throne, fill the soul with his light, power, and life; and, in a word, "destroy the works of the devil." These are done in us; without which we cannot be saved unto eternal life. But these acts done in us are consequent on the acts done for us: for had He not been incarnated, suffered, and died in our stead, we could not receive either pardon or holiness; and did he not cleanse and purify our hearts, we could not enter into the place where all is purity: for the beatific vision is given to them only who are purified from all unrighteousness; for it is written, "Blessed are the pure in heart, for they shall see God." Nothing is purified by death;—nothing in the grave; nothing in heaven. The living stones of the temple, like those of that at Jerusalem, are hewn, squared, and cut here, in the church militant, to prepare them to enter into the composition of the church triumphant.

This perfection is the restoration of man to the state of holiness from which he fell, by creating him anew in Christ Jesus, and restoring to him that image and likeness of God which he has lost. A higher meaning than this it cannot have; a lower meaning it must not have. God made man in that degree of perfection which was pleasing to his own infinite wisdom and goodness. Sin defaced this divine image; Jesus came to restore it. Sin must have no triumph; and the Redeemer of mankind must have his glory. But if man be not perfectly saved from all sin, sin does triumph, and Satan exult, because they have done a mischief that Christ either cannot or will not remove. To say he cannot, would be shocking blasphemy against the infinite power and dignity of the great Creator; to say he will not, would be equally such against the infinite benevolence and holiness of his nature. All sin, whether in power, guilt, or defilement, is the work of the devil; and he, Jesus, came to destroy the work of the devil; and as all unrighteousness is sin, so his blood cleanseth from all sin, because it cleanseth from all unrighteousness.

Many stagger at the term *perfection* in Christianity; because they think that what is implied in it is inconsistent with a state of probation, and savours of pride and presumption: but we must take good heed how we stagger at any word of God; and much more how we deny or fritter away the meaning of any of his sayings, lest he reprove us, and we be found liars before him. But it may be that the term is rejected because it is not understood. Let us examine its import.

The word "perfection," in reference to any person or thing, signifies that such person or thing is complete or finished; that it has nothing redundant, and is in nothing defective. And hence that observation of a learned civilian is at once both correct and illustrative, namely, "We count those things perfect which want nothing requisite for the end whereto they were instituted." And *to be perfect* often signifies "to be blameless, clear, irreproachable;" and, according to the above definition of Hooker, a man may be said to be perfect who answers the end for which God made him; and as

God requires every man to love him with all his heart, soul, mind, and strength, and his neighbour as himself; then he is a perfect man that does so; he answers the end for which God made him; and this is more evident from the nature of that love which fills his heart: for, as love is the principle of obedience, so he that loves his God with all his powers will obey him with all his powers; and he who loves his neighbour as himself will not only do no injury to him, but, on the contrary, labour to promote his best interests. Why the doctrine which enjoins such a state of perfection as this should be dreaded, ridiculed, or despised, is a most strange thing; and the opposition to it can only be from that carnal mind that is enmity to God; "that is not subject to the law of God, neither indeed can be." And had I no other proof that man is fallen from God, his opposition to Christian holiness would be to me sufficient.

The whole design of God was to restore man to his image, and raise him from the ruins of his fall; in a word, to make him perfect; to blot out all his sins, purify his soul, and fill him with holiness; so that no unholy temper, evil desire, or impure affection or passion shall either lodge, or have any being within him; this and this only is true religion, or Christian perfection; and a less salvation than this would be dishonourable to the sacrifice of Christ, and the operation of the Holy Ghost; and would be as unworthy of the appellation of "Christianity," as it would be of that of "holiness or perfection." They who ridicule this are scoffers at the word of God; many of them totally irreligious men, sitting in the seat of the scornful. They who deny it, deny the whole scope and design of divine revelation and the mission of Jesus Christ. And they who preach the opposite doctrine are either speculative Antinomians, or pleaders for Baal.

When St. Paul says he "warns every man, and teaches every man in all wisdom, that he may present every man PERFECT in Christ Jesus," he must mean something. What then is this *something?* It must mean "that holiness without which none shall see the Lord." Call it by what name we please, it must imply the pardon of all transgression, and the removal of the whole body of sin and death; for this must take place before we can be like him, and see him as he is, in the effulgence of his own glory. This fitness, then, to appear before God, and thorough preparation for eternal glory, is what I plead for, pray for, and heartily recommend to all true believers, under the name of *Christian perfection*. Had I a better name, one more energetic, one with a greater plenitude of meaning, one more worthy of the efficacy of the blood that bought our peace, and cleanseth from all unrighteousness, I would gladly adopt and use it. Even the word "perfection" has, in some relations, so many qualifications and abatements that cannot comport with that full and glorious salvation recommended in the Gospel, and bought and sealed by the blood of the cross, that I would gladly lay it by, and employ a word more positive and unequivocal in its meaning, and more worthy of the merit of the infinite atonement of Christ, and of the energy of his almighty Spirit; but there is none in our language; which I deplore as an inconvenience and a loss.

Why then are there so many, even among sincere and godly ministers and people, who are so much opposed to the term, and so much alarmed at the profession? I answer, Because they think no man can be fully saved from sin in this life. I ask, Where is this, in unequivocal words, written in the New Testament? Where, in that book, is it intimated that sin is never wholly destroyed till death takes place, and the soul and the body are separated? Nowhere. In the popish baseless doctrine of purgatory, this doctrine, not with more rational consequences, is held: this doctrine allows that, so inveterate is sin, it cannot be wholly destroyed even in death; and that a penal fire, in a middle state between heaven and hell, is necessary to atone for that which the blood of Christ had not cancelled; and to purge from that which the energy of the almighty Spirit had not cleansed before death.

Even papists could not see that a moral evil was detained in the soul through its physical connection with the body; and that it required the dissolution of this physical connection before the moral contagion could be removed. Protestants, who profess, and most certainly possess, a better faith, are they alone that maintain the deathbed purgatory; and how positively do they hold out death as the complete deliverer from all corruption, and the final destroyer of sin, as if it were revealed in every page of the Bible! Whereas, there is not one passage in the sacred volume that says any such thing. Were this true, then death, far from being the last enemy, would be the last and best friend, and the greatest of all deliverers: for if the last remains of all the indwelling sin of all believers is to be destroyed by death, (and a fearful mass this will make,) then death, that removes it, must be the highest benefactor of mankind. The truth is, he is neither the cause nor the means of its destruction. It is the blood of Jesus alone that cleanseth from all unrighteousness.

It is supposed that indwelling sin is useful even to true believers, because it humbles them and keeps them low in their own estimation. A little examination will show that this is contrary to the fact. It is generally, if not universally allowed, that pride is of the essence of sin, if not its very essence; and the root whence all moral obliquity flows. How then can pride humble us? Is not this absurd? Where is there a sincere Christian, be his creed what it may, that does not deplore his proud, rebellious, and unsubdued heart and will, as the cause of all his wretchedness; the thing that mars his best sacrifices, and prevents his communion with God? How often do such people say or sing, both in their public and private devotions, —

"But pride, that busy sin,
Spoils all that I perform!"

Were there no pride, there would be no sin; and the heart from which it is cast out has the humility, meekness, and gentleness of Christ implanted in its stead.

But still it is alleged, as an indubitable fact, that "a man is humbled under a sense of indwelling sin." I grant that they who see, and feel, and deplore their indwelling sin, are humbled: but is it the sin that humbles? No. It is the grace of God, that shows and condemns the sin, that humbles us. Neither the devil nor his work will ever show themselves. Pride works frequently under a dense mask, and will often assume the garb of humility. How true is that saying, and of how many is it the language!

"Proud I am my wants to see,
Proud of my humility."

And, to conceal his working, even Satan himself is transformed into an angel of light! It appears then that we attribute this boasted humiliation to a wrong cause. We never are humbled under a sense of indwelling sin till the Spirit of God drags it to the light, and shows us, not only its horrid deformity, but its hostility to God; and he manifests it, that he may take it away: but a false opinion causes man to hug the monster, and to contemplate their chains with complacency!

It has been objected to this perfection, this perfect work of

God in the soul, that "the greater sense we have of our own sinfulness, the more will Christ be exalted in the eye of the soul: for, if the thing were possible that a man might be cleansed from all sin in this life, he would feel no need of a Saviour; Christ would be undervalued by him as no longer needing his saving power." This objection mistakes the whole state of the case. How is Christ exalted in the view of the soul? How is it that he becomes precious to us? Is it not from a sense of what he has done for us; and what he has done in us? Did any man ever love God till he had felt that God loved him? Do we not "love him because he first loved us?" Is it the name JESUS that is precious to us? or Jesus the Saviour saving us from our sins? Is all our confidence placed in him because of some one saving act? or, because of his continual operation as the Saviour? Can any effect subsist without its cause? Must not the cause continue to operate in order to maintain the effect? Do we value a good cause more for the instantaneous production of a good and important effect, than we do for its continual energy, exerted to maintain that good and important effect? All these questions can be answered by a child. What is it that cleanseth the soul and destroys sin? Is it not the mighty power of the grace of God? What is it that keeps the soul clean? Is it not the same power dwelling in us? No more can an effect subsist without its cause, than a sanctified soul abide in holiness without the indwelling Sanctifier. When Christ casts out the strong-armed man he takes away that armour in which he trusted, he spoils his goods, he cleanses and enters into the house, so that the heart becomes the habitation of God through the Spirit. Can then a man undervalue that Christ who not only blotted out his iniquity, but cleansed his soul from all sin; and whose presence and inward mighty working constitute all his holiness and all his happiness? Impossible! Jesus was never so highly valued, so intensely loved, so affectionately obeyed, as now. The great Saviour has not his highest glory from his atoning and redeeming acts, but from the manifestation of his saving power.

"But the persons who profess to have been made thus perfect are proud and supercilious, and their whole conduct says to their neighbour, 'Stand by, I am holier than thou.'" No person that acts so has ever received this grace. He is either a hypocrite or a self-deceiver. Those who have received it are full of meekness, gentleness, and long suffering: they love God with all their hearts, they love even their enemies; love the whole human family, and are servants of all. They know they have nothing but what they have received. In the splendour of God's holiness they feel themselves absorbed. They have neither light, power, love, nor happiness, but from their indwelling Saviour. Their holiness, though it fills the soul, yet is only a drop from the infinite Ocean. The flame of their love, though it penetrate their whole being, is only a spark from the incomprehensible Sun of righteousness. In a spirit and in a way which none but themselves can fully comprehend and feel, they can say or sing, —

> "I loathe myself when God I see,
> And into nothing fall:
> Content that Christ exalted be;
> And God is all in all."

It has been no small mercy to me, that, in the course of my religious life, I have met with many persons who professed that the blood of Christ had saved them from all sin, and whose profession was maintained by an immaculate life; but I never knew one of them that was not of the spirit above described. They were men of the strongest faith, the purest love, the holiest affections, the most obedient lives, and the most useful in society. I have seen such walking with God for many years: and as I had the privilege of observing their walk in life, so have I been privileged with their testimony at death, when their sun appeared to grow broader and brighter at its setting; and, though they came through great tribulation, they found that their robes were washed and made white through the blood of the Lamb. They fully witnessed the grand effects which in this life flow from justification, adoption, and sanctification; namely, assurance of God's love, peace of conscience, joy in the Holy Ghost, increase of grace, and perseverance in the same to the end of their lives. O God! let my death be like that of these righteous! and let my end be like theirs! Amen.

It is scarcely worth mentioning another objection that has been started by the ignorant, the worthless, and the wicked. "The people that profess this leave Christ out of the question; they either think that they have purified their own hearts, or that they have gained their pretended perfection by their own merits." Nothing can be more false than this calumny. I know *that people* well in whose creed the doctrine of "salvation from all sin in this life" is a prominent article. But that people hold most conscientiously that all our salvation, from the first dawn of light in the soul to its entry into the kingdom of glory, is all by and through Christ. He alone convinces the soul of sin, justifies the ungodly, sanctifies the unholy, preserves in this state of salvation, and brings to everlasting blessedness. No soul ever was or can be saved but through his agony and bloody sweat, his cross and passion, his death and burial, his glorious resurrection and ascension, and continued intercession at the right hand of God.

If men would but spend as much time in fervently calling upon God to cleanse the blood that he has not cleansed, as they spend in decrying this doctrine, what a glorious state of the church should we soon witness! Instead of compounding with iniquity, and tormenting their minds to find out with how little grace they may be saved, they would renounce the devil and all his works; and be determined never to rest till they had found that He had bruised him under their feet, and that the blood of Christ had cleansed them from all unrighteousness. Why is it that men will not try how far God will save them? nor leave off praying and believing for more and more, till they find that God has held his hand? When they find that their agonizing faith and prayer receive no farther answer, then, and not till then, they may conclude that God will be no farther gracious, and that he will not save to the uttermost them who come to him through Christ Jesus.

But it is farther objected, that even St. Paul himself denies this doctrine of perfection, disclaiming it in reference to himself: "Not as though I had already attained, either were already perfect; but I follow after," Phil. 3: 12. This place is mistaken: the apostle is not speaking of his restoration to the image of God; but to completing his ministerial course, and receiving the crown of martyrdom; as I have fully shown in my notes on this place, and to which I must beg to refer the reader. There is another point that has been produced, at least indirectly, in the form of an objection to this doctrine: "Where are those adult, those perfect Christians? We know none such; but we have heard that some persons professing those extraordinary degrees of holiness have become scandalous in their lives." When a question of this kind is asked by one who fears God, and earnestly desires his salvation, and only wishes to have full evidence that the thing is attainable, that he may shake himself from the dust, and arise and go out, and possess the good land—it deserves to be seriously answered. To such I would say, There may be several, even in the circle of your own religious acquaintance, whose evil tempers and unholy affections God has destroyed; and having filled them with his own holiness, they are enabled to love him with all their heart, soul, mind, and strength; and their neighbour as themselves. But such make no public professions: their conduct, their spirit, the whole tenor of their life, is their testimony. Again: there may be none such among your religious acquaintance, because they do not know their privilege, or they unfortunately sit under a ministry where the doctrine is decried; and in such congregations and churches holiness never abounds; men are too apt to be slothful, and unfaithful to the grace they have received; they need not their minister's exhortations to beware of looking for or expecting a heart purified from all unrighteousness; striving or agonizing to "enter in at the strait gate" is not pleasant work to flesh and blood; and they are glad to have any thing to countenance their spiritual indolence; and such ministers have always a powerful coadjutor; the father of lies, and the spirit of error will work in the unrenewed heart, filling it with darkness, and prejudice, and unbelief. No wonder, then, that in such places, and under such a ministry, there is no man that can be "presented perfect in Christ Jesus." But wherever the trumpet gives a certain sound, and the people go forth to battle, headed by the Captain of their salvation, there the foe is routed, and genuine believers brought into the liberty of the children of God.

As to some having professed to have received this salvation, and afterward become scandalous in their lives, (though in all my long ministerial labours, and extensive religious acquaintance, I never found but one example,) I would just observe that they might possibly have been deceived; thought they had what they had not; or they might have become unfaithful to that grace and lost it; and this is possible through the whole range of a state of probation. There have been angels who kept not their first estate; and we all know, to our cost, that he who was the head and fountain of the whole human family, who was made in the image and likeness of God, sinned against God, and fell from that state. And so may any of his descendants fall from any degree of the grace of God while in their state of probation; and any man and every man must fall, whenever he or they cease to watch unto prayer, and cease to be "workers together with God." Faith must ever be kept in lively exercise, working by love; and that love is only safe when found exerting its energies in the path of obedience. An objection of this kind against the doctrine of Christian perfection will apply as forcibly against the whole revelation of God as it can do against one of the doctrines; because that revelation brings the account of the defection of angels and of the fall of man. The truth is, no doctrine of God stands upon the knowledge, experience, faithfulness, or unfaithfulness of man; it stands on the veracity of God who gave it. If there were not a man to be found who was justified freely through the redemption that is by Jesus; yet the doctrine of "justification by faith" is true; for it is a doctrine that stands on the truth of God. And suppose not one could be found in all the churches of Christ whose heart was purified from all unrighteousness, and who loved God and man with all his regenerated powers, yet the doctrine of Christian perfection would still be true; for Christ was manifested that he might destroy the work of the devil; and his blood cleanseth from all unrighteousness. And suppose every man be a liar, God is true.

It is not the profession of a doctrine that establishes its truth; it is the truth of God, from which it has proceeded. Man's experience may illustrate it; but it is God's truth that confirms it.

In all cases of this nature, we must for ever cease from man, implicitly credit God's testimony, and look to Him in and through whom all the promises of God are yea and amen.

To be filled with God is a great thing; to be filled with *the fulness* of God is still greater; to be filled with *all the fulness* of God is greatest of all. This utterly bewilders the sense and confounds the understanding, by leading at once to consider the immensity of God, the infinitude of his attributes, and the absolute perfection of each! But there must be a sense in which even this wonderful petition was understood by the apostle, and may be comprehended by us. Most people, in quoting these words, endeavour to correct or explain the apostle by adding the word *communicable*. But this is as idle as it is useless and impertinent. Reason surely tells us that St. Paul would not pray that they should be filled with what could not be communicated. The apostle certainly meant what he said, and would be understood in his own meaning; and we may soon see what this meaning is.

By the "fulness of God," we are to understand all the gifts and graces which he has promised to bestow on man in order to his full salvation here, and his being fully prepared for the enjoyment of glory hereafter. To be filled with all the fulness of God is to have the heart emptied of and cleansed from all sin and defilement, and filled with humility, meekness, gentleness, goodness, justice, holiness, mercy, and truth, and love to God and man. And that this implies a thorough emptying of the soul of every thing that is not of God, and leads not to him, is evident from this, that what God fills neither sin nor Satan can fill, nor in any wise occupy; for, if a vessel be filled with one fluid or substance, not a drop or particle of any other kind can enter it, without displacing the same quantum of the original matter as that which is afterward introduced. God cannot be said to fill the whole soul while any place, part, passion, or faculty is filled, or less or more occupied, by sin or Satan: and as neither sin nor Satan can be where God fills and occupies the whole, so the terms of the prayer state that Satan shall neither have any dominion over that soul nor being in it. A fulness of humility precludes all pride; of meekness, precludes anger; of gentleness, all ferocity; of goodness, all evil; of justice, all injustice; of holiness, all sin; of mercy, all unkindness and revenge; of truth, all falsity and dissimulation: and where God is loved with all the heart, soul, mind, and strength, there is no room for enmity or hatred to him, or to any thing connected with him; so, where a man loves his neighbour as himself, no ill shall be worked to that neighbour; but, on the contrary, every kind affection will exist toward him; and every kind action, so far as power and circumstances can permit, will be done to him. Thus the being filled with God's fulness will produce constant, pious, and affectionate obedience to him, and unvarying benevolence toward one's neighbour; that is, any man, any and every human being. Such a man is saved from all sin; the law is fulfilled in him; and he ever possesses and acts under the influence of that love to God and man which is the fulfilling of the law. It is impossible, with any Scriptural or rational consistency, to understand these words in any lower sense; but how much more they imply, (and more they do imply,) who can tell?

Many preachers, and multitudes of professing people, are

studious to find out how many imperfections and infidelities, and how much inward sinfulness, are consistent with a safe state in religion; but how few, very few, are bringing out the fair Gospel standard to try the height of the members of the church; whether they be fit for the heavenly army; whether their stature be such as qualifies them for the ranks of the church militant! "the measure of the stature of the fulness" is seldom seen; the measure of the stature of littleness, dwarfishness, and emptiness, is often exhibited.

Some say, "The body of sin in believers is, indeed, an enfeebled, conquered, and deposed tyrant, and the stroke of death finishes its destruction." So, then, the death of Christ and the influences of the Holy Spirit were only sufficient to depose and enfeeble the tyrant sin; but our death must come in to effect his total destruction! Thus our death is, at least partially, our Saviour; and thus that which was an effect of sin, ("for sin entered into the world, and death by sin,") becomes the means of finally destroying it: that is, the effect of a cause can become so powerful as to react upon that cause and produce its annihilation! The divinity and philosophy of this sentiment are equally absurd. It is the blood of Christ alone that cleanses from all unrighteousness; and the sanctification of a believer is no more dependent on death than his justification. If it be said that "believers do not cease from sin till they die," I have only to say they are such believers as do not make a proper use of their faith: and what can be said more of the whole herd of transgressors and infidels? They cease to sin when they cease to breathe. If the Christian religion bring no other privileges than this to its upright followers, well may we ask, "Wherein doth the wise man differ from the fool, for they have both one end?" But the whole Gospel teaches a contrary doctrine.

It is strange there should be found a person believing the whole Gospel system and yet living in sin! "Salvation from sin" is the long continued sound, as it is the spirit and design, of the Gospel. Our Christian name, our baptismal covenant, our profession of faith in Christ, and avowed belief in his word, all call us to this: can it be said that we have any louder calls than they? Our self-interest, as it respects the happiness of a godly life, and the glories of eternal blessedness; the pains and wretchedness of a life of sin, leading to the worm that never dies, and the fire that is not quenched; second, most powerfully, the above calls. Reader, lay these things to heart, and answer this question to God: "How shall I escape if I neglect so great salvation?" And then, as thy conscience shall answer, let thy mind and thy hand begin to act.

As there is no end to the merits of Christ incarnated and crucified; no bounds to the mercy and love of God; no let or hinderance to the almighty energy and sanctifying influence of the Holy Spirit; no limits to the improvability of the human soul; so there can be no bounds to the saving influence which God will dispense to the heart of every genuine believer. We may ask and receive, and our joy shall be full! Well may we bless and praise God, "who has called us into such a state of salvation;" a state in which we may be thus saved; and, by the grace of that state, continue in the same to the end of our lives!

As sin is the cause of the ruin of mankind, the Gospel system, which exhibits its cure, is fitly called "good news, or glad tidings;" and it is good news, because it proclaims Him who saves his people from their sins; and it would indeed be dishonourable to that grace, and the infinite merit of Him who procured it, to suppose, much more to assert, that sin had made wounds which grace would not heal. Of such a triumph Satan shall ever be deprived.

"He that committeth sin is of the devil." Hear this, ye who plead for Baal, and cannot bear the thought of that doctrine that states believers are to be saved from all sin in this life! He who committeth sin is a child of the devil, and shows that he has still the nature of the devil in him; "for the devil sinneth from the beginning:" he was the father of sin,—brought sin into the world, and maintains sin in the world by living in the hearts of his own children, and thus leading them to transgression; and persuading others that they cannot be saved from their sins in this life, that he may secure a continual residence in their heart. He also knows that if he has a place throughout life he will probably have it at death; and, if so, throughout eternity.

"That is," say some, "he does not sin habitually as he formerly did." This is bringing the influence and privileges of the heavenly birth very low indeed. We have the most indubitable evidence that many of the heathen philosophers had acquired, by mental discipline and cultivation, an entire ascendency over all their wonted vicious habits. Perhaps my reader will recollect the story of the physiognomist, who, coming into the place where Socrates was delivering a lecture, his pupils, wishing to put the principles of the man's science to proof, desired him to examine the face of their master, and say what his moral character was. After a full contemplation of the philosopher's visage, he pronounced him "the most gluttonous, drunken, brutal, and libidinous old man that he had ever met." As the character of Socrates was the reverse of all this, his disciples began to insult the physiognomist. Socrates interfered, and said, "The principles of his science may be very correct; for such I was, but I have conquered it by my philosophy." O ye Christian divines! ye real or pretended Gospel ministers! will ye allow the influence of the grace of Christ a sway not even so extensive as that of the philosophy of a heathen who never heard of the true God?

Many tell us that "no man can be saved from sin in this life." Will these persons permit us to ask, How much sin may we be saved from in this life? Something must be ascertained on this subject: 1. That the soul may have some determinate object in view. 2. That it may not lose its time, or employ its faith and energy, in praying for what is impossible to be attained. Now, as Christ was manifested to take away our sins, to destroy the works of the devil; and as his blood cleanseth from all sin and unrighteousness, is it not evident that God means that believers in Christ shall be saved from all sin? For if his blood cleanses from all sin, if he destroys the works of the devil, (and sin is the work of the devil,) and if he who is born of God does not commit sin, then he must be cleansed from all sin; and while he continues in that state he lives without sinning against God, for the seed of God remaineth in him, and he cannot sin, because he is born, or begotten, of God.

How strangely warped and blinded by prejudice and system must men be who, in the face of such evidence as this, will still dare to maintain that no man can be saved from his sin in this life; but must daily commit sin in thought, word, and deed, as the Westminster divines have asserted! that is, every man is laid under the fatal necessity of sinning as many ways against God as the devil does through his natural wickedness and malice; for even the devil himself can have no other way of sinning against God, except by thought, word, and deed. And yet, according to these and others of the same creed, "even the most regenerate sin against God as long as they live." It is a miserable salvo to say "they do not sin so much as they used to do; and they do not sin habitually, only occasionally." Alas for this system! Could not the grace that saved them partially save them perfectly? Could not that power of God that saved them from habitual sin save them from occasional or accidental sin? Shall we suppose that sin, how potent soever it may be, is as potent as the Spirit and grace of Christ? And may we not ask, If it was for God's glory and their good that they were partially saved, would it not have been more for God's glory and their good if they had been perfectly saved? But the letter and spirit of God's word, and the design and end of Christ's coming, is to save his people from their sins.

The perfection of the Gospel-system is not that it makes allowances for sin, but that it makes an atonement for it; not that it tolerates sin, but that it destroys it.

However inveterate the disease of sin may be, the grace of the Lord Jesus can fully cure it.

God sets no bounds to the communications of his grace and Spirit to them that are faithful. And as there are no bounds to the graces, so there should be none to the exercise of those graces. No man can ever feel that he loves God too much, or that he loves man too much for God's sake.

Be so purified and refined in your souls, by the indwelling Spirit, that even the light of God shining into your hearts shall not be able to discover a fault that the love of God has not purged away.

"Be thou perfect, and thou shalt be perfections," that is, altogether perfect: be just such as the holy God would have thee to be, as the almighty God can make thee, and live as the all-sufficient God shall support thee; for He alone who makes the soul holy can preserve it in holiness. Our blessed Lord appears to have these words pointedly in view, "Ye shall be perfect, as your Father who is in heaven is perfect," Matt. v, 48. But what does this imply? Why, to be saved from all the power, the guilt, and the contamination of sin. This is only the negative part of salvation, but it has also a positive part; to be made perfect—to be perfect as our Father who is in heaven is perfect, to be filled with the fulness of God, to have Christ dwelling continually in the heart by faith, and to be rooted and grounded in love. This is the state in which man was created; for he was made in the image and likeness of God. This is the state from which man fell; for he broke the command of God. And this is the state into which every human soul must be raised who would dwell with God in glory; for Christ was incarnated and died to put away sin by the sacrifice of himself. What a glorious privilege! And who can doubt the possibility of its attainment who believes in the omnipotent love of God, the infinite merit of the blood of atonement, and the all-pervading and all- purifying energy of the Holy Ghost? How many miserable souls employ that time to dispute and cavil against the possibility of being saved from their sins, which they should devote to praying and believing that they might he saved out of the hands of their enemies! But some may say, "You overstrain the meaning of the term; it signifies only, Be sincere; for, as perfect obedience is impossible, God accepts of sincere obedience." If by *sincerity* the objection means "good desires, and generally good purposes, with an impure heart and spotted life," then I assert that no such thing is implied in the text, nor in the original word. But if the word *sincerity* be taken in its proper and literal sense, I have no objection to it. Sincere is compounded of *sine cera,* "without wax;" and, applied to moral subjects, is a metaphor taken from clarified honey, from which every atom of the comb or wax is separated. Then let it be proclaimed from heaven, "Walk before me, and be sincere! Purge out the old leaven, that ye may be a new lump unto God; and thus ye shall be perfect, as your Father who is in heaven is perfect." This is sincerity. Reader, remember that the blood of Christ cleanseth from all sin. Ten thousand quibbles on insulated texts can never lessen, much less destroy, the merit and efficacy of the Great Atonement.

God never gives a precept but he offers sufficient grace to enable thee to perform it. Believe as he would have thee, and act as he shall strengthen thee, and thou wilt believe all things savingly, and do all things well.

God is holy; and this is the eternal reason why all his people should be holy—should be purified from all filthiness of the flesh and spirit, perfecting holiness in the fear of God. No faith in any particular creed, no religious observance, no acts of benevolence and charity, no mortification, attrition, or contrition can be a substitute for this. We must be made partakers of the divine nature. We must be saved from our sins—from the corruption that is in the world, and be holy within and righteous without, or never see God.

For this very purpose Jesus Christ lived, died, and revived, that he might purify us unto himself; that through faith in his blood our sins might be blotted out, and our souls restored to the image of God. Reader, art thou hungering and thirsting after righteousness? Then, blessed art thou, for thou shalt be filled.

God is ever ready, by the power of his Spirit, to carry us forward to every degree of life, light, and love, necessary to prepare us for an eternal weight of glory. There can be little difficulty in attaining the end of our faith, the salvation of our souls from all sin, if God carry us forward to it; and this he will do, if we submit to be saved in his own way, and on his own terms. Many make a violent outcry against the doctrine of perfection; that is, against the heart being cleansed from all sin in this life, and filled with love to God and man; because they judge it to be impossible! Is it too much to say of these, that they know neither the Scripture nor the power of God? Surely the Scripture promises the thing, and the power of God can carry us on to the possession of it.

The object of all God's promises and dispensations was to bring fallen man back to the image of God, which he had lost. This, indeed, is the sum and substance of the religion of Christ. We have partaken of an earthly, sensual, and devilish nature; the design of God, by Christ, is to remove this, and to make us partakers of the divine nature, and save us from all the corruption, in principle and fact, which is in the world.

It is said that Enoch not only "walked with God," setting him always before his eyes—beginning, continuing, and ending every work to his glory—but also that "he pleased God," and had "the testimony that he did please God." Hence we learn that it was then possible to live so as not to offend God: consequently, so as not to commit sin against him, and to have the continual evidence or testimony that all that a man did and purposed was pleasing in the sight of Him who searches the heart, and by whom devices are weighed: and if it was possible then, it is surely, through the same grace, possible now; for God, and Christ, and faith are still the same.

The petition, "Thy will be done in earth, as it is in heaven," certainly points out a deliverance from all sin; for nothing that is unholy can consist with the divine will; and, if this be fulfilled in man, surely sin shall be banished from his soul. Again: the holy angels never mingle iniquity with their loving obedience; and, as our Lord teaches us to pray that we do his will here as they do it in heaven, can it be thought he would put a petition into our mouths the fulfilment of which was impossible?

The reader is probably amazed at the paucity of large stars in the whole firmament of heaven. Will he permit me to carry his mind a little farther, and either stand astonished at, or deplore with me the fact that, out of the millions of Christians in the vicinity and splendour of the eternal Sun of righteousness, how very few are found of the first order! How very few can stand examination by the test laid down in 1 Cor. xiii! How very few love God with all their heart, soul, mind, and strength, and their neighbours as themselves! How few mature Christians are found in the Church! How few are, in all things, living for eternity! How little light, how little heat, and how little influence and activity, are to be found among them that bear the name of Christ! How few stars of the first magnitude will the Son of God have to deck the crown of his glory! Few are striving to excel in righteousness; and it seems to be a principal concern with many, to find out how little grace they may have, and yet escape hell; how little conformity to the will of God they may have, and yet get to heaven. In the fear of God I register this testimony, that I have perceived it to be the labour of many to lower the standard of Christianity, and to soften down, or explain away, those promises of God that himself has linked with duties; and, because they know they cannot be saved by their good works, they are contented to have no good works at all; and thus the necessity of Christian obedience, and Christian holiness, makes no prominent part of some modern creeds. Let all those who retain the apostolic doctrine, that the blood of Christ cleanseth from all sin in this life, press every believer to go on to perfection, and expect to be saved, while here below, into the fulness of the blessing of the Gospel of Jesus. To all such my soul says, Labour to show yourselves approved unto God; workmen that need not be ashamed, rightly dividing the word of truth; and may the pleasure of the Lord prosper in your hands! Amen.

Many employ that time in brooding and mourning over their impure hearts, which should be spent in prayer and faith before God, that their impurities might be washed away. In what a state of nonage are many members of the Christian church!

I am afraid that what some persons call their *infirmities* may rather be called their *strengths;* the prevailing and frequently ruling power of pride, anger, ill will, &c.; for how few think evil tempers to be sins! The gentle term "infirmity" softens down the iniquity; and as St. Paul, so great and so holy a man, say they, had his infirmities, how can they expect to be without theirs? These should know that they are in a dangerous error; that St. Paul means nothing of the kind; for he speaks of his sufferings, and of these alone.

One word more: would not the grace and power of Christ appear more conspicuous in slaying the lion than in keeping him chained? in destroying sin, root and branch, and filling the soul with his own holiness, with love to God and man, with the mind, all the holy, heavenly tempers that were in himself, than in leaving these impure and unholy tempers ever to live, and often to reign, in the heart? The doctrine is discreditable to the Gospel, and wholly antichristian.

"If they sin against thee, for there is no man that sinneth not," 1 Kings viii, 46. On this verse we may observe that the second clause, as it is here translated, renders the supposition in the first clause entirely nugatory; for if there be no man that sinneth not, it is useless to say, "If they sin;" but this contradiction is taken away by reference to the original, which should be translated, "If they shall sin against thee;" or, "Should they sin against thee; for there is no man that may not sin;" that is, There is no man impeccable; none infallible; none that is not liable to transgress. This is the true meaning of the phrase in various parts of the Bible, and so our translators have understood the original; for, even in the thirty- first verse of this chapter, they have translated *yecheta,* "If a man trespass;" which certainly implies he might or might not do it: and in this way they have translated the same word, "If a soul sin," in Lev. v, 1; vi, 2; 1 Sam. ii, 25; 2 Chron. vi, 22; and in several other places. The truth is, the Hebrew has no mood to express words in the permissive or optative way; but to express this sense, it uses the future tense of the conjugation *kal.* This text has been a wonderful stronghold for all who believe that there is no redemption from sin in this life; that no man can live without committing sin; and that we cannot be entirely freed from it till we die. 1. The text speaks no such doctrine; it only speaks of the possibility of every man sinning; and this must be true of a state of probation. 2. There is not another text in the divine records that is more to the purpose than this. 3. The doctrine is flatly in opposition to the design of the Gospel; for

Jesus came to save his people from their sins, and to destroy the works of the devil. 4. It is a dangerous and destructive doctrine, and should be blotted out of every Christian's creed. There are too many who are seeking to excuse their crimes by all means in their power; and we need not embody their excuses in a creed, to complete their deception, by stating that their sins are unavoidable.

The soul was made for God, and can never be united to him, nor be happy, till saved from sin. He who is saved from his sin, and united to God, possesses the utmost felicity that the human soul can enjoy, either in this or the coming world.

Where a soul is saved from all sin, it is capable of being fully employed in the work of the Lord: it is then, and not till then, fully fitted for the Master's use.

All who are taught of Christ are not only saved, but their understandings are much improved. True religion, civilization, mental improvement, common sense, and orderly behaviour, go hand in hand.

When the light of Christ dwells fully in the heart, it extends its influence to every thought, word, and action; and directs its possessor how he is to act in all places and circumstances.

Our souls can never be truly happy till our wills be entirely subjected to, and become one with, the will of God.

While there is an empty, longing heart, there is a continual overflowing fountain of salvation. If we find, in any place, or at any time, that the oil ceases to flow, it is because there are no empty vessels there; no souls hungering and thirsting for righteousness. We find fault with the dispensations of God's mercy, and ask, "Why were the former days better than these?" Were we as much in earnest for our salvation as our forefathers were for theirs, we should have equal supplies, and as much reason to sing aloud of Divine mercy.

"Be ye holy," saith the Lord, "for I am holy." He who can give thanks at the remembrance of his holiness is one who loves holiness; who hates sin; who longs to be saved from it, and takes encouragement at the recollection of God's holiness, as he seeth in this the holy nature which he is to share, and the perfection which he is here to attain. But most who call themselves Christians hate the doctrine of holiness; never hear it inculcated without pain; and the principal part of their studies, and those of their pastors, is to find out with how little holiness they can rationally expect to enter into the kingdom of heaven. O fatal and soul-destroying delusion! How long will a holy God suffer such abominable doctrines to pollute his church, and destroy the souls of men.

Increase in the image and favour of God. Every grace and divine influence which ye have received is a seed, a heavenly seed, which, if it be watered with the dew of heaven from above, will endlessly increase and multiply itself. He who continues to believe, love, and obey, will grow in grace, and continually increase in the knowledge of Jesus Christ, as his Sacrifice, Sanctifier, Counsellor, Preserver, and final Saviour. The life of a Christian is a growth: he is at first born of God, and is a little child: becomes a young man and a father in Christ. Every father was once an infant; and, had he not grown, he would never have been a man. Those who content themselves with the grace they received when converted to God, are, at best, in a continual state of infancy; but we find, in the order of nature, that the infant that does not grow, and grow daily too, is sickly, and soon dies: so, in the order of grace, those who do not grow up into Jesus Christ are sickly, and will soon die — die to all sense and influence of heavenly things. There are many who boast of the grace of their conversion; persons who were never more than babes, and have long since lost even that grace, because they did not grow in it. Let him that readeth understand.

In order to get a clean heart, a man must know and feel its depravity, acknowledge and deplore it before God, in order to be fully sanctified. Few are pardoned, because they do not feel and confess their sins; and few are sanctified and cleansed from all sin, because they do not feel and confess their own sore and the plague of their hearts. As the blood of Jesus Christ, the merit of his passion and death, applied by faith, purges the conscience from all dead works, so the same cleanses the heart from all unrighteousness. As all unrighteousness is sin, so he that is cleansed from all unrighteousness is cleansed from all sin. To attempt to evade this, and plead for the continuance of sin in the heart through life, is ungrateful, wicked, and blasphemous; for, as he who says he has not sinned makes God a liar, who has declared the contrary through every part of his revelation, so he that says the blood of Christ either cannot or will not cleanse us from all sin in this life gives also the lie to his Maker, who has declared the contrary, and thus shows that the word, the doctrine of God, is not in him. Reader, it is the birthright of every child of God to be cleansed from all sin, to keep himself unspotted from the world, and so to live as never more to offend his Maker. All things are possible to him that believeth, because all things are possible to the infinitely meritorious blood and energetic Spirit of the Lord Jesus.

Every man whose heart is full of the love of God is full of humility; for there is no man so humble as he whose heart is cleansed from all sin. It has been said that indwelling sin humbles us; never was there a greater falsity: pride is the very essence of sin; he who has sin has pride; and pride, too, in proportion to his sin: this is a mere popish doctrine; and, strange to tell, the doctrine on which their doctrine of merit is founded! They say, God leaves concupiscence in the heart of every Christian, that, in striving with and overcoming it from time to time, he may have an accumulation of meritorious acts. Certain Protestants say, "It is a true sign of a very gracious state when a man feels and deplores his inbred corruption." How near do these come to the Papists, whose doctrine they profess to detest and abhor! The truth is, it is no sign of grace whatever; it only argues, as they use it, that the man has got light to show him his corruptions, but he has not yet got grace to destroy them. He is convinced that he should have the mind of Christ, but he feels that he has the mind of Satan; he deplores it; and, if his bad doctrine do not prevent him, he will not rest till he feels the blood of Christ cleansing him from all sin.

Can any man expect to be saved from his inward sin in the other world? None, except such as hold the popish, anti-scriptural doctrine of purgatory. "But this deliverance is expected at death." Where is the promise that it shall then be given? There is not one such in the whole Bible! And to believe for a thing essential to our glorification, without any promise to support that faith in reference to the point on which it is exercised, is a desperation that argues as well the absence of true faith as it does of right reason. Multitudes of such persons are continually deploring their want of faith, even where they have the clearest and most explicit promises; and yet, strange to tell, risk their salvation at the hour of death on a deliverance that is nowhere promised in the sacred oracles! "But who has got this blessing?" Every one who has come to God in the right way for it. "Where is such a one?" Seek the blessing as you should do, and you will soon be able to answer the question. "But it is too great a blessing to be expected." Nothing is too great for a believer to expect, which God has promised, and Christ has purchased with his blood. "If I had such a blessing, I should not be able to retain it." All things are possible to him that believeth. Besides, like all other gifts of God, it comes with a principle of preservation with it; "and upon all thy glory there shall be a defence." "Still, such an unfaithful person as I cannot expect it." Perhaps the infidelity you deplore came through the want of this blessing: and as to worthlessness, no soul under heaven deserves the least of God's mercies. It is not for thy worthiness that he has given thee any thing, but for the sake of his Son. You can say, "When I felt myself a sinner, sinking into perdition, I did then flee to the atoning blood, and found pardon: but this sanctification is a far greater work." — No; speaking after the manner of men, justification is far greater than sanctification. When thou wert a sinner, ungodly, an enemy in thy mind by wicked works, a child of the devil, an heir of hell, God pardoned thee on thy casting thy soul on the merit of the great sacrificial Offering: thy sentence was reversed, thy state was changed, thou wert put among the children, and God's Spirit witnessed with thine that thou wert his child. What a change! and what a blessing! What then is *this* complete sanctification? It is the cleansing of the blood that has not been cleansed; it is washing the soul of a true believer from the remains of sin; it is the making one who is already a child of God more holy, that he may be more happy, more useful in the world, and bring more glory to his heavenly Father. Great as this work is, how little, humanly speaking, is it when compared with what God has already done for thee! But suppose it were ten thousand times greater, is any thing too hard for God? Are not all things possible to him that believes? And does not the blood of Christ cleanse from all unrighteousness? Arise, then, and be baptized with a greater effusion of the Holy Ghost, and wash away thy sin, calling on the name of the Lord.

Art thou weary of that carnal mind which is enmity to God? Canst thou be happy while thou art unholy? Dost thou know any thing of God's love to thee? Dost thou not know that he has given his Son to die for thee? Dost thou love him in return for his love? Hast thou even a little love to him? And canst thou love him a little, without desiring to love him more? Dost thou not feel that thy happiness grows in proportion to thy love and subjection to him? Dost thou not wish to be happy? And dost thou not know that holiness and happiness are as inseparable as sin and misery? Canst thou have too much happiness or too much holiness? Canst thou be made holy and happy too soon? Art thou not weary of a sinful heart? Are not thy bad tempers, pride, anger, peevishness, fretfulness, covetousness, and the various unholy passions that too often agitate thy soul, a source of misery and woe to thee? And canst thou be unwilling to have them destroyed? Arise, then, and shake thyself from the dust, and call upon thy God! His ear is not heavy that it cannot hear: his hand is not shortened that it cannot save. Behold, now is the accepted time! Now is the day of salvation! It was necessary that Jesus Christ should die for thee, that thou mightest be saved; but he gave up his life for thee eighteen hundred years ago! and himself invites thee to come, for all things are now ready. Such is the nature of God that he cannot be more willing to save thee in any future time than he is now. He wills that thou shouldst love him now with all thy heart; but he knows that thou canst not thus love him till the enmity of the carnal mind is removed; and this he is willing this moment to destroy. The power of the Lord is therefore present to heal. Turn from every sin; give up every idol; cut off every right hand; pluck out every right eye. Be willing to part with thy enemies that thou mayest receive thy chief friend. Thy day is far spent, the night is at hand, the graves are ready for thee, and here thou hast no abiding city. A month, a week, a day, an hour, yea, even a moment, may send thee into eternity. And if thou die in thy sins, where God is thou shalt never come. Do not expect redemption in death: it can do nothing for thee even under the best consideration: it is thy last enemy. Remember then that nothing but the blood of Jesus can cleanse thee from all unrighteousness. Lay hold, therefore, on the hope that is set before thee. The gate may appear strait; but strive, and thou shalt pass through! "Come unto me," says Jesus. Hear his voice, believe at all risks, and struggle into God. Amen and Amen!

In no part of the Scriptures are we directed to seek holiness *gradatim*. We are to come to God as well for an instantaneous and complete purification from all sin, as for an instantaneous pardon. Neither the *seriatim* pardon, nor the *gradatim* purification, exists in the Bible. It is when the soul is purified from all sin that it can properly grow in grace, and in the knowledge of our Lord Jesus Christ:—as the field may be expected to produce a good crop, and all the seed vegetate, when the thorns, thistles, briers, and noxious weeds of every kind are grubbed out of it.

From every view of the subject, it appears that the blessing of a clean heart, and the happiness consequent on it, may be obtained in this life; because here, not in the future world, are we to be saved. Whenever, therefore, such blessings are offered, they may be received: but all the graces and blessings of the Gospel are offered at all times; and when they are offered, they may be received. Every sinner is exhorted to turn from the evil of his way, to repent of sin, and supplicate the throne of grace for pardon. In the same moment in which he is commanded to turn, in that moment he may and should return. He does not receive the exhortation to repentance to-day that he may become a penitent at some future time. Every penitent is exhorted to believe on the Lord Jesus that he may receive remission of sins:—he does not, he cannot understand that the blessing thus promised is not to be received to-day, but at some future time. In like manner, to every believer the new heart and the right spirit are offered in the present moment; that they may, in that moment, be received. For as the work of cleansing and renewing the heart is the work of God, his almighty power can perform it in a moment, in the twinkling of an eye. And as it is this moment our duty to love God with all our heart, and we cannot do this till he cleanse our hearts, consequently he is ready to do it this moment, because he wills that we should in this moment love him. Therefore we may justly say, "Now is the accepted time, now is the day of salvation." He who in the beginning caused light in a moment to shine out of darkness, can in a moment shine into our hearts, and give us to see the light of his glory in the face of Jesus Christ. This moment, therefore, we may be emptied of sin, filled with holiness, and become truly happy.

Such cleansed people never forget the horrible pit and miry clay out of which they have been brought. And can they then be proud? No! they loathe themselves in their own sight. They can never forgive themselves for having sinned against so good a God and so loving a Saviour. And can they undervalue Him by whose blood they were bought, and by whose blood they were cleansed?

No! That is impossible: they now see Jesus as they ought to see him; they see him in his splendour, because they feel him in his victory and triumph over sin. To them that thus believe he is precious; and he was never so precious as now. As to their not needing him when thus saved from their sins, we may as well say, As soon may the creation not need the sustaining hand of God, because the works are finished! Learn this, that as it requires the same power to sustain creation as to produce it; so it requires the same Jesus who cleansed to keep clean. They feel that it is only through his continued indwelling that they are kept holy, and happy, and useful. Were he to leave them, the original darkness and kingdom of death would soon be restored.

XIII. – THE MORAL LAW.

THE giving of the law on Mount Sinai was the most solemn transaction which ever took place between God and man: and, therefore, it is introduced in the most solemn manner. In the morning of that day in which this law was given, (which many learned chronologists suppose to have been May 30, in the year of the world 2513, before the incarnation 1491, that day being the pentecost,) the presence of Jehovah became manifest by thunders and lightnings,—a dense cloud on the mountain,—and a terrific blast of a trumpet,—so that the whole assembly were struck with terror and dismay. Shortly after, the whole mount appeared on fire; columns of smoke arose from it as the smoke of a furnace; and an earthquake shook it from top to base; the trumpet continued to sound, and the blast grew longer, and louder and louder. Then Jehovah, the sovereign Lawgiver, came down upon the mount, and called Moses to ascend to the top, where, previously to his delivering this law, he gave him directions concerning the sanctification of the people.

There are two points of view under which this law of God appears both singular and important:

1. It is the most ancient code or system of law ever given to man.

2. It was written in alphabetical characters invented by God himself; as it is most probable that, previously to this, no such characters had been known in the world.

THE FIRST COMMANDMENT.

Against mental and theoretical idolatry. – We must not attempt to form conceptions of the supreme Being as if confined to form, to any kind of limits, to any particular space or place. As Jehovah, he is in every respect inconceivable: no mind can grasp him; he is an infinite Spirit; equally in every place, and in all points of duration.

The Divine Being we must sanctify in our hearts: — that is, we must separate all transitory, material, and, particularly, earthly things, from the notion we form of him.

This commandment also forbids all inordinate attachment to earthly and sensible things: — that is, things that are the objects of our senses, and for the possession of which our appetites and affections are intensely occupied.

THE SECOND COMMANDMENT.

Against making and worshipping images – Image worship is a positive breach of this command. It attempts to humanize God, and fills the miserable idolater with the opinion that God is like to himself, if not altogether so: and image worshippers in general have no other idea of God than that of a gigantic man, of amazing dimensions, of vast strength, wisdom, and skill; — no other kind of being having any such strength or wisdom, thence, among the Roman Catholics, God is represented as a very grave, venerable old man, with a triple crown, (which, however, their popes borrow,) to signify his sovereignty over heaven, earth, and hell; angels, men, and devils, being subject to him. All these, as well as the triple crown, their symbol, have the popes of Rome, by their doctrines, traditions, and pretensions, arrogated to themselves. They have the keys of both worlds; they open, and no man shutteth; they shut, and no man openeth! It is a matter of the highest astonishment that the blasphemous pretensions of these individuals should have been acknowledged, and conceded to them, for so long a time, by all the powers of Europe! They have raised up and put down emperors and kings at pleasure; have absolved, as in a moment, all their officers and subjects from the most solemn oaths of allegiance, and their obligations of obedience:—and for all this, they have given them indulgences, purgatory, transubstantiation, image worship, worship of the Virgin Mary, as queen of heaven; saints and angels as mediators and intercessors; prayers for the dead, and uncertain and contradictory traditions in place of the Bible! All these must be received on their authority; and he who disputes their authenticity is a heretic: that is, one that the Church of Rome orders to be burned alive: and those who reject their authority incur the divine displeasure, and, if not reconciled to them and their church, shall be banished from the presence of God, and the glory of his power, to all eternity! What blasphemous pretensions! what gross idolatry!

This commandment is also directed against the idolatry of Egypt and against all idolatry, whether found among the savage tribes in North America; the worshippers of the visible heavens in China; the devotees of Brahma, Siva, and Mahadeo in Hindostan; the followers of Budhoo in Ceylon, and Java, and Ava; or the corrupt Christians in the Church of Rome.

THE THIRD COMMANDMENT.

Against false swearing, blasphemy, and irreverent use of the name of God.—This precept not only forbids all false oaths, but all common swearing, where the name of God is used, or where he is appealed to as a witness of the truth. It also necessarily forbids all light and irreverent mention of God, or any of his attributes; and we may safely add, that every prayer, ejaculation, and supplication, that is not accompanied with deep reverence, and the genuine spirit of piety, is here condemned also. So, also, is the wicked mode of turning the name of God, of the throne of his glory, into interjections, and words to express surprise, wonder, amazement, &c.: as, "O God! O Lord! O heavens! Good God! O my God!" &c., &c.; when it is evident, from the character of the persons, their habits, the nature of the circumstances in which they then were, that their souls were as truly without the fear of God as their tongues were without respect to the company or reverence of their Maker.

But the command may be and is broken in thousands of instances, in the prayers, whether read or offered extempore, of inconsiderate, bold, and presumptuous worshippers. Were every blasphemer among us to be stoned to death, how many of the people would fall in every corner of the land! God is long suffering; may this lead them to repentance! We have excellent laws against all profaneness, but alas for our country! they are not enforced; and he who attempts to put the laws in force against profane swearers, &c., is considered a litigious man, and a disturber of the peace of society. Will not God visit for these things? This is not only contempt of God's holy word and commandments, but rebellion against the law.

A common swearer is constantly perjuring himself. Such a person should never be trusted.

The best way is to have as little to do as possible with oaths. An oath will not bind a knave or a liar; and an honest man needs none, for his character and conduct swear for him.

He who uses any oath except what he is solemnly called by the magistrate to make, so far from being a Christian, does not deserve the reputation either of decency or common sense.

THE FOURTH COMMANDMENT.

Against profanation of the Sabbath, and idleness on the other days of the week. – "Remember the Sabbath day to keep it holy." As this was the most ancient institution, God calls upon them to remember it. As if he had said, "Do not forget that when I had finished the creation of the heavens and the earth, and all that is in them, I instituted the Sabbath; and remember why I did so, and for what purposes."

The word *shabath* signifies "he rested," and hence *shabath*, or "sabbath," the seventh day, or the day of rest, or rest simply. "In six days God created the heavens and the earth, and rested," that is, ceased to create, "on the seventh day;" and has consecrated it as a day of rest for man; rest to the body from labour and toil; and rest to the soul from all worldly cares and anxieties. He who labours with his mind on the Sabbath day is as culpable as he who labours with his hands in his ordinary calling. It is by the authority of God, that the Sabbath is set apart for rest and religious purposes, as the six days of the week are appointed for labour. How wise is this provision! How gracious this command! It is essentially necessary not only to the body of man, but to all the animals employed in his service. Take this away, and the labour is too great; both man and beast would fail under it. Without this consecrated day, religion itself would fail; and the human mind, becoming sensualized, would soon forget its origin and end.

Even as a political regulation, it is one of the wisest and most beneficent in its effects of any ever instituted. Those who habitually disregard its moral obligation are to a man not only good for nothing, but are wretched in themselves, a curse to society, and often end their lives miserably. The idler is next to the Sabbath-breaker. As God has formed both the body and mind of man on principles of activity, so he designed him proper employment: and it is his decree, that the mind shall improve by exercise, and the body find increase of vigour and health in honest labour. He who idles away his time on the six days is equally culpable in the sight of God as he who works on the seventh. The idle person is ordinarily clothed in rags; and it has ever been remarked in all Christian countries that Sabbath-breakers generally come to an ignominious death.

The appointment of the Sabbath is the first command ever given to man: and that the sanctification of it was of great consequence in the sight of God, we may learn from the various repetitions of this law; and we may observe that it has still for its object not only the benefit of the soul, but the health and comfort of the body also.

Because this commandment has not been particularly mentioned in the New Testament, as a moral precept binding on all, therefore some have presumptuously inferred that there is no Sabbath under the Christian dispensation. Were there none, Christianity itself would soon become extinct, and religion would soon have an end. But why is not the moral obligation of it insisted on by our Lord and the apostles? They have sufficiently insisted on it; they all kept it sacred, and so invariably did all the primitive Christians; though some observed the last day of the week, the Jewish Sabbath, instead of the first day, in commemoration not only of God's resting from his work of creation, but also of the resurrection of Christ from the dead. But to insist on the necessity of observing it was not requisite, because none doubted of its moral obligation; the question itself had never been disturbed; not so with circumcision and other Mosaic rites. The truth is, it is considered as a type—all types are of full force till the things signified by them take place:—but the thing signified by the Sabbath is that rest in glory which remains for the people of God; and in this light it evidently appears to have been considered by the apostle, Heb. iv. As, therefore, the antitype remains, the moral obligation of the Sabbath must continue till time be swallowed up in eternity. The world was never without a Sabbath, and never will be. And there is scarcely a people on the face of the earth, whether civilized or uncivilized, that has not agreed in the propriety of having a Sabbath, or something analogous to it; but it has been objected that the Sabbath could be only of partial obligation, and affect those only whose day and night were divisible into twenty-four hours; and would never be intended to apply to the inhabitants of either of the polar regions, where their days and nights alternately consist of several months each. This objection is very slight. The object of the divine Being is evidently to cause men to apply the seventh part of time to rest; and this may be as easily done at Spitzbergen as at any place under the equator. Nor is it of particular consequence when a nation or people may begin their Sabbath observances;—whether it fall in with our, or the Jewish, or even the Mohammedan Sabbath, provided they continue regular in the observance, and hallow to religious uses this seventh part of time.

In His mercy the divine Being has limited our labour to six days out of seven. In order to destroy the institution of God, the "French National Assembly" divided time into *decades,* and ordered every tenth day to be kept as a day of relaxation, dissipation, and merriment. The offended God wrought no miracle to bring back his institution; but, in the course of his providence, he annihilated them and their devices, and restored the Sabbath, in spite of legislative enactments to the contrary; and the people, bad as they were, rejoiced to be put in possession of the Sabbath which God had consecrated to rest and religious uses from the foundation of the world.

But let us remember, as before noted, that while we rest on the Sabbath we do not idle away the other six days. The Lord commands, "Six days shalt thou labour, and do all thy work," Exod. xx, 9. Therefore, it has been justly observed that he who idles away time on the six days is equally guilty before God as he who does his ordinary work on the Sabbath. An idle person, though able to discourse like an angel, or pray like an apostle, cannot be a

Christian; all such are hypocrites and deceivers; the true members of the church of Christ walk, work, and labour.

No work should be done on the Sabbath that can be done on the preceding day, or can be deferred to the ensuing week. Works of absolute necessity and mercy are alone excepted. He who works by his servants or cattle is equally guilty as if he worked himself; for God has commanded that both the cattle and the male and female servants shall rest also. Yea, the slave himself is included; for so the original word often signifies. But in what a state of moral depravity must those slave-holders be, who reduce their slaves to such a state of wretchedness that they allow them only the Sabbath day to cultivate those grounds from which they are to derive their subsistence; having no food allowed them but what they are able to bring out of the earth on that day in which the supreme Lord has commanded their masters to give them rest, and to require no manner of labour from them. Such enemies to God must expect no common judgment from the justice of the Most High, whatsoever countries they may inhabit.

Where men are unmerciful to their own species, no wonder that they have no feeling for the beasts that perish. Hiring out horses, &c., for pleasure or business, going on journeys, paying worldly visits, or taking jaunts on the Lord's day, are breaches of this law. "Doth God care for oxen?" Yes, and he mentions them with tenderness: "that thine ox and thine ass may rest." How criminal to employ the labouring cattle on the Sabbath, as well as on the other days of the week! In stage coaches, and on canals, horses are in continual labour. In general there is no Sabbath observed by the proprietors of those vehicles. Yet so tender and scrupulous are some proprietors, that they will not, on any account, do any of these things themselves; but they can be shareholders in stage coaches, wagons, canal boats, &c., &c., where the Sabbath is constantly profaned, and from which they derive an annual profit! Good souls! ye would not do these things yourselves; you only hire other persons to do them, and you live by the profit! Take heed that you enter all these things punctually in your leger, for the day is at hand in which you must render a strict account. More cattle are destroyed in England than in any other part of the world, in proportion, by continual labour. The noble horse in general has no Sabbath. Does God look on this with an indifferent eye? Surely he does not.

"England," said a foreigner, "is the paradise of women, the purgatory of servants and the hell of horses."

On this head, I conclude with, Reader, remember that thou keep holy the Sabbath day: thou needest the rest of it for thy body; and the religious ordinances of it for thy soul. God has hallowed it for these purposes: observe it as thou oughtest, and it will bring health to thy body, and peace to thy mind. So be it! Amen.

THE FIFTH COMMANDMENT.

See the Chapter **PARENTS AND CHILDREN.**

THE SIXTH COMMANDMENT.

Against murder and cruelty. — God is the Fountain and Author of life. No creature can give life to another: an archangel cannot give life to an angel; an angel cannot give life to man; man cannot give life even to the meanest of the brute creation. As God alone gives life, so he alone has the right to take it away; and he who, without the authority of God, takes away life, is properly a murderer. This commandment, which is general, prohibits murder of every kind: —

All actions by which the life of our fellow creatures may be suddenly taken away or abridged.

All wars for extending empire, commerce, &c.

All sanguinary laws, by the operation of which the lives of men may be taken away for offences of comparatively trifling demerit.

All bad dispositions which lead men to wish evil to, or meditate mischief against, each other; for the Scripture says, "He that hateth his brother in his heart is a murderer."

All want of charity and humanity to the helpless and distressed; for he who has it in his power to save the life of another, by a timely application of succour, food, raiment, medicine, &c., and does not do it, and the life of the person either falls or is abridged on this account, he is in the sight of God a murderer. He who neglects to save life is, according to an incontrovertible maxim in law, the same as he who takes it away.

All who, by immoderate and superstitious fastings,

macerations of the body, and wilful neglect of health, destroy or abridge life, are murderers; whatever a false religion and ignorant superstitious priests may say of them, God will not have murder for sacrifice.

All duellists are murderers, almost the worst of murderers; each meets the other with the design of killing him. He who shoots his antagonist dead is a murderer; he who is shot is a murderer also. The surviver should be hanged; the slain should be buried at a crossway, and the hanged murderer laid by his side.

All who put an end to their own lives by hemp, steel, poison, drowning, &c., are murderers, whatever coroners' inquests may say of them; unless it be clearly proved that the deceased was radically insane.

All who are addicted to riot and excess, to drunkenness and gluttony, to extravagant pleasures, to inactivity and slothfulness; in short and in sum, all who are influenced by indolence, intemperance, and disorderly passions, by which life is prostrated and abridged, are murderers.

A man who is full of fierce and furious passions, who has no command of his own temper, may in a moment destroy the life even of his friend, his wife, or his child. All such fell and ferocious men are murderers; they ever carry about with them the murderous propensity, and are not praying to God to subdue and destroy it.

A vindictive man excludes himself from all hope of eternal life, and himself seals his own damnation.

Malice and envy are never idle, they incessantly hunt the person they intend to make their prey.

Reader, hast thou a child or servant who has offended thee, and humbly asks forgiveness? Hast thou a debtor or a tenant who is insolvent, and asks for a little longer time? And hast thou not forgiven that child or servant? Hast thou not given time to that debtor or tenant? How, then, canst thou ever expect to see the face of the just and merciful God? Thy child is banished or kept at a distance; thy debtor is cast into prison, or thy tenant sold up; yet the child offered to fall at thy feet; and the debtor or tenant, utterly insolvent, prayed for a little longer time, hoping God would enable him to pay thee all; but to these things thy stony heart and seared conscience paid no regard! O monster of ingratitude! Scandal to human nature, and reproach to God! If thou canst, go hide thyself, even in hell, from the face of the Lord!

THE SEVENTH COMMANDMENT.

Against adultery, fornication, and uncleanness. – One principal part of the criminality of adultery consists in its injustice: – 1. It robs a man of his right, by depriving him of the affection of his wife; 2. It does him a wrong, by fathering on him, and obliging him to maintain as his own, a spurious offspring, a child which is not his. The act itself, and every thing leading to the act, are here prohibited; and also fornication, as well as all impure books, songs, paintings, &c., which tend to inflame and debauch the mind.

THE EIGHTH COMMANDMENT.

Against stealing and dishonesty. – All rapine and theft are here forbidden; as well national and commercial wrongs, as petty larceny, highway robberies, house- breaking, private stealing, knavery, cheating, and frauds of every kind: also, the taking advantage of a buyer's or seller's ignorance, to give the one less, and make the other pay more for a commodity than it is worth, is a breach of this sacred law. All withholding of rights, and doing of wrongs, are against the spirit of it.

But the word is principally applicable to clandestine stealing; though it may undoubtedly include all political injustice and private wrongs: and, consequently, all kidnapping, crimping, and slave-dealing are prohibited here, whether practised by individuals, the state, or its colonies. I greatly doubt whether the impress service stands clear here. Crimes are not lessened in their demerit by the number or political importance of those who commit them. A state that enacts bad laws is as criminal before God as the individual who breaks good ones.

Stealing, overreaching, defrauding, purloining, &c., are consistent with no kind of religion that acknowledges the true God. If Christianity does not make men honest, it does nothing for them. Those who are not saved from dishonesty, fear not God, though they may dread man.

No man, from what is called a principle of charity or generosity, should give that in alms which belongs to his creditors.

Generosity is godlike; but justice has ever, both in law and Gospel, the first claim.

I have known many decent, respectable people, who feared a lie and trembled at an oath, who, when brought either by failure of trade, sudden fall of some article of commerce, speculation in business, through the hope of what they considered honest gain, by which they might be enabled to pay every man his due,—were led to forge bills—borrow money—impose upon even their own relations—cover one bad bill with another as bad, hoping that ere the time of payment they might, by the speculations or promises that were still in abeyance, be able to pay every one his due. Reader, if thou be a man in business or trade, and art about to he straitened in thy circumstances, pray most fervently to God that thou mayest not fall into abject poverty, lest thou complete thy wretchedness by lying, cheating, false promising, false swearing, and other dirty acts; by which many, once respectable, honest, and upright, have been drowned in destruction of property, and perdition of character and life; and so the Lord have mercy on thy soul!

Among all thieves and knaves, he is the most execrable who endeavours to rob another of his character, that he may enhance his own; lessening his neighbour, that he may aggrandize himself. This is that pest of society who is full of kind assertions tagged with *buts*. "He is a good kind of man; *but* —every bean has its black! Such a one is very friendly; *but*— it is in his own way! My neighbour N. can be very liberal; *but* —you must catch him in the humour." Persons like these speak well of their neighbours, merely that they may have the opportunity to neutralize all their commendations, and make them suspected whose character stood deservedly fair, before the traducer began to pilfer his property. He who repents not for these injuries, and does not make restoration, if possible, to his defrauded neighbour, will hear, when God comes to take away his soul, these words, more terrible than the knell of death: "Thou shalt not steal."

A man, for instance, of a good character, is reported to have done something evil; the tale is spread, and the slanderers, whisperers, and backbiters carry it about: and thus the man is stripped of his fair character, of his clothing of righteousness, truth, and honesty. And yet the whole report may be false; or the person, in an hour of the power of darkness, may have been tempted and overcome; may have been wounded in the cloudy and dark day; and now deeply mourns his fall before God! Who that has not the heart of a demon would not strive rather to cover than to make bare the fault in such circumstances! Those who, as the proverb says, "Feed like the flies, passing over all a man's whole parts to light upon his sores," will take up the tale and carry it about. Such, in the course of their diabolic work, carry the story of scandal, among others, to the righteous man; to him who loves his God and his neighbour: but what reception has the tale-bearer? The good man taketh it not up, he will not bear it; it shall not be propagated by or from him. He cannot prevent the detracter from laying it down; but it is in his power not to take it up; and thus the progress of the slander may be arrested. "He taketh not up a reproach against his neighbour; and, by this means, the tale-bearer may be discouraged from bearing it to another door. If there were no takers up of defamation, there would be fewer detracters in the land. If there were no receivers of stolen goods, there would be no thieves. And hence another proverb, founded on the justest principle, "The receiver is as bad as the thief." And is not the whisperer, the backbiter, and the tale-bearer the worst of thieves? robbing not only individuals, but whole families, of their reputation! scattering firebrands, arrows, and death! Yes, they are the worst of felons. O, how many a fair fame has been tarnished by this most Satanic practice! But, bad as the accidental retailer of calumny is, he who makes it his business to go about to collect stories of scandal, and who endeavours to have vouchers for his calumnies, is yet worse; whether the stories be true or false, whether they make the simple relation, or exaggerate the fact,—whether they present a simple lens, through which to view the character they exhibit, or an *anamorphosis* by which every feature is distorted, so that, in a monstrosity of appearance, every trait or similitude of goodness is lost: and then the reporter himself takes advantage of his own inferences, "O, sir, how bad is this! But—but, there is worse behind." This insinuation is like a drag-net, gathering as it goes, and bringing every thing into its vortex: the good and the bad are found in one indiscriminate assembly.

Suppose the stories to be true, or founded in truth, what benefit does society or the church ever derive from this underhand detailing? None. There are but few cases ever occurring, where the misunderstanding between the members of the church of Christ should be brought before two witnesses, much less before the church: but there are some such, and our Lord orders us to treat these with the greatest caution and forbearance.

All the above, with the whole family of defamers, false accusers, calumniators, detracters, destroyers of the good reputation of others, traducers, and libellers, however they may rank here, shall have one lot in the eternal world; none of them shall become residents on the hill of God's holiness; and should not here be permitted to sojourn in his tabernacle, or militant church. Reader, pray God to save thee from the spirit and conduct of these bad men; have no communion with them, drive them from thy door, yet labour to convert them if thou canst. But if they will still continue as disturbers of the peace of society, of the harmony of families, and of the union of Christ's church, let them be to thee as heathen men and publicans; the basest, the lowermost, the most dejected, most underfoot, and downtrodden vassals of perdition.

There are busybodies, impertinent meddlers with other people's business; prying into other people's circumstances and domestic affairs; magnifying or minifying, mistaking or underrating, every thing; news- mongers and telltales; an abominable race, the curse of every neighbourhood where they live, and a pest to religious society.

Do not open your ear to the tale-bearer, to the slanderer, who comes to you with accusations against your brethren, or with surmisings and evil speakings. These are human devils; they may be the means of making you angry, even without any solid pretence; therefore give them no place, that you may not be angry at any time. But if, unhappily, you should be overtaken in this fault, let not the sun go down upon your wrath; go to your brother, against whom you have found your spirit irritated, tell him what you have heard, and what you fear; let your ears be open to receive his own account; carefully listen to his own explanation; and, if possible, let the matter be finally settled, that Satan may not gain advantage over either.

The grand maxim of the Roman law and government, to condemn no man unheard, and to confront the accusers with the accused, should be a sacred maxim with every magistrate and minister, and among all private Christians. How many harsh judgments and uncharitable censures would this prevent! Conscientiously practised in all Christian societies, detraction, calumny, tale-bearing, whispering, backbiting, misunderstandings, with every unbrotherly affection, would be necessarily banished from the church of God.

THE NINTH COMMANDMENT.

Against false testimony, perjury, lying, and deceit. – Not only false oaths to deprive a man of his life or of his right, are here prohibited; but also all whispering, tale-bearing, calumny, and slander, where the object is to bring the neighbour to pain, loss, or punishment. In a word, whatever is deposed as a truth, which is false in fact, and tends to injure another in his body, goods, or influence, is against the spirit and letter of this law.

What is a lie? It is any action done or word spoken, whether true or false in itself, which the doer or speaker wishes the observer or hearer to take in a contrary sense to that which he knows to be true. It is, in a word, any action done or speech delivered with the intention to deceive, though both may be absolutely true and right in themselves.

Do not deceive each other; speak the truth in all your dealings; do not say, "My goods are so, and so," when you know them to be otherwise; do not undervalue the goods of your neighbour when your conscience tells you that you are not speaking the truth. "It is naught, it is naught, saith the buyer; but afterward he boasteth;" that is, he underrates his neighbour's property till he gets him persuaded to part with it for less than it is worth; and when he has thus got it, he boasts what a good bargain he has made. Such a knave speaks not truth with his neighbour.

A liar has always some suspicion that his testimony is not credited, for he is conscious to his own falsity, and is therefore naturally led to support his assertions by oaths.

To pretend much love and affection for those for whom we have neither; to use toward them complimentary phrases, to which we affix no meaning, but that they mean nothing, is highly offensive in the sight of that God by whom actions are weighed and words judged.

THE TENTH COMMANDMENT.

Against covetousness. – The covetousness which is placed on forbidden objects is that which is here prohibited and condemned. To covet in this sense is intensely to long after, in order to enjoy, as a property, the person or thing coveted. He breaks this commandment who by any means endeavours to deprive a man of his house, or farm, by some underhand and clandestine bargain with the original landlord; what is called, in some countries, "taking a man's house and farm over his head." He breaks it, also, who lusts after his neighbour's wife, and endeavours to ingratiate himself into her affections by striving to lessen her husband in her esteem: and he also breaks it who endeavours to possess himself of the servants, cattle, &c., of another, in any clandestine or unjustifiable manner.

By covetousness many lives and many souls have been destroyed; and yet the living lay it not to heart! Who fears the love of money, provided he can get riches? Through the intensity of this desire, every part of the surface of the earth, and, as far as possible, its bowels, are ransacked to get wealth; and God alone can tell, who sees all things, to how many private crimes, frauds, and dissimulations, this gives birth; by which the wrath of God is brought down upon the community at large! Who is an enemy to his country? The sinner against his God. An open foe may be resisted and repelled, because he is known; but the covetous man, who, as far as his personal safety will admit, is outraging all the requisitions of justice, is an unseen pestilence, sowing the seeds of desolation and ruin in society. Achan's covetousness, which led him to break the law of God, had nearly proved the destruction of the Israelitish camp; nor would the Lord turn away from his displeasure till the evil was detected, and the criminal punished.

The spirit of covetousness cancels all bonds and obligations, makes wrong right, and cares nothing for father or brother.

A covetous man is, in effect, and in the sight of God, a murderer: he wishes to get all the gain that can accrue to any or all who are in the same business that he follows; no matter to him how many families starve in consequence. This is the very case with him who sets up shop after shop in different parts of the same town or neighbourhood, in which he carries on the same business, and endeavours to undersell others in the same trade, that he may get all into his own hand.

How apt are men to decry the goods they wish to purchase, in order that they may get them at a cheaper rate; and when they have made their bargain, and carried it off; boast to others at how much less than its value they have received it! Are such honest men? Is such knavery actionable? Can such be punished only in another world? St. Augustine tells us a pleasant story on this subject: "A certain mountebank published in the full theatre that at the next entertainment he would show to every man present what was in his heart. The time came, and the concourse was immense: all waited, with deathlike silence, to hear what he would say to each. He stood up, and in a single sentence redeemed his pledge: — 'You all wish to buy cheap, and sell dear.' He was applauded; for every one felt it to be a description of his own heart, and was satisfied that all others were similar."

How often does charity serve as a cloak for covetousness! God is sometimes robbed of his right under the pretence of devoting what is withheld to some charitable purpose to which there was no intention ever to give it.

If thou be too nice in endeavouring to find out who are the impostors among those who profess to be in want, the real object may perish, which otherwise thou mightest have relieved, and whose life might have been thereby saved. The very punctilious and scrupulous people, who will sift every thing to the bottom in every case, and before they will act must be fully satisfied in all points, seldom do any good, and are themselves generally good for nothing. While they are observing the clouds and the rain, others have "joined hands with God, and made a poor man live."

XIV. – PUBLIC WORSHIP.

By adoration we are to understand that reverence that is due to the highest and best of beings. The word "adoration" signifies that act of religious worship which was expressed by lifting the hand to the mouth, and kissing it, in token of the highest esteem and the most profound reverence and subjection. It implies a proper contemplation of His excellences, so as to excite wonder and admiration; and of His goodness and bounty, so as to impress us with the liveliest sense of his ineffable goodness to us, and our deep unworthiness. It implies the deepest awe of his divine Majesty while even approaching him with the strongest sensations of filial piety; a trembling before him while rejoicing in him; the greatest circumspection in every act of religious worship; the mind wholly engrossed with the object while the heart is found in the deepest prostration at his feet; the soul abstracted from every outward thing; no thought indulged but what relates to the act of worship in which we are engaged, nor a word uttered in prayer or praise the meaning of which is not felt by the heart; no unworthy conceptions of such a Majesty permitted to arise in the mind; the same worshipping in spirit and in truth; no carelessness of manner, no boldness of expression, permitted to appear; the body prostrated while the soul, in all its powers and faculties, adores; no lip service, no animal labour, allowed to take place; nothing felt, nothing seen, but the supreme God, and the soul made by his hand and redeemed by his blood.

Worship, or worthship, implies that proper conception we should have of God, as the great governor of heaven and earth, of angels and men. How worthy He is in his nature, and in the administration of his government, of the highest praises we can offer, and of the best services we can render! Every act we perform should bear testimony to the sense we have of the excellence of his Majesty, and of the worthiness of his acts. "Speak, Lord, thy servant heareth," is the language of the true worshipper. He seeks to know the will of his Lord, that he may do that will. Every prayer is offered up in the spirit of subjection and obedience; and in the deepest humility he waits to receive the commands of his heavenly Master, and the power to fulfil them. He feels that he cannot choose; he knows that his Lord cannot err. "Thy will be done on earth as it is in heaven," is not an unmeaning petition while proceeding from his mouth. His soul feels it; his heart desires it. Obedience is the element in which his soul lives, and in which it thrives, and increases in happiness. In his sight God is worthy of all glory, and praise, and dominion, and power, because He is not only the Fountain of being, but also the Source of mercy. He waits on his God, and he finds that his God waits to be gracious to him. He waits on his God, and he finds that this God, who is his friend, condescends to be his companion through life: therefore his heart is fixed; nor is he afraid of evil tidings; for he trusts in the name of the Lord. He draws nigh to God in every act of worship, and has communion with the Father and the Son through the Holy Ghost. He is kept in perfect peace, for his mind is stayed upon God, because he trusts in him. All his powers are sensible of this truth, "Thou God seest me;" and his experience proves that God is the "rewarder of them that diligently seek him."

The very eyes should be guarded: they often affect the heart in such a way as to mar and render unprofitable this most solemn act of devotion. The objects that they see will present images to the mind which call off or divide the thoughts, and produce that wandering of heart so frequently complained of by many religious people, whose own unguarded eyes and thoughts are the causes of those wanderings which spoil their devotions. I never could understand how any man can have a collected mind or proper devotion in prayer, who, while he is engaged in it, has his eyes open; not indeed fixed on one point, but wandering through the house, beholding the evil and the good. He must be distracted, and his prayers such, unless technical or got off by heart; then indeed he may *say* his prayers, but he cannot *pray* them.

Were it not for public, private worship would soon be at an end. To this, under God, the church of Christ owes its being and its continuance. Where there is no public worship there is no religion. It is by this that God is acknowledged, and he is the universal Being; and by his bounty and providence all live; consequently it is the duty of every intelligent creature publicly to acknowledge Him, and offer him that worship which himself has prescribed in his word.

The wisest and best of men have always felt it their duty and their interest to worship God in public. As there is nothing more necessary, so there is nothing more reasonable: he who acknowledges God in all his ways may expect all his steps to be directed. The public worship of God is one grand line of distinction between the atheist and the believer. He who uses not public worship has either no God or has no right notion of his being; and such a person, according to the rabbins, is a bad neighbour; it is dangerous to live near him; for neither he nor his can be under the protection of God. No man should be forced to attend a particular place of worship, but every man should be obliged to attend some place; and he who has any fear of God will not find it difficult to get a place to his mind.

We see the vast importance of worshipping God according to his own mind. No sincerity, no uprightness of intention, can atone for the neglect of positive commands, delivered in divine revelation, when the revelation is known. He who will bring a eucharistic offering instead of a sacrifice, while a sin-offering lieth at the door, as he copies Cain's conduct, may expect to be defeated in the same manner. Reader, remember that thou hast an entrance into the holiest through the veil, that is to say, his flesh; and those who come in this way God will in nowise cast out.

Were the religion of Christ stripped of all that state policy, fleshly interest, and gross superstition have added to it, how plain and simple, (and may we not add?) how amiable and glorious, would it appear! Well may we say of human inventions in divine worship, what one said of the paintings on old cathedral windows, "Their principal tendency is to prevent the light from coming in." Nadab and Abihu could perform the worship of God, not according to his command, but in their own way; and God not only would not receive the sacrifice from their hands, but, while encompassing themselves with their own sparks, and warming themselves with their own fire, this had they from the hand of the Lord, — they lay down in sorrow; "for there went out a fire from the Lord, and devoured them." What is written above is to be understood of persons who make a religion for themselves, leaving divine revelation; for, being wilfully ignorant of God's righteousness, they go about to establish their own. This is a high offence in the sight of God. Reader, God is a Spirit, and they who worship him must worship him in spirit and in truth. Such worshippers the Father seeketh.

To worship God publicly is the duty of every man; and no man can be guiltless who neglects it. If a person cannot get such public worship as he likes, let him frequent such as he can get.

XV. – PRAYER.

PRAYER has been defined, "an offering of our desire to God for things needful, with an humble confidence to obtain them through the alone merits of Christ, to the praise of the mercy, truth, and power of God." And "its parts are said to be invocation, adoration, confession, petition, pleading, dedication, thanksgiving, and blessing." Though the definition be imperfect, yet, as far as it goes, it is not objectionable; but the parts of prayer, as they are called, (except the word *petition,*) have scarcely any thing to do with the nature of prayer. They are, in general, separate acts of devotion; and attention to them in what is termed "praying," will entirely mar it, and destroy its efficacy.

It was by following this division, that long prayers have been introduced among Christian congregations, by means of which the spirit of devotion has been lost: for, where such prevail most, listlessness and deadness are the principal characteristics of the religious services of such people; and these have often engendered formality, and frequently total indifference to religion. Long prayers prevent kneeling, for it is utterly impossible for man or woman to keep on their knees during the time such last; where these prevail, the people either stand or sit. Technical prayers, I have no doubt, are odious in the sight of God; for no man can be in the spirit of devotion who uses such: it is a drawing nigh to God with the lips, while the heart is, almost necessarily, far from him.

A proper idea of prayer is, "the pouring out the soul before

God, with the hand of faith placed on the head of the sacrificial offering; imploring mercy, and presenting itself a free-will offering unto God; giving up body, soul, and spirit, to be guided and governed as may seem good to his heavenly wisdom, desiring only perfectly to love him, and serve him with all its powers, at all times, while he has a being."

It is not merely to tell God our wants, or to show him our state, that we are to pray; (for he knows this state and these wants much better than ourselves;) but to get a suitable feeling of the pressure of these wants, and the necessity of having them supplied: and this we obtain by looking into our own hearts and lives; for here, particularly, the eye affects the heart, and, from the urgency of the necessity, we feel excited to pray earnestly to God for his mercy; and our confessing them before him affects us still more deeply; induces us to be more fervent; and shows us that none but God can save and defend.

Prayer is not designed to inform God, but to give man a sight of his misery; to humble his heart, to excite his desire, to inflame his faith, to animate his hope, to raise his soul from earth to heaven, and to put him in mind that there is his Father, his country, and inheritance.

Prayer is the most secret intercourse of the soul with God, and, as it were, the conversation of one heart with another.

Prayer is the language of dependance; he who prays not is endeavouring to live independently of God; this was the first curse, and continues to be the great curse of mankind.

Prayer requires more of the heart than of the tongue. The eloquence of prayer consists in the fervency of desire and the simplicity of faith. The abundance of fine thoughts, studied and vehement motions, and the order and politeness of the expressions, are things which compose mere human harangue, not an humble and Christian prayer. Our trust and confidence should proceed from that which God is able to do in us, and not from what we say to him.

Unmeaning words, useless repetitions, and complimentary phrases in prayer, are, in general, the result of heathenism, hypocrisy, or ignorance.

A fluency in prayer is not essential to praying: a man may pray most powerfully, in the estimation of God, who is not able to utter even one word. The unutterable groan is big with meaning, and God understands it, because it contains the language of his own Spirit. Some desires are too mighty to be expressed; there is no language expressive enough to give them proper form and distinct vocal sound: such desires show that they come from God; and as they come from him, so they express what God is disposed to do, and what he has purposed to do.

"Wherefore criest thou unto me?" We hear not one word of Moses' praying, and yet here the Lord asks him why he cries unto him: from which we may learn that the heart of Moses was deeply engaged with God, though it is probable he did not articulate one word; but the language of sighs, tears, and desires is equally intelligible to God with that of words. This consideration should be a strong encouragement to every feeble, discouraged mind: thou canst not pray, but thou canst weep; if even tears are denied thee, (for there may be deep and genuine repentance where the distress is so great as to stop up these channels of relief,) then thou canst sigh; and God, whose Spirit has thus convinced thee of sin, righteousness, and judgment, knows thy unutterable groanings, and reads the inexpressible wish of thy burthened soul,—a wish of which himself is the Author, and which he has breathed into thy heart with the purpose to satisfy it.

Prayer is the language of a conscious dependance on God; and he who considers that his being is an effect of the divine power, the continuance of that being an effect of an ever active Providence, and his well-being an effect of infinite grace and mercy, will feel the necessity of praying to God, that the great purpose for which this being was given may be accomplished, and his soul saved unto eternal life. And he will feel this necessity the more forcibly when he considers this: his Maker, Preserver, and Redeemer is under no obligation to continue those exertions of his power and goodness by which his being is continued, his life preserved, or his soul saved. Did it comport with the requisition of divine justice, we might expect to see every prayerless soul blotted out of the list of intelligent beings, or annihilated from the place it occupied in the creation of God. To see such ungodly, unthankful, unholy, profligate, and perishing from the blessedness of both worlds, vessels of wrath fitted for destruction, can be no matter of surprise to those who know that they who pray not cannot be saved.

He who has the spirit of prayer has the highest interest in the court of heaven; and the only way to retain it, is to keep it in constant employment. Apostasy begins in the closet. No man ever backslid from the life and power of Christianity who continued constant and fervent, especially in private prayer. He who prays without ceasing is likely to rejoice evermore.

Where Abram has a tent, there God must have an altar, as he well knows there is no safety but under the divine protection. How few who build houses ever think on the propriety and necessity of building an altar to their Maker! The house in which the worship of God is not established cannot be considered as under the divine protection.

"I will therefore that men pray everywhere:"—In every place; that they should always have a praying heart, and this will ever find a praying place. This may refer to a Jewish superstition. They thought, at first, that no prayer could be acceptable that was not offered at the temple at Jerusalem; afterward this was extended to the Holy Land; but, when they became dispersed among the nations, they built oratories, or places of prayer, principally by rivers, and by the seaside; and in these they were obliged to allow that public prayer might be legally offered, but nowhere else. In opposition to this, the apostle, by the authority of Christ, commands men to pray everywhere; that all places belong to God's dominions; and, as he fills every place, in every place he may be worshipped and glorified. As to ejaculatory prayer, they allowed that this might be performed standing, sitting, leaning, lying, walking by the way, and during their labour.

God is the object of prayer; and the word of God, and especially his promises, are also the objects of prayer.

God on his mercy-seat is the object of prayer; and to fix the mind, and prevent it from wavering, the supplicant should consider him under such attributes as are best suited to his own state and wants. There are three general views which may be taken of this divine object: infinite wisdom, infinite power, infinite goodness. There are few blessings which we want that do not come from one or other of these three sources: We are either ignorant, and want instruction; weak, and need power; wretched, and need mercy. As we feel, so we should pray; and in order to feel aright, and pray successfully, we should endeavour to find out our state, to discover our most pressing wants; and to find these, we need much light, which the Holy Spirit alone can impart. Hence, strange as it may appear, we must pray before we begin to pray. We must pray for light to discover our state, that our eye may affect our heart, in order to go successfully to the great object of prayer. To get our wants summarily supplied we must pray first to see what we need; and then we shall pray to get our wants supplied.

Prayer to God is considered among the Mohammedans in a very important point of view. It is declared by the Mosliman doctors to be "the corner stone of religion, and the pillar of faith." They hold the following points to be essentially requisite to the efficacy of prayer: 1. That the person be free from every species of defilement. 2. That all sumptuous, gaudy apparel be laid aside. 3. That the attention accompany the act, and be not suffered to wander to any other object. 4. That the prayer be performed with the face toward the temple of Mecca.

What can any man think of himself, who, in his addresses to God, can either sit on his seat or stand in the presence of the Maker and Judge of all men? Would they sit while addressing any person of ordinary respectability? If they did so, they would be reckoned very rude indeed. Would they sit in the presence of the king of their own land? They would not be permitted so to do. Is God, then, to be treated with less respect than a fellow-mortal? Paul kneeled in praying, Acts xx, 36; xxi, 5. Stephen kneeled when he was stoned, Acts vii, 60. And Peter kneeled when he raised Tabitha, Acts ix, 40.

I suppose the grossly absurd and perfectly ungodly custom of sitting during prayer is out of the question. It was so perfectly unlike every thing that was becoming in divine worship, and so expressive of a total want of reverence in the worshipper, and of that consciousness of his wants and deep sense of his own worthlessness which he ought to have, that the church of God never tolerated it: a custom that even heathenism itself had too much light either to practice or sanction. Among the most ancient and most enlightened nations, kneeling was ever considered to be the proper posture of supplication; as it expressed humility, contrition, and subjection.

At a public meeting a pious brother went to prayer; I kneeled on the floor, having nothing to lean against, or to support me. He prayed forty- eight minutes. I was unwilling to rise, and several times was nigh fainting. What I suffered I cannot describe. After the meeting was over, I ventured to expostulate with the good man; and, in addition to the injury I sustained by his unmerciful prayer, I had the following reproof: "My brother, if your mind had been more spiritual, you would not have felt the prayer too long." More than twenty years have elapsed since this transaction took place, but the remembrance of what I then suffered still rests on my mind with a keen edge. The good man is still alive, will probably read this paper, will no doubt recollect the circumstance, and I hope will feel that he has since learned more prudence and more charity.

What satisfaction must it be to learn from God himself, with what words, and in what manner, he would have us pray to him, so as not to pray in vain!

Even they who use the Lord's Prayer in their public devotions, seem to use it in the wrong place. Should we not begin our addresses to God with this prayer? and then after that manner continue our requests to a reasonable length? But whether used in the beginning, middle, or end, let it never be forgotten.

Can he who sees himself a slave of the devil, beg with too much earnestness to be delivered from his thraldom?

"This is the confidence," — the liberty of access and speech, "that if we ask any thing according to his will;" that is, which he has promised in his word. His word is a revelation of his will, in the things which concern the salvation of man. All that God has promised we are justified in expecting; and what he has promised, and we expect, we should pray for. Prayer is the language of the children of God. He who is begotten of God speaks this language. He calls God, "Abba, Father!" in the true spirit of supplication. Prayer is the language of dependence on God; where the soul is dumb, there is neither life, love, nor faith. Faith and prayer are not boldly to advance claims upon God; we must take heed that what we ask and believe for, is agreeable to the revealed will of God. What we find promised, that we may plead.

Come with confidence to the throne of grace. Know that it is such; and that He who sits on it is gracious. When you approach, you have an Intercessor there: he will introduce you: he will recommend your suit, plead in your behalf, give you full liberty to use his name, to appropriate to yourselves the infinite merit of his passion and death, his resurrection and mediation; and to avail yourselves of that indescribable nearness he has to the Father, as his beloved Son, in whom he is well pleased; and his affinity to you, as "God manifested in the flesh." It is impossible that any thing can be added, to strengthen this confidence; or by a more powerful argument to ensure a success which, from the above considerations, must be certain and absolute.

"In the morning will I direct my prayer unto thee." Here seems to be a metaphor taken from an archer. He sees his mark; puts his arrow in his bow; directs his shaft to the mark, that is, takes his aim; lets fly; and then looks up, to see if he has hit his mark. Prayers that have a right aim will have a prompt answer: and he who sends up his petitions to God through Christ, from a warm, affectionate heart, may confidently look up for an answer: for it will come. If an immediate answer be not given, let not the upright heart suppose that the prayer is not heard. It has found its way to the throne, and there it is registered.

In approaching the throne of grace, we keep Jesus, as our sacrificial victim, continually in view. Our prayers should be directed through him to the Father: and, under the conviction that his passion and death have purchased every possible blessing for us, we should, with humble confidence, ask the blessings we need; and, as in him the Father is ever well pleased, we should most confidently expect the blessings he has purchased.

The prayer that is not sent up through the influence of the Holy Ghost is never likely to reach heaven.

Worldly men, if they pray at all, ask for temporal things: "What shall we eat? what shall we drink? and wherewithal shall we be clothed?" Most of the true religious people go into another extreme; they forget the body, and ask only for the soul: and yet there are "things requisite and necessary as well for the body as the soul," and things which are only at God's disposal. The body lives for the soul's sake; its life and comfort are in many respects essentially requisite to the salvation of the soul; and therefore the things necessary for its support should be earnestly asked from the God of all grace, the Father of bounty and providence. "Ye have not, because ye ask not," may be said to many poor, afflicted religious people; and they are afraid to ask, lest it should appear mercenary, or that they sought their portion in this life. They should be better taught. Surely to none of these will God give a stone if they ask bread; He who is so liberal of his heavenly blessings will not withhold earthly ones, which are infinitely of less consequence. Reader, expect God's blessing on thy honest industry; pray for it, and believe that God does not love thee less, who hast taken refuge in the same hope, than he loved Isaac. Plead not only his promises, but plead on the precedents he has set before thee. "Lord, thou didst so and so to Abraham, to Isaac, to Jacob, and to others who trusted in thee; bless my field, bless my flocks, prosper my labour, that I may be able to provide things honest in the sight of all men, and have something to dispense to those who are in want." And will not God hear such prayers? Yea, and answer them too, for he does not willingly afflict the children of men. And we may rest assured that there is more affliction and poverty in the world than either the justice or providence of God requires. There are, however, many who owe their poverty to their want of diligence and economy; they sink down into indolence, and forget that word," Whatsoever thy hand findeth to do, do it with thy might;" nor do they consider that "by idleness a man is clothed in rags." Be diligent in business, and fervent in spirit, and God will withhold from thee no manner of thing that is good.

We must ask only what is necessary for our support; God having promised neither luxuries nor superfluities. Daily support for our bodies, and daily support for our souls, is all that we need; and this we should pray for; and this we have reason to expect from a bountiful and merciful God; and then leave it to him to care for that body and that soul as he pleases. We are his servants: he calls us to labour; and no man will expect his servants to fulfil their task, if they have nothing to eat. God, our heavenly Master, will give us bread for both worlds.

He who prays for "riches," prays for snares, vanity, and vexation of spirit. He who prays for "poverty," prays for what few can bear: and should his prayer be heard, and he become poor, he will most probably steal, and take the name of the Lord in vain.

God's way is ever best. We know not what we ask, nor what we ought to ask, and therefore often ask amiss when we petition for such secular things as belong to the dispensations of God's providence. For things of this kind we have no revealed directory; and when we ask for them, it should be with the deepest submission to the divine will, as God alone knows what is best for us. With respect to the soul, every thing is clearly revealed, so that we may ask and receive, and have a fulness of joy; but as to our bodies, there is much reason to fear that the answer of our petitions would be, in numerous cases, our inevitable destruction. How many prayers does God in mercy shut out!

When a man has any doubts whether he has grieved God's Spirit, and his mind feels troubled, it is much better for him to go immediately to God, and ask forgiveness, than spend any time in finding excuses for his conduct, or labouring to divest it of its seeming obliquity. Restraining or suppressing prayer, in order to find excuses or palliations for infirmities, indiscretions, or improprieties of any kind, which appear to trench on the sacred limits of morality and godliness, may be to a man the worst of evils: humiliation and prayer for mercy and pardon can never be out of its place to any soul of man, who, surrounded with evils, is ever liable to offend.

Prayer is a part of the worship which God expects from his creatures. "Ask," says he, "and you shall receive; seek," says he, "and you shall find: knock," he adds, "and it shall be opened unto you." This is the voice of a Father: now, would any man that had the heart of a parent give his hungry dying child a stone when he asked for bread? would he give him a serpent when he asked for fish? or would he give him a scorpion when he entreated for an egg? Surely, no! And would God, the Father of the spirits of all flesh, do otherwise? His word says, "No:" his Spirit says, "No:" his church says, "No:" and his own eternal and loving nature says, "No." God the Father will, for Christ's sake, for his own name's sake, and for his truth's sake, "give his Holy Spirit to them that ask him." Have not the fathers of our flesh cared for us, laboured for us, fed us, clothed us, instructed us, and defended us? Have they not even risked their lives for us? And what will not our heavenly Father do? Is it not from him that all love, all bounty, all affection, all parental tenderness proceed? And when the streamlets are abundant, what may not be expected from the fountain,—rather from the shoreless, bottomless, inexhaustible ocean of eternal love! He is seeking for those who pray and adore; seeking for an opportunity to do them good; seeking to save them, to pardon, sanctify, and seal them heirs of eternal life.

As God has graciously promised to give salvation to every

soul that comes unto him through his Son, and has put his Spirit into their hearts, inducing them to cry unto him incessantly for it; the goodness of his nature and the promise of his grace bind him to hear the prayers they offer unto him, and to grant them all that salvation which he has led them by his promise and Spirit to request.

He who does not pray is not humble; and an un-humbled searcher after truth never yet found it to the salvation of his soul.

God never inspires a prayer but with the design to answer it. What goodness is there equal to this of God? — to give not only what we ask, and more than we ask, but to reward even prayer itself!

The only return that God requires is, that we ask for more! Who is like God? One reason why we should never more come to a fellow mortal for a favour is, we have received so many already. A strong reason why we should claim the utmost salvation of God is, because we are already so much in debt to his mercy. Now, this is the only way we have of discharging our debts to God; and yet, strange to tell, every such attempt to discharge the debt only serves to increase it. Yet, notwithstanding, the debtor and Creditor are represented as both pleased, both profited, and both happy in each other! Reader! pray to Him, invoke his name; receive the cup; accept the abundance of salvation which He has provided thee, that thou mayest love and serve him with a perfect heart.

It is a modern refinement in theology which teaches that no man can know when God hears and answers his prayers but by an induction of particulars, and by an inference from his promises. And on this ground, how can any man fairly presume that he is heard or answered at all? May not his inductions be no other than the common occurrences of providence? And may not providence be no more than the necessary occurrence of events? And is it not possible that, on this skeptic ground, there is no God to hear or answer? True religion knows nothing of these abominations; it teaches its votaries to pray to God, to expect an answer from him, and to look for the Holy Spirit to bear witness with their spirits that they are the sons and daughters of God.

God has put it in the power of every man to know whether the religion of the Bible be true or false. The promises relative to enjoyments in this life are the grand tests of divine revelation. These must be fulfilled to all them who, with deep repentance and true faith, turn unto the Lord, if the revelation which contains them be of God. Let any man, in this spirit, approach his Maker, and plead the promises that are suited to his case, and he will soon know whether the doctrine be of God. He shall taste, and then see, that the Lord is good, and that the man is blessed who trusts in him. This is what is called "experimental religion," the living operative knowledge that a true believer has that he is passed from death to life; that his sins are forgiven him for Christ's sake, the Spirit himself bearing witness with his spirit that he is a child of God.

Prayer is always heard after one manner or another. No soul can pray in vain that prays as Christ directs. The truth and faithfulness of the Lord Jesus are pledged for its success. Bring Christ's word and Christ's sacrifice with thee, and not one of Heaven's blessings can be denied thee.

One person full of faith and prayer may be the means of drawing down innumerable blessings on his family and acquaintance.

How true is that word, "The energetic faithful prayer of a righteous man availeth much!" Abraham draws near to God by affection and faith, and in the most devout and humble manner makes prayer and supplication; and every petition is answered on the spot. Nor does God cease to promise to show mercy till Abraham ceases to intercede! What encouragement does this hold out to them that fear God to make prayer and intercession for their sinful neighbours and ungodly relatives! Faith in the Lord Jesus endues prayer with a species of omnipotence; whatsoever a man asks of the Father in his name he will do it. Prayer has been termed "the gate of heaven;" but without faith that gate cannot be opened. He who prays as he should, and believes as he ought, shall have the fulness of the blessing of the Gospel of peace.

Prayer not only necessarily supposes the being of a God, (for he that cometh unto God must believe that he is,) but also the providence of God. For why should we pray to him to avert evil, if we do not acknowledge that he exercises a universal providence in the world! Why should we pray to be preserved in and from dangers, if we be not convinced that he has sway everywhere, and that all things serve the purposes of his gracious will? And why should men in every place who pray and make supplication expect to be heard, unless it be an incontrovertible truth that God is omnipotent, and that he can and will so interfere with, and interpose in, the matters that concern them? And should evil be coming against them in direct course, he can divert it, turn it entirely back, so that it shall have no operation near them; or, if he permit it to come on, convert it to their great spiritual advantage, by counter-working the bad effects which it would otherwise produce, and thus, by his providence (in answer to their prayers) working together with his grace, cause all those things which would otherwise be mischievous to work for their present good and future happiness.

"Hear what the unjust judge saith." Our blessed Lord intimates that we should reason thus with ourselves: "If a person of such an infamous character as this judge was, could yield to the pressing and continual solicitations of a poor widow for whom he felt nothing but contempt, how much more ready must God be, who is infinitely good and merciful, and who loves his creatures in the tenderest manner, to give his utmost salvation to all them who diligently seek it!"

"Which cry day and night unto him," &c. This is a genuine characteristic of the true elect, or disciples of Christ. They feel they have neither light, power, nor goodness, but as they receive them from him; and as he is the desire of their soul, they incessantly seek that they may be upheld and saved by him.

The reason which our Lord gives for the success of his chosen is, 1. They cry unto him day and night. 2. He is compassionate toward them. In consequence of the first, they might expect justice even from an unrighteous judge; and, in consequence of the second, they are sure of salvation, because they ask it from that God who is toward them a Father of eternal love and compassion. There was little reason to expect *justice* from the unrighteous judge: 1. Because he was unrighteous; and 2. Because he had no respect for man: no, not even for a poor desolate widow. But there is all the reason under heaven to expect *mercy* from God: 1. Because he is righteous, and he has promised it; and 2. Because he is compassionate toward his creatures; being ever prone to give more than the most enlarged heart can request of Him.

XVI. – PRAISE.

ALL intelligent beings are especially called to praise Him who made them in his love, and sustains them by his beneficence. Man particularly, in all the stages of his being, infancy, youth, manhood, and old age; all human beings have their peculiar interest in the great Father of the spirits of all flesh: he loves man, wheresoever found, of whatsoever colour, in whatever circumstances, and in all the stages of his pilgrimage from his cradle to his grave. Let the lisp of the infant, the shout of the adult, and the sigh of the aged, ascend to the universal Parent, as a gratitude-offering. He guards those who hang upon the breast; controls and directs the headstrong and the giddy; and sustains old age in its infirmities, and sanctifies to it the sufferings that bring on the termination of life. Reader, this is thy God! how great! how good! how merciful! how compassionate! Breathe thy soul up to him; breathe it into him, and let it be preserved in his bosom, till mortality be swallowed up of life, and all that is imperfect be done away! Jesus is thy sacrificial offering: Jesus is thy mediator: he has taken thy humanity, and placed it on the throne! He creates all things new; and faith in his blood will bring thee to his glory! Amen! Hallelujah.

Were I like Mohammed's feigned angel, having to my lot seventy thousand heads, each actuated by as many tongues, and each of these uttering seventy thousand distinct voices, with my present ideas of the divine Being, I should think their eternal vibrations in his praise an almost no-tribute to a God immeasurably good! And yet, where am I going? I have but *one* tongue, and that speaks but very inexpressively; the choicest blessings of heaven are given unto me, and how, how seldom, comparatively, is it used in showing forth his excellency, or acknowledging how deep his debtor I am! O my God! what reason have I to be ashamed and confounded? But thou wilt have mercy. Again: I discover that God can only be viewed in the above light through God made man, that is, manifested in the flesh; and this sets forth the Redeemer in the most amiable and absolutely important point of view. God through him is altogether lovely! But remove this medium, and this my beautiful system is lost in chaos, in the twinkling of an eye. Glory be to God for Christ! Amen.

God is to receive praise in reference to that attribute which he has exhibited most in the defence or salvation of his followers. Sometimes he manifests his power; sometimes his mercy; sometimes his wisdom, his long-suffering, his fatherly care, his good providence, his holiness, his justice, his truth, &c. Whatever attribute or perfection he exhibits most, that should be the chief subject of his children's praise. One wants teaching, prays for it, and is deeply instructed; he will naturally celebrate the wisdom of God. Another feels himself beset with the most powerful adversaries, with the weakest of whom he is not able to cope; he cries to the almighty God for strength; he is heard, and strengthened with strength in his soul: he therefore will naturally magnify the all-conquering power of the Lord: another feels himself lost—condemned—on the brink of hell; he calls for mercy; is heard, and saved: mercy, therefore, will be the chief subject of his praise, and the burden of his song.

The deliverance of mariners from imminent danger, and in a way which clearly shows the divine interposition, demands not only gratitude of heart, and the tongue of praise, at the end of the storm; but when they come to shore, they should publicly acknowledge it in the congregation of God's people. I have been often pleased, when in seaport towns, to see and hear notes sent to the minister from pious sailors, returning thanks to the Almighty for preservation from shipwreck; and, in general, from the dangers of the sea; and for bringing them back in safety to their own port. Thus "they exalt the Lord in the congregation, and praise him in the assembly of the elders."

Though I never hail a personal quarrel with the singers in any place, yet I have never known one case, where there was a choir of singers, that they did not make disturbance in the societies. And it would be much better in every case, and in every respect, to employ a precentor, or a person to raise the tunes; and then the congregation would learn to sing, the purpose of singing would be accomplished, every mouth would confess to God, and a horrible evil would be prevented—the bringing together in the house of God, and making them the almost only instruments of celebrating his praises, such a company of gay, airy, giddy, and ungodly men and women as are generally grouped in such choirs; for voice and skill must be had, let decency of behaviour and morality be where they will. Every thing must be sacrificed to a good voice, in order to make the choir complete and respectable. Many scandals have been brought into the church of God by choirs and their accompaniments. Why do not the Methodist preachers lay this to heart?

The singing which is recommended, Col. iii, 16, is widely different from what is commonly used in most Christian congregations; a congeries of unmeaning sounds, associated to bundles of nonsensical and often ridiculous repetitions, which at once both deprave and disgrace the church of Christ. Melody, which is allowed to be the most proper for devotional music, is now sacrificed to an exuberant harmony, which requires not only many different kinds of voices, but different musical instruments to support it. And by these preposterous means the simplicity of the Christian worship is destroyed, and all edification totally prevented. And this kind of singing is amply proved to be very injurious to the personal piety of those employed in it: even of those who enter with a considerable share of humility and Christian meekness, how few continue to sing with grace in their hearts unto the Lord!

It does appear that singing psalms or spiritual hymns was one thing that was implied in what is termed *prophesying*, in the Old Testament, as is evident from I Sam. x, 5, 6, 10, &c. And when this came through an immediate afflatus, or inspiration of God, there is no doubt that it was exceedingly edifying; and must have served greatly to improve and excite the devotional spirit of all that were present. But I rather suppose that their singing consisted in solemn, well measured recitative, than in the jingling and often foolish sounds which we use when a single monosyllable is sometimes shivered into a multitude of semiquavers! Here it may not be improper to remark, that the spirit and the understanding are seldom united in our congregational singing. Those whose hearts are right with God have generally no skill in music; and those who are well skilled in music have seldom a devotional spirit, but are generally proud, self-willed, contentious, and arrogant. Do not these persons entirely overrate themselves? Of all the liberal arts, surely music is the least useful, however ornamental it may be. And should any thing be esteemed in the church of God but in proportion to its utility. A good singer among the people of God, who has not the life of God in his soul, is *vox et praeterea nihil*, as Heliogabalus said of the nightingale's brains, on which he desired to sup, "He is nothing but a sound." Some of those persons, I mean those who sing with the understanding without the spirit, suppose themselves of great consequence in the church of Christ; and they find foolish superficial people whom they persuade to be of their own mind, and soon raise parties and contentions, if they have not every thing their own way; and that way is generally as absurd as it is unscriptural and contrary to the spirit and simplicity of the Gospel.

It is very likely that the singing of the Jews was only a kind of recitative or chanting, such as we still find in the synagogues. It does not appear that God had especially appointed these singers, much less any musical instruments, the silver trumpets excepted, to be employed in his service. Musical instruments in the house of God are, at least, under the Gospel, repugnant to the spirit of Christianity, and tend not a little to corrupt the worship of God. Those who are fond of music in the theatre are fond of it in the house of God, when they go thither; and some, professing Christianity, set up such a spurious worship, in order to draw people to hear the Gospel. This is doing evil, that good may come of it; and, by this means, light and trifling people are introduced into the church of Christ; and, when in, are generally very troublesome, hard to be pleased, and difficult to be saved.

Did ever God ordain instruments of music to be used in his worship? Can they be used in Christian assemblies according to the spirit of Christianity? Has Jesus Christ, or his apostles, ever commanded or sanctioned the use of them? Were they ever used anywhere in the apostolic church? Does the use of them at present, in Christian congregations, ever increase the spirit of devotion? Does it ever appear that hands of musicians, either in their collective or individual capacity, are more spiritual, or as spiritual, as the other parts of the church of Christ? Is there more pride, self-will, stubbornness, insubordination, lightness, and frivolity, among such persons, than among the other professors of Christianity found in the same religious society? Is it ever remarked or known that musicians, in the house of God, have ever attained to any depth of piety, or superior soundness of understanding, in the things of God? Is it ever found that those churches and Christian societies which have and use instruments of music in divine worship, are more holy, or as holy, as those societies which do not use them? And is it always found that the ministers who affect and recommend them to be used in the worship of almighty God, are the most spiritual men, and the most spiritual and useful preachers? Can mere sounds, no matter how melodious, where no word or sentiment is or can be uttered, be considered as giving praise to God? Is it possible that pipes or strings of any kind can give God praise? Can God be pleased with sounds which are emitted by no sentient being, and have in themselves no meaning? If these questions cannot be answered in the affirmative, then is not the introduction of such instruments into the worship of God antichristian, calculated to debase and ultimately ruin the spirit and influences of the Gospel of Jesus Christ? And should not all who wish well to the spread and establishment of pure and undefiled religion lift up their hand, their influence, and their voice against them? The argument from their use in the Jewish service is futile in the extreme, when applied to Christianity.

In a representative system of religion, such as the Jewish, there must have been much outside work, all emblematical of better things; no proof that such things should be continued under the Gospel dispensation, where outsides have disappeared, shadows flown away, and the substance alone is presented to the hearts of mankind. He must be ill off for proofs in favour of instrumental music in the church of Christ, who has recourse to practices under the Jewish ritual!

Moses had not appointed any musical instruments to be

used in the divine worship; there was nothing of the kind under the first tabernacle. The trumpets, or horns, then used, were not for song, nor for praise, but, as we use bells, to give notice to the congregation of what they were called to perform, &c. But David did certainly introduce many instruments of music into God's worship; for which, we have already seen, he was solemnly reproved by the Prophet Amos, chap. vi, 1-6. Here, however, the author of this book states he had the commandment of the Prophet Nathan, and Gad, the king's seer; and this is stated to have been the commandment of the Lord by his prophets. But the Syriac and Arabic give this a different turn: "Hezekiah appointed the Levites in the house of the Lord, with instruments of music, and the sound of harps, and with the hymns of David, and the hymns of Gad, the king's prophet; for David sang the praises of the Lord his God, as from the mouth of the prophets." It was by the hand or commandment of the Lord and his prophets, that the Levites should praise the Lord; for so the Hebrew text may be understood; and it was by the order of David that so many instruments of music should be introduced into the divine service. But were it even evident, which it is not, either from this or any other place in the sacred writings, that instruments of music were prescribed by divine authority under the law, could this he adduced with any semblance of reason that they ought to be used in Christian worship? No, the whole spirit, soul, and genius of the Christian religion are against this; and those who know the church of God best, and what constitutes its genuine spiritual state, know that these things have been introduced as a substitute for the life and power of religion, and that where they prevail most there is least of the power of Christianity. Away with such portentous baubles from the worship of that infinite Spirit who requires his followers to worship him in spirit and in truth! for to no such worship are those instruments friendly.

I have no doubt but the gross perversion of the simplicity of Christian worship, by the introduction of various instruments of music into churches and chapels, if not a species of idolatry, will at least rank with will-worship and superstitious rites and ceremonies. Where the Spirit and unction of God do not prevail in Christian assemblies, priests and people being destitute of both, their place, by general consent, is to be supplied by imposing ceremonies, noise, and show.

The Church of Rome, in every country where it either prevails or exists, has so blended a pretended Christian devotion with heathenish and Jewish rites and ceremonies, two parts of which are borrowed from pagan Rome, the third from the Jewish ritual ill understood, and grossly misrepresented, and the fourth part from other corruptions of the Christian system. Nor is the Protestant church yet fully freed from a variety of matters in public worship which savours little of that simplicity and spirituality which should ever designate the worship of that infinitely pure Spirit who cannot be pleased with any thing incorporated with his worship that has not been prescribed by himself, and has not a direct tendency to lead the heart from earth and sensual things to heaven, and to that holiness without which none shall see the Lord. The singing, as it is practiced in several places, and the heathenish accompaniments of organs and musical instruments of various sorts, are as contrary to the simplicity of the Gospel, and the spirituality of that worship which God requires, as darkness is contrary to light. And if these abuses are not corrected, I believe the time is not far distant when singing will cease to be a part of the divine worship. It is now, in many places, such as cannot be said to be any part of that worship which is in spirit and according to truth. May God mend it!

Charles Wesley, A.M., was the best Christian poet in reference to hymnology that has flourished in either ancient or modern times. The hymns used in the religious services of the Methodists were composed principally by him; and such a collection exists not among any other people. Most collections among other sects of Christians are indebted to his compositions for some of their principal excellences.

XVII. – THE CHRISTIAN CHURCH.

THE word *church* simply means an "assembly" or "congregation," and must have some other word joined to it to determine its nature: namely, the "church of God;" the congregation collected by God, and devoted to his service: the "church of Christ;" the whole company of Christians wheresoever found; because, by the preaching of the Gospel, they are called out of the spirit and maxims of the world, to live according to the precepts of the Christian religion. This is sometimes called the "catholic" or "universal" church, because constituted of all the professors of Christianity in the world, to whatsoever sects or parties they may belong; and hence the absurdity of applying the term "catholic," which signifies "universal," to that very small portion of it, the Church of Rome. In primitive times, before Christians had any stated buildings, they worshipped in private houses; the people that had been converted to God meeting together in some one dwelling house of a fellow convert more convenient and capacious than the rest; hence "the church that was in the house of Aquila and Priscilla," Rom. xvi, 3, 5; and 1 Cor. xvi, 19; and "the church that was in the house of Nymphas," Col. iv, 15. Now, as these houses were dedicated to the worship of God, each was termed *kuriou oikos*, the "house of the Lord;" which word, in process of time, became contracted into *kurioik,* and *kuriake;* and hence the *kirk* of our northern neighbours, and *kirik,* of our Saxon ancestors, from which, by corruption, changing the hard Saxon C into *ch,* we have made the word "church." This term, though it be generally used to signify the people worshipping in a particular place, yet by a metonymy, the container being put for the contained, we apply, as it was originally, to the building which contains the worshipping people.

The church of Christ was considered an enclosure; a field, or vineyard, well hedged or walled. Those who were not members of it were considered without; that is, not under that especial protection and defence which the true followers of Christ had. This has been since called, "the pale of the church," from *palus,* a stake; or, as Dr. Johnson defines it, "A narrow piece of wood, joined above and below to a rail, to enclose grounds." As to be a Christian was essential to the salvation of the soul, so to be in the church of Christ was essential to the being a Christian; therefore it was concluded "there was no salvation out of the pale of the church." Now this is true in all places where the doctrines of Christianity are preached: but when one description of people professing Christianity, with their own peculiar mode of worship and creed, arrogate to themselves, exclusive of all others, the title of " THE church;" and then, on the ground of a maxim which is true in itself, but falsely understood and applied by them, assert that, as they are THE church, and there is no church beside, then you must be one of them, believe as they believe, and worship as they worship, or you will be infallibly damned;—I say, when this is asserted, every man who feels he has an immortal spirit is called on to examine the pretensions of such spiritual monopolists. Now as the church of Christ is formed on the foundation of the prophets and apostles, Jesus Christ being the chief corner stone, the doctrines of this Christian church must be sought for in the sacred Scriptures. As to fathers, councils, and human authorities of all kinds, they are, in this question, lighter than vanity; the book of God alone must decide. The church which has been so hasty to condemn all others, and, by its own *soi-disant* or self-constituted authority, to make itself the deter-miner of the fates of men, dealing out the mansions of glory to its partisans, and the abodes of endless misery to all those who are out of its antichristian and inhuman pale; this church, I say, has been brought to this standard, and proved by the Scriptures to be fallen from the faith of God's elect, and to be most awfully and dangerously corrupt; and to be within its pale, of all others professing Christianity, would be the most likely means of endangering the final salvation of the soul. Yet even in it many sincere and upright persons may be found, who, in spirit and practice, belong to the true church of Christ. Such persons are to be found of all religious persuasions, and in all sorts of Christian societies.

Of this glorious church every Christian soul is an epitome: for as God dwells in the church at large, so he dwells in every believer in particular: each is a habitation of God through the Spirit. In vain are all pretensions among sects and parties to the privilege of the church of Christ, if they have not the doctrine and life of Christ. Traditions and legends are not apostolic doctrines, and showy ceremonies are not the life of God in the soul of man.

Religion has no need of human ornaments or trappings; it shines by its own light, and is refulgent with its own glory. Where it is not in life and power, men have endeavoured to produce a specious image, dressed and ornamented with their own hands. Into this, God never breathed; therefore, it can do no good to man, and only imposes on the ignorant and credulous by a vain show of lifeless pomp and splendour. This phantom, called "true religion," and "the church," by its votaries, is in heaven denominated "vain superstition;" the speechless symbol of departed piety.

The government of the church of Christ is widely different from secular governments. It is founded in humility and brotherly love: it is derived from Christ, the great head of the church, and is ever conducted by his maxims and Spirit. When political matters are brought into the church of Christ, both are ruined. The church has more than once ruined the state; the state has often corrupted the church: it is certainly for the interests of both to be kept separate. This has already been abundantly exemplified in both cases, and will continue to be, over the whole world, wherever the church and state are united in secular matters.

"The chief priests were sore displeased," or, "were incensed." Incensed at what? At the purification of the profane temple! This was a work they should have done themselves, but for which they had neither grace nor influence; and their pride and jealousy will not suffer them to permit others to do it. Strange as it may appear, the priesthood itself, in all corrupt times, has ever been the most forward to prevent a reform in the church. Was it because they were conscious that a reformer would find them no better than money-changers in, and profaners of, the house of God, and that they and their system must be overturned, if the true worship of God were restored? Let him who is concerned answer this to his conscience.

"No secular arm, no human prudence, no earthly policy, in suits at law, shall ever be used for the founding, extension, and preservation of my church." But the spirit of the world says, "These are all means to which we must have recourse; otherwise the cause of God may be ruined." Satan, thou liest!

How strange it is that people professing Christianity can suppose, that, with a worldly spirit, worldly companions, and their lives governed by worldly maxims, they can be in the favour of God, or ever get to the kingdom of heaven! When the world gets into the church, the church becomes a painted sepulchre; its spiritual vitality becomes extinct.

I believe God never intended that his church should have the civil government of the world. His church, like its Founder and Head, will never be a ruler and divider among men. The men who, under pretence of superior sanctity, affect this, are not of God: the truth of God is not in them; they are puffed up with pride, and fall into the condemnation of the devil. "Woe unto the inhabiters of the earth," when the church takes the civil government of the world into its hands! Were it possible that God should trust religious people with civil government, anarchy would soon ensue; for every professed believer in Christ would consider himself on a par with any other and every other believer: the right to rule and the necessity to obey would be immediately lost, and every man would do what was right in his own eyes; for, where the grace of God makes all equal, who can presume to say, "I have divine authority to govern my fellows?" The Church of Rome has claimed this right; and the pope, in consequence, became a secular prince: but the nations of the world have seen the vanity and iniquity of the claim, and refused allegiance. Those whom it did govern, with force and cruelty did it rule them; and the odious yoke is now universally cast off. Certain enthusiasts and hypocrites, not of that church, have also attempted to set up a fifth monarchy, a civil government by the saints! — and diabolic saints they were. To such pretenders God gives neither countenance nor support. The secular and spiritual government God will ever keep distinct: and the church shall have no power but that of doing good; and this only in proportion to its holiness, heavenly- mindedness, and piety to God.

XVIII. – BAPTISM.

IN what form baptism was originally administered, has been deemed a subject worthy of serious dispute. Were the people dipped or sprinkled? for it is certain Βαπτω and Βαπτιζω mean both. "They were all dipped," say some. Can any man suppose that it was possible for John to dip all the inhabitants of Jerusalem and Judea, and of all the country round about the Jordan? Were both men and women dipped? for certainly both came to his baptism. This could never have comported either with safety or with decency. Were they dipped in their clothes? This would have endangered their lives, if they had not with them change of raiment: And as such a baptism as John's (however administered) was, in several respects, a new thing in Judea, it is not at all likely that the people would come thus provided. But suppose these were dipped, which I think it would be impossible to prove, does it follow that in all regions of the world men and women must be dipped, in order to be evangelically baptized? In the eastern countries bathings were frequent, because of the heat of the climate, it being there so necessary to cleanliness and health; but could our climate, or a more northerly one, admit of this with safety, for at least three fourths of the year? We may rest assured that it could not. And may we not presume that if John had opened his commission in the north of Great Britain, for many months of the year, he would have dipped neither man nor woman, unless he could have procured a tepid bath? Those who are dipped or immersed in water, in the name of the holy Trinity, I believe to be evangelically baptized: those who are washed or sprinkled with water, in the name of the Father, and of the Son, and of the Holy Ghost, I believe to be equally so; and the repetition of such a baptism I believe to be profane. Others have a right to believe the contrary if they see good. After all, it is the thing signified, and not the mode, which is the essential part of the sacrament.

Though "little children," they were capable of receiving Christ's blessing. If Christ embraced them, why should not his church embrace them? Why not dedicate them to God by baptism?—whether that be performed by sprinkling, washing, or immersion; for we need not dispute about the mode: on this point let every one be fully persuaded in his own mind. I confess it appears to me grossly heathenish and barbarous, to see parents who profess to believe in that Christ who loves children, and among them those whose creed does not prevent them from using infant baptism, depriving their children of an ordinance by which no soul can prove that they cannot be profited, and through an unaccountable bigotry or carelessness withholding from them the privilege of even a nominal dedication to God; and yet these very persons are ready enough to fly for a minister to baptize their child when they suppose it to be at the point of death! It would be no crime to pray that such persons should never have the privilege of hearing "My father!" or "My mother!" from the lips of their own child.

It is easy to carry things to extremes on the right hand and on the left. In this controversy there has been much asperity on all sides. It is high time this were ended. To say that water baptism is nothing, because a baptism of the Spirit is promised, is not correct. Baptism, however administered, is a most important rite in the church of Christ. To say that sprinkling or aspersion is no Gospel baptism is as incorrect as to say immersion is none. Such assertions are as unchristian as they are uncharitable; and should be carefully avoided by all those who wish to promote the great design of the Gospel, glory to God, and peace and good will among men. Lastly, to assert that infant baptism is unscriptural, is as rash and reprehensible as any of the rest. Myriads of conscientious people choose to dedicate their infants to God by public baptism. They are in the right!—and, by acting thus, follow the general practice of the

Jewish and Christian church—a practice from which it is as needless as it is dangerous to depart.

Baptism is a standing proof of the divine authenticity of the Christian religion, and a seal of the truth of the doctrine of justification by faith, through the blood of the covenant.

To the baptism of water a man was admitted when he became a proselyte to the Jewish religion; and in this baptism he promised in the most solemn manner to renounce idolatry, to take the God of Israel for his God, and to have his life conformed to the precepts of the divine law. But the water which was used on the occasion was only an emblem of the Holy Ghost. The soul was considered as in a state of defilement, because of past sin; now, as by that water the body was washed, cleansed, and refreshed, so by the influences of the Holy Spirit the soul was to be purified from its defilement, and strengthened to walk in the way of truth and holiness.

When John came baptizing with water, he gave the Jews the plainest intimations that this would not suffice; that it was only typical of that baptism of the Holy Ghost, under the similitude of fire, which they must all receive from Jesus Christ. Therefore our Lord asserts that a man must be born of water and the Holy Spirit, that is, of the Holy Ghost, which, represented under the similitude of water, cleanses, refreshes, and purifies the soul. Reader, hast thou never had any other baptism than that of water? If thou hast not had any other, take Jesus Christ's word for it, thou canst not in thy present state enter into the kingdom of God. I would not say to thee merely, "Read what it is to be born of the Spirit;" but "pray, O pray to God incessantly till he give thee to feel what is implied in it!" Remember it is Jesus only who baptizes with the Holy Ghost.

XIX. – THE LORD'S SUPPER.

"DO THIS in remembrance of ME," is a command by which our blessed Lord has put both the affection and piety of his disciples to the test. If they love him they will keep his commandments, for, to them that love, his commandments are not grievous. It is a peculiar excellence of the Gospel economy, that all the duties it enjoins become the highest privileges to those that obey.

Among the ordinances prescribed by the Gospel, that commonly called the "sacrament of the Lord's supper" has ever held a distinguished place; and the church of Christ, in all ages, has represented the due religious celebration of it as a duty incumbent on every soul that professed faith in Jesus Christ, and sought for salvation through his blood alone. Hence, it was ever held in the highest estimation and reverence, and the great High Priest of his church has shown, by more than ordinary influences of his blessed Spirit on the souls of the faithful, that they had not mistaken his meaning, nor believed in vain, while, by eating of that bread, and drinking of that cup, they endeavoured to show forth his death, and realize the benefits to be derived from it.

If any respect should be paid to the primitive institution in the celebration of this divine ordinance, then unleavened; unyeasted bread should be used. In every sign or type, the thing signifying or pointing out that which is beyond itself should either have certain properties, or be accompanied with certain circumstances as impressive as possible of the things signified. Bread, simply considered in itself, may be an emblem apt enough of the body of our Lord Jesus, which was given for us; but the design of God was evidently that it should not only point out this, but also the disposition required in those who should celebrate both the antitype and the type; and this the apostle explains to be sincerity and truth, the reverse of malice and wickedness. The very taste of the bread was instructive: it pointed out to every communicant that he who came to the table of God with malice or ill will against any soul of man, or with wickedness, a profligate or sinful life, might expect to eat and drink judgment to himself; as not discerning that the Lord's body was sacrificed for this very purpose, that all sin might be destroyed.

Blessing and touching the bread are merely popish ceremonies, unauthorized either by Scripture or the practice of the pure church of God; necessary of course to them who pretend to transmute, by a kind of spiritual incantation, the bread and wine into the real body and blood of Jesus Christ — a measure, the grossest in folly, and most stupid in nonsense, to which God in judgment ever abandoned the fallen spirit of man.

The breaking of the bread I consider highly necessary to the proper performance of this solemn and significant ceremony, because this act was designed by our Lord to shadow forth the wounding, piercing, and breaking of his body upon the cross; and all this was essentially necessary to the making a full atonement for the sin of the world; so it is of vast importance that this apparently little circumstance, the breaking of the bread, should be carefully attended to, that the godly communicant may have every necessary assistance to enable him to discern the Lord's body while engaged in the most important and divine of all God's ordinances.

I have learned, with extreme regret, that in many churches and chapels a vile compound, wickedly denominated wine, not the offspring of the vine, but of the alder, gooseberry, or currant tree, and not unfrequently the issue of the sweepings of a grocer's shop, is substituted for wine, in the sacrament of the Lord's supper. That this is a most wicked and awful perversion of our Lord's ordinance, needs, I am persuaded, no proof.

As the passover was to be celebrated annually, to keep the original transaction in memory, and to show forth the true paschal Lamb, the Lamb of God that taketh away the sin of the world, so after the once offering of Christ our passover on the cross, he himself ordained that bread and wine should be used to keep "that, his precious death, in remembrance, until his coming again." Now, as the paschal lamb, annually sacrificed, brought to the people's remembrance the wonderful deliverance of their fathers from the Egyptian bondage and tyranny; so the bread and wine, consecrated and received according to our Saviour Jesus Christ's holy institution, was designed by himself to keep up a continual remembrance and lively representation of the great atonement made by his death upon the cross. The doing this is not intended merely to keep up a recollection of Christ, as a kind and benevolent friend, which is the utmost some allow; but to keep in remembrance his body broken for us, and his blood poured out for us. For as the way to the holiest was ever through his blood, and as no man can ever come to the Father but by him, and none can come profitably who have not faith in his blood; it was necessary that this great help to believing should be frequently furnished; as, in all succeeding ages, there would be sinners to be saved, and saints to be confirmed and established in their holy faith. Those, therefore, who reject the Lord's supper sin against their own mercies, and treat their Maker with the basest ingratitude.

Let no man deceive his own soul by imagining he can still have all the benefits of Christ's death, and yet have nothing to do with the sacrament. It is a command of the living God, founded on the same authority as "Thou shalt do no murder;" none, therefore, can disobey it and be guiltless. Again: let no man impose on himself by the supposition that he can enjoy this supper spiritually without using what too many impiously call the "carnal ordinance;" that is, without eating bread and drinking wine in remembrance of the death of Christ. Is not this a delusion? What says the sovereign will of God? "DO THIS" What is THIS? Why, "Take bread, break, and eat it. Take the cup and drink ye all of it." THIS, and only this, is fulfilling the will of God. Therefore the eating of the sacramental bread, and the drinking of the consecrated wine, are essential to the religious performance of our Lord's command.

Every institution has its letter as well as its spirit, as every word must refer to something of which it is the sign or signification. The Gospel has both its letter and its spirit; and multitudes of professing Christians, by resting in the letter, receive not the life which it is calculated to impart. Water, in baptism, is the letter that points out the purification of the soul; they who rest in the letter are without this purification, and, dying in that state, they die eternally. Bread and wine, in the sacrament of the Lord's supper, are the letter; the atoning efficacy of the death of Jesus, and the grace communicated by this to the soul of a believer, are the spirit. Multitudes rest in this letter, simply receiving these symbols without reference to the atonement or to their guilt; and thus lose the benefit of the atonement and the salvation of their souls.

Improper communicants are in a very awful state. These may be divided into two classes: the inconsiderate and the ungodly. Of the former class, there are multitudes among the different societies of Christians. They know not the Lord, and discern not the operation of his hands: hence they go to the Lord's table from a mere sense of duty or propriety, without considering what the sacred elements represent, and without feeling any hunger after the bread that endureth unto eternal life. These really profane the ordinance, either by not devoting it to the end of its institution, or by perverting that end. Among these may probably be ranked those who believe not in the vicarious sufferings and death of the blessed Redeemer. They also receive the Lord's supper; but they do it as a testimony, of respect and, friendly remembrance: these do not discern the Lord's body, do not see that this bread represents his body which was broken for them, and his blood, which was spilled for the remission of sins.

Of the ungodly, as comprehending transgressors of all descriptions, little need be said in proof of their unworthiness. Such, coming to the table of the Lord, eat and drink their own condemnation; as they profess by this religious act to acknowledge the virtue of that blood which cleanseth from all unrighteousness, while themselves are slaves of sin. None such should ever be permitted to approach the table of the Lord; if they, through that gross ignorance which is the closely wedded companion of profligacy, are intent on their own destruction, let the ministers of God see that the ordinance be not profaned by the admission of such disreputable and iniquitous guests. For can it be expected that God will manifest his approbation when the pale of his sanctuary is broken down; and the beasts of the forest introduced into the Holy of Holies!

It may be here asked, "Who then should approach this awful ordinance?" I answer, 1. Every believer in Christ Jesus who is saved from his sins has a right to come. Such are of the family of God; and this bread belongs to the children. On this there can be but one opinion. 2. Every genuine penitent is invited to come, and consequently has a right, because he needs the atoning blood; and by this ordinance, the blood shed for the remission of sins is expressly represented. "But I am not worthy." And who is? There is not a saint upon earth, nor an archangel in heaven, who is worthy to sit down at the table of the Lord. None are excluded but the impenitent, the transgressors, and the profane. Believers, however weak, have a right to come; and the strongest in faith need the grace of this ordinance. Penitents should come, as all the promises of pardon mentioned in the Bible are made to such; and he that is athirst may take of the water of life freely. None is worthy of the entertainment, though all these will partake of it worthily; but it is freely provided by Him who is the Lamb of God, who was slain for us, and is worthy to receive glory and majesty, dominion and power, for ever and ever.

Every soul who wishes not to abjure his right to the benefits of Christ's passion and death, should make it a point with God and his conscience to partake of this ordinance, if not twelve times, at least four or six times in the year; and continue thus to show forth the Lord's death till he come.

The accredited minister, the man who was set apart according to the custom of his community, was the only person who was ever conceived to have a right to administer this ordinance; as he alone could judge of the persons who were proper to be admitted. Where private persons have assumed this important function, they have brought the ordinance of God into contempt; and they, and their deluded partisans, have generally ended in confusion and apostasy.

Not only the sacred elements should be of the purest and best quality, but also the holy vessels, of whatever metal, perfectly clean, and decently arranged on the table. The communicants, in receiving the bread and wine, should not be hurried, so as to endanger their dropping the one or spilling the other; as accidents of this kind have been of dreadful consequence to some weak minds. No communicant should receive with a glove on: this is indecent, not to say irreverent. Perhaps the best way of receiving the bread is, to open the hand, and let the minister lay it upon the palm, whence it may be taken by the communicant with readiness and ease.

In the apparatus of this feast, a contribution for the support of the poor should never be neglected. This was a custom religiously observed from the very remotest antiquity of the Christian era.

A few reasons for frequenting the table of the Lord. and profiting by this ordinance: —

1. Jesus Christ has commanded his disciples to do this in remembrance of him; and, were there no other reason, this certainly must be deemed sufficient by all those who respect his authority as their Teacher and Judge.

2. As the oft-repeated sacrifices in the Jewish church, and particularly the passover, were intended to point out the Son of God till he came; so, it appears, our blessed Lord designed that the eucharist should be a principal means of keeping in remembrance his passion and death; and thus show forth Him who *has died* for our offences, as the others did Him who in the fulness of time *should die*.

3. As it is the duty of every Christian to receive the holy eucharist, so it is the duty of every Christian minister to see that the people of God neither neglect nor lose sight of this ordinance.

4. It is a standing and inexpugnable proof of the authenticity of the Christian religion.

In this place a question of very great importance should be considered: is the ungodliness of the minister any prejudice to the ordinance itself, or to the devout communicant? I answer, 1. None who is ungodly should ever be permitted to minister in holy things, on any pretence whatever; and in this ordinance, in particular, no unhallowed hand should ever be seen. 2. As the benefit to be derived from the eucharist depends entirely on the presence and blessing of God, it cannot be reasonably expected that he will work through the instrumentality of the profligate or the profane. Many have idled away their time in endeavouring to prove "that the ungodliness of the minister is no prejudice to the worthy communicant:" but God has disproved this by ten thousand instances, in which he has, in a general way, withheld his divine influence, because of the wickedness or worthlessness of him who ministered, whether bishop, priest, minister, or preacher.

Profanity and sin will certainly prevent the divine Spirit from realizing the sign in the souls of worthless ministers and sinful communicants; but the want of episcopal ordination in the person, or consecration in the place, can never prevent Him who is not confined to temples made by hands, and who sends by whom he will send, from pouring out his Spirit upon those who call faithfully upon his name, and who go to meet him in his appointed ways.

I should prefer the sacrament to be administered in our form. We must yield a little in innocent matters to inveterate prejudice, but keep as near to our plan as you possibly can. Methodism in Scotland was ruined by building it by a Presbyterian model. Keep this in your eye. You should by all means give the sacrament to all united with you: do not send them elsewhere to receive it. May the holy Trinity have you in his continual keeping!

Scarcely any thing is more unbecoming than to see the majority of communicants, as soon as they have received, posting out of the church or chapel; so that at the conclusion of the ordinance very few are found to join together in a general thanksgiving to God for the benefits conferred by the passion and death of Christ by means of this blessed ordinance.

XX. – HUSBAND AND WIFE.

"A MAN shall leave," wholly give up, "both father and mother;" the matrimonial union being more intimate and binding than even paternal or filial affection: and shall be closely united; shall be firmly cemented to his wife: a beautiful metaphor, which most forcibly intimates that nothing but death can separate them: as a well glued board will break sooner in the whole wood than in the glued joint.

"And they twain shall be one flesh:" not only meaning that they should be considered as one body, but also as two souls in one body, with a complete union of interests, and an indissoluble partnership of life and fortune, comfort and support, desires and inclinations, joys and sorrows.

Here is a grand rule, according to which every husband is called to act: "Love your wife as Christ loved the church." But how did Christ love the church? "He gave himself for it:" he laid down his life for it. So then husbands should, if necessary, lay down their lives for their wives: and there is more implied in the words than mere protection and support; for, as Christ gave himself for the church to save it, so husbands should, by all means in their power, labour to promote the salvation of their wives and their constant edification in righteousness. Thus we find that the authority of the man over the woman is founded on his love to her, and this love must be such as to lead him to risk his life for her. As the care of the family devolves on the wife, and the children must owe the chief direction of their minds and formation of their manners to the mother, she has need of all the assistance and support which her husband can give her; and if she performs her duty well, she deserves the utmost of his love and affection.

The husband is to love his wife, the wife to obey and venerate her husband; love and protection on the one hand, affectionate submission and fidelity on the other. The husband should provide for his wife without encouraging profuseness; watch over her conduct without giving her vexation; keep her in subjection without making her a slave; love her without jealousy; oblige her without flattery; honour her without making her proud; and be hers entirely, without becoming either her footman or her slave. In short, they have equal rights and equal claims; but superior strength gives the man dominion; affection and subjection entitle the woman to love and protection. Without the woman, man is but half a human being; in union with the man, the woman finds her safety and perfection.

How few wives feel it their duty to pray to God to give them grace to behave as wives! How few husbands pray for the grace suited to their situation that they may be able to fulfil its duties! The like may be said of children, parents, servants, and masters. As every situation in life has its peculiar duties, trims, &c., so to every situation there is peculiar grace appointed. No man can fulfil the duties of any station without the grace suited to that station. The grace suited to him, as a member of society in general, will not be sufficient for him as a husband, father, or master. Many proper marriages become unhappy in the end, because the parties have not earnestly besought God for the grace necessary for them as husbands and wives. This is the origin of family broils in general; and a proper attention to the apostle's advice would prevent them all.

Those who imagine they can encounter the cares of life with just the same measure of grace which was sufficient for them in a single state, will find themselves greatly mistaken. For to every situation in life peculiar and suitable grace is requisite. Most new-married people, even among those who are religious, think nothing of this. Hence it is often found that the new-married pair soon decline in the divine life; and, instead of getting forward, either go halting in the heavenly road, or turn back to the world.

I am perfectly of Solomon's opinion, that "he who findeth a wife findeth a good thing." Even in any circumstances, matrimony is better than celibacy; and hence I execrate the addition made here by the Targum, and some other would-be menders of the word of God, who have added "good;" a truth, indeed, that a child could have told; a truism and an *actum agere* very unworthy of the wisdom of Solomon; for most assuredly he that finds a good thing finds a good thing. Please to enter this beautiful criticism in your *adversaria*.

God pronounces the state of celibacy to be a bad state, or, if the reader please, "not a good one:" "And the Lord God said, It is not good for man to be alone." This is God's judgment. Councils, and fathers, and doctors, and synods have given a different judgment; but on such a subject they are worthy of no attention. The word of God abideth for ever. God made the woman *for* the man, and thus he has shown us that every son of Adam should be united to a daughter of Eve to the end of the world. God made the woman *out* of the man, to intimate that the closest union and the most affectionate attachment should subsist in the matrimonial connection; so that the man should ever consider and treat the woman as a part of himself; and as no one ever hated his own flesh, but nourishes and supports it, so should a man deal with his wife; and on the other hand, the woman should consider that the man was not made for her, but that she was made for the man, and derived, under God, her being from him; therefore the wife should see that she reverence her husband. Gen. ii, 23, 24, contain the very words of the marriage ceremony: "This is flesh of my flesh, and bone of my bone: therefore shall a man leave his father and his mother, and shall cleave unto his wife, and they two shall be one flesh." How happy must such a state be where God's institution is properly regarded, when the parties are married, as the apostle expresses it, "in the Lord;" when each, by acts of the tenderest kindness, lives only to prevent the wishes, and contribute in every possible way to the comfort and happiness of the other! Marriage might still be what it was in its original institution, pure and suitable; and in its first exercise, affectionate and happy: but how few such marriages are there to be found! Passion, turbulent and irregular, not religion; custom founded by these irregularities, not reason; worldly prospects, originating and ending in selfishness and earthly affections, not in spiritual ends, are the grand producing causes of the great majority of matrimonial alliances. How then can such turbid and bitter fountains send forth pure and sweet waters?

Unfitness of minds, more than circumstances, is what in general mars the marriage union. Where minds are suited, means of happiness and contentment are ever within reach.

I scruple not to say that those who marry for money are committing adultery as long as they live.

A conversation on board ship between Leith and Lerwick. — "How is it," says one, "that the most simple and unadorned rings are used in the matrimonial ceremony?" — "Because, I believe, the canon law requires that no other should be used." — A. C. "I am not aware, that there is any law on this part of the subject. The law states that a metal ring shall be used, and not one of leather, straw, thread, &c.; and the reason to me appears to be this: — The ring itself points out the duration of the union; it is without end in reference to the natural lives of the parties. Metal is less liable to destruction than flax, leather, straw, &c. Gold is generally preferred, not only because it is the most precious, but the most perfect of metals, being less liable to destruction or deterioration by oxidizement. Life will wear out by labours, trials, &c.; and so will gold by attrition, frequent use, &c. Therefore, life and the metal shadow forth each other, properly enough. As to the ring being simple and unadorned, I think it has its reason in the case itself, and in the feelings and apprehension of the spouse who produces it. He has chosen, according to his feelings, one whom he esteems the most perfect of her kind: she is to him superior to every other female, adorned with every charm. To use then, in this state of the case, any ornament, would be a tacit confession that her person was defective, and needed something to set it off, and must be more or less dependant on the feeble aid of dress." — Mrs. Frembly. "But, sir, there is soon added what is called a guard; and this is, if circumstances will admit, highly ornamented with pearls or brilliants." — A. C. "True, madam; and this is not without much signification. The unadorned ring supposes the fact of the bride's great superiority as already mentioned, and her suitable feelings toward her spouse; but the guard is afterward added. In order to preserve this perfection, the husband feels it necessary to add ornaments to the union, that is, endearments, attentions, and obligations, to keep his wife steady to the character which he has given her to assume; and without attention to the support of the character, and the continuance of endearing conduct, he knows the progress of married life will soon remove all false or too sanguine expectations of each other's character. The bubble, if it were one, would soon burst; animosities and mutual recriminations would soon embitter wedded life, and show how false and empty the high-formed estimation and expectations of each other were at the beginning. Thus the guard, as well as the ring, are not without their respective significations."

XXI. – PARENTS AND CHILDREN.[9]

To many God gives children in place of temporal good. To many others he gives houses, lands, and thousands of gold and silver; and with them the womb that beareth not; and these are their inheritance. The poor man has from God a number of children, without lands or money; these are his inheritance: and God shows himself their Father, feeding and supporting them by a chain of miraculous providences. Where is the poor man who would give up his six children, with the prospect of having more, for the thousands or millions of him who is the centre of his own existence; and has neither root nor branch, but his forlorn solitary self, upon the face of the earth? Let the fruitful family, however poor, lay this to heart: "Children are a heritage of the Lord; and the fruit of the womb is his reward." And he who gave them will feed them; for it is a fact, and the maxim formed on it has never failed: "Wherever God sends mouths he sends meat." "Murmur not," said an Arab to his friend, "because thy family is large; know that it is for their sakes that God feeds thee."

Education is generally defined, "that series of means by which the human understanding is gradually enlightened, and the dispositions of the heart are corrected, formed, and brought forth

---

[9] The reading of Dr. Clarke's interesting "Memoirs of the Wesley Family, by all parents and children, has my warmest recommendation. – S.D.

between early infancy and the period when a young person is considered as qualified to take a part in active life." Whole nations have been corrupted, enfeebled, and destroyed, through the want of proper education: through this, multitudes of families have degenerated; and a countless number of individuals have come to an untimely end. Parents who neglect this, neglect the present and eternal interests of their offspring.

A spirit of inquiry is common to every child. The human heart is ever panting after knowledge; and if not rightly directed when young, will, like that of our first mother, go astray after forbidden science. If we wish our children to be happy, we should show them where happiness is to be found. If we wish them to be wise, we should lead them unto God, by means of his word and ordinances. It is natural for a child to inquire, "What do you mean by this baptism? by this sacrament? by praying? by singing psalms and hymns?" &c. And what fine opportunities do such questions give pious and intelligent parents to instruct their children in every article of the Christian faith, and every fact on which these articles are established! O why is this neglected, while the command of God is before our eyes, and the importance of the measure so strikingly obvious?

A child should be taught what is necessary for it to know, as soon as that necessity exists, and the child is capable of learning. Among children there is a great disparity of intellect, and in the power of apprehension and comprehension. Many children have such a precocity of intellect as to be more capable of learning to read at two than others are at five years of age: and it would be high injustice indeed to prevent them from acquiring much useful knowledge and some hundreds, if not thousands of ideas, by waiting for a prescribed term of "five" years. When a child is capable of learning any thing, give that teaching: but let the teaching be regularly graduated; let it go on from step to step, never obliging it to learn what it cannot yet comprehend. We begin very properly with letters, or the elementary signs of language; teach the child to distinguish them from each other, and give them in their names some notion of their power. We then teach them to combine them into simple syllables; syllables into words; words into sentences; sentences into speeches, or regular discourse. This process is as philosophic as it is natural: but who follows it through the successive steps of education? Scarcely any. Because a child can understand a little, and shows aptness in learning, parental fondness, or the teacher's ignorance, comes into powerful operation; and the child is pushed unnaturally forward to departments of learning to which it has not been gradually inducted. The mind is puzzled and bewildered; a great gulf is left behind which cuts off all connection with what has been already learned, and what is now proposed to the understanding; and the issue is, the child is confounded and discouraged, and falls either under the power of hebetude, or learns superficially, and never becomes a correct scholar. A child must understand what it is doing before it can do what it ought.

"A young saint, an old devil," was a maxim of such unaccountable prevalence formerly, that even parents have been afraid to discover any tendency to early piety in their children, lest the proverb should be verified in them: and I have known some who, in their tender years, deeply feared God, who were afraid to encourage such heavenly feelings, lest they should be a prelude to their endless perdition! On this very ground piety to God was rarely cultivated on the infant mind; and both parents and teachers thought it best to instruct children in their simple duties, without showing the basis on which they should rest, or the spring from which they should flow. Hence, though they were generally taught what God had done for their souls, they were seldom, if at all, shown what God must do in them, in order to their being saved unto eternal life.

It is not to be wondered at, that infant piety was formerly very rare, when we consider the influence of the above diabolic proverb, with the general listlessness of parents, who were glad to omit duties which they found little disposition to perform, under the apprehension that early piety would most likely degenerate, in advanced life, into a more than ordinary degree of profligacy or irreligion.

A most injurious and destructive maxim has lately been advanced by a few individuals, which it is to be hoped is disowned by the class of Christians to which they belong, though the authors affect to be thought Christians, and rational ones too. The sum of the maxim is this: "Children ought not to be taught religion, for fear of having their minds biased to some particular creed; but they should be left to themselves till they are capable of making a choice, and choose to make one." This maxim is in flat opposition to the command of God, and those who teach it show how little they are affected by the religion they profess. If they felt it to be good for any thing, they would certainly wish their children to possess it; but they do not teach religion to their children, because they feel it to be of no use to themselves. Now, the Christian religion properly applied saves the soul, and fills the heart with love to God and man; for the love of God is shed abroad in the heart of a genuine believer by the Holy Ghost given to him. These persons have no such love, because they have not the religion that inspires it; and the spurious religion which admits of the maxim above mentioned is not the religion of God, and consequently better untaught than taught. But what can be said of those parents who, possessing a better faith, equally neglect the instruction of their children in the things of God? They are highly criminal; and if their children perish through neglect, which is very probable, what a dreadful account must they give in the great day! PARENTS! hear what the Lord saith unto you: Ye shall diligently teach your children that there is one Lord, Jehovah, Elohim; the Father, the Son, and the Holy Ghost; and that they must love him with all their heart, with all their soul, and with all their might. And as children are heedless, apt to forget, liable to be carried away by sensible things; repeat and re-repeat the instruction, and add line upon line, precept upon precept, here a little and there a little, carefully studying time, place, and circumstances, that your labour be not in vain: show it in its amiableness, excite attention by exciting interest; show how good, how useful, how blessed, how ennobling, how glorious it is. Whet these things on their hearts, till the keenest edge is raised on the strongest desire, till they can say, "Whom have I in heaven but thee? and there is none upon earth that I desire beside thee!"

Initiate the child at the opening of his path. When he comes to the opening of the way of life, being able to walk alone, and to choose; stop at this entrance, and begin a series of instructions, how he is to conduct himself in every step he takes. Show him the duties, the dangers, and the blessings of the path; give him directions how to perform the duties, how to escape the dangers, and how to secure the blessings, which all lie before him. Fix these on his mind by daily inculcation, till their impression is become indelible: then lead him to practice by slow and almost imperceptible degrees, till each indelible impression becomes a strongly radicated habit. Beg incessantly the blessing of God on all this teaching and discipline; and then you have obeyed the injunction of the wisest of men. Nor is there any likelihood that such impressions shall ever be effaced, and that such habits shall ever be destroyed.

Teach a child that "whom the Lord loveth he chasteneth." Teach him that God suffers men to hunger and be in want, that he may try them if they will be faithful, and do them good in their latter end. Teach him that he who patiently and meekly bears providential affliction shall be relieved and exalted in due time. Teach him that it is no sin to die in the most abject poverty and affliction, brought on in the course of divine providence; but that any attempts to alter his condition by robbery, knavery, cozening, and fraud, will be distinguished with heavy curses from the Almighty, and necessarily end in perdition and ruin. A child thus educated is not likely to abandon himself to unlawful courses.

We do not know of how much religious instruction our little ones are capable. Nothing of this kind, rightly spoken and suitably recommended, is lost. A child seldom forgets any thing by which it is interested. In the morning sow thy seed: speak to them lovingly; instruct them affectionately; encourage them powerfully; upbraid them as little as possible; and commend them as much as you can. Tell them about Jesus; and how he loves them; and what he has done for them; and what he will do in them; and how happy he will eternally make them! No tale affects the heart so much, whether of old or young, as that of Christ crucified; — and, let me add, there is no tale that God will bless so much as this; for there is nothing else that is, or can be, the power of God unto salvation. He was delivered for our offences; he rose again for our justification; and ever liveth to make intercession for us! How unspeakable is his mercy! How boundless is his grace!

How powerful are the effects of a religions education, enforced by pious example! It is one of God's especial means of grace. Let a man only do justice to his family, by bringing them up in the fear of God, and he will crown it with his blessing. How many excuse the profligacy of their family, which is often entirely owing to their own neglect, by saying, "O we cannot give them grace!" No, you cannot; but you can afford them the means of grace.

This is your work, that is the Lord's. If, through your neglect of precept and example, they perish, what an awful account must you give to the Judge of quick and dead! It was the sentiment of a great man, that should the worst of times arrive, and magistracy and ministry were both to fail, yet, if parents would be faithful to their trust, pure religion would be handed down to posterity, both in its form and in its power.

Early habits are not easily rooted out, especially those of a bad kind. Next to the influence and grace of the Spirit of God is a good and religious education. Parents should teach their children to despise and abhor low cunning, to fear a lie, and tremble at an oath; and, in order to be successful, they should illustrate their precepts by their own regular and conscientious example.

It is no wonder that the great mass of children are so wicked when so few are put under the care of Christ by humble, praying, believing parents.

Were a proper line of conduct pursued in the education of children, how few profligate sons and daughters, and how few broken-hearted parents should we find! The neglect of early religious education, connected with a wholesome and affectionate restraint, is the ruin of millions. Many parents, to excuse their indolence and most criminal neglect, say, "We cannot give our children grace." What do they mean by this? That God, not themselves, is the Author of the irregularities and viciousness of their children! They may shudder at this imputation; but when they reflect that they have not given them right precepts; have not brought them under firm and affectionate restraint; have not shown them, by their own spirit, temper, and conduct, how they should be regulated in theirs; when either the worship of God has not been established in their houses, or they have permitted their children, on the most trifling pretences, to absent themselves from it: when all these things are considered, they will find that, speaking after the manner of men, it would have been a very extraordinary miracle indeed if the children had been found preferring a path in which they did not see their parents conscientiously tread. Let those parents who continue to excuse themselves by saying, "We cannot give grace to our children," lay their hand on their conscience, and say whether they ever knew an instance where God withheld his grace while they were, in humble subserviency to him, performing their duty? The real state of the case is this: parents cannot do God's work, and God will not do theirs; but, if they use the means, and train up the child in the way he should go, God will never withhold his blessing.

It is not parental fondness nor parental authority, taken separately, that can produce this beneficial effect. A father may be as fond of his offspring as Eli was, and his children be sons of Belial: he may be as authoritative as the Grand Turk, and his children despise and plot rebellion against him. But let parental authority be tempered with fatherly affection; and let the rein of discipline be steadily held by this powerful but affectionate hand; and there shall the pleasure of God prosper; there will he give his blessing, even life for evermore. Many fine families have been spoiled, and many ruined, by the separate exercise of these two principles. Parental affection, when alone, infallibly degenerates into foolish fondness; and parental authority frequently degenerates into brutal tyranny when standing by itself. The first sort of parents will be loved, without being respected; the second sort will be dreaded, without either respect or esteem. In the first case obedience is not exacted, and is therefore felt to be unnecessary, as offences of great magnitude pass without punishment or reprehension. In the second case, rigid exaction renders obedience almost impossible; and the smallest delinquency is often punished with the extreme of torture, which, hardening the mind, renders duty a matter of perfect indifference. Parents, lay these things to heart: remember Eli and his sons; remember the dismal end of both! Teach your children to fear God; use wholesome discipline; be determined; begin in time; mingle severity and mercy together in all your conduct; and earnestly pray to God to second your godly discipline with the power and grace of his Spirit.

"Fathers, provoke not your children to wrath:" avoid all severity; this will hurt your own souls, and do them no good; on the contrary, if punished with severity or cruelty, they will only be hardened and made desperate in their sins. Cruel parents generally have bad children. He who corrects his children according to God and reason will feel every blow on his own heart more sensibly than his child feels it on his body. Parents are called to correct, not to punish, their children. Those who punish them do it from a principle of revenge; those who correct them do it from a principle of affectionate concern.

Mrs. Wesley taught her children from their earliest age their duty to their parents. She had little difficulty in breaking their wills, or reducing them to absolute subjection. They were early brought by rational means under a mild yoke; they were perfectly obsequious to their parents; and were taught to wait their decision in every thing they were to have, and in every thing they were to perform. They were taught also to ask a blessing upon their food, to behave quietly at family prayers, and to reverence the Sabbath. They were never permitted to command the servants, or to use any words of authority in their addresses to them. Mrs. Wesley charged the servants to do nothing for any of the children unless they asked it with humility and respect: and the children were duly informed that the servants had such orders. This is the foundation, and indeed the essence, of good breeding. Insolent, impudent, and disagreeable children are to be met with everywhere; because this simple, but important, mode of bringing up is neglected. "Molly, Robert, be pleased to do so and so," was the usual method of request both from the sons and the daughters; and because the children behaved thus decently, the domestics reverenced and loved them; were strictly attentive, and felt it a privilege to serve them. They were never permitted to contend with each other: whatever differences arose the parents were the umpires, and their decision was never disputed. The consequence was, there were few misunderstandings among them, and no unbrotherly and vindictive passions; and they had the common fame of being the most loving family in the county of Lincoln! How much evil may be prevented, and how much good may be done, by judicious management in the education of children! Mrs. Wesley never considered herself discharged from the care of her children. Into all situations she followed them with her prayers and counsels; and her sons, even when at the university, found the utility of her wise and parental instructions. They proposed to her all their doubts, and consulted her in all difficulties.

I consider the time spent at boarding school in teaching girls music, drawing, painting, and dancing, as almost totally lost. Reason and the necessities of the case, if consulted, would dictate that young women should be taught such things as might fit them for social and domestic life. But this is so far from being the case, that, when married, they are generally found utterly ignorant of the several duties incumbent on them; therefore the expectations of the husband are disappointed; he finds to his sorrow that the *fine, well bred young lady* knows better how to play on the harpsichord, drop a courtesy, sketch a landscape, or paint a rose, than to behave herself as a wife and mother, or conduct her domestic affairs with discretion. All these things, therefore, should be considered so many useless conformities to the world, which can be of no advantage in the most important departments and relations of life.

It is easier for most men to walk with a perfect heart in the church, or even in the world, than in their own families. How many are as meek as lambs among others, when at home they are wasps or tigers! The man who, in the midst of family provocations, maintains a Christian character, being meek, gentle, and long suffering, to his wife, children, and his servants, has got a perfect heart, and adorns the doctrine of God his Saviour in all things.

How can that family expect the blessing of God where the worship of God is not daily performed? No wonder their servants are wicked, their children profligate, and their goods cursed. What an awful reckoning shall such heads of families have with the Judge in the great day, who have refused to petition for that mercy which they might have had for asking!

How ruinous are family distractions! A house divided against itself cannot stand. Parents should take good heed that their own conduct be not the first and most powerful cause of such dissensions, by exciting envy in some of their children through undue partiality to others: but it is in vain to speak to most parents on the subject; they will give way to foolish predilections, till, in the prevailing distractions of their families, they meet with the punishment of their imprudence, when regrets are vain, and the evil past remedy.

It may not be well in general for parents to tell their children of their former failings or vices, as this might lessen their authority or respect, and the children might make a bad use of it in the extenuation of their own sins. But there are certain cases which, from the nature of their circumstances, may often occur, where a candid acknowledgment, with suitable advice, may prevent those children from repeating the evil; but this should be done with great delicacy and caution, lest even the advice itself should serve as an incentive to the evil.

Sovereign of the heavens and of the earth, behold this my daughter on the anniversary of her birthday! I bring her especially before thee; fill her with thy light, life, and power; as in thee she lives, moves, and has her being, so may she ever live to thee. Strengthen her, O thou Almighty! Instruct and counsel her, O thou Omniscient! Be her prop, her stay, her shield, and her Lord. Put all her enemies under her feet; deck her with glory and honour; make her an example to her family, a pattern of piety to her friends, a solace to the poor, and a teacher of wisdom to those who are ignorant and out of the way; and on all her glory let there be a defence to preserve, and in every respect to render it efficient! By her may thy name ever be glorified; and in her may the most adorable Saviour ever see the travail of his soul and he satisfied. Amen, amen! So be it! and let her heart hear and feel thy amen, which is, So it shall be — hallelujah.

Woe to those parents who strive, for filthy lucre's sake, to prevent their son from embracing a call to preach Jesus to their perishing countrymen, or to the heathen, because they see that the life of a true evangelist is a life of comparative poverty; and they would rather he should gain money than save souls.

How strange is the infatuation, in some parents, which leads them to desire worldly or ecclesiastical honours for their children! He must be much in love with the *cross* who wishes to have his child a minister of the Gospel; for, if he be such as God approves of in the work, his life will be a life of toil and suffering; he will be obliged to *sip*, at least, if not to drink largely of the cup of Christ. We know not what we ask when, in getting our children into the church, we take upon ourselves to answer for their call to the sacred office, and for the salvation of the souls that are put under their care. Blind parents! rather let your children beg their bread than thrust them into an office to which God has not called them; and in which they will not only ruin their souls, but be the means of damnation to hundreds; for, if God has not sent them, they shall not profit the people at all.

We may easily learn from the child what the man will be. In general they give indications of those trades and callings for which they are adapted by nature. And, on the whole, we cannot go by a surer guide in preparing our children for future life than by observing their early propensities. The future engineer is seen in the little handicraftsman of two years old. Many children are crossed in these early propensities to a particular calling, to their great prejudice, and the loss of their parents; as they seldom settle at, or make much out at, the business to which they are tied, and to which nature has given them no tendency. These infantine predilections to particular callings, we should consider as indications of divine providence, and its calling them to that work for which they are peculiarly fitted.

I have no high opinion of Polyglot businesses, though I am an admirer of Polyglot Bibles. A chemist, a druggist, a grocer, a bookseller, are too much at once. A chemist, if properly understood, is a business of science and practice, sufficient to occupy the whole of a man's life. A chemist is a student by fire, and his eyes should ever be awake to behold the operations of nature, and the synthesis and analysis of endlessly varied substances, which require such an accuracy of observation, and such a patience of investigation, in order to find out all the double and single multitudinous elective attractions as would require the attention of a first- rate mind. As a druggist, he should understand the chemical nature and actions of all simples that enter into the composition of the whole *materia medica,* and the proper method of dispensing the recipes of physicians. As to a grocer, whether he be a wholesale or retail person in that line, he requires not only a knowledge of the simples in which he deals, but also an acquaintance with the state of the commercial relations of his own country with those of the nations with which we hold commercial traffic and trade, each of which requires particular knowledge. Now, as to the book-selling, it is a science as well as a trade, of great extent and difficulty. The man who professes it should have an accurate knowledge of the whole operations of typography, compositions of papers and inks, of spacing, pointing, registering, &c.; and, in short, of bibliography, without which he cannot give a proper character of a book; be enabled to point out the characteristics of a good from a bad, a genuine from a spurious edition, and be able to judge of the merits of the different editions. I might say much more on all these topics; but I forbear. If, however, "chemist" mean only one who sells some matters prepared by the chemists, without knowing any thing of the science itself; a "druggist," the seller of those matters used by apothecaries, and prescribed by physicians to their patients, without knowing a tittle of their hygeian properties; or, whether they are calculated in the case (*pro re nata*) to kill or to cure; the "*grocer,*" the dealer in pounds or pennyworths of tea, sugar, spices, raisins, soap, starch, blue, &c., &c.; and the "*bookseller,*" merely a vender of Reading-made-Easys, geography, histories of England, and the snivellings and drivellings of the sentimental writers; all these may be dealt in by the same person, and collected together in the same shop, if it be only large enough. I must confess I pay great deference to ancient adages, and among them I remember, "Jack of all trades, and master of none." "He who has too many irons in the fire, — some of them must cool."

A match of a man's own making, when guided by reason and religion, will necessarily be a happy one. When fathers and mothers make matches for their children, which are dictated by motives, not of affection, but merely of convenience, worldly gain, &c., &c., such matches are generally wretched; it is Leah in the place of Rachel to the end of life's pilgrimage.

If I be asked, "Should Christian parents lay up money for their children?" I answer: it is the duty of every parent, who can, to lay up what is necessary to put every child in a condition to earn its bread. If he neglect this, he undoubtedly sins against God and nature. "But should not a man lay up, beside this, a fortune for his children, if he can honestly?" I answer: Yes, if there be no poor within his reach; no good work which he can assist; no heathen region on the earth to which he can contribute to send the Gospel of Jesus; but not otherwise. God shows, in the course of his providence, that this laying up of fortunes for children is not right; for there is scarcely ever a case, where money has been saved up to make the children independent and gentlemen, in which God has not cursed the blessing. It was saved from the poor, from the ignorant, from the cause of God; and the canker of his displeasure consumed this ill-saved property.

Christ loves little children, because he loves simplicity and innocence; he has sanctified their very age by passing through it himself. The holy Jesus was once a little child.

There is no evidence in the whole Book of God that any child dies eternally for Adam's sin. Nothing of this kind is intimated in the Bible; and, as Jesus took upon him human nature, and condescended to be born of a woman in a state of perfect helpless infancy, he has, consequently, sanctified this state, and has said, without limitation or exception, "Suffer little children to come unto me, and forbid them not; for of such is the kingdom of God." We may justly infer, and all the justice as well as the mercy of the Godhead supports the inference, that all human beings, dying in an infant state. are regenerated by that "grace of God which bringeth salvation to all men," Titus ii, 11, and go infalliby to the kingdom of heaven.

Who can account for the continual preservation and support of little children, while exposed to so many dangers, but on the ground of a peculiar and extraordinary providence?

Youth is the time, and the time alone, in which learning can be attained. I find that I can now remember very little but what I learned when I was young. I have, it is true, acquired many things since, but it has been with great labour and difficulty; and I find I cannot retain them as I can those things which I gained in my youth. Had I not got rudiments and principles in the beginning, I should certainly have made but little out in life.

Hear, ye children: God has given us only ten commandments, essentially necessary to our happiness in our religious, civil, and domestic life; and one of the ten speaks of, and strongly recommends, obedience to parents. Nature and common sense teach us that there is a degree of affectionate respect which is owing to parents, and which no other persons can properly claim. For a considerable time, parents stand, in some sort, in the place of God to their children; and, therefore, rebellion against their lawful commands has been considered as rebellion against God. This precept, therefore, prohibits, not only all injurious acts, irreverent and unkind speeches to parents, but enjoins all necessary acts of kindness, filial respect, and obedience.

We can scarcely suppose that man honours his parents who, when they fall weak, blind, or sick, does not exert himself to the uttermost in their support. In such cases God as truly requires the children to provide for their parents, as he required the parents to feed, nourish, instruct, support, and defend the children, when they were in the lowest state of helpless infancy.

All the reasonable commands of parents, children, while they are under their jurisdiction, should punctually obey. And even in cases where parents have no right to command, (as in matters of religion, which refer only to God and the conscience, and in the choice of partners for life, in which the parties themselves are alone interested, because they are to dwell together for life,) their counsel and advice should be respectfully sought, as their age and experience often enable them to speak seasonably on such a subject.

There is little room to doubt that the untimely deaths of many young persons were the judicial consequences of their disobedience to their parents. Most who come to an untimely end are obliged to confess that this, with the breach of the Sabbath, were the principal causes of their ruin. Reader, art thou guilty? Humble thyself, therefore, before God, and repent.

The duty of children to their parents only ceases when the parents are laid in their graves, and this duty is the next in order and importance to the duty we owe to God. No circumstances can alter its nature or lessen its importance. "Honour thy father and thy mother," is the sovereign everlasting command of God. While the relations of parent and child exist, this commandment will be in full force.

Filial affection is one of the first duties man owes upon earth: only his duty to God is paramount. There cannot be a nearer representation of an impoverished Christ, to the eye of a child, than a parent in distress; nor will the approbation of God be more strongly expressed in the day of final retribution than to that child who has honoured the Lord with his substance, in supplying the wants of those from whom, under God, he has derived his being. And those who have ministered to the necessities of their parents will be found at the top of the list of those of whom the Fountain of justice and Father of mercies speaks when he says, "I was hungry, and ye gave me meat; thirsty, and ye gave me drink; naked, and ye clothed me; sick, and in prison, and ye ministered unto me."

XXII. – MASTERS AND SERVANTS.[10]

JUSTICE and equity require that servants should have proper food, proper raiment, due rest, and no more than moderate work. This is a lesson that all masters throughout the universe should carefully learn. Do not treat your servants as if God had made them of an inferior blood to yours.

Mr. S. Wesley, jun., had not only the friendship of Lord Oxford, but his intimacy also; and frequently dined at his house. But this was an honour for which he was obliged to pay a grievous tax, ill suited to the narrowness of his circumstances. *Vales* to servants, that sovereign disgrace to their masters, were in those days quite common, and, in some instances, seem to have stood in the place of wages. A whole range of liverymen generally stood in the lobby with eager expectation and rapacity when any gentleman came out from dining at a nobleman's table; so that no person who was not affluent could afford to enjoy that privilege. One day on returning from his lordship's table, and seeing the usual range of greedy expectants, Mr. Wesley addressed them thus: "My friends, I must make an agreement with you suited to my purse; and shall distribute so much (naming the sum) once in the month, and no

---

[10] As I have found very little on this subject in Dr. Clarke's writings, I shall perhaps be excused if I refer the reader to a small work recently published, the title of which is, "A Present for Female Servants: or, the Secret of their getting and keeping good Places." – S.D.

more." This becoming generally known, was not only the means of checking that troublesome importunity, but also of redressing the evil; for their master, whose honour was concerned, commanded them to "stand back in their ranks when a gentleman retired;" and prohibited their begging! Many eminent men have endeavoured to bring this vile custom into deserved disgrace; Dryden, Addison, Swift, &c.; but it still continues, though under another form: leaving taverns out of the question, (where the lowest menial expects to be paid if he condescends to answer a civil question,) cooks, chambermaids, waiters, errand boys, &c., &c.: all expect money, if you lodge in their master's house but a single night! And they expect to be paid, too, in proportion to the treatment you have received from their master, and in proportion to his credit and respectability, and not to your means or purse. The gentry of the land should rise up as one man against this disgraceful custom, as the Board of Excise have done against the bribes taken by their officers. Let a servant, on being hired, hear, "Your wages for which you agree shall be duly and faithfully paid: I shall not require the aid of my friends to make up the deficiencies of my servants. The day on which I am informed that you receive any thing from my guests, you shall be dismissed from my service." If all agree to act thus, this grievous tax upon our friends will soon be abolished. There are few cases where the friendly visit does not cost him who pays it five times more than his maintenance would have done at his own house.

It is possible for an unfaithful servant to wrong and defraud his master in a great variety of ways without being detected; but let all such remember what is here said: "He that doeth wrong shall receive for the wrong which he has done:" God sees him and will punish him for his breach of honesty and trust. Wasting, or not taking proper care of the goods of your master, is such a wrong as God will resent. He that is unfaithful in that which is little, will be unfaithful in much, if he have opportunity; and God alone is the defence against an unfaithful servant.

A good servant never disputes, speaks little, and always follows his work.

XXIII. – RULERS AND SUBJECTS.[11]

THE different forms of civil government which have obtained in the world: —

I. PATRIARCHAL. —Government by the heads of families.

II. THEOCRACY. —The government of the Jews by God himself, as lawgiver, monarch, and judge.

III. MONARCHY. —Government exercised, laws made and executed, by the authority and will of an individual. Under this form may be classed, 1. Autocracy; a government in which an individual rules by himself without ministry, counsel, or advice. 2. Gynaeocracy. This is simply a case where the male issue fails, and the crown descends in the female line: but it has nothing in its civil constitution to distinguish it from monarchy, &c. 3. Despotism. Formerly *despot* signified no more than "master or teacher." It is now used only in a bad sense, and frequently confounded with tyranny. 4. Tyranny. Originally the term *tyranny* appears to have meant no more than "monarchy;" but the abuse, or lawless exercise of power, brought the words *tyrant* and *despot* to imply "a cruel and relentless governor; an unreasonable and oppressive ruler." 5. King signifies properly "the knowing person, the wise man."

IV. ARISTOCRACY. —Government by the nobles. Aristocracy generally prevails in a regency, where the hereditary governor is a

---

[11] Dr. Clarke published two very instructive tracts, entitled, "The Rights of God and Caesar;" and The Origin and End of Civil Government." —S.D.

minor, or under age. Under aristocracy may be ranked OLIGARCHY: a state in which a few men, whether of the nobles or plebeians, but particularly the latter, have the supreme rule. This frequently prevails under revolutions, where the rightful governor is deposed or destroyed.

V. DEMOCRACY. — A government administered by representatives chosen by the people at large. Nearly allied to this is "republicanism." There is rather an affected than real difference between this and democracy: both are of the people, though the latter pretends to be of a more liberal type than the former. FEDERALISM: A government framed out of several states, each having its own representatives, and sending them to a general congress or diet.

VI. ANARCHY. — Where the legislative and executive power is acknowledged as existing nowhere, or rather equally in every individual: and where, consequently, there is no rule; all is confusion, every one doing what is right in his own eyes.

At present only three kinds of governments prevail in the world: — 1. Monarchy; 2. Aristocracy; 3. Democracy: and these are only distinguished, by being more or less limited by law, more or less rigid in execution, or more or less mild in general operation.

Every man owes to Caesar, that is, the civil government under which he lives,

I. HONOUR. He who respects not civil institutions, and those who in the course of God's providence are clothed with political authority, will scarcely regard civil obligations: and the men who can speak evil of such dignities will, in general, be found such as have little reverence for God himself. It is therefore most evident that every man should honour and reverence civil authority, in whomsoever it is invested: 1. Because it comes from God. 2. Because without it society could not subsist. 3. Because in every case it promotes, in a less or greater degree, the public welfare; and, 4. Because, in its support and preservation, his own happiness is intimately concerned. If Caesar, in his official character, do not receive that honour which, from the origin, nature, and end of government, is due to him, public order and tranquillity must soon be at an end.

II. OBEDIENCE. There can be no government without laws: and laws, howsoever good in themselves, are useless if not obeyed.

In the order of God, to Caesar is entrusted the civil sword; and the laws show how he is to wield it. While it is "a terror to evil doers," it is a "praise to them that do well." Where the laws are right, and equal justice is maintained, no honest man need fear the sword. Obedience to the laws is absolutely necessary; for, when the spirit of insubordination takes place, no man can ever have his right; nothing but wrong prevails; and the property of the honest and industrious man will soon be found in the hands of the knave. Those who have nothing to lose, and to whom the state owes nothing, are the first to cry out of wrongs; and the first to disturb civil order, that they may enrich themselves with the spoils of those who by legal inheritance, or honest industry, have obtained wealth. Wherever the spirit of disobedience and insubordination appears, it should be discountenanced and opposed by every honest man.

III. TRIBUTE. Nothing can be more reasonable than the principle of taxation. Every country must have a government. Every government has three grand duties to perform in behalf of the governed: 1. To maintain domestic order. 2. To distribute impartial justice. 3. To protect from foreign enemies. For the first, many civil officers, and a militia, are generally required. For the second, courts of justice, judges, &c., must be provided. For the third, a strong military and naval force, particularly in times of war, or danger, must be always on foot, or in readiness, in order to save the state.

Now, all these expenses are incurred for the public; and by the public they ought to be borne: and taxation is the only mode by which money can be raised to defray these expenses. Every man, therefore, who shares in the blessings of domestic peace; who glories in the administration of impartial justice; and who wishes the land of his nativity, the constitution of his country, and its civil and religious institutions, to be preserved to himself and his dependants; should cheerfully bear his part of the public burdens, by giving that tribute to Caesar, through whom and from whom, according to the constitution, under the superintendence of God's providence, all these inestimable blessings are derived. He should support the government, that the government may support him: and the principle of justice is the same here as in the performance of any civil contract, or the remuneration of any kind of service. The justice that obliges me to pay the hireling his wages equally obliges me to pay tribute to Caesar. I have had the hireling's labour; he has had my pay. I have had the protection of the state; it has had my respect, obedience, and support. In both cases obligation and interest are mutual. The state is bound to protect the subject; the subject is bound to obey and support the state. When the subject is protected in all his rights and privileges, the state has done its duty. When the subject honours the state, obeys the laws, and contributes his quota for the support of government, he has done his duty. The subject cannot live without the support of the state; the state cannot exist without the obedience and support of the subject.

Reader, if thou hast the happiness to live under the British constitution, be thankful to God. Here, the will, the power, and utmost influence of the king, were he even so disposed, cannot deprive the meanest subject of his property, his liberty, or his life. All the solemn legal forms of justice must be consulted; the culprit, however accused, be heard by himself and his counsel; and in the end twelve honest, impartial men, chosen from among his fellows, shall decide on the validity of the evidence produced by the accuser. For the trial by jury may God make the inhabitants of Great Britain thankful!

XXIV. – RICH AND POOR.

HAPPINESS must have its seat in the mind, and, like that, be of a spiritual nature; consequently earthly goods cannot give it: so far are they from either producing or procuring it, that they always engender care and anxiety, and often strifes and contentions.

Affluence is a slippery path: few have ever walked in it without falling. It is possible to be faithful in the unrighteous mammon: but it is very difficult. No man should desire riches; for they bring with them so many snares and temptations as to be almost unmanageable. Rich men, even when pious, are seldom happy: they do not enjoy the consolations of religion. A good man, possessed of very extensive estates, unblamable in his whole deportment, once said to me, "There must be some strange malignity in riches, thus to keep me in continual bondage, and deprive me of the consolations of the Gospel." Perhaps to a person, to whom his estates are a snare, the words of our Lord may be literally applicable: "Sell what thou hast, and give to the poor and thou shalt have treasure in heaven; and come, take up thy cross, and follow me." But "he went away sorrowful; for he had great possessions!"

To be rich is in general a great misfortune: but what rich man can be convinced of this? It is only God himself who, by a miracle of mercy, can do this.

A godly man must save both time and money. Before he was converted he lost much time, and squandered his money. All this he now saves, and therefore wealth and riches must be in his house: and if he do not distribute to the necessities of the poor, they will continue to accumulate till they be his curse; or God will, by his providence, sweep them away.

What art thou, O rich man? Why, thou art a steward to whom God has given substance, that thou mayest divide with the poor. They are the right owners of every farthing thou hast to spare from thy own support and that of thy family; and God has given thee surplus for their sakes. Dost thou, by hoarding up this treasure, deprive the right owners of their property? If this were a civil case, the law would take thee by the throat, and lay thee up in prison: but it is a case in which God alone judges. And what will he do to thee? Hear! "He shall have judgment without mercy who hath showed no mercy." Read, feel, tremble, and act justly.

In the order of God the rich and the poor live together, and are mutually helpful to each other. Without the poor, the rich could not be supplied with the articles they consume; for the poor include all the labouring classes of society: and without the rich the poor could get no vent for the produce of their labour; nor, in many cases, labour itself. The poor have more time to labour than the mere necessaries of life require; their extra time is employed in providing a multitude of things which are called the superfluities of life, and which the rich especially consume. All the poor man's time is thus employed; and he is paid for his extra labour by the rich. The rich should not despise the poor, without whom he can neither have his comforts, nor maintain his state. The poor should not envy the rich, without whom he could neither get employment nor the necessaries of life. Both the states are in the order of God's providence; and both are equally important in his sight. Merely considered as men, God loves the simple artificer, or labourer, as much as he does the king; though the office of the latter, because of its entering into the plan of his government of the world, is of infinitely greater consequence than the trade of the poor artificer. Neither should despise the other; neither should envy the other. Both are useful; both important; both absolutely necessary to each other's welfare and support; and both are accountable to God for the manner in which they acquit themselves in those duties of life which God has respectively assigned them. The abject poor, those who are destitute of health and. the means of life, God in effect lays at the rich man's door, that by his superfluities they may be supported. How wise is that ordinance which has made the rich and the poor! Pity it were not better understood! Great possessions are generally accompanied with pride, idleness, and luxury, and these are the greatest enemies to salvation.

What opinion should we form of a rich man who, in a collection for a public charity, only threw in a handful of halfpence?

What blindness is it for a man to lay up that as a treasure which must necessarily perish! A heart designed for God and eternity is terribly degraded by being fixed on those things which are subject to corruption. "But may we not lay up treasure innocently?" Yes, 1. If you can do it without setting your heart on it, which is almost impossible: and, 2. If there be neither widows nor orphans, destitute nor distressed persons, in the place where you live.

In every man professing Christianity, the religion of Jesus Christ says most authoritatively, "With every man who is pinched by poverty, share what the providence of God has not made absolutely necessary for thy own support."

A rich man is a man who gets all he can, saves all he can, and keeps all he has gotten. Speak, reason! Speak, conscience! (for God has already spoken,) Can such a person enter into the kingdom of God? All, *No!*

A man of the world cannot be a truly religious character. He who gives his heart to the world robs God of it; and, in snatching at the shadow of earthly good, loses substantial and eternal blessedness.

The affluently rich, full of sensuality, and pampered with the good things of this life, are only occupied with what they shall eat, what they shall drink, how they shall amuse and sport themselves, and wherewithal they shall be clothed according to the endless changes in fantastic flippery fashions; are too busy or too brutally happy to attend to the call of the Gospel; and because it would break in upon their gratifications, they hate religion, despise a crucified Saviour and the men who proclaim salvation through his name alone.

Who, whatsoever his authority might be, or his qualifications, has been able to make many favourable impressions on the souls of mighty, and particularly rich and opulent men, so as to stem the torrent of fashionable impiety, and to establish among them the "form," or, if already established, imbue it with the "power of godliness?"

Neither good nor evil can be known by the occurrences of this life. Every thing argues the certainty of a future state, and the necessity of a day of judgment. They who are in the habit of marking casualties (especially if those whom they love not be the subjects of them) as tokens of divine displeasure, only show an ignorance of God's dispensations, and a malevolence of mind, that would fain arm itself with the celestial thunders, in order to transfix those whom they deem their enemies.

"Blessed are the poor!" This is God's word: but who believes it? Do we not say, "Yea, rather, blessed is the rich?"

A man may be grievously afflicted, and yet have his eye bent on temporal good; from his afflictions he can derive no benefit, though many think that their glorification must be a necessary consequence of their afflictions; and hence we do not unfrequently hear among the afflicted poor, "Well, we shall not suffer both here and in the other world too! Afflictions may be the means of preparing us for glory, if during them we receive grace to save the soul." But afflictions of themselves have no spiritual nor saying tendency; on the contrary, they sour the unregenerated mind, and cause murmurings against the dispensations of divine providence. Let us, therefore, look to God, that they may be sanctified; and when they are, then we may say exultingly, "These light afflictions, which are but for a moment, work for us a far more exceeding and eternal weight of glory." O world to come, in exchange for the present! O eternity, for a moment! O eternal communion in the holy, blessed, and eternal life of God, for the sacrifice of a poor, miserable, and corrupted life here on earth!

I have had occasion to remark in many thousands of cases, during the observations of a long life, made in various parts, that true religion makes as little way among the miserably poor as among the affluently rich. The former, full of unbelief, baseness of mind, and pining bitterness, neither pray to God, nor care to hear about the provision he has made for their salvation. Who has ever been able to spread religion with much success among the occupants of a parish workhouse?

And now, ye poor: arise and shake yourselves from the dust,

and cry unto the Lord. Has not your present wretchedness proceeded either from your slothfulness, or the abuse of mercies already received? God may bring back your captivity: search your hearts, humble yourselves before him; who knows but he will return to you with mercies, and your expectation shall not perish for ever?

Be prudent; be cautions; neither eat, drink, nor wear, but as you pay for every thing. Live not on trust, for that is the way to pay double; and by this means the poor are still kept poor. He who takes credit, even for food or raiment, when he has no probable means of defraying the debt, is a dishonest man. It is no sin to die through lack of the necessaries of life when the providence of God has denied the means of support; but it is a sin to take up goods without the probability of being able to pay for them. Poor man! suffer poverty a little; perhaps God is only trying thee for a time; and who can tell if he will not turn again thy captivity. Labour hard to live honestly; if God still appear to withhold his providential blessing, do not despair; leave it all to him; do not make a sinful choice; he cannot err. He will bless thy poverty, while he curses the ungodly man's blessings.

The most indigent may exercise the works of mercy and of charity; seeing even a "cup of cold water," given in the name of Jesus, shall not lose its reward. How astonishing is God's kindness! It is not the rich merely whom he calls on to be charitable; but even the poor, and the most impoverished of the poor!

We can scarcely ever speak of poverty and affliction in an absolute sense; they are only comparative. Even the poor are called to relieve those who are poorer than themselves; and the afflicted, to comfort those who are more afflicted than they are. The poor and afflicted churches of Macedonia felt this duty, and therefore came forward to the uttermost of their power to relieve their more impoverished and afflicted brethren in Judea.

"I have been young, and now am old; yet have I not seen the righteous forsaken, nor his seed begging bread." I believe this to be literally true in all cases. I am now grey-headed myself, I have travelled in different countries, and have had many opportunities of seeing and conversing with religions people in all situations of life; and I have not, to my knowledge, seen one instance to the contrary. I have seen no righteous man forsaken, nor any children of the righteous begging their bread. God puts this honour upon all that fear him; and thus careful is he of them and of their posterity.

XXV. – MINISTERS AND PEOPLE.[12]

YOUR call is not to instruct men in the doctrines and duties of Christianity merely, but to convert them from sin to holiness. A doctrine can be of little value that does not lead to practical effect; and the duties of Christianity will be preached in vain to all who have not the principle or obedience.

It is the prerogative of God both to call and qualify a man to be a successful preacher of his word. All men are not thus called; among the millions professing Christianity very few are employed in the work of the ministry in the ordinary course of providence; and still fewer by especial call. Every revival of religion is the proof of the dispensation of an extraordinary influence; for in such outpourings of God's Spirit we ever find extraordinary means and instruments used.

You are either among these ordinary or extraordinary messengers; and you have either an ordinary or extraordinary call. But as you belong not, as a Christian minister, to any established form of religion in the land, you are an extraordinary messenger, or no minister at all; and you have either an extraordinary call, or you have no call whatever.

---

[12] Few selections have been made from the doctor's "Letter to a Preacher." It is presumed that those who feel an interest in the contents of this chapter will purchase that interesting pamphlet. It deserves the attention of all ministers of the Gospel, and to Methodist preachers is invaluable. – S.D.

I hold this to be a matter of prime importance; for long experience has shown me that he among us who is not convinced that he has an extraordinary call to the ministry will never seek for extraordinary help, will sink under discouragements and persecutions, and consequently, far from being a light of the world, will be salt without savour; and, in our connection, a slothful, if not a wicked servant, who should be cast out of the sacred fold, as an encumberer of the inheritance of the Lord.

It is the prerogative of God to call and ordain his own ministers: it may be the prerogative of the church to appoint them where to labour; though, frequently, this also comes by an especial divine appointment.

To be properly qualified for a minister of Christ, a man must be—1. Filled with the Spirit of holiness; 2. Called to his particular work; 3. Instructed in its nature, &c.; and, 4. Commissioned to go forth, and testify the Gospel of the grace of God. These are four different gifts which a man must receive from God by Christ Jesus. To these let him add all the human qualifications he can possibly attain; as in his arduous work he will require every gift and every grace.

Jesus Christ never made an apostle of any man who was not first his scholar or disciple.

He who has nothing but a net, and leaves that for the sake of doing good to the souls of men, leaves his all.

Those who are really called of God to the sacred ministry are such as have been brought to a deep acquaintance with themselves, feel their own ignorance, and know their own weakness. They know also the awful responsibility that attaches to the work; and nothing but the authority of God can induce such to undertake it. They whom God never called run because of worldly honour and emolument; the others hear the call with fear and trembling, and can go only in the strength of Jehovah.

> "How ready is the man to go,
> Whom God hath never sent!
> How tim'rous, diffident, and slow
> God's chosen instrument!"

None should be appointed to ecclesiastical offices who is not able, by sound doctrine, both to exhort and convince the gainsayers. The powers necessary for this are partly natural, partly gracious, and partly acquired. 1. If a man have not good natural abilities, nothing but a miracle from heaven can make him a proper preacher of the Gospel; and to make a man a Christian minister who is unqualified for any function of civil life, is sacrilege before God. 2. If the grace of God do not communicate ministerial qualifications, no natural gifts, however splendid, can be of any avail. To be a successful Christian minister, a man must feel the worth of immortal souls in such a way as God only can show it, in order to spend and be spent in the work. He who has never passed through the travail of the soul in the work of regeneration in his own heart can never make plain the way of salvation to others. 3. He who is employed in the Christian ministry should cultivate his mind in the most diligent manner; he can neither learn nor know too much. If called of God to be a preacher, (and without such a call he had better be a galley slave,) he will be able to bring all his knowledge to the assistance and success of his ministry. If he have human learning, so much the better; and if he be accredited, and appointed by those who have authority in the church, it will be to his advantage; but no human learning, no ecclesiastical appointment, no mode of ordination, whether Popish, Episcopal, Protestant, or Presbyterian, can ever supply the divine unction, without which he never can convert and build up the souls of men. The piety of the flock must be faint and languishing when it is not animated by the heavenly zeal of the pastor; they must be blind if he be not enlightened; and their faith must be wavering when he can neither encourage nor defend it.

O ye rulers of the church! be careful, as ye shall answer it to God, never to lay hands on the head of a man whom ye have not just reason to believe God has called to the work; and whose eye is single, and whose heart is pure. Let none be sent to teach Christianity who have not experienced it to be the power of God to the salvation of their own souls. If ye do, though they have your authority, they never can have the blessing or the approbation of God. "I sent them not: therefore they shall not profit this people at all, saith the Lord."

In consequence of the appointment of improper persons to the Christian ministry, there has been not only a decay of piety but also a corruption of religion. No man is a true Christian minister who has not grace, gifts, and fruit. If he have the grace of God, it will appear in his holy life and godly conversation. If to this he add genuine abilities he will give full proof of his ministry: and if he give full proof of his ministry he will have fruit; the souls of sinners will be converted to God through his preaching, and believers will be built up on their most holy faith. How contemptible must that man appear in the eyes of common sense who boasts of his clerical education, his sacerdotal order, his legitimate authority to preach, administer the Christian sacraments, &c., while no soul is benefited by his ministry! Such a person may have legal authority to take tithes, but as to an appointment from God, he has none; else his word would be with power, and his preaching the means of salvation to his perishing hearers.

What should ministers of the Gospel feel on such subjects? Is not their charge more important and more awful than that of Moses? How few consider this! It is respectable, it is honourable, to be in the Gospel ministry; but who is sufficient to guide and feed the flock of God? If through the pastor's unfitness or neglect any soul should go astray, or perish through want of proper spiritual nourishment, or through not getting his portion in due season, in what a dreadful state is the pastor! That soul, says God, shall die in his iniquities, but his blood will I require at the watchman's hands! Were these things duly considered by those who are candidates for the Gospel ministry, who could be found to undertake it? We should then indeed have the utmost occasion to pray the Lord of the harvest to thrust out labourers into the harvest; as no one, duly considering those things, would go, unless thrust out by God himself. O ye ministers of the sanctuary! tremble for your own souls, and the souls of those committed to your care, and go not into this work unless God go with you. Without his presence, unction, and approbation ye can do nothing.

Who is capable of these things? Is it such a person as has not intellect sufficient for a common trade or calling? No; a preacher of the Gospel should be a man of the soundest sense, the most cultivated mind, the most extensive experience, one who is deeply taught of God, and who has deeply studied man; one who has prayed much, read much, and studied much; one who takes up his work as from God, does it as before God, and refers all to the glory of God; one who abides under the inspiration of the Almighty, and who has hidden the word of God in his heart, that he might not sin against him. No minister formed by man call ever be such as is required here. The school of Christ, and that alone, can ever form such a preacher.

The ministers of the Gospel are signets or seals of Jesus Christ; he uses them to stamp his truth, to accredit it, and give it currency. But as a seal can mark nothing of itself unless applied by a proper hand, so the ministers of Christ can do no good, seal no truth, impress no soul, unless the great Owner condescend to use them.

A wicked man can neither have nor communicate authority to dispense heavenly mysteries; and a fool, or a blockhead, can never teach others the way of salvation. The highest abilities are not too great for a preacher of the Gospel; nor is it possible that he can have too much human learning. But all is nothing unless he can bring the grace and Spirit of God into all his ministrations; and these will never accompany him unless he live in the spirit of prayer and humility, fearing and loving God, and hating covetousness.

The word of him who has this commission from heaven shall be as a fire and as a hammer; sinners shall be convinced and converted to God by it. But the others, though they steal the word from their neighbour, borrow or pilfer a good sermon; yet they do not profit the people at all, because God did not send them; for the power of God does not in their ministry accompany the word.

For my own part, I should ever feel disposed to bow with respect to that rare dispensation of providence and grace which should, in similar circumstances, with as clear and distinct a call, raise up a woman of such talents and piety to labour in the Gospel, where the people were perishing for lack of knowledge, and so snatch the brands from eternal burning. Who so prejudiced as not to see that God put no honour on Inman, the curate, but chose Susanna Wesley to do the work of the evangelist? The abundance of gracious fruit which sprang from this seed proved that the master sower was Jesus, the Lord of the harvest. Lord, thou wilt send by whomsoever thou pleasest; and wilt hide pride from man, in order to prove that the excellence of the power is of thee!

When the Great Head of the church calls a man to preach the Gospel, he in effect says, "Go into all the world, and preach the

Gospel to every creature." He never confines his own gift and call absolutely to any place; but leaves them under the direction and management of his own providence. The call of God to preach is a missionary call; and they who have it know that they are not their own, and must do the Master's work in the Master's own way, place, and time. Hence all the ministers of his Gospel have a missionary spirit; let providence direct, as it chooses, their way.

Does any man inquire what is the duty of a Gospel minister? Send him to the second chapter of the Epistle to Titus for a complete answer. There he will find what he is to believe, what he is to practise, and what he is to preach. Even his congregation is parcelled out to him. The old and the young of both sexes, and those who are in their employment, are considered to be the objects of his ministry; and a plan of teaching, in reference to those different descriptions of society, is laid down before him. He finds here the doctrine which he is to preach to them, the duties which he is required to inculcate, the motives by which his exhortations are to be strengthened, and the end which both he and his people should invariably have in view.

The charge of St. Paul to the pastors of the church of Christ at Ephesus and Miletus contains much that is interesting to every Christian minister:—1. If he be sent of God at all, he is sent to feed the flock. 2. But, in order to feed them, he must have the bread of life. 3. This bread he must distribute in its due season, that each may have that portion that is suitable to time, place, and state. 4. While he is feeding others, he should take care to have his own soul fed: it is possible for a minister to be the instrument of feeding others, and yet starve himself. 5. If Jesus Christ entrust to his care the souls he has bought by his own blood, what an awful account will he have to give in the day of judgment, if any of them perish through his neglect! Though the sinner, dying in his sins, has his own blood upon his head, yet, if the watchman has not faithfully warned him, his blood will be required at the watchman's hand. Let him who is concerned read Ezekiel xxxiii, 3-5, and think of the account which he is shortly to give unto God.

The very discoveries which are really useful have been made by men who feared God, and conscientiously credited divine revelation; witness Newton, Boyle, Pascal, and many others. But all the skeptics and deists, by their schemes of natural religion and morality, have not been able to save one soul! No sinner has ever been converted from the error of his ways by their preaching or writings.

In all this enumeration, where the apostle gives us all the officers and gifts necessary for the constitution of a church, we find not one word of bishops, presbyters, or deacons; much less of the various officers and offices which the Christian church at present exhibits. Perhaps the bishops are included under the apostles, the presbyters under the prophets, and the deacons under the teachers. As to the other ecclesiastical officers with which the Romish Church teems, they may seek them who are determined to find them, anywhere out of the New Testament.

It is natural for men to run into extremes; and there is no subject on which they have run into wider extremes than that of the necessity of human learning; for, in order to a proper understanding of the sacred Scriptures, on one hand, all learning has been cried down, and the necessity of the inspiration of the Holy Spirit, as the sole interpreter, strongly and vehemently argued. On the other, all inspiration has been set aside, the possibility of it questioned, and all pretensions to it ridiculed in a way savouring little of Christian charity or reverence for God. That there is a middle way from which these extremes are equally distant, every candid man who believes the Bible must allow. That there is an inspiration of the Spirit which every conscientious Christian may claim, and without which no man can be a Christian, is sufficiently established by innumerable scriptures, and by the uninterrupted and universal testimony of the church of God; this has been frequently proved in the preceding notes. If any one, professing to be a preacher of the Gospel of Jesus, denies, speaks, or writes against this, he only gives awful proof to the Christian church how utterly unqualified he is for his sacred function. He is not sent by God, and therefore he shall not profit the people at all. With such, human learning is all in all; it is to be a substitute for the unction of Christ, and the grace and influences of the Holy Spirit.

But while we flee from such sentiments as from the influence of a pestilential vapour, shall we join with those who decry learning and science, absolutely denying them to be of any service in the work of the ministry, and often going so far as to assert that they are dangerous, and subversive of the truly Christian temper and spirit, engendering little beside pride, self-sufficiency, and intolerance?

That there have been pretenders to learning, proud and intolerant, we have too many proofs of the fact to doubt it; and that there have been pretenders to divine inspiration, not less so, we have also many facts to prove. But such are only pretenders; for a truly learned man is ever humble and complacent; and one who is under the influence of the divine Spirit is ever meek, gentle, and easy to be entreated. The proud and the insolent are neither Christians nor scholars. Both religion and learning disclaim them, as being a disgrace to both.

But it is not the ability merely to interpret a few Greek and Latin authors that can constitute a man a scholar, or qualify him to teach the Gospel. Thousands have this knowledge who are neither wise unto salvation themselves, nor capable of leading those who are astray into the path of life. LEARNING is a word of extensive import; it signifies knowledge and experience; the knowledge of God and of nature in general, and of man in particular; of man in all his relations and connections; his history in all the periods of his being, and in all the places of his existence; the means used by divine Providence for his support; the manner in which he has been led to employ the power and faculties assigned to him by his Maker; and the various dispensations of grace and mercy by which he has been favoured. To acquire this knowledge, an acquaintance with some languages, which have long ceased to be vernacular, is often not only highly expedient, but in some cases indispensably necessary. But how few of those who pretend most to learning, and who have spent both much time and much money in seats of literature in order to obtain it, have got this knowledge! All that many of them have gained is merely the means of acquiring it; with this they become satisfied, and most ignorantly call it *learning*. These resemble persons who carry large unlighted tapers in their hand, and boast how well qualified they are to give light to them who sit in darkness; while they neither emit light nor heat, and are incapable of kindling the taper they hold. Learning, in one proper sense of the word, is the means of acquiring knowledge; but multitudes who have the means seem utterly unacquainted with their use, and live and die in a learned ignorance. Human learning, properly applied and sanctified by the divine Spirit, is of inconceivable benefit to a Christian minister in teaching and defending the truth of God. No man possessed more of it in his day than St. Paul. And no man better knew its use. In this, as well as in many other excellences, he is a most worthy pattern to all the preachers of the Gospel. By learning a man may acquire knowledge; by knowledge, reduced to practice, experience; and from knowledge and experience wisdom is derived. The learning that is got from books, or the study of languages, is of little use to any man, and is of no estimation, unless practically applied to the purposes of life. He whose learning and knowledge have enabled him to do good among men, and who lives to promote the glory of God and the welfare of his fellow creatures, can alone, of all the *literati,* expect to hear in the great day, "Well done, good and faithful servant! Enter thou into the joy of thy Lord."

How necessary learning is at present to interpret the sacred writings, any man may see who reads with attention; but none can be so fully convinced of this as he who undertakes to write a comment on the Bible. Those who despise helps of this kind are to be pitied. Without them, they may, it is true, understand enough for the mere salvation of their souls; and yet even much of this they owe, under God, to the teaching of experienced men. After all, it is not a knowledge of Latin and Greek merely that can enable a man to understand the Scriptures, or interpret them to others; if the Spirit of God take not away the veil of ignorance from the heart, and enlighten and quicken the soul with his all-pervading energy, all the learning under heaven will not make a man wise unto salvation.

Paul was not brought into the Christian ministry by any rite ever used in the Christian church. Neither bishop nor presbyter ever laid hands on him; and he is more anxious to prove this, because his chief honour arose from being sent immediately by God himself: his conversion and the purity of his doctrine showed whence he came. Many since his time, and in the present day, are far more anxious to show that they are legitimately appointed by man than by God; and are fond of displaying their human credentials. These are easily shown; those that come from God are out of their reach. How idle and how vain is a boasted succession from the apostles, while ignorance, intolerance, pride, and vain glory prove that those very persons have no commission from Heaven! Endless cases may occur where man sends, and yet God will not sanction. And that man has no right to preach, nor administer the sacraments of the church of Christ, whom God has not sent, though the whole assembly of apostles had laid their hands on him. God never sent, and never will send, to convert others, a man who is not converted himself. He will never send him to teach meekness, gentleness, and long suffering, who is proud, overbearing, intolerant, and impatient. He, in whom the Spirit of Christ does not dwell, never had a commission to preach the Gospel; he may boast of his human authority, but God will laugh him to scorn. On the other hand, let none run before he is sent; and when he has got the authority of God, let him be careful to take that of the church with him also.

By the kind providence of God, it appears that he has not permitted any apostolic succession to be preserved; lest the members of his church should seek that in uninterrupted succession which must be found in the HEAD alone. The Papists or Roman Catholics, who boast of an uninterrupted succession, which is a mere fable, that never was and never can be proved, have raised up another head, the *pope*. And I appeal to themselves, in the fear of God, whether they do not in heart and in speech trace up all their authority to him; and only compliment Christ as having appointed Peter to be the first bishop of Rome; (which is an utter falsity, for he was never appointed to such an office there, nor ever held such an office in that city; nor, in their sense, anywhere else;) and they hold also that the popes of Rome are not so much Peter's successors, as God's vicars; and thus both God and Peter are nearly lost sight of in their papal enumerations. With them the authority of the church is all in all; the authority of Christ is seldom mentioned.

It is idle to employ time in proving that there is no such thing as an uninterrupted succession of this kind; it does not exist, it never did exist. It is a silly fable, invented by ecclesiastical tyrants, and supported by clerical coxcombs. But were it even true, it has nothing to do with the text, Heb. v, 4. It speaks merely of the appointment of a high priest, the succession to be preserved in the tribe of Levi, and in the family of Aaron. But even this succession was interrupted and broken, and the office itself was to cease on the coming of Christ, after whom there could be no high priest; nor can Christ have any successor, and therefore he is said to be a "priest for ever," for he ever liveth the intercessor and sacrifice for mankind. The verse, therefore, has nothing to do with the clerical office, with preaching God's holy word, or administering the sacraments; and those who quote it in this way show how little they understand the Scriptures, and how ignorant they are of the nature of their own office.

If Christ be a priest for ever, there can be no succession of priests; and if he have all power in heaven and in earth, and if he be present wherever two or three are gathered together in his name, he can have no vicars; nor can the church need one to act in his place, when he, from the necessity of his nature, fills all places and is everywhere present. This one consideration nullifies all the pretensions of the Romish pontiff, and proves the whole to be a tissue of imposture.

A man may be well taught in the things of God, and be able to teach others, who has not had the advantages of a liberal education.

Teachers who preach for hire, having no motive to enter into the ministry but to get a living, as it is called ominously by some; however they may bear the garb and appearance of the innocent useful sheep, the true pastors commissioned by the Lord Jesus, or to whatever name, class, or party they may belong, are, in the sight of the heart-searching God, no other than ravenous wolves, whose design is to feed themselves with the fat, and clothe themselves with the fleece, and thus ruin, instead of save the flock.

He who preaches to get a living, or to make a fortune, is guilty of the most infamous sacrilege.

Even in our enlightened country, we find prophets who prefer hunting the hare or the fox, and pursuing the partridge and pheasant, to visiting the sick, and going after the strayed, lost sheep of the house of Israel. Poor souls! they know neither God nor themselves; and if they did visit the sick, they could not speak to them to exhortation, edification, or comfort. God never called them to his work, therefore they know nothing of it. But O what an account have these pleasure-taking false prophets to render to the Shepherd of souls!

"His blood will I require at thy hand:"—I will visit thy soul for the loss of his. O how awful is this! Hear it, ye priests,—ye preachers,—ye ministers of the Gospel; ye, especially, who have entered into the ministry for a living: ye who gather a congregation to yourselves that ye may feed upon their fat, and clothe yourselves with their wool; in whose parishes and in whose congregations souls are dying unconverted from day to day, who have never been solemnly warned by you, and to whom you have never shown the way of salvation,—probably because ye know nothing of it yourselves. O, what a perdition awaits you! To have the blood of every soul that has died in your parishes or in your congregations unconverted, laid at your door! To suffer a common damnation for every soul that perishes through your neglect! How many loads of endless woe must such have to bear! Ye take your tithes, your stipends, or your rents, to the last grain, and the last penny; while the souls over whom you made yourselves watchmen have perished, and are perishing through your neglect! O worthless and hapless men! better for you had ye never been born! Vain is your boast of apostolical authority, while ye do not the work of apostles. Vain your boast of your orthodoxy, while ye neither show nor know the way of salvation;—vain your pretensions to a divine call, when ye do not the work of evangelists. The state of the most wretched of the human race is enviable to that of such ministers, pastors, teachers, and preachers.

We did not seek temporal emolument; nor did we preach the Gospel for a cloak to our covetousness: God is witness that we did not; we sought you, not yours. Hear this, ye that preach the Gospel! Can ye call God to witness that in preaching it ye have no end in view by your ministry but his glory in the salvation of souls? Or do ye enter into the priesthood for a morsel of bread, or for what is ominously and impiously called "a living, a benefice?" In better days your place and office were called "a cure of souls;" what care have you for the souls of them by whose labours you are in general more than sufficiently supported? Is it your study, your earnest labour, to bring sinners to God, to preach among your heathen parishioners the unsearchable riches of Christ?

But I should speak to the thousands who have no parishes, but who have their chapels, their congregations, pew and seat rents, &c. Is it for the sake of these that ye have entered or continue in the Gospel ministry? Is God witness that, in all these things, ye have no cloak of covetousness? Happy is the man who can say so, whether he has the provision which the law of the land allows him, or whether he lives on the free-will offerings of the people.

Christian ministers, who preach the whole truth, and labour

in the word and doctrine, are entitled to more than respect; the apostle commands them to be esteemed, abundantly, and superabundantly; and this is to be done in love; and as men delight to serve those whom they love, it necessarily follows that they should provide for them, and see that they want neither the necessaries nor conveniences of life; I do not say comforts, though these also should be furnished; but of these the genuine messengers of Christ are frequently destitute. However, they should have food, raiment, and lodging for themselves and their household. This they ought to have for their work's sake.

Many canons, at different times, have been made to prevent ecclesiastics from intermeddling with secular employments. He who will preach the Gospel thoroughly, and wishes to give full proof of his ministry, had need to have no other work. He should be wholly in this thing, that his profiting may appear unto all. There are many who sin against this direction. They love the world, and labour for it, and are regardless of the souls committed to their charge. But what are they, either in number or guilt, compared to the immense herd of men professing to be Christian ministers, who neither read nor study, and, consequently, never improve? These are too conscientious to meddle with secular affairs, and yet have no scruple of conscience to while away time, be among the chief in needless self-indulgence, and, by their burdensome and monotonous ministry, become an encumbrance to the church! Do you inquire, In what sect or party are these to be found? I answer, In all: idle drones,

"Born to consume the produce of the soil,"

disgrace every department in the Christian church. They cannot teach, because they will not learn.

That minister who neglects the poor, but is frequent in his visits to the rich, knows little of his Master's work, and has little of his Master's spirit.

Time-servers and flatterers; persons who pretend to be astonished at the greatness, goodness, sagacity, learning, wisdom, &c., of rich and great men, hoping thereby to acquire money, influence, power, friends, and the like: all the flatterers of the rich are of this kind; and especially those who profess to be ministers of the Gospel, and who, for the sake of a more advantageous settlement or living, will sooth the rich even in their sins. With such persons a rich man is every thing; and, if he have but a grain of grace, his piety is extolled to the skies. I have known several ministers of this character, and wish them all to read the sixteenth verse of Jude.

"Neither as being lords over God's heritage." This is the voice of St. Peter in his catholic epistle to the catholic church. According to him, there are to be no lords over God's heritage; the bishops and presbyters, who are appointed by the Head of the church, are to feed the flock, to guide and to defend it, not to fleece and waste it; and they are to look for their reward in another world, and in the approbation of God in their consciences. And in humility, self-abasement, self- renunciation, and heavenly mindedness, they are to be ensamples, types to the flock, moulds of a heavenly form, into which the spirits and lives of the flock may be cast, that they may come out after a perfect pattern. We need not ask, Does the church that arrogates to itself the exclusive title of "Catholic," and do its supreme pastors who affect to be the successors of Peter, and the vicars of Jesus Christ, act in this way? They are in every sense the reverse of this. But we may ask, Do the other churches, which profess to be reformed from the abominations of the above, keep the advice of the apostle in their eye? Have they pastors according to God's own heart, who feed them with knowledge and understanding? Jer. iii, 15. Do they feed themselves, and not the flock? Are they lords over the heritage of Christ, ruling with a high ecclesiastico-secular hand, disputing with their flocks about penny-farthing tithes and stipends, rather than contending for the faith once delivered to the saints? Are they heavenly moulds, into which the spirits and conduct of their flocks may be cast? I leave those who are concerned to answer these questions; but I put them, in the name of God, to all the preachers in the land. How many among them properly care for the flock? Even among those reputed evangelical teachers, are there not some who, on their first coming to a parish or congregation, make it their first business to raise the tithes and the stipends, where, in all good conscience, there was before enough to provide them and their families with not only the necessaries, but all the conveniences and comforts of life? conveniences and comforts which neither Jesus Christ nor his servant Peter ever enjoyed. And is not the great concern among ministers to seek for those places, parishes, and congregations, where the provision is the most ample, and the work the smallest? Preacher or minister, whosoever thou art who readest this, apply not the word to thy neighbour, whether he be state-appointed, congregation-appointed, or self-appointed; take all to thyself; *mutato nomine de te fabula narratur.* See that thy own heart, views, and conduct be right with God.

The church of God has ever been troubled with such pretended pastors; men who feed themselves, not the flock; men who are too proud to beg, and too lazy to work; who have neither grace nor gifts to plant the standard of the cross on the devil's territories, and by the power of Christ make inroads upon his kingdom, and spoil him of his subjects. On the contrary, by sowing the seeds of dissension, by means of doubtful disputations, and the propagation of scandals; by glaring and insinuating speeches, (for they affect elegance and good breeding,) they rend Christian congregations, form a party for themselves, and thus live on the spoils of the church of God.

How can worldly minded, hireling, fox-hunting, and card-playing priests read Ezek. xxxiv, 2, &c., without trembling to the centre of their souls? Woe to those parents who bring up their children merely for church honours and emoluments! Suppose a person have all the church's revenues, if he have God's woe, how miserable is his portion! Let none apply this censure to any one class of preachers exclusively.

How many, by their attachment to filthy lucre, have lost the honour of becoming or continuing ambassadors for the Most High!

How unutterable must the punishment of those be who are chaplains to princes or great men, and who either flatter them in their vices, or wink at their sins!

Were men as zealous to catch souls as they are to support their particular creeds and forms of worship, the state of Christianity would be more flourishing than it is at present.

There are multitudes of scribes, Pharisees, and priests; of reverend and right reverend men; but there are few that work. Jesus wishes for labourers, not gentlemen who are either idle drones or slaves to pleasure and sin.

Alas! Alas! how many preachers are there who appear

prophets in their pulpits; how many writers, and other evangelical workmen, the miracles of whose labour, learning, and doctrine we admire; who are nothing, and worse than nothing, before God, because they perform not his will, but their own! What an awful consideration, that a man of eminent gifts, whose talents are a source of public utility, should only be as a waymark, or fingerpost, in the way to eternal bliss, pointing out the road to others, without walking in it himself!

Where is the grand difference between the teaching of scribes and Pharisees, the self-created or men-made ministers, and those whom God sends? The first may preach what is called very good and sound doctrine; but it comes with no authority from God to the souls of the people. Therefore, the unholy is unholy still; because preaching can only be effectual to the conversion of men, when the unction of the Holy Spirit is in it; and, as these are not sent by the Lord, therefore they shall not profit the people at all.

It is requisite that he who is to be judge of so many cases of conscience should clearly understand them. But is this possible, unless he have passed through those states and circumstances on which these cases are founded? I trow not. He who has not been deeply exercised in the furnace of affliction and trial is never likely to be a workman that needeth not to be ashamed, rightly dividing the word of truth. How can a man unexperienced in spiritual trials build up the church of Christ!

He who boasts of his ancestry, talks of his mighty sacrifices, and insinuates that he has descended from much dignity, respectability, ease, and affluence, in order to become a Methodist preacher, is the character of which Mr. Wesley speaks, Rule 8. Such a one affects the gentleman, wishes to be thought so by others, may be thought so by persons as empty as himself; but, in the light of every man of good common sense, is a vain, conceited, empty ass; is unworthy of the ministry, should be cast out of the vineyard, and hooted from society.

Preach the law and its terrors to make way for the Gospel of Christ crucified. But take heed, lest, while you announce the terrors of the Lord, in order to awaken sinners and prepare them for Christ, that you do not give way to your own spirit, especially if you meet with opposition.

Beware of discouraging the people; therefore, avoid

continually finding fault with them. This does very much hurt. If you find a society fallen or falling, examine as closely as you can to find out all the good that is among them; and, copying Christ's conduct toward the seven Asiatic churches, preface all that you have to say on the head of their backsliding with the good that remains in them; and make that good which they still possess, the reason why they should shake themselves from the dust, take courage, and earnestly strive for more.

Avoid the error of those who are continually finding fault with their congregations because more do not attend. Bring Christ with you, and preach his truth in the love thereof, and you will never be without a congregation, if God have any work for you to do in that place.

A preacher of the Gospel should have nothing about him which savours of effeminacy and worldly pomp: he is awfully mistaken who thinks to prevail on the world to hear him and receive the truth, by conforming himself to its fashions and manners. Excepting the mere colour of his clothes, we can scarcely now distinguish a preacher of the Gospel, whether in the establishment of the country, or out of it, from the merest worldly man. Ruffles, powder, and fribble seem universally to prevail. Thus the church and the world begin to shake hands, the latter still retaining its enmity to God. How can those who profess to preach the doctrine of the cross act in this way? Is not a worldly minded preacher, in the most peculiar sense, an abomination in the eyes of the Lord?

Let it be well observed that the preacher who conforms to the world in his clothing is never in his element but when he is frequenting the houses and tables of the rich and great.

The first preachers, historians, and followers of the doctrines of the Gospel were men eminent for the austerity of their lives, the simplicity of their manners, and the sanctity of their conduct; they were authorized by God, and filled with the most precious gifts of his Spirit.

He who makes use of God's gift to feed and strengthen his pride and vanity will be sure to be stripped of the goods wherein he trusts, and fall down into the condemnation of the devil.

He is not a seedsman of God who desires to sow by the wayside, and not on the proper ground; that is, he who loves to preach only to genteel congregations, to people of sense and fashion, and feels it a pain and a cross to labour among the poor and the ignorant.

The ambition which leads to spiritual lordship is one great cause of murmurings and animosities in religions societies, and has proved the ruin of the most flourishing churches in the universe.

Every kind of lordship and spiritual domination over the church of Christ, like that exercised by the Church of Rome, is destructive and anti-christian.

Preachers of the Gospel, and especially those who are instruments in God's hand of many conversions, have need of much heavenly wisdom; that they may know to watch over, guide, and advise those who are brought to a sense of their sin and danger. How many auspicious beginnings have been ruined by men's proceeding too hastily, endeavouring to make their own designs take place, and to have the honour of that success themselves, which is due only to God!

How often is the work of God marred and discredited by the folly of men! for nature will always, and Satan too, mingle themselves as far as they can in the genuine work of the Spirit, in order to discredit and destroy it. Nevertheless, in great revivals of religion, it is almost impossible to prevent wild-fire from getting in among the true fire; but it is the duty of the ministers of God to watch against and prudently check this; but if themselves encourage it, then there will be "confusion and every evil work."

A minister of the Gospel of God should, above all men, be continent of his tongue; his enemies, in certain cases, will crowd question upon question, in order so to puzzle and confound him that he may speak unadvisedly with his lips, and thus prejudice the truth he was labouring to promote and defend. The following is a good prayer, which all who are called to defend or proclaim the truths of the Gospel may confidently offer to their God: "Let thy wisdom and light, O Lord, disperse their artifice and my darkness! Cast the bright beams of thy light upon those who have to defend themselves against subtle and deceitful men! Raise and animate their hearts, that they may not be wanting to the cause of truth. Guide their tongue, that they may not be deficient in prudence, nor expose thy truth by any indiscretions or unseasonable transports of zeal. Let meekness, gentleness, and long suffering influence and direct their hearts; and may they ever feel the full weight of that truth: 'The wrath of man worketh not the righteousness of God!'" The following advice of one of the ancients is good: "Stand thou firm as a beaten anvil; for it is the part of a good soldier to be flayed alive, and yet conquer."

A minister of God should act with great caution: every man, properly speaking, is placed between the secret judgment of God and the public censure of men. He should do nothing rashly, that he may not justly incur the censure of men; and he should do nothing but in the loving fear of God, that he may not incur the censure of his Maker. The man who scarcely ever allows himself to be wrong is one of whom it may be safely said, "He is seldom right." It is possible for a man to mistake his own will for the will of God, and his own obstinacy for inflexible adherence to his duty. With such persons it is dangerous to have any commerce. Reader, pray to God to save thee from an inflated and self-sufficient mind.

Zeal for God's truth is essentially necessary for every minister; and prudence is not less so. They should be wisely tempered together, but this is not always the case. Zeal without prudence is like a flambeau in the hands of a blind man; it may enlighten and warm, but it may also destroy the spiritual building. Human prudence should be avoided as well as intemperate zeal; this kind of prudence consists in a man's being careful not to bring himself into trouble, and not to hazard his reputation, credit, interest, or fortune, in the performance of his duty. Evangelical wisdom consists in our suffering and losing all things, rather than be wanting in the discharge of our obligations.

Discipline must be exercised in the Christian church; without this it will soon differ but little from the wilderness of this world. But what judgment, prudence, piety, and caution are requisite in the execution of this most important branch of a minister's duty! He may be too easy and tender, and permit the gangrene to remain till the flock be infected with it. Or he may be rigid and severe, and destroy parts that are vital, while only professing to take away what is vitiated. A backslider is one who once knew less or more of the salvation of God. Hear what God says concerning such: "Turn, ye backsliders, for I am married unto you." See how unwilling he is to give them up! He suffers long, and is kind: do thou likewise; and when thou art obliged to cut off the offender from the church of Christ, follow him still with thy best advice and heartiest prayers.

There are some who seem to take a barbarous pleasure in expelling members from the church. They should be continued in as long as possible: while they are in the church, under its ordinances and discipline, there is some hope that their errors may be corrected; but when once driven out again into the world, that hope must necessarily become extinct. As judgment is God's strange work, so excommunication should be the strange, the last, and the most reluctantly performed work of every Christian minister.

"Without preferring one before another."—Without prejudice. Promote no man's cause; make not up thy mind on any case, till thou hast weighed both sides and heard both parties, with their respective witnesses, and then act impartially, as the matter may appear to be proved. Do not treat any man, in religions matters, according to the rank he holds in life, or according to any personal attachment thou mayest have for him. Every man should be dealt with in the church as he will be dealt with at the judgment seat of Christ. A minister of the Gospel, who, in the exercise of discipline in the church, is swayed and warped by secular considerations, will be a curse rather than a blessing to the people of God. Accepting the persons of the rich, in ecclesiastical matters, has been a source of corruption in Christianity. With some ministers, the show of piety in a rich man goes farther than the soundest Christian experience in the poor. What account can such persons give of their stewardship?

A useful, zealous preacher, though unskilled in learned languages, is much greater in the sight of God, and in the eye of sound common sense, than he who has the gift of those learned tongues; "except he interpret:" and we seldom find great scholars good preachers. This should humble the scholar, who is too apt to be proud of his attainments, and despise his less learned but most useful brother. This judgment of St. Paul is too little regarded.

Ever let your ear be open to the cry of the afflicted and dying; in the warmest and most affectionate manner give them directions and exhortations, open to them the Fountain of mercy, and lead them straight to God through the sacrifice of his Son. Show them, prove to them, that with him is mercy, and with him a plenteous salvation; and that in very faithfulness he has afflicted them. While you are ready at every call, make use of all your prudence to prevent the reception of contagion. Do not breathe near the infected person. Contagion is generally taken into the stomach by means of the breath; not that the breath goes into the stomach, but the noxious effluvia are by inspiration brought into the mouth, and immediately connect themselves with the whole surface of the tongue and fauces, and, in swallowing the saliva, are taken down into the stomach, and, there mixing with the aliment in the process of digestion, are conveyed, by means of the lacteal vessels, through the whole of the circulation, corrupting and assimilating to themselves the whole mass of blood, and thus carry death to the heart, lungs, and to the utmost of the capillary system. In visiting fever cases, I have been often conscious of having taken the contagion. On my returning home, I have drunk a few mouthfuls of warm water, and then with the small point of a feather, irritated the stomach to cause it to eject its contents. By these means I have frequently, through mercy, been enabled to escape many a danger and many a death. Never swallow your saliva in a sick room, especially where there is contagion; keep a handkerchief for this purpose, and wash your mouth frequently with tepid water. Keep to windward of every corpse you bury. Never go out with an empty stomach, nor let your strength be prostrated by long abstinence from food.

In a thousand instances an apostolic preacher, who goes into the wilderness to seek the lost sheep, will be exposed to hunger and cold, and to other inconveniences; he must therefore resign himself to God, depending on his providence for the necessaries of life. If God have sent him, he is bound to support him, and will do it: anxiety, therefore, in him, is a double crime; as it insinuates a bad opinion of the Master who has employed him. Every missionary should make himself master of this subject.

Augustine, archbishop of Tarragon, was one of the most learned men of the age: he gave literally all he had to the poor; so that when he died, in 1586, there was not found sufficient cash in his coffers to procure him a decent burial. To any of his archiepiscopal brethren, "Go thou and do likewise," might be esteemed a hard saying.

Let a minister of Christ but impair his health by his pastoral labours; presently "he is distracted; he has not the least conduct nor discretion." But let a man forget his soul, let him destroy his health by debaucheries, let him expose his life through ambition, and he may, notwithstanding, pass for a very prudent and sensible man!

Men who have laboured to bring the mass of the common people from ignorance, irreligion, and general profligacy of manners, to an acquaintance with themselves and God, and to a proper knowledge of their duty to him and to each other, have been often branded as being disaffected to the state, and as movers of sedition among the people!

A minister's trials and comforts are permitted and sent, for the benefit of the church. What a miserable preacher must he be who has all his divinity by study and learning, and nothing by experience! If his soul have not gone through all the travail of regeneration, if his heart have not felt the love of God shed abroad in it by the Holy Ghost, he can neither instruct the ignorant nor comfort the distressed.

A minister of Christ is represented as a day-labourer: he comes into the harvest, not to become lord of it, not to live on the labour of others, but to work, and to labour his day. Though the work may be very severe, yet, to use a familiar expression, there is good wages in the harvest home; and the day, though hot, is but a short one.

When Christ shall appear to judge the world in righteousness, ye who have fed his flock, who have taken the superintendence of it, not by constraint, not for "filthy lucre's sake," not as lords over the heritage, but with a "ready mind," employing body, soul, spirit, time, and talents, in endeavouring to pluck sinners as brands from eternal burnings, and build up the church of Christ on its most holy faith; YE shall "receive a crown of glory" that "fadeth not away;" an eternal nearness and intimacy with the ineffably glorious God; so that ye who have turned many to righteousness shall shine, not merely as stars, but as suns, in the kingdom of your Father! O ye heavenly minded, diligent, self-denying pastors after God's own heart, whether ye be in the church established by the state, or in those divisions widely separated from or nearly connected with it, take courage; preach Jesus; press through all difficulties in the faith of your God; fear no evil while meditating nothing but good. Ye are stars in the right hand of Jesus, who walks among your golden candlesticks, and has lighted that lamp of life which ye are appointed to trim; fear not, your labour in the Lord cannot be in vain! Never, never can ye preach one sermon in the spirit of your office which the God of all grace shall permit to be unfruitful; ye carry and sow the seed of the kingdom by the command and on the authority of your God; ye sow it, and the heavens shall drop down dew upon it. Ye may go forth weeping, though bearing this precious seed; but ye shall doubtless come again with rejoicing, bringing your sheaves with you. Amen, even so, Lord Jesus!

God does not reward his servants according to the success of their labour, because that depends on himself; but he rewards them according to the quantum of faithful labour which they bestow on his work. In this sense none can say, "I have laboured in vain, and spent my strength for naught."

On the other hand, if they be faithful, their labour shall not be in vain, and their safety shall be great. He that toucheth them toucheth the apple of God's eye, and none shall be able to pluck them out of his hand. They are the angels and ambassadors of the Lord; their persons are sacred; they are the messengers of the churches, and the glory of Christ. Should they lose their lives in the work, it will be only a speedier entrance into an eternal glory.

> "The rougher the way, the shorter their stay;
> The troubles that rise
> Shall gloriously hurry their souls to the skies."

Go on in the name of God; I am your invariable friend; I labour early and late for you; I feel the people as if they were members of my own family. As to small friends, value them not. God is with you, and therefore the devil must be against you. Preach Jesus and his present and full salvation. This will carry you through, because God will infallibly bear testimony to the doctrine that puts due honour on the sacrificial blood of his Son. No other doctrine, however highly it may speak of Him who shed it, does honour to the great design of God, than that which shows that it saves from the power and guilt of sin, and cleanses from all unrighteousness; not in a future world, but in this; and in the present time.

Go on; fear nothing; God is with you, and nothing can

withstand the all-conquering blood and mighty Spirit of the Lord Jesus. Proclaim loudly to the poor sinners that Jesus Christ tasted death for every man; and that his blood cleanses from all unrighteousness. This is the doctrine which God will own. What has the wretched stuff of C——n done for the world? Produced a spurious Christianity, and left the people in their sins! Walk with God, and you need fear no reproach. Luther said, *Evangelium predicare, est furorem mundi in te derivare.* Yes, he who preaches the unadulterated doctrines of the God who bought him will be hated by the Christian world. Jesus and his apostles were persecuted, not by the heathens, but by Jews professing godliness; so spurious Christians are the prime persecutors of the genuine followers of the Lord Jesus. Fear them not; our God is mightier than their devil! Amen. Selah. Whiskey and tobacco will also fall before the Spirit of Christ: reason mildly with those who are addicted to them; in this respect you will gain ground by degrees.

Be urgent, whether the times be prosperous or adverse, whenever there is an opportunity; and when there is none, strive to make one. The Judge is at the door, and to every man eternity is at hand! Wherever thou meetest a sinner, speak to him the word of reconciliation. Do not be contented with stated times and accustomed places merely; all time and place belong to God, and are proper for his work. Wherever it can be done, there it should be done. Satan will omit neither time nor place where he can destroy. Omit thou none where thou mayest be the instrument of salvation to any.

He who wishes to save souls will find few opportunities to rest. As Satan is going "about as a roaring lion seeking whom he may devour," the messenger of God should imitate his diligence, that he may counteract his work.

Let no minister of God think he has delivered his own soul till he has made an offer of salvation to every city and village within his reach.

I have taken care that your credit should ever be preserved. For I think it fatal to our missionary work in any place, to dishonour the bill of a missionary; or to trifle with his just demands so as to render his credit suspicious. Take care to be ever prudent and economic; and while God spares me in reference to your station, I shall take care that your credit shall be preserved.

A scandal or heresy in the church of God is ruinous at all times, but particularly so when the cause is in its infancy; and therefore the messengers of God cannot be too careful to lay the foundation well in doctrine, to establish the strictest discipline, and to be very cautious whom they admit and accredit as members of the church of Christ. It is certain that the door should be opened wide to admit penitent sinners; but the watchman should ever stand by, to see that no improper person enter in. Christian prudence should ever be connected with Christian zeal. It is a great work to bring sinners to Christ; it is a greater work to preserve them in the faith; and it requires much grace and much wisdom to keep the church of Christ pure, not only by not permitting the unholy to enter, but by casting out those who apostatize or work iniquity. Slackness in discipline generally precedes corruption of doctrine; the former generating the latter.

The ministers of God are compared to stewards, of whom the strictest fidelity is required. 1. Fidelity to God, in publishing his truth with zeal, defending it with courage, and recommending it with prudence. 2. Fidelity to Christ, whose representatives they are, in honestly and fully recommending his grace and salvation on the ground of his passion and death, and preaching his maxims in all their force and purity. 3. Fidelity to the church, in taking heed to keep up a godly discipline, admitting none into it but those who have abandoned their sins; and permitting none to continue in it that do not continue to adorn the doctrine of God their Saviour. 4. Fidelity to their own ministry, walking so as to bring no blame on the Gospel; avoiding the extremes of indolent tenderness on one hand, and austere severity on the other; considering the flock, not as *their* flock, but the flock of Jesus Christ; watching, ruling, and feeding it according to the order of their Divine Master.

A preacher who is not a man of prayer cannot have a proper knowledge of the nature and design of the Gospel ministry; cannot be alive to God in his own soul; nor is likely to become instrumental in the salvation of others. In order to do good, a man must receive good: prayer is the way in which divine assistance is received; and in the work of the ministry, no man can do any thing unless it be given him from above. In many cases the success of a preacher's labours depends more on his prayers than on his public preaching.

Live to God, pray much, read much, labour hard, and have

immeasurable faith.

Earnest frequent prayer to God, and keeping up a living sense of your acceptance with him, are of the first and last necessity. Breathe continually in the divine atmosphere, and then the contagion of sin will not be able to reach you. Keep yourselves in the love of God, and then that wicked one shall not touch you.

In all my long experience I have been led to see that ninety-nine out of the hundred of offences that take place in the sacred ministry are occasioned by unguarded conversation with women, and incautiously touching spirituous liquors. Against both these you cannot be too much on your guard. Among people of simple manners, the first is peculiarly dangerous; because, when confidence takes place, all distance is forgotten, familiarity ensues, intimacy becomes grafted on that, and then irregular affections are easily produced. "Converse sparingly with women," says Mr. Wesley, "especially with young women." Those who are naturally of a free and affectionate disposition are, in this case, in most danger. A supercilious carriage ill becomes a minister of Christ, whose avocation binds him to be servant of all. To the young act as brothers; to the old as respectful children: keep a due distance; do not go too far off; do not approach too near. The first will excite prejudice against you; the latter will lead almost imperceptibly to the gulf whence there is no returning.

As to a total abstinence from spirituous liquors where no other beverage can be found, I know not well what to say. If any be taken, it should be very little, or well diluted; a little in cold water, without any sweetening, would be best. Try toast and water: even oat bread, where wheaten cannot be found, will do: toast either well, till perfectly brown throughout, and then pour boiling water on it, cover it up, and let it stand two hours at least before you use it. This is a most wholesome and diluting beverage.

Only to shine is but vanity; and to burn without shining will never edify the church of God. Some shine, and some burn, but few both shine and burn; and many there are who are denominated pastors, who neither shine nor burn. He who wishes to save souls must both burn and shine: the clear light of the sacred records must fill his understanding; and the holy flame of loving zeal must occupy his heart. Zeal without knowledge is continually blundering; and knowledge without zeal makes no converts to

Christ.

Never take a text which you do not fully understand; and make it a point of conscience to give the *literal* meaning of it to the people: this is a matter of great and solemn importance. To give God's words a different meaning to what he intended to convey by them, or to put a construction upon them which we have not the fullest proof he has intended, is awful indeed!

Never appear to contradict the Holy Spirit by what is called treating a subject negatively and positively. Seldom take a very short text. Never take a text which, out of its proper connection, can mean nothing. I would most solemnly guard you against what is termed fine or flowery preaching. I do not mean preaching in elegant, correct, and dignified language; as every thing of this kind is quite in place, when employed in proclaiming and illustrating the records of our salvation; but I mean a spurious birth, which endeavours to honour itself by this title. Some preachers think they greatly improve their own discourses by borrowing the fine sayings of others; and when these are frequently brought forward in the course of a sermon, the preacher is said to be a flowery preacher. Such flowers, used in such a way, bring to my remembrance the custom in some countries of putting full-blown roses, or sprigs of rosemary, lavender, and thyme, in the hands of the dead, when they are put in their coffins.

But the principal fault in this kind of preaching is the using a vast number of words long and high sounding, to which the preacher himself appears to have fixed no specific ideas, and which are often foreign, in the connection in which he places them, to the meaning which they radically convey.

How careful should the ministers of Christ be that they proclaim nothing as truth, and accredit nothing as truth, but what comes from their Master! They should take heed lest, after having preached to others, themselves should be castaways; lest God should say unto them as he said of Coniah, "As I live, saith the Lord, though Coniah, the son of Jehoiakim, were the signet upon my right hand, yet would I pluck thee hence."

It is worthy of remark, that in all the revivals of religion with which we are acquainted God appears to have made very little use of human eloquence, even when possessed by pious men. His own nervous truths, announced by plain common sense, though in homely phrase, have been the general means of the conviction and conversion of sinners. Human eloquence and learning have often been successfully employed in defending the outworks of Christianity; but simplicity and truth have preserved the citadel.

We should be cautious how we appeal to heathens, however eminent, in behalf of morality; because much may be collected from them on the other side. In like manner we should take heed how we quote the fathers in proof of the doctrines of the Gospel; because he who knows them best, knows that on many of those subjects they blow hot and cold.

In most Christian churches there appears to be but one office, that of preacher; and one gift, that by which he professes to preach. The apostles, prophets, evangelists, pastors, and teachers, are all compounded in the class "preachers;" and many, to whom God has given nothing but the gift of exhortation, take texts to explain them; and thus lose their time, and mar their ministry.

"Not handling the word of God deceitfully."—Not using the doctrines of the Gospel to serve any secular or carnal purpose; not explaining away their force so as to palliate or excuse sin; not generalizing its precepts so as to excuse many in particular circumstances from obedience, especially in that which most crossed their inclinations. There were deceitful handlers of this kind in Corinth, and there are many of them still in the garb of Christian ministers; persons who disguise that part of their creed which, though they believe it is of God, would make them unpopular; affecting moderation in order to procure a larger audience and more extensive support; not attacking prevalent and popular vices; calling dissipation of mind *relaxation;* and worldly and carnal pleasures *innocent amusements,* &c.: in a word, turning with the tide, and shifting with the wind, of popular opinion, prejudice, fashion, &c.

The truth of God should be so preached to all the members of the church of God, that they may all receive an increase of grace and life; so that each, in whatever state he may be, may get forward in the way of truth and holiness. In the church of Christ there are persons in various states: the careless, the penitent, the lukewarm, the tempted, the diffident, the little child, the young man, and the father. He who has got a talent for the edification of only one of these classes should not stay long in a place, else the whole body cannot grow up in all things under his ministry.

A preacher whose mind is well stored with divine truths, and who has a sound judgment, will suit his discourses to the circumstances and states of his hearers. He who preaches the same sermon to every congregation gives the fullest proof that, however well he may speak, he is not a scribe who is instructed in the kingdom of heaven.

In preaching on parables and similitudes, great care should be taken to discover their object and design, and those grand and leading circumstances by which the author illustrates his subjects.

Every preacher of God's word should take heed that it is God's message that he delivers to the people. Let him not suppose, because it is according to his own creed or confession of faith, that therefore it is God's word. False doctrines and fallacies without end are foisted on the world in this way. Bring the creed first to the word of God, and scrupulously try whether it be right; and when this is done, leave it where you please; take the Bible, and warn them from God's word recorded there.

Avoid paraphrasing a whole book or epistle in a set of discourses; it is tedious, and often produces many sleepers.

From one of the royal household of George III., I have received the following anecdote: "The late Bishop F., of Salisbury, having procured a young man of promising abilities to preach before the king, and the young man having, to his lordship's apprehension, acquitted himself well, the bishop, in conversation with the king afterward, wishing to get the king's opinion, took the liberty to say, 'Does not your majesty think that the young man who had the honour to preach before your majesty is likely to make a good clergyman, and has this morning delivered a very good sermon?' To which the king, in his blunt manner, hastily replied, 'It might have been a good sermon, my lord, for aught I know; but I consider no sermon good that has nothing of Christ in it!'"

In 1790 the conference was held in Bristol, the last in which that most eminent man of God, John Wesley, presided; who seemed to have his mind particularly impressed with the necessity of making some permanent rule that might tend to lessen the excessive labour of the preachers, which he saw was shortening the lives of many useful men. In a private meeting with some of the principal and senior preachers, which was held in Mr. Wesley's study, to prepare matters for the conference, he proposed that a rule should be made that no preacher should preach thrice on the same day. Messrs. Mather, Pawson, Thompson, and others said this would be impracticable; as it was absolutely necessary, in most cases, that the preachers should preach thrice every Lord's day, without which the places could not be supplied. Mr. W. replied, "It must be given up; we shall lose our preachers by such excessive labour." They answered, "We have all done so; and you, even at an advanced age, have continued to do so." "What I have done," said he, "is out of the question; my life and strength have been under an especial Providence; besides, I know better than they how to preach without injuring myself; and no man can preach thrice a day without killing himself sooner or later; and the custom shall not be continued." They pressed the point no farther, finding that he was determined; but they deceived him after all, by altering the minute thus, when it went to the press: No preacher shall any more preach three times in the same day (to the same congregation)." By which clause the minute was entirely neutralized. He who preaches the Gospel as he ought, must do it with his whole strength of body and soul; and he who undertakes a labour of this kind thrice every Lord's day will infallibly shorten his life by it. He who, instead of preaching, talks to the people, merely speaks about good things, or tells a religious story, will never injure himself by such an employment; such a person does not labour in the word and doctrine; he tells his tale, and as he preaches, so his congregation believes, and sinners are left as he found them.

Go from your knees to the chapel. Get a renewal of your commission every time you go to preach, in a renewed sense of the favour of God. Carry your authority to declare the Gospel of Christ not in your hand, but in your heart. When in the pulpit, be always solemn: say nothing to make your congregation laugh. Remember you are speaking for eternity; and trifling is inconsistent with such awful subjects as the great God, the agony and death of Christ, the torments of hell, and the blessedness of heaven.

Never assume an air of importance while in the pulpit; you stand in an awful place, and God hates the proud man. Never be boisterous or dogmatical. Self-confidence will soon lead to a forgetfulness of the presence of God; and then you will speak your own words, and perhaps in your own spirit too.

Avoid all quaint and fantastic attitudes; all queer noddings, ridiculous stoopings, and erections of your body, skipping from side to side of the desk, knitting your brows; and every other theatrical or foppish air, which tends to disgrace the pulpit, and to render yourself contemptible. Never shake or flourish your handkerchief; this is abominable: nor stuff it into your bosom; this is unseemly. Do not gaze about on your congregation. Endeavour to gain their attention. Remind them of the presence of God.

Give out the page and measure of the hymn, and the hymn itself, distinctly and with a full voice. While praying, keep your eyes closed: at such a time you have nothing to do with outward objects; the most important matters are at issue between God and you; and he is to be contemplated with the eye of the mind. If you wish the people to join with you in this part of the worship, speak so as to be heard, even at the beginning. Whispering petitions to God may be genteel, for aught I know; but I am certain it is not to the use of edification. In your prayers avoid long prefaces and circumlocutions: you find none of these in the Bible. Some have got a method of complimenting the Most High on the dignity of his nature, and the glory of his heavens: this you should studiously avoid. Read your text distinctly, and begin to speak about the middle of your voice, not only that you may be readily heard, but that you may rise or fall as occasion may require: Never drop your voice at the end of a sentence; this is barbarous and intolerable.

Be sure to have the matter of your text well arranged in your own mind before you come into the pulpit, that you may not be confused while speaking. But beware of too much dividing and subdividing; by these means the word of God has been made to speak something, any thing, or nothing, according to the creed or prejudice of the preacher. In whatever way you handle your text, take care, when you have exhausted the matter of it, not to go over it again. Apply every thing of importance as you go along; and when you have done, learn to make an end. There are some who sing long hymns, and pray long prayers, merely to fill up the time: this is a shocking profanation of these sacred ordinances, and has the most direct tendency to bring them into contempt.

While you are engaged in the pulpit in recommending the salvation of God, endeavour to feel the truth you preach, and diffuse a divine animation through every part. As the preacher appears to preach the people hear and believe. You may set it down as an incontrovertible truth, that none of your hearers will be more affected with your discourse than yourself. A dull, dead preacher makes a dull, dead congregation.

Shun all controversies about politics; and especially that disgrace of the pulpit, political preaching. I have known this do much evil; but though I have often heard it, I never knew an instance of its doing good.

A sentence or two of affectionate prayer in different parts of the discourse has a wonderful tendency to enliven it, and to make the people hear with concern and interest.

Never ape any person, however eminent he may be for piety or ministerial abilities. Every man has a fort, as it is called, of his own; and if he keep within it he is impregnable.

A fine appearance and a fine voice cover many weaknesses and defects, and strongly and forcibly recommend what is spoken, though not remarkable for depth of thought or solidity of reasoning. Many popular orators have little beside their persons and their voice to recommend them.

When you baptize, let it be, if possible, in the face of the congregation; and not in the vestry, nor in private. Take occasion in a few words to explain its nature and importance, both to the congregation and to the parents; and insist on the personal attendance of the latter, that you may give them those directions and charges relative to their training up their children in the discipline and admonition of the Lord which the case requires; and take heed that all whom you baptize be properly registered; and let the register book be kept in the most secure place, because it is of great importance; and in all cases in which a baptismal register can be applied, these registers are complete evidences in law.

In administering the sacrament of the Lord's supper, be deeply reverent and devout in all your deportment. Pour out the wine into the cups leisurely, and take heed that you spill not one drop of it. Shedding the wine on the table cloth, to say the least of it, is highly unbecoming and ungraceful: keep firm hold both of the bread and the cup, till you feel the communicant has hold with yourself.

The only preaching worth any thing, in God's account, and which the fire will not burn up, is that which labours to convict and convince the sinner of his sin, to bring him into contrition for it, to convert him from it; to lead him to the blood of the covenant, that his conscience may be purged from its guilt,—to the Spirit of judgment and burning, that he may be purified from its infection,— and then to build him up on this most holy faith, by causing him to pray in the Holy Ghost, and keep himself in the love of God, looking for the mercy of our Lord Jesus Christ unto eternal life: this is the system pursued by the apostles, and it is that alone which God will own to the conversion of sinners. I speak from the experience of nearly fifty years in the public ministry of the word: this is the most likely mode to produce the active soul of divinity, while the body is little else but the preacher's creed.

A man who preaches in such a language as the people cannot comprehend may do for a stage player or a mountebank, but not for a minister of Christ.

How foolish the preacher who uses fine and hard words in his preaching, which, though admired by the shallow, convey no instruction to the multitude.

A harsh, unfeeling method of preaching the promises of the Gospel, and a smiling manner of producing the terrors of the Lord, are equally reprehensible. Some preachers are always severe and magisterial; others are always mild and insinuating: neither of these can do God's work; and it would take two such to make one preacher.

How injudicious must that preacher be who frequently brings his people abstract questions concerning civil rights and civil wrongs, party politics, reasons of state, financial blunders, royal prerogatives, divine right of kings, questions on which a thousand things may be said *pro* and *con:* and, after all, a wise and dispassionate man finds it extremely difficult, after bearing both sides, to make up his mind as to that which he should from duty and interest attach himself.

Rhetoric or oratory is studied by many much more than divinity. A copious flow and elegance of language, words of splendid sound, imposing epithets, and striking figures and similes are everywhere sought, in order to form harmonious sentences and finely turned periods;—a fustian language, misnamed *oratory*, is thus introduced into the church of Christ; but when the words of this are analyzed, they are found, however musically arranged, to be destitute of force; so that a dozen of such expressions will labour in vain to produce one single impressive idea that can illuminate the understanding, correct the judgment, or persuade the conscience either to hate sin or love righteousness. "How forcible are right words," can never be applied to such sermons; they may please the giddy and superficial, but they neither edify the saint, nor bring conviction into the bosom of the sinner. And what redounds to their reproach and discredit is, they are flowers meanly stolen from the gardens of others.

Ministers continually harping on, "Ye are dead, ye are dead; there is little or no Christianity among you," &c., &c., are a contagion in a church, and spread desolation and death wheresoever they go. It is far better to say, in such cases, "Ye have lost ground, but ye have not lost all your ground; ye might have been much farther advanced, but through mercy ye are still in the way. The Spirit of God is grieved by you, but it is evident he has not forsaken you. Ye have not walked in the light as ye should, but your candlestick is not yet removed, and still the light shines. Ye have not much zeal, but ye have a little. In short, God still strives with you, still loves you, still waits to be gracious to you; take courage, set out afresh, come to God through Christ; believe, love, obey, and you will soon find days more blessed than you have ever yet experienced." Exhortations and encouragements of this kind are sure to produce the most blessed effects; and under such the work of God infallibly revives.

Stay in your own lodging as much as possible, that you may have time for prayer and study.

He who knows the value of time, and will redeem it from useless chitchat and trifling visits, will find enough for all the purposes of his own salvation, the cultivation of his mind, and the work of the ministry.

He to whom time is not precious, and who lives not by rule, never finds time sufficient for any thing, is always embarrassed, always in a hurry, and never capable of bringing one good purpose to proper effect.

Seldom frequent the tables of the rich or great. If you do, it will unavoidably prove a snare to you: the unction of God will perish from your mind; and your preaching be only a dry, barren repetition of old things. The bread of God in your hands will be like the dry, mouldy, Gibeonitish crusts, mentioned Josh. 9:5. Visit the people, and speak to them about their souls as often and as much as you can; but be not at their mercy of every invitation to go out for a morsel of bread. If you take not this advice, you will do no good, get no good, and utterly evaporate your influence and consequence.

I have such high notions of literary merit, and the academical distinctions to which it is entitled, that I would not, in conscience, take, or cause to be taken, in my own behalf, any step to possess the one, or to assume the other: every thing of this kind should come, not only unbought, but unsolicited. I should as soon think of being learned by proxy, as of procuring academical honours by influence; and could one farthing purchase me the highest degree under the sun, I would not give it: not that I lightly esteem such honours; I believe them, when given through merit, next to those which come from God; but I consider them misplaced when conferred in consequence of influence or recommendation, in which the party concerned has any part, near or remote.

Bodies of divinity I do most heartily dislike: they tend to supersede the Bible; and, independently of this, they are exceedingly dangerous; they often give false notions, bring their own kind of proofs to confirm those notions, and by their mode of quoting insulated texts of Scripture, greatly pervert the true meaning of the word of God. This is my opinion of them: the ministers who preach from them fill the heads of their hearers with systematic knowledge.

In dead languages it is well to select the best authors, and establish them as standards of pure and elegant composition; for, in such languages no farther excellence can be expected. But in those languages which continue to be vernacular, the case is widely different; they may still be improved and polished, therefore no writer should be set up as a standard of unsurpassable excellence. Why may not the English, for instance, expect writers who shall as far excel Addison, Steele, Johnson, Spenser, Shakespeare, Milton, and Pope, as they have surpassed their predecessors? Certainly the English language and the British genius, notwithstanding their almost unrivalled excellence, are still capable of greater perfection.

A good pastor will not, like a miser, keep what he has to himself, to please his fancy; nor, like a merchant, traffic with it to enrich himself, but, like a bountiful father or householder, distribute it with a liberal, though judicious hand, for the comfort and support of the whole heavenly family.

A late morning student is a lazy one, and will rarely make a true scholar; and he who sits up late at night, not only burns his life's candle at both ends, but puts a red-hot poker to the middle.

PEOPLE — Be very cautious of receiving evil reports against those whose business it is to preach to others, and correct their vices. Do not consider an elder as guilty of any alleged crime, unless it be proved by two or three witnesses. This the law of Moses required in respect to all. Among the Romans, a plebeian might be condemned on the deposition of one credible witness; but it required two to convict a senator. The reason of this difference is evident: those whose business it is to correct others will usually have many enemies; great caution, therefore, should be used in admitting accusations against such persons.

God requires that his people should pray for his ministers; and it is not to be wondered at, if they who pray not for their preachers should receive no benefit from their teaching. How can they expect God to send a message by him for whom they who are the most interested have not prayed? If the grace and Spirit of Christ be not worth the most earnest prayers which a man can offer, they, and the heaven to which they lead, are not worth having.

Even the success of the apostles depended, in a certain way, on the prayers of the church. Few Christian congregations feel, as they ought, that it is their bounden duty to pray for the success of the Gospel, both among themselves and in the world. The church is weak, dark, poor, and imperfect, because it prays little.

There are some people who are unwilling to grant the common necessaries of life to those who watch over them in the Lord. For there are such people even in the Christian church! If the preachers of the Gospel were as parsimonious of the bread of life as some congregations and Christian societies are of the bread that perisheth; and if the preacher gave them a spiritual nourishment as base, as mean, and as scanty as the temporal support which they afford him, their souls must, without doubt, have nearly a famine of the bread of life.

St. Paul contends that a preacher of the Gospel has a right to his support; and he has proved this from the law, from the Gospel, and from the common sense and consent of men. If a man who does not labour takes his maintenance from the church of God, it is not only a domestic theft, but a sacrilege. He that gives up his time to this labour has a right to the support of himself and family. Those who refuse the labourer his hire are condemned by God and good men. How liberal are many to public places of amusement, or to some popular charity, where their names are sure to be published abroad; while the man who watches over their souls is fed with the most parsimonious hand! Will not God abate this pride, and reprove this hard heartedness?

Contribute to the support of the man who has dedicated himself to the work of the ministry, and who gives up his time and his life to preach the Gospel. It appears that some of the believers in Galatia could receive the Christian ministry without contributing to its support. This is both ungrateful and base. We do not expect that a common schoolmaster will give up his time to teach our children their alphabet without being paid for it; and can we suppose that it is just for any person to sit under the preaching of the Gospel in order to grow wise unto salvation by it, and not contribute to the support of the spiritual teacher? It is unjust.

Let all churches, all congregations of Christians, from whom their ministers and preachers can claim nothing by law, and for whom the state makes no provision, ask themselves: "Do we deal with these in a manner worthy of God, and worthy of the profession we make? Do we suffer them to lack the bread that perisheth, while they minister to us with no sparing hand the bread of life?" Let a certain class of religious people, who will find themselves out when they read this, consider whether, when their preachers have ministered to them their certain or stated time, and are called to go and serve other churches, they send them forth in a manner worthy of God, making a reasonable provision for the journey which they are obliged to take. In the itinerant ministry of the apostles, it appears that each church bore the expenses of the apostle to the next church, or district, to which he was going to preach the word of life. So it should be still in the mission and itinerant ministry.

I have seen many aged and worn-out ministers reduced to great necessity, and almost literally obliged to beg their bread among those whose opulence and salvation were, under God, the fruits of their ministry! Such persons may think they do God service by disputing "tithes, as legal institutions long since abrogated," while they permit their worn-out ministers to starve: but how shall they appear in that day when Jesus shall say, "I was hungry, and ye gave me no meat; thirsty, and ye gave me no drink; naked, and ye clothed me not?"

The religion that costs us nothing, is to us worth nothing.

It is the privilege of the churches of Christ to support the ministry of his Gospel among them. Those who do not contribute their part to the support of the Gospel ministry either care nothing for it, or derive no good from it.

Nothing can be more reasonable than to devote a portion of the earthly good which we receive from the free mercy of God, to his own service; especially when by doing it we are essentially serving ourselves. If the ministers of God give up their whole time, talents, and strength, to watch over, labour for, and instruct the people in spiritual things, justice requires that they shall receive their support from the work. How worthless and wicked must that man be who is continually receiving good from the Lord's hands without restoring any part for the support of true religion and for charitable purposes! To such God says, "Their table shall become a snare to them," and that he will curse their blessings. God expects returns of gratitude in this way from every man; he that has much should give plenteously; he that has little should do his diligence to give of that little.

It is an honour to be permitted to do any thing for the support of public worship; and he must have a strange, unfeeling, ungodly heart, who does not esteem it a high privilege to have a stone of his own laying or procuring in the house of God. How easily might all the buildings necessary for the purpose of public worship be raised, if the money that is spent in needless self-indulgence by ourselves, our sons, and our daughters, were devoted to this purpose! By sacrifices of this kind the house of the Lord would be soon built, and the "top stone brought on with shouting, Grace, grace unto it!"

Though I had been almost exhausted with my yesterday's work, yet they insisted on my preaching at Lisburne at eleven, as it was their quarterly meeting. In vain I urged and expostulated. They said, "Surely, you came out to preach, and why should you not preach at every opportunity?" "I must rest." "Surely, you can rest after preaching!" I replied, "I must preach to-morrow at Lurgan, and shall have but little time to rest." "O, the more you preach, the more strength you will get." "I came out for the sake of health and rest." "O, rest when you return home." "I cannot rest at home, as I have got more work to do there than I can manage." "Then," said they, "you shall get rest in the grave." I give this specimen of the inconsiderateness and unfeelingness of many religious people, who care little how soon their ministers are worn out; because they find their excessive labours comfortable to their own minds; and should the preacher die through his extraordinary exertions, they have this consolation, "God can soon raise up another."

No teacher should be exalted above, or opposed to, another. As the eye could not say to the hand, "I have no need of thee;" so, luminous Apollos could not say to laborious Paul, "I can build up and preserve the church without thee." As the foot planted on the ground to support the whole fabric; and as the hands which swing at liberty; and as the eye that is continually taking in near and distant objects, are all necessary to the whole, and mutually helpful to and dependant on each other; so also are the different ministers and members of the church of Christ.

The doctrine and teacher most prized and followed by worldly men, and by the gay, giddy, and garish multitude, are not from God; they savour of the flesh, lay on no restraints, prescribe no cross-bearing, and leave every one in full possession of his heart's lusts and easily besetting sins. And by this, false doctrine and false teachers are easily discerned.

Happy they who, on hearing of the salvation of Christ, immediately attach themselves to its Author! Delays are always dangerous; and, in this case, often fatal. Reader! hast thou ever had Christ as a sacrifice for thy sin pointed out unto thee? If so, hast thou followed him? If not, thou art not in the way to the kingdom of God. Lose not another moment! Eternity is at hand! and thou art not prepared to meet thy God. Pray that he may alarm thy conscience, and stir up thy soul to seek till thou hast found.

If thou art seriously inquiring where Christ dwelleth, take the following for an answer: He dwells not in the tumult of worldly affairs, nor in profane assemblies, nor in worldly pleasures, nor in the place where drunkards proclaim their shame, nor in carelessness and idleness. But he is found in his temple, where two or three are gathered together in his name, in secret prayer, in self-denial, in fasting, in self-examination. He also dwells in the humble, contrite spirit, in the spirit of faith, of love, of forgiveness, of universal obedience: in a word, he dwells in the heaven of heavens, whither he graciously purposes to bring thee, if thou wilt come and learn of him, and receive the salvation which he has bought for thee with his own blood.

The church or chapel in which the blind and lame are not healed has no Christ in it, and is not worthy of attendance.

Those who come, under the influence of God's Spirit, to places of public worship, will undoubtedly meet with Him who is the comfort and salvation of Israel.

The soul that relishes God's word is ever growing in grace by it.

Those who suppose themselves to excel all others in piety, understanding, &c., while they are harsh, censorious, and overbearing, prove that they have not the charity that "thinketh no evil;" and in the sight of God are only "as sounding brass and a tinkling cymbal." There are no people more censorious or uncharitable than those among some religious people who pretend to more light and a deeper communion with God. They are generally carried away with a sort of sublime high-sounding phraseology, which seems to argue a wonderfully deep acquaintance with divine things: stripped of this, many of them are like Samson without his hair.

The mere preaching of the Gospel has done much to convince and convert sinners; but the lives of the sincere followers of Christ, as illustrative of the truth of these doctrines, have done much more. Truth represented in action seems to assume a body, and thus renders itself palpable. In heathen countries, which are under the dominion of Christian powers, the Gospel, though established there, does little good, because of the profane and irreligious lives of those who profess it. Why has not the whole peninsula of India been long since evangelized? The Gospel has been preached there; but the lives of the Europeans professing Christianity there have been, in general, profligate, sordid, and base. From them sounded out no good report of the Gospel; and therefore the Mohammedans continue to prefer their Koran, and the Hindoos their Vedas and Shasters, to the Bible.

Do not suppose that ye have no need of continual instruction; without it ye cannot preserve the Christian life, nor go on to perfection. God will ever send a message of salvation by each of his ministers to every faithful, attentive hearer. Do not suppose that ye are already wise enough; you are no more wise enough than you are holy enough; they who slight or neglect the means of grace, and especially the preaching of God's holy word, are generally vain, empty, self-conceited people, and exceedingly superficial both in knowledge and piety.

"Ever learning, and never able to come to the knowledge of the truth." There are many professors of Christianity still who answer the above description. They hear, repeatedly hear, it may be, good sermons; but, as they seldom meditate on what they hear, they derive little profit from the ordinances of God. They have no more grace now than they had several years ago, though hearing all the while, and perhaps not wickedly departing from the Lord. They do not meditate, they do not think, they do not reduce what they hear to practice; therefore, even under the preaching of an apostle, they could not become wise to salvation.

Should the most nutritive aliment be received into the stomach, if not mixed with the above juices, it would be rather the means of death than of life; or, in the words of the apostle, it would not profit, because not thus mixed. Faith in the word preached, in reference to that God who sent it, is the grand means of its becoming the power of God to the salvation of the soul. It is not likely that he who does not credit a threatening when he comes to hear it, will be deterred by it from repeating the sin against which it is levelled; nor can he derive comfort from a promise who does not believe it as a pledge of God's veracity and goodness. Faith, therefore, must be mixed with all that we hear, in order to make the word of God effectual to our salvation.

The seed of the kingdom can never produce much fruit in any heart till the thorns and thistles of vicious affections and impure desires be plucked up by the roots and burned.

It is very difficult to get a worldly minded and self-righteous man brought to Christ. Examples signify little to him. Urge the example of an eminent saint, he is discouraged at it. Show him a profligate sinner converted to God, him he is ashamed to own and follow; and as to the conduct of the generality of the followers of

Christ, it is not striking enough to impress him.

How many of those who are called Christians suffer the kingdom, the graces, and the salvation which they had in their hands to be lost; while West India negroes, American Indians, Hindoo Polytheists, and atheistic Hottentots obtain salvation.

Many, after having done their duty, as they call it, in attending a place of worship, forget the errand that brought them thither, and spend their time, on their return, rather in idle conversation than in reading or conversing about the word of God. It is no wonder that such should be always "learning, and never able to come to a knowledge of the truth."

It is not, therefore, the nation, kindred, profession, mode or form of worship, that the just God regards; but the character, the state of heart, and the moral deportment. For what are professions, &c., in the sight of that God who trieth spirits, and by whom actions are weighed! He looks for the grace he has given, the advantages he has afforded, and the improvement of all these. Let it be observed farther, that no man can be accepted with this just God who does not live up to the advantages of the state in which Providence has placed him.

It is possible for a man to credit the four evangelists, and yet live and die an infidel, as far as his own salvation is concerned.

God says to the swearer and the profane, "Thou shalt not take the name of the Lord thy God in vain;" and yet common swearing and profaneness are most scandalously common among multitudes who bear the Christian name, and who presume on the mercy of God to get at last to the kingdom of heaven! He says also, "Remember the Sabbath day to keep it holy; thou shalt not kill; thou shalt not commit adultery; thou shalt not steal; thou shalt not bear false witness; thou shalt not covet;" and sanctions all these commandments with the most awful penalties: and yet with all these things before them, and the professed belief that they came from God, Sabbath-breakers, men-slayers, adulterers, fornicators, thieves, dishonest men, false witnesses, liars, slanderers, backbiters, covetous men, "lovers of the world more than lovers of God," are found by hundreds and thousands! What were the crimes of the poor half-blind Egyptian king, when compared with these? He sinned against a comparatively "unknown God;" these sin against the God of their fathers—against the God and Father of Him whom they call their Lord and Saviour, Jesus Christ! They sin with the Bible in their hand, and a conviction of its divine authority in their hearts. They sin against light and knowledge; against the checks of their consciences, the reproofs of their friends, the admonitions of the messengers of God; against Moses and Aaron in the law; against the testimony of all the prophets; against the evangelists, the apostles, the Maker of heaven and earth, the Judge of all men, and the Saviour of the world! What were Pharaoh's crimes to the crimes of these? On comparison, his atom of moral turpitude is lost in their world of iniquity. And yet who supposes these to be under any necessitating decree to sin on, and go to perdition? Nor are they; nor was Pharaoh. In all things God has proved both his justice and mercy to be clear in this point.

I shall now take the liberty of giving you a few directions how to hear the word profitably.

Endeavour to get your minds deeply impressed with the value of God's word.

If possible, get a few minutes for private prayer before you go to the house of God, that you may supplicate his throne for a blessing on your own soul, and on the congregation.

When you get to the chapel, consider it as the house of God, the dwelling place of the Most High; that he is there to bless his people; and that you cannot please him better than by being willing to receive the abundant mercies which he is ready to communicate.

Mingle all your hearing with prayer.

Hear with faith. Receive the Scriptures as the words of God.

Receive the preacher as the ambassador of God, sent particularly to *you* with a message of salvation. Listen attentively to every part of the sermon; there is a portion for you somewhere in it: hear all, and you are sure to discern what belongs to yourself.

Do not suppose that you know even all the outlines of the plan of salvation. There is a height, length, breadth, and depth in the things of God, of which you have as yet but a very inadequate conception.

Do not think that this or the other preacher cannot instruct you. He may be, comparatively speaking, a weak preacher; but the meanest servant of God's sending will at all times be directed to bring something to the wisest and holiest Christians which they have not fully known or enjoyed before.

Never absent yourself from the house of God when you can possibly attend.

Consider how great the blessing is which you enjoy! What would a damned soul give for the privilege of sitting five minutes in your place, to hear Jesus preached, with the same possibility of being saved?

Do not divide the word with your neighbour; hear for yourself. Share your clothes, money, bread, &c., with him, but do not divide the word preached.

Consider, this may be the last sermon you shall ever be permitted to hear.

That your being blessed does not consist in your remembering heads, divisions, &c., but in feeling the divine influence.

After the sermon is over, get as speedily home as you can, and spend a few moments on your knees in private prayer. Meditate on what you have heard.

Pray for your preachers, that God may fill them with the unction of his Spirit.

And, when you read the Holy Scriptures, consider that it is God's word which you read, and that his faithfulness is pledged to fulfil both its promises and threatenings.

Read the whole Bible, and read it in order; two chapters in the Old Testament, and one in the New, daily, if you can possibly spare time.

Think that the eye of God is upon you while you are reading; and remember that the word is not sent to particular persons, as if by name; and do not think you have no part in it, because you are not named there. It is not thus sent: it is addressed to particular characters; to saints, sinners, the worldly minded, the proud, &c. Therefore, examine your own state, and see to which of these characters you belong, and then apply the word spoken to the character in question to yourself; for it is as surely spoken to you as if your name were found printed in the Bible, and placed there by divine inspiration itself.

When you meet with a threatening, and know, from your own state, that this awful word is spoken against you, stop, and implore God, for the sake of the sufferings and death of his Son, to pardon the sin that exposes you to the punishment threatened.

When you meet with a promise made to the penitent, tempted, afflicted, &c., having found out your own case, stop, and implore God to fulfil that promise.

Should you find, on examination, that the threatening has been averted by your having turned to God; that the promise has been fulfilled through your faith in Christ; stop here also, and return God thanks. Thus you will constantly find matter, in reading the book of God, to excite repentance, to exercise faith, to produce confidence and consolation, and to beget gratitude; and gratitude will never fail to beget obedience.

It is always useful to read a portion of the Scriptures before prayer, whether performed in the family or in the closet.

Keep the eye of your mind steadily fixed upon Him who is the end of the law, and the sum of the Gospel.

Let the Scriptures, therefore, lead you to that Holy Spirit by which they were inspired; let that Spirit lead you to Jesus Christ, who has ransomed you by his death. And let this Christ lead you to the Father, that he may adopt you into the family of heaven; and thus, being taught of him, justified by his blood, and sanctified by his Spirit, you shall be saved with all the power of an endless life.

XXVI. – GOOD AND BAD ANGELS.

GOOD ANGELS – Our word "angel" comes from the Greek *angelos,* which literally signifies "a messenger," or, as translated in some of our old Bibles, "a tidings-bringer." It is applied indifferently to a human agent or messenger, 2 Sam. ii, 5; to a prophet, Haggai i, 13; to a priest, Mal. ii, 7; to celestial spirits, Psalm ciii, 19, 20, 22; civ. 4.

The doctrine of the ministration of angels has been much abused, not only among the heathens, but also among Jews and Christians, and most among the latter. Angels, with feigned names, titles, and influences, have been and still are invoked and worshipped by a certain class of men, because they have found that God has been pleased to employ them to minister to mankind; and hence they have made supplications to them to extend their protection, to shield, defend, instruct, &c. This is perfectly absurd. 1. They are God's instruments, not self-determining agents. 2. They can only do what they are appointed to perform, for there is no evidence that they have any discretionary power. 3. God helps man by ten thousand means and instruments; some intellectual, as angels; some rational, as men; some irrational, as brutes; and some merely material, as the sun, wind, rain, food, raiment, and the various productions of the earth. He therefore helps by whom he will help, and to him alone belongs all the glory; for, should he be determined to destroy, all these instruments collectively could not save. Instead, therefore, of worshipping them, we should take their own advice: "See thou do it not; worship God."

Evil spirits may attempt to injure thee; but they shall not be able. The angels of God shall have an especial charge to accompany, defend, and preserve thee; and against their power the influence of evil spirits cannot prevail. These will, when necessary, turn thy steps out of the way of danger; ward it off when it comes in thy ordinary path; suggest to thy mind prudent counsels, profitable designs, and pious purposes; and thus minister to thee as a child of God and an heir of salvation.

Previously to our Lord's ascension to heaven these holy beings could have little knowledge of the necessity, reasons, and economy of human salvation, nor of the nature of Christ as God and man. St. Peter informs us that the angels desire to look into these things, 1 Pet. i, 12. And St. Paul says the same thing, Eph. iii, 9, 10, when speaking of the revelation of the Gospel plan of salvation, which he calls "the mystery which from the beginning of the world had been hid in God;" and which was now published, that "unto the principalities and powers in heavenly places might be made known by the church the manifold wisdom of God." Even those angelic beings have got an accession to their blessedness by an increase of knowledge in the things which concern Jesus Christ, and the whole scheme of human salvation, through his incarnation, passion, death, resurrection, ascension, and glorification.

BAD ANGELS — There are many demons mentioned in Scripture; but the word *Satan,* or *Devil,* is never found in the originals of the Old and New Testaments in the plural number. Hence we reasonably infer that all evil spirits are under the government of one chief, the devil, who is more powerful and more wicked than the rest. From the Greek διαβολος comes the Latin *diabolus,* the Spanish *diablo,* the French *diable,* the Italian *diavolo,* the German *teuffel,* the Dutch *duivel,* the Anglo-Saxon *deovle,* and the English *devil,* which some would derive from "the evil;" the evil one, or wicked one.

I have remarked, among the simple, honest inhabitants of the counties of Antrim and Londonderry, in Ireland, that the common name for the devil or Satan was "the sorrow;" a good sense of the original word, — "the wicked one, the evil one, the sorrow;" he who is miserable himself, and whose aim is to make all others so.

It is now fashionable to deny the existence of this evil spirit; and this is one of what St. John, Rev. ii, 24, calls "the depths of Satan;" as he well knows that they who deny his being will not be afraid of his power and influence; will not watch against his wiles and devices; will not pray to God for deliverance from the evil one; will not expect him to be trampled down under their feet, who has no existence; and, consequently, they will become an easy and unopposing prey to the enemy of their souls. By leading men to disbelieve and deny his existence, he throws them off their guard, and is then their complete master, and they are led captive by him at his will. It is well known that, among all those who make any profession of religion, those who deny the existence of the devil are they who pray little or none at all; and are, apparently, as careless about the existence of God, as they are about the being of a devil. Piety to God is with them out of the question; for those who do not pray, especially in private, (and I never met with a devil-denier who did,) have no religion of any kind, whatsoever pretensions they may choose to make.

Those who deny the existence of Satan are generally men of desperate characters and desperate fortunes; and, as they will not listen to the voice of reason, nor to the sacred oracles, they must be left to their own desperation.

Because men cannot see as far as the Spirit of God does, therefore they deny his testimony. "There was no devil; there can be none." Why? "Because we have never seen one, and we think the doctrine absurd." Excellent reason! And do you think that any man who conscientiously believes his Bible will give any credit to you? Men sent from God, to bear witness to the truth, tell us there were demoniacs in their time; you say, "No; they were only diseases." Whom shall we credit? the men sent from God, or you?

Is the doctrine of demoniacal influence false? If so, Jesus took the most direct method to perpetuate the belief of that falsity by accommodating himself so completely to the deceived vulgar. But this was impossible; therefore the doctrine of demoniacal influence is a true doctrine, otherwise Christ would never have given it the least countenance or support.

God has often permitted demons to act on and in the bodies of men and women; and it is not improbable that the principal part of unaccountable and inexplicable disorders still come from the same source.

Satan was once in the truth, in righteousness and true holiness; and he fell from that truth into sin and falsehood, so that he became the father of lies, and the first murderer.

God, in his endless mercy, has put enmity between men and Satan; so that, though all mankind love his service, yet all invariably hate himself. Were it otherwise, who could be saved? A great point gained toward the conversion of a sinner is, to convince him that it is Satan he has been serving; that it is to him he has been giving up his soul, body, goods, &c. He starts with horror when this conviction fastens on his mind, and shudders at the thought of being in league with the old murderer.

It is very seldom that God permits Satan to waste the substance, or afflict the body, of any man; but at all times this malevolent spirit may have access to the mind of any man, and inject doubts, fears, diffidence, perplexities, and even unbelief. And here is the spiritual conflict. Now, their wrestling is not with flesh and blood; with men like themselves, nor about secular affairs; but they have to contend with angels, principalities, and powers, and the rulers of the darkness of this world, and spiritual wickednesses in high places. In such cases Satan is often permitted to diffuse darkness into the understanding, and envelope the heavens with clouds. Hence are engendered false views of God and his providence; of men and of the spiritual world; and particularly of the person's own state and circumstances. Every thing is distorted, and all seen through a false medium. Indescribable distractions and uneasiness are hereby induced. The mind is like a troubled sea, tossed by a tempest that seems to confound both heaven and earth. Strong temptations to things which the soul contemplates with abhorrence are injected, and which are followed by immediate accusations, as if the injections were the offspring of the heart itself; and the trouble and dismay produced are represented as the sense of guilt from a consciousness of having in heart committed these evils. Thus Satan tempts, accuses, and upbraids, in order to perplex the soul, induce skepticism, and destroy the empire of faith. Behold here the permission of God; and behold also his sovereign control: all this time the grand tempter is not permitted to touch the heart, the seat of the affections; nor to do even the slightest violence to the will. The soul is cast down, but not destroyed; perplexed, but not in despair. It is on all sides harassed: without are fightings; within are fears; but the will is inflexible on the side of God and truth, and the heart, with all its train of affections and passions, follows it. The man does not wickedly depart from his God; the outworks are violently assailed, but not taken; the city is still safe, and the citadel impregnable. Heaviness may endure for the night, but joy cometh in the morning. Jesus is seen walking upon the waters. He speaks peace to the winds and the sea; immediately there is a calm. Satan is bruised down under the feet of the sufferer; the clouds are dispersed; the heavens reappear; and the soul, to its surprise, finds that the storm, instead of hindering, has driven it nearer the haven whither it should be.

Satan's ordinary method in temptation is to excite strongly to sin, to blind the understanding and inflame the passions; and when he succeeds, he triumphs by insults and reproaches. No one so ready then to tell the poor soul how deeply, disgracefully, and ungratefully it has sinned! Reader, take heed!

A part of Job's sufferings probably arose from appalling representations made to his eye, or to his imagination, by Satan and his agents: I think this neither irrational nor improbable. That he and his demons have power to make themselves manifest on especial occasions, has been credited in all ages of the world; not by the weak, credulous, and superstitious only, but also by the wisest, the most learned, and the best of men. I am persuaded that many passages in the book of Job refer to this; and admit of an easy interpretation on this ground.

Satan, who works in the heart of the children of disobedience, possesses himself of the corrupt nature of man, produces bad motives in a bad heart, blinds the understanding, excites irregular appetites, and thence bad tempers, evil words, and unholy actions.

Satan is ever going about as a roaring lion seeking whom he may devour; in order to succeed, he blinds the understanding of sinners, and then finds it an easy matter to tumble them into the pit of perdition.

What a wide-wasting woe and evil is one sinner! He spreads desolation and death wherever he comes. Satan drives, and he runs; or, spontaneous with the tempter, he is led captive by him at his will. By the instrumentality of one wicked man Satan can do ten thousand times more evil than he can in his own person. He deceiveth the world, waters the infernal seed, and powerfully works in the hearts of the children of disobedience. What a dishonour to be a servant, and much more to be a slave, of the devil! O why do not sinners lay this to heart!

Satan takes advantage of our natural temper, state of health, and outward circumstances, to plague and ruin our souls.

An unholy spirit is the only place where Satan can have his full operation, and show forth the plenitude of his destroying power.

Neither the devil nor his servants ever speak truth but when they expect to accomplish some bad purpose by it.

Satan makes himself master of the heart, the eyes, and the tongue of the sinner. His heart he fills with the love of sin; his eyes he blinds, that he may not see his guilt and the perdition that awaits him; and his tongue he hinders from prayer and supplication, though he gives it increasing liberty in blasphemies, lies, slanders, &c. None but Jesus can redeem from this threefold captivity.

After having sown his seed, Satan disappears. Did he appear as himself, few would receive solicitation to sin; but he is seldom discovered in evil thoughts.

Satan has a shoot of iniquity for every shoot of grace and when God revives his work, Satan revives his also. No marvel, therefore, if we find scandals arising suddenly to discredit a work of grace where God has begun to pour out his Spirit.

It is the interest of Satan to introduce hypocrites and wicked persons into religious societies, in order to discredit the work of God, and to favour his own designs.

Men, through sin, are become the very house and dwelling place of Satan, having, of their own accord, surrendered themselves to this unjust possessor; for, whoever gives up his soul to sin gives it up to the devil. It is Jesus, and Jesus alone, who can deliver from the power of this bondage. When Satan is cast out, Jesus purifies and dwells in the heart.

Since a demon cannot enter even into a swine without being sent by God himself, how little is the power or malice of any of them to be dreaded by those who have God for their portion and protection.

The devil himself has his chains; and he who often binds

others is always bound himself.

A man must consent to sin before he can sin. God has so constituted the human will that it cannot be forced. Satan may present false images to the imagination, darken the mind, and confound the memory; but he cannot force the will. He may flatter, sooth, and promise pleasure in order to gain over the will, but before he can ruin us he must have our consent. Were the case otherwise, we could not possibly be saved.

Satan is never permitted to block up our way without the providence of God making a way through the wall. God ever makes a breach in his otherwise impregnable fortification. Should an upright soul get into difficulties and straits, he may rest assured that there is a way out as there was a way in; and that the trial shall never be above the strength that God shall give him to bear it.

The devil cannot conquer you if you continue to resist. Strong as he is, God never permits him to conquer the man who continues to resist him. He cannot force the human will. He who in the terrible name of JESUS opposes even the devil himself, is sure to have a speedy and glorious conquest. He flees from that name, and from his conquering blood.

Be vigilant: awake and keep awake; be always watchful; never be off your guard; your enemies are alert, they are never off theirs. Your "adversary the devil:" This is a reason why ye should be sober and vigilant; ye have an ever active, implacable, subtle enemy to contend with. He "walketh about:"—He has access to you everywhere: he knows your feelings and your propensities, and informs himself of all your circumstances; only God can know more and do more than he, therefore your care must be cast upon God. As a "roaring lion:"—Satan tempts under three forms: 1. The subtle serpent; to beguile our senses, pervert our judgment, and enchant our imagination. 2. As an angel of light; to allure us with false views of spiritual things, refinement in religion, and presumption on the providence and grace of God. 3. As a roaring lion; to beat us down, and destroy us by violent opposition, persecution, and death.

What a comfortable thought it is to the followers of Christ, that neither men nor demons can act against them but by the permission of their heavenly Father; and that he will not suffer any of those who trust in him to be tried above what they are able to bear, and will make the trial issue in their greater salvation, and in his glory!

"Every man has his price," was the maxim of a great statesman, Sir Robert Walpole, "But you have not bought such a one." "No, because I would not go up to his price. He valued himself at more than I thought him worth, and I could get others cheaper, who, in the general muster, would do as well!" No doubt Sir R. met with many such; and the devil, many more. But still God has multitudes that will neither sell their souls, their consciences, nor their country, for any price; who, though God should slay them, will nevertheless trust in him, and be honest men, howsoever tempted by the devil and his vicegerents: so did Job; so have thousands; so will all do, in whose hearts Christ dwells by faith.

XXVII. – TEMPTATIONS.

THE process of temptation is often as follows: —1. A simple: evil thought. 2. A strong imagination, or impression made on the imagination by the thing to which we are tempted. 3. Delight in viewing it. 4. Consent of the will to perform it. Thus lust is conceived, sin is finished, and death brought forth.

Temptation is a part of our Christian warfare; and Jesus, our Lord and pattern, was tempted, and sorely tempted too; and has, by his temptation, showed us how we may foil our adversary, and glorify our God in the day of such a visitation.

And man may be tempted, and be in a state of temptation, without entering into it: "entering into it" implies giving way, closing in with, and embracing it. That man has entered into a temptation who feels his heart inclined to it, and would act accordingly, did time, place, and opportunity serve. Christ was tempted even to worship the devil; but he entered not into any of the temptations of his adversary: the prince of this world came and found nothing in him, no evil nature within to join with the evil temptation without. Now a man may be on the verge of falling by some powerful and well circumstanced sin, —he may be in it; but the timely help of God may succour him, and prevent him from entering into it; and thus a brand is plucked from the burning. He was heated, yea, scorched by it, but was saved from the desolating and ruinous act.

The temptation that leads us astray may be as sudden as it is successful. We may lose in one moment the fruit of a whole life! How frequently is this the case, and how few lay it to heart! A man may fall by the means of his understanding, as well as by the means of his passions.

Ye have many enemies, cunning and strong; many trials, too great for your natural strength; many temptations, which no human power is able successfully to resist; many duties to perform, which cannot be accomplished by the strength of man; therefore you need divine strength; ye must have might; and ye must be strengthened everywhere, and every way fortified by that might; mightily and most effectually strengthened.

To know when to fight, and when to fly, is of great importance in the Christian life. Some temptations must be manfully met, resisted, and thus overcome; from others we must fly. He who stands to contend or reason, especially in such a case as that mentioned here, is infallibly ruined. *Principiis obsta*, "resist the first overtures of sin," is a good maxim. After remedies come too late.

No man, howsoever holy, is exempted from temptation; for God manifested in the flesh was tempted by the devil.

To be tempted even to the greatest abominations, (while a person resists,) is not sin; for Christ was tempted to worship the devil.

The state of our bodily health and worldly circumstances may afford our adversary many opportunities of doing us immense mischief.

We must shut our senses against dangerous objects, to avoid the occasion of sin. There is no temptation which is from its own nature, or favouring circumstances, irresistible. God has promised to bruise even Satan under our feet.

The fear of being tempted may become a most dangerous snare. Men often part with some member of the body, at the discretion of a surgeon, that they may preserve the trunk, and die a little later; and yet they will not deprive themselves of a look, a touch, a small pleasure, which endanger the eternal death of the soul.

Human strength and human weakness are only names in religion. The mightiest man, in the hour of trial, can do nothing without the strength of God; and the weakest woman can do all things, if Christ strengthen her.

Do not yield to temptation. It is no sin to be tempted; the sin lies in yielding. While the sin exists only in Satan's solicitation, it is the devil's sin, not ours: when we yield, we make the devil's sin our own; then we enter into temptation.

We should be on our guard against what are called little sins, and all occasions and excitements to sin. Take heed what company you frequent. One thing apparently harmless may lead by almost imperceptible links to sins of the deepest die.

The best way to foil the adversary is by the sword of the Spirit, which is the word of God.

He who, through the grace of God, resists and overcomes temptation, is always bettered by it.

A more than ordinary measure of divine consolation shall be the consequence of every victory.

Perhaps nothing tends so much to discover what we are, as trials either from men or devils.

The trials, disappointments, insults, and wants of the followers of Christ become, in the hand of the all-wise God, subservient to their best interests: hence nothing can happen to them without their deriving profit from it, unless it be their own fault.

The advantage of trials is to make us know our weakness, so as to oblige us to have recourse to God by faith in Christ.

Trials put religion and all the graces of which it is composed to proof; the man that stands in such trials gives proof that his religion is sound, and the evidence afforded to his own mind induces him to take courage, bear patiently, and persevere.

XXVIII. – AFFLICTIONS.

ALL men in the present life must be frequently in danger, necessity, and tribulation: dangers from which they cannot by their own strength or wisdom escape: necessities which no prudence or providence of theirs can supply: and tribulations through which it will be impossible for them to pass, unless they have divine help, both in the water and in the fire.

The labours of the day in several of the avocations of life are performed in perilous situations. Mining, in which hundreds of thousands are employed, is a tissue of dangers; in every moment life is exposed to imminent and various deaths, by what is called the fire damp, and the falling of parts of the pit on the miners. Those who travel by land or by water are not less exposed. By common stage coaches, accidents are not only frequent, but often mortal: weekly accounts from public registers are full of details of such calamitous events. Those who travel by water are yet more exposed than those who travel by land. On sea, there is never more than a few inches of plank between any man and death. In a sudden squall, a ship may easily founder; in a gale blowing on a lee shore, she may soon be dashed to pieces, and every hand lost. A ship may spring a leak which no industry or skill may be able to stop; and, after incredible labour of the crew, fill and go to the bottom, and every person be consigned to a watery grave. In cases where the weather has been dark and tempestuous for several days, so that no observation could be taken, and the reckoning, because of the conflicting and thwarting tides, has been necessarily imperfect; in a hazy state of the atmosphere the ship may make land in a breeze or gale, either by night or day, and be suddenly dashed in pieces: some of these perilous states I have witnessed. Beside these, there is a multitude of other dangers which unavoidably accompany a seafaring life; and which, in numerous cases, are destructive of human life: what need of an almighty Preserver!

I have known persons, in endeavouring to run out of the way of carts and coaches, actually run into the way of danger. I have known one who, walking along the parapet, was crushed to pieces by a cart wheel against the wall. I have seen a woman striving to see the raree-show of an illumination, fall from a garret, and dashed to pieces on the pavement. I have seen a man who had got too much liquor, riding furiously,—his horse fell, and he was killed on the spot. I have seen another who, getting on forbidden ground, was shot dead on the spot. I have known another who fell over a bank, and was dead before he could be taken up. In short, I have known many who ran into various kinds of dangers, and have paid for their imprudence, temerity, or what was called the "accident," by the loss of their life. In crossing the streets of London, or other large cities and towns, let us remember the proverb, that "there are always two hundred yards more of room behind a coach than before it:" of this many are sadly unmindful, and run across public streets before horses and carriages driving at full trot; and not a few have either lost life or limb by this folly.

As the religion of Christ gives no quarter to vice, so the vicious will give no quarter to this religion, or to its professors.

Can any man who pretends to be a scholar or disciple of Jesus Christ expect to be treated well by the world? Will not the world love its own, and them only? Why then so much impatience under sufferings, such an excessive sense of injuries, such delicacy? Can you expect any thing from the world better than you receive? If you want the honour that comes from it, abandon Jesus Christ, and it will again receive you into its bosom. But you will, no doubt, count the cost before you do this. Take the converse, abandon the love of the world, &c., and God will receive you.

If, in order to please a father or brother who is opposed to vital godliness, we abandon God's ordinances and followers, we are unworthy of any thing but hell.

It is no certain proof of the displeasure of God, that a whole people, or an individual, may be found in a state of great oppression and distress; nor are affluence and prosperity any certain signs of his approbation. God certainly loved the Israelites better than he did the Egyptians; yet the former were in the deepest adversity, while the latter were in the height of prosperity.

Though religion is frequently persecuted, and religious people suffer at first, where they are not fully known; yet a truly religious and benevolent character will in general be prized wherever it is well known. The envy of men is a proof of the excellence of that which they envy.

Reader, be thankful to God, who, in pity to thy weakness, has called thee to believe and enjoy, and not to suffer for his sake. It is not for us to covet seasons of martyrdom; we find it difficult to be faithful even in ordinary trials; yet, as offences may come, and times of sore trial and proof may occur, we should be prepared for them; and we should know that nothing less than Christ in us, the hope of glory, will enable us to stand in the cloudy and dark day. Let us, therefore, put on the whole armour of God; and, fighting under the Captain of our salvation, expect the speedy destruction of every inward foe; and triumph in the assurance that death, the last enemy, will, in his destructions, shortly be brought to a perpetual end. Hallelujah! The Lord God Omnipotent reigneth. Amen and Amen.

Eminent communications of the divine favour prepare for, and entitle to, great services and great conflicts.

Jan. 19th, 1830.—My purpose is to bear the evils and calamities of life with less pain of spirit; if I suffer wrong, to leave it to God to right me; to murmur against no dispensation of his providence; to bear ingratitude and unkindness, as things totally beyond my control, and consequently things on account of which I should not distress myself; and, though friends and confidants should fail, to depend more on my everlasting
Friend, who never can fail, and to the unkindly treated will cause all such things to work together for their good.

It is not likely that God, who has preserved thee so long, and fed and supported thee all thy life long, girding thee when thou knewest him not, is less willing to save and provide for thee and thine now than he was when probably thou trustedst less in him. He who made and gave his Son to redeem thee, can never be indifferent to thy welfare; and if he gave thee power to pray and to trust in him, is it at all likely that he is now seeking an occasion against thee, in order to destroy thee? Add to this, the very light that shows thy wretchedness, ingratitude, and disobedience, is, in itself, a proof that he is waiting to be gracious to thee; and the penitential pangs thou feelest, and thy bitter regret for thy unfaithfulness, argue that the light and fire are of God's own kindling, and are sent to direct and refine, not to drive thee out of the way and destroy thee. Nor would he have told thee such things of his love, mercy, and kindness, and unwillingness to destroy sinners, as he has told thee in his sacred Word, if he had been determined not to extend his mercy to thee.

Many have been humbled under afflictions, and taught to know themselves and humble themselves before God, that probably without this could have never been saved; after this, they have been serious and faithful. Affliction sanctified is a great blessing; unsanctified, is an additional curse.

Sometimes there is a kind of necessity that the followers of God should be afflicted: when they have no trials, they are apt to get careless; and when they have secular prosperity, they are likely to become worldly minded. "God," said a good man, can neither trust me with health nor money, therefore I am poor and afflicted." But the disciples of Christ may be very happy in their souls, though grievously afflicted in their bodies and in their estates.

God may bring his followers into severe straits and difficulties, that they may have the better opportunity of both knowing and showing their own faith and obedience; and that he may seize on those occasions to show them the abundance of his mercy, and thus confirm them in righteousness all their days. There is a foolish saying among some religious people, which cannot be too severely reprobated: "Untried grace is no grace." On the contrary, there may be much grace, though God, for good reasons, does not think proper for a time to put it to any severe trial or proof. But grace is certainly not fully known but in being called to trials of severe and painful obedience. But as all the gifts of God should be used, (and they are increased and strengthened by exercise,) it would be unjust to deny trials and exercises to grace, as this would be to preclude it from the opportunities of being strengthened and increased.

God never permits any tribulation to befall his followers, which he does not design to turn to their advantage. When he permits us to hunger, it is that his mercy may be the more observable in providing us with the necessaries of life. Privations, in the way of providence, are the forerunners of mercy and goodness abundant.

Multitudes, who condemn the conduct of this miserable Egyptian king, act in a similar manner. They relent when smarting under God's judgments, but harden their hearts when these judgments are removed. Of this kind I have witnessed numerous cases. To such God says by his prophet, "Why should ye be stricken any more? Ye will revolt more and more." Reader, are not the vows of God upon thee? Often when afflicted in thyself or family, hast thou not said like Pharaoh, "Now, therefore, forgive, I pray thee, my sin only this once," and "take away" from me "this death only?" And yet, when thou hadst respite, didst thou not harden thy heart, and, with returning health and strength, didst thou not return unto iniquity? And art thou not still in the broad road of transgression? "Be not deceived; God is not mocked:" he warns thee, but he will not be mocked by thee. What thou sowest, that thou must reap. Think, then, what a most dreadful harvest thou mayest expect from the seeds of vice which thou hast already sown!

It is not a mark of much grace to be longing to get to heaven because of the troubles and difficulties of the present life; they who love Christ are ever willing to suffer with him; and he may be as much glorified by patient suffering, as by the most active faith or laborious love. There are times in which, through affliction or other hinderances, we cannot do the will of God, but we can suffer it; and in such cases he seeks a heart that bears submissively, suffers patiently, and endures, as seeing Him who is invisible, without repining or murmuring. This is as full a proof of Christian perfection as the most intense and ardent love. Meekness, gentleness, and long suffering, are in our present state of more use to ourselves and others, and of more consequence in the sight of God, than all the ecstasies of the spirits of just men made perfect, and than all the raptures of an archangel. That church or Christian society, the members of which manifest the work of faith, labour of love, and patience of hope, is most nearly allied to heaven, and is on the suburbs of glory.

How vain were the attempts of men and devils to destroy the light of the Gospel by persecution and death! In spite of these it grew; and under them it flourished! The gates of hell, though opened wide to pour out all its hosts, could not prevail against it; and persecution, like a good broad- cast sowing, dispersed the seed of eternal life throughout the world. The persecuted went everywhere preaching the word of the truth of the Gospel: and had not the primitive Christians been burned out by persecution at Jerusalem, humanly speaking, it would have been a long time before Syria, Asia Minor, Greece, and Italy, could have heard the words of eternal life! Satan and his children persecuted and drove them from city to city. One company ran, and sowed the good seed of the kingdom; another, driven by the same agency, followed after them, and watered the seed; and God continued to reap a "plentiful harvest." Never was the wise and experienced devil farther out in his calculations than when he counted on the destruction of Christianity by fire and sword. Under him the Jews distinguished themselves in the first instance, and instead of casting down Christianity, they stumbled and fell, and rose no more! Heathen Rome followed in the same track; the sword, the fire, the axe, the gibbet, with the fangs and teeth of ferocious beasts, were tried in vain; and at last, by the power of Christianity, she and her idols, and her instruments of cruelty, were defeated and cast down, even down to the ground. Papal Rome, having apostatized from the spirit and power of the Gospel, copied her ancient mother, and most grievously persecuted all who held the truth of God against corrupt doctrines and the uncertain traditions of men; but she prevailed not; the secular and spiritual power were conjoined to annihilate those who testified against its corruptions and its crimes; and now, that truth which entered a solemn protest against those corruptions is rapidly spreading over the earth; and by it more than half the world has received that heavenly light concentrated in the Bible, which that church had first obscured by false interpretations; and at last violently snatched out of the hands of the people. But God has reclaimed his own Word, delivered it over to mankind; and they who would not walk in the light, but persecuted to death those who did, are now consigned to their native weakness, darkness, frippery, and folly; and her secular power is cast down for ever: and after ruling the earth with her iron sceptre, she has vanished as a power from the nations of the earth! Where now is her terror? Where now is her fear? and where her respect? The mighty angel has taken up the stone, like a "great millstone," and cast it "into the sea," saying, "Thus with violence shall that great city Babylon be thrown down, and shall be found no more at all!" Rejoice over her, thou heaven, and ye holy apostles and prophets, for the blood of prophets and of saints, and of all that were slain upon the earth. While we say, "Alas, alas, for this great city!" let us pray that, while her Antichristian power is crushed and dissolved, a Christian Rome may arise, clothed with the sun, having the moon under her feet; and thus, illustrated with sound doctrine, unspotted holiness, and useful learning, be once more respectable among the nations, and a blessing to the earth! Amen! Amen!

If men had uninterrupted comforts here, perhaps not one soul would seek a preparation for heaven. Human trials and afflictions, the general welfare of human life, are the highest proof of a Providence as benevolent as it is wise. Were the state of human affairs different from what it is, hell would be more thickly peopled; and there would be fewer inhabitants in glory. There is reason to doubt whether there would be any religion upon earth, had we nothing but temporal prosperity.

XXIX. – PROVIDENCE.

THAT God has general laws by which he governs the universe, I am fully aware; I see them through universal nature: and that he has a general providence suited to those laws, I equally believe; but as all generals imply the particulars of which they are composed, so I believe God has his particular laws; and, suited to them, his particular providence, adapted to every occurrence, and applicable to all possible varieties of persons, place, and circumstance; that nothing can occur to which he cannot adapt a particular influence by which that occurrence shall be so directed, or counteracted, as to prevent the evil, and produce the necessary good.

And should there be no occurrences which appear to be under the control of no particular laws, and should there be no natural means to meet such occurrences, guide their operation, or direct their mal- influence; so sovereign is he, that without laws and means, he can, by the omnific volitions of his own mind, counterwork the evil and produce the good. And this he is constantly doing, in numberless cases, in answer to prayer: and, indeed, every answer to prayer is a proof as well of this particular and especial providence, as of his innate and eternal goodness.

This providence is not only general, taking in the earth and its inhabitants, *en masse;* giving and establishing laws by which all things shall be governed; but it is also particular; it takes in the multitudes of the isles, as well as the vast continents; the different species, as well as the genera; the individual, as well as the family. As every whole is composed of its parts, without the smallest of which it could not be whole; so all generals are composed of particulars. And by the particular providence of God, the general providence is formed: he takes care of each individual; and, therefore, he takes care of the whole. Therefore, on the particular providence of God the general providence is built. And the general providence could not exist without the particular, any more than a whole could subsist independently of its parts. It is by this particular providence that God governs the multitude of the isles, notices the fall of a sparrow, bottles the tears of the mourner, and numbers the hairs of his followers. Now, as God is an infinitely wise and good being, and governs the world in wisdom and goodness, the earth may well rejoice and the multitude of the isles be glad.

It is granted that this is a subject which cannot be comprehended. And why? Because God is infinite: he acts from his own counsels, which are infinite, in reference to ends which are also infinite; therefore the reasons of his government cannot be comprehended by the feeble limited powers of man.

The providence of God in renewing the wastes of nature, and in fructifying barren tracts, so as to make the wilderness a fruitful field, and even the steril rocks a vegetable surface, is a subject of astonishing beauty and contrivance; and as such is worthy of the contemplation of angels and men; and is a sovereign proof of the being and love of the great First Cause and Preserver of all things.

God disposes and governs the affairs of the universe, descending to the minutest particulars, and managing the great whole by directing and influencing all its parts. This particular or especial providence is not confined to work by general laws; it is wise and intelligent, for it is the mind, the will, and energy of God; it steps out of common ways, and takes particular directions, as endlessly varied human necessities may need, or the establishment and maintenance of godliness in the earth may require.

That Divine Providence which arranges and conducts the whole, and under whose especial guidance and control the course of the present state is ordered, so that all operations in the natural, civil, and moral world, issue in manifesting the glory, justice, and mercy of the supreme Being, lies farther out of the view of men, and by most is little regarded: hence a multitude of events appear to have either no intelligent cause, or no one adequate to their production; and because the operations of the divine hand are not regarded, historians and biographers often disquiet themselves in vain to find out the causes and reasons of the circumstances and transactions which they record.

How exactly does every thing in the conduct of Providence occur! and how completely is every thing adapted to time, place, and occasion! All is in weight, measure, and number. Those simple occurrences which men snatch at, and press into the service of their own wishes, and call them "providential openings," may indeed be links of a providential chain, in reference to some other matters; but unless they be found to speak the same language in all their parts, occurrence corresponding with occurrence, they are not to be construed as indications of the divine will in reference to the claimants. Many persons, through these misapprehensions, miscarrying, have been led to charge God foolishly for the unsuccessful issue of some business in which their passions, not his providence, prompted them to engage.

Nothing escapes his merciful regards, not even the smallest things, of which he may be said to be only the Creator and Preserver; how much less those of whom he is the Father, Saviour, and endless Felicity!

There is not a circumstance in our life, not an occurrence in our business, but God will make subservient to our salvation, if we have a simple heart and teachable spirit.

Nothing is more astonishing than the care and concern of God for his followers. The least circumstances of their life are regulated, not merely by the general providence which extends to all things, but by a particular providence, which fits and directs all things to the design of their salvation, causing them all to cooperate for their present and eternal good.

"If God be for us, who can be against us?" He who is infinitely wise has undertaken to direct us: he who is infinitely powerful has undertaken to protect us: he who is infinitely good has undertaken to save us. What cunning, strength, or malice can prevail against his wisdom, power, and goodness? None. Therefore we are safe who love God, and not only shall sustain no essential damage by the persecutions of ungodly men, but even these things work together for our good.

The person whom Christ terms "happy" is one who is not under the influence of fate or chance, but is governed by an all-wise providence, having every step directed to the attainment of immortal glory, being transformed by the power into the likeness of the ever blessed God.

The belief of an all-wise, all-directing providence, is a powerful support under the most grievous accidents of life.

Let man, who is made for God and eternity, learn from a flower of the field how low the care of Providence stoops.

It is the property of a wise and tender father to provide necessaries, and not superfluities, for his children. Not to expect the former is an offence to his goodness; to expect the latter is injurious to his wisdom.

The passage from distrust to apostasy is very short and easy; and a man is not far from murmuring against providence who is dissatisfied with its conduct. We should depend as fully upon God for preservation of his gifts as for the gifts themselves.

To rely so much upon Providence as not to use the very powers and faculties with which the divine Being has endowed us, is to tempt God.

That God has promised to protect and support his servants admits of no dispute; but, as the path of duty is the way of safety, they are entitled to no good when they walk out of it.

XXX. – APOSTASY.

THERE has been much spoken against the doctrine of what is called free will by persons who seem not to have understood the term. Will is a free principle. Free will is as absurd as bound will: it is not will if it be not free; and if it be bound, it is no will. Volition is essential to the being of the soul, and to all rational and intellectual beings. This is the most essential discrimination between matter and spirit. Matter can have no choice, spirit has. Ratiocination is essential to intellect; and from these volition is inseparable. God uniformly treats man as a free agent; and on this principle the whole of divine revelation is constructed, as is also the doctrine of future rewards and punishments. If a man be forced to believe, he believes not at all: it is the forcing power that believes, not the machine forced. If he be forced to obey, it is the forcing power that obeys; and he, as a machine, shows only the effect of this irresistible force. If a man be incapable of willing good and willing evil, he is incapable of being saved as a rational being; and if he acts only under an overwhelming compulsion, he is as incapable of being damned. In short, this doctrine reduces him either to a *punctum stans*, which by the *vis inertiae* is incapable of being moved, but as acted upon by foreign influence; or, as an intellectual being, to nonentity.

The power to will and the power to act must necessarily come from God, who is the Author both of the soul and the body, and of all their powers and energies; but the act of volition and the act of working come from the man. God gives power to will: man wills through that power; God gives power to act, and man acts through that power. Without the power to will man can will nothing; without the power to work, man can do nothing. God neither wills for man, nor works in man's stead, but he furnishes him with power to do both; he is, therefore, accountable to God for these powers.

It is only in the use of lawful means that we have any reason to expect God's blessing and help. One of the ancients has remarked, "Though God has made man without himself, he will not save him without himself;" and therefore man's own concurrence of will, and co-operation of power with God, are essentially necessary to his preservation and salvation. This co-operation is the grand condition, *sine qua non*, of which God will help or save. But is not this endeavouring to merit salvation by our own works? No: for this is impossible, unless we could prove that all the mental and corporeal powers which we possess come from and of ourselves, and that we hold them independently of the power and beneficence of our Creator; and that every act of these was of infinite value, to make it an equivalent for the heaven we wished to purchase. Putting forth the hand to receive the alms of a benevolent man, can never be considered a purchase price for the bounty bestowed. For ever shall that word stand true in all its parts, "Christ is the Author of eternal salvation to all them that obey him."

It is not for want of holy resolutions and heavenly influences that men are not saved, but through their own unsteadiness; they do not persevere, they forget the necessity of continuing in prayer, and thus the Holy Spirit is grieved, departs from them, and leaves them to their own darkness and hardness of heart. When we consider the heavenly influences which many receive who draw back to perdition, and the good fruits which, for a time, they bore, it is blasphemy to say, They had no genuine, or saving grace. They had it, they showed it, they trifled with it, and sinned against it; and therefore are lost.

What a comfortable thought it is to the followers of Christ, that neither men nor demons can act against them but by the permission of their heavenly Father, and that he will not suffer any of those who trust in him to be tried above what they are able to bear, and will make the trial end in their greater salvation, and in his glory!

Slothfulness is natural to man; it requires much training to induce him to labour for his daily bread: if God should miraculously send it, he will wonder and eat it; and that is the whole. "Strive to enter in at the strait gate," is an ungracious word to many; they profess to trust in God's mercy, but labour not to enter that rest. God will not reverse his purpose to meet their slothfulness: they alone who overcome shall sit with Jesus on his throne. Reader, "take unto thee the whole armour of God, that thou mayest be able to stand in the evil day, and, having done all, to stand." And remember that he only who endures to the end shall be saved.

If to "watch" be to employ ourselves chiefly about the business of our salvation, alas! how few of those who are called Christians are there who do watch! how many who slumber! how many who are asleep! how many seized with a lethargy! how many quite dead!

You have many enemies; be continually on your guard; be always circumspect: 1. Be watchful against evil. 2. Watch for opportunities to do good. 3. Watch over each other in love. 4. Watch that none may draw you aside from the belief and unity of the Gospel.

He that is self-confident is already half fallen. He who professes to believe that God will absolutely keep him from falling finally, and neglects watching unto prayer, is not in a safer state. He who lives by the moment, walks in the light, and maintains his communion with God, is in no danger of apostasy.

Will it avail any of us how near we get to heaven, if the door be shut before we arrive? How dreadful the thought, to have only *missed* being eternally saved! to aim well and yet to permit the devil, the world, or the flesh, to hinder in the few last steps! Reader, watch and be sober.

For want of a little more dependance upon God, how often does an excellent beginning come to an unhappy conclusion! Many who were on the borders of the promised land, and about to cross Jordan, have, through an act of unfaithfulness, been turned back to wander many a dreary year in the wilderness. Reader, be on thy guard. Trust in Christ, and watch unto prayer.

He who changes from opinion to opinion, and from one sect

or party to another, is never to be depended on; there is much reason to believe that such a person is either mentally weak, or has never been rationally and divinely convinced of the truth.

The apostle shows here five degrees of apostasy: 1. Consenting to sin; being deceived by its solicitations. 2. Hardness of heart through giving way to sin. 3. Unbelief in consequence of this hardness, which leads them to call even the truth of the Gospel in question. 4. This unbelief causing them to speak evil of the Gospel, and the provision God has made for the salvation of their souls. 5. Apostasy itself, or falling off from the living God, and thus extinguishing all the light that was in them, and finally grieving the Spirit of God, so that he takes his flight, and leaves them to a seared conscience and reprobate mind. He who begins to give the least way to sin is in danger of final apostasy: the best remedy against this is, to get the evil heart removed; as one murderer in the house is more to be dreaded than ten without.

Every believer in Christ is in danger of apostasy while any remains of the evil heart of unbelief are found in him. God has promised to purify the heart, and the blood of Christ cleanses from all sin. It is, therefore, the highest wisdom of genuine Christians to look to God for the complete purification of their souls; this they cannot have too soon, and for this they cannot be too much in earnest.

Who can adequately describe the misery and wretchedness of that soul which has lost its union with the Fountain of all good, and, in losing this, has lost the possibility of happiness till the simple eye be once more given, and the straight line once more drawn?

How strange is it that there should be found any backslider! that one who once felt the power of Christ should ever turn aside! But it is still stranger that any one who has felt it, and given, in his life and conversation, full proof that he has felt it, should not only let it slip, but at last deny that he ever had it, and even ridicule a work of grace in the heart! Such instances have appeared among men.

Where there are so many snares and dangers, it is impossible to be too watchful and circumspect. Satan, as a roaring lion, as a subtle serpent, or in the guise of an angel of light, is momentarily going about seeking whom he may deceive, blind, and devour; and, when it is considered that the human heart, till entirely renewed, is on his side, it is a miracle of mercy that any soul escapes perdition: no man is safe any longer than he maintains the spirit of watchfulness and prayer; and to maintain such a spirit, he has need of all the means of grace. He who neglects any of them which the mercy of God has placed in his power, tempts the devil to tempt him. As a preventive of backsliding and apostasy, the apostle recommends mutual exhortation. No Christian should live for himself alone; he should consider his fellow Christian as a member of the same body, and feel for him accordingly, and love, succour, and protect him. When this is carefully attended to in religions society, Satan finds it very difficult to make an inroad on the church; but when coldness, distance, and want of brotherly love take place, Satan can attack each singly, and, by successive victories over individuals, soon make an easy conquest of the whole.

"But he that lacketh these things:" he, whether Jew or Gentile, who professes to have faith in God, and has not added to that faith, fortitude, knowledge, temperance, patience, godliness, brotherly kindness, and universal love, "is blind," his understanding is darkened, and cannot see afar off, shutting his eyes against the light, winking, not able to look truth in the face, nor to behold that God whom he once knew was reconciled to him; and thus it appears he is wilfully blind, "and hath forgotten that he was purged from his old sins" — has at last, through the non-improvement of the grace which he received from God, his faith ceasing to work by love, lost the evidence of things not seen: for, having grieved the Holy Spirit by not showing forth the virtues of Him who called him into his marvellous light, he has lost the testimony of his sonship; and then darkness and hardness having taken the place of light and filial confidence, he first calls all his former experience into doubt; — questions whether he has not put enthusiasm in the place of religion. By these means his darkness and hardness increase, his memory becomes indistinct and confused, till at length he forgets the work of God on his soul, next denies it, and at last asserts that the knowledge of salvation by the remission of sins is impossible, and that no man can be saved from sin in this life. Indeed, some go so far as to deny the Lord that bought them; to renounce Jesus Christ as having made atonement for them; and finish their career of apostasy by utterly denying his godhead. Many cases of this kind have I known; and they are all the consequence of believers not continuing to be workers together with God, after they had experienced his pardoning love.

Here (2 Peter ii, 22) is a sad proof of the possibility of falling from grace, and from very high degrees of it too. These had escaped from the contagion that was in the world; they had had true repentance, and cast up "their sour-sweet morsel of sin;" they had been washed from all their filthiness, and this must have been through the blood of the Lamb; yet, after all, they went back, got entangled with their old sins, swallowed down their formerly rejected lusts, and rewallowed in the mire of corruption. It is no wonder that God should say, "The latter end is worse with them than the beginning:" reason and nature say, "It must be so;" and divine justice says, "It ought to be so;" and the person himself must confess that it is right that it should be so. But how dreadful is this state! How dangerous, when the person has abandoned himself to his old sins! Yet it is not said that it is impossible for him to return to his Maker; though his case be deplorable, it is not utterly hopeless; the leper may yet be made clean, and the dead may be raised. Reader, is thy backsliding a grief and burden to thee? Then thou art not far from the kingdom of God; believe on the Lord Jesus, and thou shalt be saved.

The backslider's soul, before influenced by the Spirit of God, dilated and expanded under its heavenly influences, becomes more capable of refinement in iniquity, as its powers are more capacious than formerly. Evil habits are formed and strengthened by relapses; and relapses are multiplied, and become more incurable, through new habits.

A soul cut off from the flock of God is in an awful state! His outward defence is departed from him; and being no longer accountable to any for his conduct, he generally plunges into unprecedented depths of iniquity, and the last state of that man becomes worse than the first. Reader, art thou without the pale of God's church? Remember, it is written, "Them that are *without*, God judgeth."

The backslider's affections and desires are no longer busied with the things of God, but gad about, like an idle person, among the vanities of a perishing world. Swept from love, meekness, and all the fruits of the Spirit; and garnished, or adorned, decorated with the vain showy trifles of folly and fashion. This may comprise also smart speeches, cunning repartees, &c., for which many who have lost the life of God are very remarkable.

In a state of probation every thing may change. While we are in life we may stand or fall. Our standing in the faith depends on our union with God; and that depends on our watching unto prayer, and continuing to possess that faith that worketh by love. The highest saint under heaven can stand no longer than he depends upon God, and continues in the obedience of faith. He that ceases to do so will fall into sin, and get a darkened understanding and a hardened heart; and he may continue in this state till God come to take away his soul. Therefore, let him who most assuredly standeth take heed lest he fall, not only partially, but finally.

When probation ends, eternity begins. In a state of trial the good may change to bad, the bad to good. It is utterly absurd to say that the day of grace may end before the day of life. It is impossible; as then the state of probation would be confounded with eternity. The Scriptures alleged by some in behalf of their sentiment are utterly misunderstood and misapplied. There can be no truer proverb than, "While there is life there is hope." Probation necessarily implies the possibility of change.

XXXI. – DEATH.

LIFE itself is a wonder, and in its principles inexplicable. Its preservation is not less so. Apparently, it depends on the circulation of the blood through the heart, the lungs, and the whole system, by means of the arteries and veins; and this seems to depend on the inspiration and expiration of the air by means of the lungs. While the pulsations of the heart continue, the blood circulates, and life is preserved. But this seems to depend on respiration, or the free inhaling of the atmospheric air, and expiration of the same. While, therefore, we freely breathe; while the lungs receive and expel the air by respiration or breathing; and the heart continues to beat, thus circulating the blood through the whole system, life is preserved. But who can explain the phenomena of respiration? And by what power do the lungs separate the oxygen of the air, for the nutrition, perfection, and circulation of the blood? And by what power is it that the heart continues to expand, in order to receive the blood, and contract; in order to repel it, so that the circulation may be continued, which must continue in order that life may be preserved? Why does the heart not get weary and rest? Why is it that, with incessant labour, for even threescore and ten years, it is not exhausted of its physical power, and so stand still? These are questions which God alone can answer satisfactorily, because life depends on him, whatsoever means he may choose to employ for its continuance and preservation.

Every man, since the fall, has not only been liable to death, but has deserved it, as all have forfeited their lives because of sin.

Death could not have entered into the world, if sin had not entered first. It was sin that not only introduced death, but has armed him with all his destroying force. The goad or dagger of death is sin; by this both body and soul are slain.

The people who know not God are in continual torment, through the fear of death, because they fear something beyond death. They are conscious to themselves that they are wicked; and they are afraid of God, and terrified at the thought of eternity. By these fears thousands of sinful, miserable creatures are prevented from hurrying themselves into the unknown world.

Reader, thou art a tenant at will to God Almighty. How soon, in what place, or in what circumstances, he may call thee to march into the eternal world, thou knowest not. But this uncertainty cannot perplex thee, if thou be properly subject to the will of God, ever willing to lose thy own in it. But thou canst not be thus subject, unless thou hast the testimony of the presence and approbation of God. How awful to be obliged to walk into the valley of the shadow of death without this! Reader, prepare to meet thy God.

Death is at no great distance; thou hast but a short time to do good. Acquire a heavenly disposition while here; for there will be no change after this life. If thou diest in the love of God and in the love of man, in that state wilt thou be found in the day of judgment. If a tree about to fall lean to the north, to the north it will fall; if to the south, it will fall to that quarter. In whatever disposition or state of soul thou diest, in that thou wilt be found in the eternal world. Death refines nothing, purifies nothing, kills no sin, helps to no glory. Let thy continual bent and inclination be to God, to holiness, to charity, to mercy, and to heaven: then, fall when thou mayest, thou wilt fall well.

I have never fallen out with life. I have borne many of its rude blasts, and I have been fostered by many of its finest breezes; and should I complain against time and the dispensations of Providence, then shame would be to me. Indeed, if God see it right, I have no objection to live on here till the day of judgment; for while the earth lasts, there will be something to do by a heart, head, and hand, like mine, as long as there is something to be learned, something to be sympathetically felt, and something to be done. I have not lived to or for myself. I am not conscious to myself that I have ever passed one such day.

It is a good antidote against the fear of death, to find, as the body grows old and decays, the soul grows young and is invigorated. By the "outward man" and the "inward man," St. Paul shows that he was no materialist. He believed that we have both a body and a soul; and so far was he from supposing that, when the body dies, the whole man is decomposed, and continues so to the resurrection, that he asserts that the decays of the one lead to the invigorating of the other; and that the very decomposition of the body itself leaves the soul in the state of renewed youth. The vile doctrine of materialism is not apostolic.

The nearer a faithful soul comes to the verge of eternity, the more the light and influence of heaven are poured out upon it: time and life are fast sinking away into the shades of death and darkness; and the effulgence of the dawning glory of the eternal world is beginning to illustrate the blessed state of the genuine Christian, and to render clear and intelligible those counsels of God, partly displayed in various inextricable providences, and partly revealed and seen as through a glass darkly in his own sacred word. Unutterable glories now begin to burst forth; pains, afflictions, persecutions, wants, distresses, sickness, and death, in any or all of its forms, are exhibited as the way to the kingdom, and as having in the order of God an ineffable glory for their result. Here are the wisdom, power, and mercy of God. Here, the patience, perseverance, and glory of the saints! Reader, are not earth and its concerns lost in the effulgence of this glory? Arise and depart, for this is not thy rest.

What do we know of the state of separate spirits? What do we know of the spiritual world? How do souls exist separate from their respective bodies? Of what are they capable, and what is their employment? Who can answer these questions? Perhaps nothing can be said much better of the state, than is said Job x, 21: "A land of obscurity like darkness, and the shadow of death;" a place where death rules, over which he projects his shadow, intercepting every light of every kind of life: "Without any order," having no arrangements, no distinctions of inhabitants; the poor and the rich are there, the master and his slave, the king and the beggar; their bodies in equal corruption and disgrace, their souls distinguished only by their moral character.

Stripped of their flesh, they stand in their naked simplicity before God, in that place. "Where the light is as darkness:" a palpable obscure. It is space and place, and has only such light or capability of distinction as renders darkness visible! It is a murky land, covered with the thick darkness of death: a land of wretchedness and obscurities, where is the shadow of death, and no order but sempiternal horror dwells everywhere: a duration not characterized or measured by any of the attributes of time: where there is no order of darkness and light, night and day, heat and cold, summer and winter. It is the state of the dead! The place of separate spirits! It is out of time, out of probation, beyond change or mutability! It is on the confines of eternity; but what is THIS? and *where? Eternity!* how can I form any conception of thee? In thee there is no order, no bounds, no substance, no progression, no change, no past, no present, no future. It is an indescribable something, to which there is no analogy in the compass of creation. It is infinity and incomprehensibility to all finite beings. It is what living I know not, and what I must die to know; and even then I shall apprehend no more of it than merely to know that it is ETERNITY.

XXXII. – JUDGMENT.

THOSE systems which contain any thing like the hope of a resurrection are borrowed from this Book. But the authors have admitted this gleam of light into their systems, as a sort of veil to cover the mass of putrefaction, which otherwise would be too horrid, and to impress their followers with the idea that their system was sacred and divine.

The justice of God is as much concerned in the resurrection of the dead, as either his power or mercy. To be freed from earthly encumbrances, earthly passions, bodily infirmities, sickness, and death; to be brought into a state of conscious existence, with a refined body, and a sublime soul, both immortal, and both ineffably happy—how glorious the privilege!

The day of judgment! what an awful word is this! what a truly terrific time! when the heavens shall be shrivelled as a scroll and the elements melt with fervent heat? when the earth and its appendages shall be burned up, and the fury of that conflagration be such, that "there shall be no more sea!" a time when the noble and ignoble dead, the small and the great, shall stand before God, and all be judged according to the deeds done in the body; yea, a time when the thoughts of the heart and every secret thing shall be brought to light; when the innumerable millions of transgressions, and embryo and abortive sins, shall be exhibited in their purposes and intents; a time when justice, eternal justice, shall sit alone upon the throne, and pronounce a sentence as impartial as irrevocable, and as awful as eternal! There is a term of human life; and every human being is rapidly gliding to it as fast as the wings of time, in their onward motion, incomprehensibly swift, can carry him! And shall not the living lay this to heart? Should we not live in order to be judged? And should we not live and die so as to live again to all eternity, not with Satan and his angels, but with God and his saints? O thou man of God! thou Christian! thou immortal spirit! think of these things!

Observe the order of this terribly glorious day: —1. Jesus, in all the dignity and splendour of his eternal majesty, shall descend from heaven to the mid region, what the apostle calls the "air," somewhere within the earth's atmosphere. 2. Then the shout or order shall be given for the dead to arise. 3. Next the archangel as the herald of Christ, shall repeat the order, "Arise, ye dead, and come to judgment!" 4. When all the dead in Christ are raised, then the "trumpet shall sound," as the signal for them all to flock together to the throne of Christ. It was by the sound of the trumpet that the solemn assemblies, under the law, were convoked; and to such convocations there seems to be here an allusion. 5. When the dead in Christ are raised, their vile bodies being made like unto his glorious body, then, 6. Those who are alive shall be changed, and made immortal. 7. These shall be "caught up together with them to meet the Lord in the air." 8. We may suppose that the judgment will now be set, and the books opened, and the dead judged out of the things written in those books. 9. The eternal states of quick and dead being thus determined, then all who shall be found to "have made a covenant with him by sacrifice," and to have "washed their robes, and made them white in the blood of the Lamb," shall be taken to his eternal glory, and "be for ever with the Lord." What an inexpressibly terrific glory will then be exhibited! I forbear to call in here the descriptions which men of a poetic turn have made of this terrible scene, because I cannot trust to their correctness; and it is a subject which we should speak of and contemplate as nearly as possible, in the words of Scripture.

XXXIII. – HELL.

HELL was made only for the devil and his angels, not for man: man is an intruder into it; no human spirit shall ever be found there, but through its own fault. He who refuses the only means of salvation is lost. God willeth not his death.

Every sinner earns everlasting perdition by long, sore, and painful service. O what pains do men take to get to hell! Early and late they toil at sin; and would not divine justice be in their debt, if it did not pay them their due wages?

Men may quibble and trifle here, but their desperate criticisms will not be urged there. There is no injustice in hell, more than there is in heaven. He who does not deserve it shall never fall into the bitter pains of eternal death.

The utmost power of human nature could not, for a moment, endure the wrath of God, the deathless worm, and the unquenchable fire. The body must die, be decomposed, and be built upon indestructible principles, before this punishment can be borne.

Could it be even supposed that moral purgation could be effected by penal sufferings, which is already proved to be absurd, we have no evidence of any such place as purgatory, in which this purgation can be effected: it is a mere fable, either collected from spurious and apocryphal writings, canonized by superstition and ignorance; or it is the offspring of the deliriums of pious visionaries, early converts from heathenism, from which they imported this part of their creed. There is not one text of Scripture, legitimately interpreted, that gives the least countenance to a doctrine, as dangerous to the souls of men as it has been gainful to its inventors: so that, if such purgation were possible, the place where it is to be effected cannot be proved to exist. Before, therefore, any dependence can be placed on the doctrines raised on this supposition, the existence of the place must be proved; and the possibility of purgation in that place demonstrated.

A purgatory was reigned by the papists, for the refinement and cleansing of offences which had not been duly satisfied for in life: and even in this place, the prayers of the church, purchased by the money of surviving friends, were of sovereign virtue, to alleviate and shorten the sufferings of the deceased culprits, and get them a speedier passport from penal fire to the paradise into which all sent thither by the church had an unalienable right to enter.

We may safely conclude that the view which damned souls have in the gulf of perdition, of the happiness of the blessed, and the conviction that they themselves might have eternally enjoyed this felicity, from which, through their own fault, they are eternally excluded, will form no mean part of the punishment of the lost.

Even in hell, a damned spirit must abhor the evil by which he is tormented, and desire that good which would free him from his torment. If a lost soul could be reconciled to its torment, and to its situation, then, of course, its punishment must cease to be such. An eternal desire to escape from evil, and an eternal desire to he united to the supreme good, the gratification of which is for ever impossible, must make a second circumstance in the misery of the lost.

The remembrance of the good things possessed in life, and now to be enjoyed no more for ever, together with the grace offered or abused, will form a third circumstance in the perdition of the ungodly.

The torments which a soul endures in the hell of fire will form, through all eternity, a continual, present source of indescribable woe.

The known impossibility of ever escaping from this place of torment, or to have any alleviation of one's misery in it, forms a fifth circumstance in the punishment of ungodly men.

The iniquitous conduct of relations and friends, who have been perverted by the bad example of those who are lost, is a source of present punishment to them.

The bitter reflection, "I might have avoided sin, but I did not; I might have been saved, but I would not," must be equal to ten thousand tormentors. What intolerable anguish must this produce in a damned soul!

There are various degrees of punishment in hell, answerable to various degrees of guilt; and the contempt manifested to, and the abuse made of, the preaching of the Gospel, will rank semi-infidel Christians in the highest list of transgressors, and purchase them the hottest hell! It will be more tolerable for certain sinners, who have already been damned nearly four thousand years, than for those who live and die infidels under the Gospel! An eternity of darkness, fears, and pains, for comparatively a moment of sensual gratification,—how terrible the thought!

To suppose that sinners shall be annihilated, is as great a heresy, though scarcely so absurd, as to believe that the pains of damnation are emendatory, and that hell fire shall burn out. There is presumptive evidence from Scripture to lead us to the conclusion that, if there be not eternal punishment, glory will not be eternal; as the same terms are used to express the duration of both. No human spirit, that is not united to God, can be saved. "Those who are far from thee shall perish;" they shall be lost, undone, ruined, and that without remedy. Being separated from God by sin, they shall never be rejoined; the great gulf must be between them and their Maker eternally. As the sinful nature continues its operations even in the place of torment, these are continual reasons why that punishment should be continued. When we can prove that the Gospel shall be preached in hell, and offers of salvation, free, full, and present, be made to the damned, then we may expect that the worm that dieth not, shall die; and the fire that is not quenched, shall burn out!

We have no evidence from Scripture or reason that there are emendatory punishments in the eternal world. The state of probation certainly extends only to the ultimate term of human life. We have no evidence, either from Scripture or reason, that it extends to another state. There is not only a deep silence on this in the divine records, but there are the most positive declarations against it. In time and life, the great business relative to eternity is to be transacted. On passing the limits of time, we enter into eternity: this is the unchangeable state. In that awful and indescribable infinitude of incomprehensible duration, we read of but two places or states: heaven and hell; glory and misery; endless suffering and endless enjoyment. In these two places or states, we read of but two descriptions of human beings: the saved and the lost; between whom there is that immeasurable gulf, over which no one can pass. In the one state we read of no sin, no imperfection, no curse: there all tears are for ever wiped away from off all faces; and the righteous shine like the sun in the kingdom of their Father. In the other we read of nothing but "weeping, wailing, gnashing of teeth;" of the worm that dieth not; and of "the fire which is not quenched." Here, the effects and consequences of sin appear in all their colourings, and in all their consequences. Here, no dispensation of grace is published; no offers of mercy made: the unholy are unholy still, nor can the circumstances of their case afford any means by which their state can be meliorated; and it is impossible that sufferings, whether penal or incidental, can destroy that cause (sin) by which they were produced.

It cannot be said that beings, in a state of penal sufferings, under the wrath and displeasure of God, (for if they suffer penally, they must be under that displeasure,) can either love or serve him. Their sufferings are the consequences of their crimes, and can form no part of their obedience. Therefore, all the ages in which they suffer, are ages spent in sinning against the first and essential law of their creation; and must necessarily increase the aggregate of their demerit, and lay the eternally successive necessity of continuance in that place and state of torment. Thus it is evident that this doctrine, so specious and promising at its first appearance, is essentially defective, and contains in itself the seeds of its own destruction. Besides, if the fire of hell could purify from sin, all the dispensations of God's grace and justice among men must have been useless: and the mission of Jesus Christ most palpably unnecessary, as all that is proposed to be effected by his grace and Spirit, might be, on this doctrine, effected by a proportionate continuance in hell fire: and there, innumerable ages are but a point in reference to eternity; and any conceivable or inconceivable duration of these torments is of no consequence in this argument, as long as, at their termination, an eternity still remains.

What this everlasting destruction consists in, we cannot tell. It is not annihilation, for their being continues; and as the destruction is everlasting, it is an eternal continuance and presence of substantial evil, and absence of all good; for a part of this punishment consists in being banished from the presence of the Lord—excluded from his approbation for ever; so that the light of his countenance can be no more enjoyed, as there will be an eternal impossibility of ever being reconciled to him. Never to see the face of God throughout eternity, is a heart-rending, soul- appalling thought, and to be banished from the glory of his power, that power the glory of which is peculiarly manifested in saving the lost and glorifying the faithful, is what cannot be reflected on without confusion and dismay.

XXXIV. – HEAVEN.

THE state of eternal glory implies three things: — 1. An absence of all suffering, pain, sin, and evil. 2. The presence of all good, both of the purest and most exalted kind. And, 3. The complete satisfaction of all the desires of the soul, at all times, and through eternity, without the possibility of decrease on the one hand, or of satiety on the other, or of any termination of the existence of the receiver or the received. This is ineffably great and glorious, but the apostle exceeds all this by saying, "an heir of God." It is therefore not heaven merely; it is not the place where no ill can enter, and where pure and spiritual good is eternally present; it is not merely a state of endless blessedness in the regions of glory; it is GOD HIMSELF; — God in his plenitude of glories; God, who, by the eternal communications of his glories, meets every wish and satisfies every desire of a deathless and imperishable spirit, which he has created for himself, and of which himself is the only portion. To a soul composed of infinite desires, what would the place or state called "heaven" be, if God were not there? God, then, is the portion of the soul, and the only portion with which its infinite powers can be satisfied. How wonderful is his lot! A child of corruption, lately a slave of sin and heir of perdition; tossed about with every storm of life; in afflictions many and privations oft; having perhaps scarcely where to lay his head; and at last prostrated by death, and mingled with the dust of the earth; but now, how changed! The soul is renewed in glory; the body fashioned after the glorious human nature of Jesus Christ; and both joined together in an indestructible bond, clearer than the indestructible moon, brighter than the sun, and more resplendent than all the heavenly spheres; for having conquered and triumphed in the church militant, it is now set down with Jesus on his throne, as he, having overcome, is set down with the Father on the Father's throne. Hallelujah! The Lord God Omnipotent reigneth! And his children, his followers and confessors, shall reign with him for ever and ever! Amen.

Eternal life is the proper object of an immortal spirit's hope, the only sphere where the human intellect can rest, and be happy in the place and state where God is; where he is seen AS HE IS ; and where he can be enjoyed without interruption in an eternal progression of knowledge and beatitude.

It is neither an earthly portion nor a heavenly portion, but God himself who is to be their portion. It is not heaven they are to inherit; it is GOD who is infinitely greater and more glorious than heaven itself. With such powers has God created the soul of man, that nothing less than himself can be a sufficient and satisfactory portion for the mind of this most astonishing creature.

The song of praise to God, through Christ, begun on earth, and protracted through all the generations of men, till the end of time, shall be continued in heaven by those who, having here received the salvation of God, and continued faithful unto death, in the resurrection of the just are taken to that ineffable glory, where, being like him, they shall see him as he is; and being raised to his right hand, have fulness of joy and pleasures for evermore: in which state, eras, limits, and periods are absorbed in one eternal duration.

It is in vain to attempt to describe this state: when we say that in it there is no sin, we at once see that in it there can be no pain, no misery, no death. From it all evil is absent, and in it all good is present. There the introduction of evil is impossible; and there the loss of good is equally so. The time of probation is only on earth: the day of trial with the blessed is for ever ended; and now they are in that state in reference to which their probation existed. This duration we often express by "world without end," that is, the world or state that has no end; sometimes by "for ever and ever," that is, one EVER or duration that is endless, succeeding one that is ended. And sometimes by a yet more forcible expression, "for evermore," that is, for ever—through the whole lapse of time; and more, the unlimited duration that shall succeed it. All these are phrases which labour to express what is at once both ineffable and inconceivable.

God never removes any of his servants till they have accomplished the work he has given them to do. Extraordinary talents are not given merely in reference to this world. They refer also to eternity; and shall there have their consummation and plenitude of employ. Far be it from God to light up such tapers to burn only for a moment in the dark night of life, and then to extinguish them for ever in the damps of death. Heaven is the region where the spirits of just men made perfect live, thrive, and eternally expand their powers in the service and to the glory of Him from whom they have derived their being.

So the truly wise man is but in his twilight here below; but he is in a state of glorious preparation for the realms of everlasting light; till at last, emerging from darkness and the shadow of death, he is ushered into the full blaze of endless felicity.

An unholy man cannot enter into heaven; and were he in it, it would be no enjoyment to him, because it is not suited to him. The nature of the resident must be suited to the place of residence. The fishes live not on the elms, and the cattle browse not in the depths of the sea. Hell is for demons and wicked men; heaven for holy angels, and the spirits of just men made perfect. There is a fellowship among devils, and those who are partakers of a diabolic nature; for aught we know,

"Devil with devil damn'd firm concord holds;"
and we know that the holy inhabitants of heaven are brethren with holy souls.

By these perpetual fountains we are to understand endless sources of comfort and happiness, which Jesus Christ will open out of his own infinite plenitude to all glorified souls. These eternal living fountains will make an infinite variety in the enjoyments of the blessed. There will be no sameness, and consequently no cloying with the perpetual enjoyment of the same things; every moment will open a new source of pleasure, instruction, and improvement; they shall make an eternal progression into the fulness of God. And as God is infinite, so his attributes are infinite; and throughout infinity more and more of those attributes will be discovered; and the discovery of each will be a new fountain or source of pleasure and enjoyment. These sources must be opening through all eternity; and yet, through all eternity, there will still remain, in the absolute perfections of the Godhead, an infinity of them to be opened! This is one of the finest images in the Bible.

Every holy soul has, throughout eternity, the beatific vision; that is, it sees God as he is, because it is like him. It drinks in beatification from the presence of the eternal Trinity.

"Pleasures for evermore," onwardly, perpetually, continually, well expressed by our translation, "ever and more," an eternal progression. Think of duration in the most extended and unlimited manner, and there is still more; more to be suffered in hell, and more to be enjoyed in heaven. Great God! grant that my readers may have this beatific sight! this eternal progression in unadulterated, unchangeable, and unlimited happiness. Hear this prayer, for His sake who found out the path of life, and who by his blood purchased an entrance into the holiest! Amen and Amen.

XXXV. – GENERAL PRINCIPLES.

1. THAT there is but one uncreated, unoriginated, infinite, and eternal Being;—the Creator, Preserver, and Governor of all things.

2. That there is in this infinite essence a plurality of what are commonly called persons; not separately subsisting, but essentially belonging to the Godhead; which persons are commonly termed Father, Son, and Holy Ghost; or God, the Logos, and the Holy Spirit; and these are generally named the Trinity, which term, though not found in the New Testament, seems properly enough applied, as we never read of more than three persons in the Godhead.

3. That the sacred Scriptures, or holy books, which form the Old and New Testaments, contain a full revelation of the will of God, in reference to man; and are alone sufficient for every thing relative to the faith and practice of a Christian; and were given by the inspiration of God.

4. That man was created in righteousness and true holiness, without any moral imperfection, or any kind of propensity to sin; but free to stand or fall.

5. That he fell from this state, became morally corrupt in his nature, and transmitted his moral defilement to all his posterity.

6. That to counteract the evil principle, and bring man into a salvable state, God, from his infinite love, formed the purpose of redeeming man from his lost estate, by Christ Jesus; and, in the interim, sent his Holy Spirit to enlighten, strive with, and convince

men of sin, righteousness, and judgment.

7. That in due time the divine Logos, called afterward Jesus the Christ, the Son of God, the Saviour, &c., became incarnated, and sojourned among men, teaching the purest truth, and working the most stupendous and beneficent miracles.

8. That this divine Person, foretold by the prophets, and described by evangelists and apostles, is really and properly God; having, by the inspired writers, assigned to him every attribute essential to the Deity; being one with Him who is called God, Jehovah, &c.[13]

9. That he is also perfect man in consequence of his incarnation; and in that man, or manhood, dwelt all the fulness of the Godhead bodily; so that his nature is twofold—divine and human, or God manifested in the flesh.

10. That his human nature is derived from the blessed Virgin Mary, through the creative energy of the Holy Ghost; but his divine nature, because God, infinite and eternal, is uncreated, underived, and unbegotten; which, were it otherwise, he could not be God in any proper sense of the word; but as he is God, the doctrine of the eternal Sonship must be false.[14]

---

[13] In addition to the many other proofs in support of the great doctrine of the Godhead of Christ, which will be found in this volume, (see page 99, &c.,) I would here recommend to the notice of the critical reader an admirable essay on the Greek article, published at the end of the doctor's notes on the Epistle to the Ephesians, by that accomplished scholar, H. S. Boyd, Esq., author of "Translations from Chrysostom," &c., who has read the Greek writers, both sacred and profane, with peculiar attention. It was carefully revised by him for the new edition of the Commentary, and was considered by Dr. Clarke the best piece ever written on the subject. The doctor's insertion of it is only one among many instances in which he showed his readiness to "sow beside all waters," and to avail himself of the talents of others to enrich his work and benefit the public.—S.D.

[14] In the Minutes of Conference for the year 1827, (p. 77,) are these words: "It is the acknowledged right, and, under existing circumstances, the indispensable duty, of every chairman of a district, to ask all candidates for admission upon trial among us, if they believe the doctrine of the eternal Sonship of our Lord Jesus Christ as it is stated by Mr. Wesley, especially in his notes upon the first chapter of the Epistle to the Hebrews, to be agreeable to the Holy Scriptures; and that it is also the acknowledged right, and, under existing circumstances, the indispensable duty, of the president of the conference for the time being, to examine particularly upon that doctrine every preacher proposed to be admitted into full connection, and to require an explicit and unreserved declaration of his assent to it, as a truth revealed in the inspired oracles."

11. That, as he took upon him the nature of man, he died for the whole human race, without respect of persons; equally for all, and for every man.

12. That on the third day after his crucifixion and burial he rose from the dead; and, after showing himself many days to his disciples and others, he ascended to heaven, where, as God manifest in the flesh, he continues, and shall continue, to be the Mediator of the human race, till the consummation of all things.

13. That there is no salvation but through him,—and that throughout the Scriptures his passion and death are considered as sacrificial; pardon and salvation being obtained by the shedding of his blood.

14. That no human being since the fall either has or can have merit or worthiness of or by himself, and therefore has nothing to claim from God, but in the way of his mercy through Christ; therefore pardon, and every other blessing promised in the Gospel, have been purchased by his sacrificial death, and are given to men, not on account of any thing they have done or suffered, or can do or suffer, but for his sake or through his merit alone.

15. That these blessings are received by faith; because not of works, nor of sufferings.

16. That the power to believe, or grace of faith, is the free gift of God, without which none can believe; but that the act of faith, or actually believing, is the act of the soul, under the influence of that power. But this power to believe, like all other gifts of God, may be slighted, not used, or misused, in consequence of which is that declaration, "He that believeth shall be saved; but he that believeth not shall be damned."

17. That justification, or the pardon of sin, is an instantaneous act of God's infinite mercy in behalf of a penitent soul, trusting only in the merits of Jesus Christ; that this act is absolute in respect of all past sin, all being forgiven where any is forgiven.

18. That the souls of all believers may be purified from all sin in this life; and that a man may live under the continual influence of the grace of Christ, without sinning against his God, all evil tempers and sinful propensities being destroyed, and his heart filled with pure love both to God and man.

19. That unless a believer live and walk in the spirit of

obedience, he will fall from the grace of God, and forfeit all his Christian privileges and rights; in which state of backsliding he may persevere, and, if so, perish everlastingly.

20. That the whole period of human life is a state of probation, in every part of which a sinner may repent and turn to God, and in every part of it a believer may give way to sin and fall from grace; and that this possibility of rising, and liability to falling, are essential to a state of trial or probation.

21. That all the promises and threatenings of the word of God are conditional, as they regard man in reference to his being here and hereafter; and that on this ground alone the sacred writings can be consistently interpreted or rightly understood.

22. That man is a free agent, never being impelled by any necessitating influence either to do evil or good, but has it continually in his power to choose the life or death that is set before him; on which ground he is an accountable being, and answerable for his own actions; and on this ground also he is alone capable of being rewarded or punished.

23. That his free will is a necessary constituent of his rational soul, without which man must be a mere machine, either the sport of blind chance, or the mere patient of an irresistible necessity; and, consequently, not accountable for any acts to which he was irresistibly impelled.

24. That every human being has this freedom of will with a sufficiency of light and power to direct its operations; and that this powerful light is not inherent in any man's nature, but is graciously bestowed by Him who is the true light that lighteneth every man that cometh into the world.

25. That as Christ has made, by his once offering himself upon the cross, a sufficient sacrifice, oblation, and satisfaction for the sins of the whole world; and that, as his gracious Spirit strives with and enlightens all men, thus putting them in a salvable state; therefore every human soul may be saved, if it be not his own fault.

26. That Jesus Christ has instituted, and commanded to be perpetuated in his church, two sacraments; baptism (sprinkling, washing with, or immersion in water) in the name of the holy and ever blessed Trinity, as a sign of the cleansing and regenerating influences of the Holy Ghost, producing a death unto sin, and a new birth unto righteousness; and the eucharist or Lord's supper, as

commemorating the sacrificial death of Christ. That by the first, once administered, every person may be initiated into the visible church; and by the second, frequently administered, all believers may be kept in mind of the foundation on which their salvation is built, and receive grace to enable them to adorn the doctrine of God their Saviour in all things.

27. That the soul is immaterial and immortal, and can subsist independently of the body.

28. That there will be a general resurrection of the dead, both of the just and unjust; that the souls of both shall be reunited to their respective bodies; and that both will be immortal, and live eternally.

29. That there will be a day of judgment, after which all shall be punished or rewarded according to the deeds done in the body; the wicked being sent to hell, and the righteous taken into heaven.

30. That these states of reward and punishment shall have no end, forasmuch as the time of probation or trial is for ever terminated, and the succeeding state must necessarily be fixed and unalterable.[15]

31. That the origin of human salvation is found in the infinite philanthropy of God; and that on this principle the unconditional reprobation of any soul is absolutely impossible.

32. The sacred writings are a system of pure, unsophisticated reason, proceeding from the immaculate mind of God; in many places, it is true, vastly elevated beyond what the reason of man could have devised or found out, but in no case contrary to human reason. They are addressed, not to the passions, but to the reason of

---

[15] The following lines were written in a lady's album: —
    I have enjoyed the spring of life;
    I have endured the toils of summer;
    I have culled the fruits of autumn;
    I am passing through the rigours of winter;
    And am neither forsaken of God,
    Nor abandoned by man.
I see, at no great distance, the dawn of a new day,
The first of a spring that shall be eternal:
It is advancing to meet me: —
    I haste to embrace it:
    Welcome! welcome! eternal spring!
        Hallelujah.
                ADAM CLARKE.

man: every command is urged with reasons of obedience, and every promise and threatening founded on the most evident reason and propriety. The whole, therefore, are to be rationally understood, and rationally interpreted. He who would discharge reason from this its noblest province, is a friend in his heart to the Antichristian maxim, "Ignorance is the mother of devotion." Revelation and reason go hand in hand. Faith is the servant of the former, and the friend of the latter: while the Spirit of God, which gave the revelation, improves and exalts reason, and gives energy and effect to faith.

XXXVI. – MISCELLANEOUS.

KNOWLEDGE

It is the will of God that Christians should be well instructed; that they should become wise and intelligent, and have their understandings well cultivated and improved. Sound learning is of great worth, even in religion; the wisest and best instructed Christians are the most steady, and may be the most useful. If a man be a child in knowledge, he is likely to be tossed to and fro, and carried about with every wind of doctrine; and often lies at the mercy of interested, designing men; the more knowledge he has, the more safe is his state. If our circumstances be such that we have few means of improvement, we should turn them to the best account. Partial knowledge is better than total ignorance. He who cannot get all he may wish must take heed to acquire all that he can. If total ignorance be a bad and dangerous thing, every degree of knowledge lessens both the evil and the danger. It must never be forgotten that the Holy Scriptures themselves are capable of making men wise unto salvation, if read and studied with faith in Christ.

Genuine wisdom is ever accompanied with meekness and gentleness. Those proud, overbearing, and disdainful men who pass for great scholars and eminent critics, may have learning, but they have not wisdom. That learning implies their correct knowledge of the structure of language, and of composition in general; but wisdom they have none, nor any self-government. They are like the blind man who carried a lantern in daylight to keep others from justling him in the street. That learning is not only of little worth, but despicable, that does not teach a man to govern his own spirit, and to be humble in his conduct toward others.

We must not suppose that eminent endowments necessarily imply gracious dispositions. A man may have much light and little love; he may be very wise in secular matters, and know but little of himself, and less of his God. There is as truly a learned ignorance as there is a refined and useful learning. One of our old writers said, "Knowledge that is not applying is like a candle which a man holds to light himself to hell." The Corinthians abounded in knowledge, and science, and eloquence, and various extraordinary gifts; but in many cases they were grossly ignorant of the genius and design of the Gospel. Many since their time have put words and observances in place of the weightier matters of the law, and the spirit of the Gospel. The apostle has taken great pains to correct these abuses among the Corinthians, and to insist on that great, unchangeable, and eternal truth,—that love to God and man, filling the heart, hallowing the passions, regulating the affections, and producing universal benevolence and beneficence, is the fulfilling of all law; and that all professions, knowledge, gifts, &c., without this, are absolutely useless.

Truth is so amiable and important in every department of knowledge, that no pains should be spared to acquire it. It is not only excellent in its source, but also in the last faint glimmerings of its farthest projected rays: to whatever distance these have shone forth, and however intermixed, they should, if possible, be analyzed, and traced back to their origin.

Truth is the contrary to falsity. Truth has been defined, "the conformity of notions to things; of words to thoughts." It declares the thing that is, and as it is; whereas falsity, in all its acceptations, is that which is not; what is pretended to be a fact, but either is no fact, or is not presented as it really is. The revelation of God to man, in reference to his salvation, is the truth, the whole truth, and nothing but the truth. It bears a strict conformity to the perfections of the divine nature. It inspires such notions as are conformable to the things of which they are the mental ectypes, and describes its subjects by such words as are conformable to the thoughts they represent.

Every Christian should study philosophy, as from it he will more evidently discover, 1. That he who is so fearfully and wonderfully made, so marvellously preserved, and so bountifully fed, should give up unreservedly his all to God, and devote the powers which he has received to the service of the Creator. 2. When atheistical notions would intrude, a few reflections on the manifold wisdom displayed in the creation may be the means of breaking the subtle snare of a designing foe. And, 3. By the study of nature, under grace, the soul becomes more enlarged, and is capable of bearing a more extensive, deeper, and better defined image of the divine perfections.

It is generally supposed that former times were full of barbaric ignorance; and that the system of philosophy which is at present in repute, and is established by experiments, is quite a modern discovery. But nothing can be more false than this, as the Bible plainly discovers to an attentive reader, that the doctrines of statics, the circulation of the blood, the rotundity of the earth, the motions of the celestial bodies, the process of generation, &c., were all known long before Pythagoras, Archimedes, Copernicus, or Newton was born.

It is very natural to suppose that God implanted the first principles of every science in the mind of his first creature; that Adam taught them to his posterity; and that tradition continued them for many generations with their proper improvements. But many of them were lost in consequence of wars, captivities, &c. Latter years have rediscovered many of them, principally by the direct or indirect aid of the Holy Scriptures; and others of them continue hidden, notwithstanding the accurate and persevering researches of the moderns.

Who taught Newton to ascertain the laws by which God governs the universe, through which discovery a new source of profit and pleasure has been opened to mankind through every part of the civilized world? No reading, no study, no example, formed his genius. God, who made him, gave him that compass and bent of mind by which he made those discoveries, and for which his name is celebrated in the earth. When I see Napier inventing the logarithms; Copernicus, Des Cartes, and Kepler, contributing to pull down the false systems of the universe, and Newton demonstrating the true one; and when I see the long list of patentees of useful inventions, by whose industry and skill long and tedious processes in the necessary arts of life have been shortened, labour greatly lessened, and much time and expense saved; I then see, with Moses, men who are wise-hearted, whom God has filled with the spirit of wisdom, for these very purposes, that he might help man by man, and that, as time rolls on, he might give to his intelligent creatures such proofs of his being, infinitely varied wisdom, and gracious providence, as should cause them to depend on him, and give him that glory which is due to his name.

The teaching of philosophy, among the ancients, became the means of the emolument of the teacher; and, while they boasted to be free, they themselves were the slaves of various evil tempers and passions; so that it was said, with great propriety, of philosophy, or wisdom, in its several stages, "Philosophy was impious under Diagoras; vicious under Epicurus; hypocritical under Zeno; impudent under Diogenes; covetous under Demochares; voluptuous under Metrodorus; fantastical under Crates; scurrilous under Menippus; licentious under Pyrrho; quarrelsome under Cleanthes; and, at last, intolerable to all men."

The Catholic writers say that St. John Damascenus was so zealous for the truth, that he resorted sometimes to pious fables to support it. Such conduct in any person leaves the difference very little between saint and sinner. The truth has no need of such support: and is always injured and rendered suspected when its votaries go to Egypt for help.

In the present age, humane and learned men have been endeavouring, so to speak, to find out a royal road to geometry: difficulties have been professedly lessened, till at last the foundations of science have been laid upon the sands. Profound literature is rarely to be met with. We have still, it is true, the splendour and brilliancy of gold: but on examination we frequently find a mass of inferior metal; and even the surface, though completely covered, yet not deeply gilt.

Our various conflicting and contradictory theories of the earth are full proofs of our ignorance, and strong evidences of our folly. The present dogmatical systems of geology itself are almost the *ne plus ultras* of brainsick visionaries and system-mad mortals. They talk as confidently of the structure of the globe, and the manner and time in which all was formed, as if they had examined every part from the centre to the circumference; though not a soul of man has ever penetrated two miles in perpendicular depth into the bowels of the earth. And with this scanty, almost no-knowledge, they pretend to build systems of the universe, and blaspheme the revelation of God! Poor souls! all these things are to them "a path which no fowl knoweth." The wisdom necessary to such investigations is out of their reach; and they have not simplicity of heart to seek it where it may be found.

If wisdom means a pursuit of the best end, by the most legitimate and appropriate means, the great mass of mankind appear to perish without it. But, if we consider the subject more closely, we shall find that all men die in a state of comparative ignorance. With all our boasted science and arts how little do we know! Do we know any thing to perfection that belongs either to the material or spiritual world? Do we understand even what matter is? What is its essence? Do we understand what spirit is? Then, what is its essence? Almost all the phenomena of nature, its grandest operations, and the laws of the heavenly bodies, have been explained on the principle of gravitation or attraction: but in what does this consist? Who can answer? We can traverse every part of the huge and trackless ocean by means of the compass: but who understands the nature of magnetism, on which all this depends? We eat and drink in order to sustain life: but what is nutrition? and how is it effected? This has never been explained. Life depends on respiration for its continuance: but by what kind of action is it, that in a moment the lungs separate the oxygen, which is friendly to life, from the nitrogen, which would destroy it; suddenly absorbing the one and expelling the other? Who, among the generation of hypothesis-framers, has guessed this out? Life is continued by the circulation of the blood: but by what power and law does it circulate? Have the systole and diastole of the heart, on which this circulation depends, been ever satisfactorily explained? Most certainly not. Alas! we die without wisdom; and must die to know these and ten thousand other matters equally unknown and equally important. To be safe, in reference to eternity, we must know the only true God and Jesus Christ whom he hath sent; whom to know is life eternal. This knowledge, obtained and retained, will entitle us to all the rest in the eternal world.

HAPPINESS.

To the soul happiness belongs: of this, it alone is capable; and as it is a spiritual being, the happiness of which it is capable must be spiritual, and must be produced by the possession, not of an earthly, but of a spiritual good. A man may have as many houses as he can inhabit, as many clothes as he can wear, as many beds as he can lie on, and as much food as he can eat, and, with all, possess sound health and strength; and yet his soul be in misery, while his body has not one wish ungratified, nor a single want unsupplied. Like may cleave to and assimilate with like. The productions of the earth are suited to animal wants: but what relation have food, raiment, gold, silver, and earthly possessions to an immortal spirit? The abundance of them does not satisfy it; the want of them does not distress it. These are not made for soul or spirit; they have nothing in their nature suited to the nature of a spiritual substance. God constituted the body so as to receive gratification and support from natural things; and endowed these natural things with such properties as render them suitable to those bodies; but he made the soul of a different nature, and designed it a happiness which no sublunary things can communicate, affect, or remove. He gave it unbounded capacities and infinite desires. I mean by this, that its capacities are not limited by created things; and its wishes extend beyond all finite good and excellence. As, therefore, the capacities of the soul extend far beyond all created material good and excellence, God alone must be its portion: he alone can satisfy its infinite desires: he alone can make it happy.

It is well, ineffably well, to have a happiness that is not affected by the great and many changes to which external objects are incident: what a blessing to be able to sit calm on the wheel of fortune, and to prosper in the midst of adversity!

The soul was made for God; and nothing but God can fill it, and make it happy. Angels could not be happy in glory, when they had cast off their allegiance to their master. As soon as his heart had departed from God, Adam would needs go to the forbidden fruit, to satisfy a desire which was only an indication of his having been unfaithful to his God. Solomon in his glory, possessing every thing heart could wish, found all to be vanity and vexation of spirit;

because his soul had not God for its portion. Ahab, on the throne of Israel, takes to his bed, and refuses to eat bread, not merely because he cannot get the vineyard of Naboth; but because he had not God in his heart, who could alone satisfy its desires. Haman, on the same ground, though the prime favourite of the king, is wretched, because he cannot have a bow from that man whom his heart even despised. O how distressing are the inquietudes of vanity! And how wretched is the man who has not the God of Jacob for his help, and in whose heart Christ dwells not by faith!

Religion is a commerce between God and man; and is intended to be the means of re-establishing him in that communion with his Maker, and the happiness consequent on it, which he has lost by the fall. All notions of religion, merely as a system of duties which we owe to God, fall, in my apprehension, infinitely short of its nature and intention. To the perfection, happiness, or gratification of the infinite mind, no creature can be necessary. Religion was not made for God, but for man. It is an institution of the divine benevolence for human happiness. Nor can God be pleased with any man's religion or faith but as far as they lead him to happiness, that is, to the enjoyment of God; without which there can be no felicity: for God is the source of intellectual happiness, and from him alone it can be derived; and in union with him alone it can be enjoyed. Animal gratifications may be acquired by means of the various matters that are suited to the senses: but gratification and happiness are widely different; the former may exist where the latter is entirely unknown.

God is a spirit, the human soul is a spirit, and the happiness suitable to the nature and state of man must be spiritual. The soul has infinite desires and wishes; and what can satisfy these wishes must be infinite. God alone is that GOOD; and in him alone is this happiness to be found.

If it be his will that the happiness lost by sin should be restored to believers in Christ, then it is his will that they should be made holy. Misery was never known till sin entered into the world; and happiness can never be known by any man, till sin be expelled from his soul. No holiness, no happiness;—and no plenary and permanent happiness, without plenary and permanent holiness. I repeat it, that to give true and permanent happiness to believers is the design of that God whose name is Mercy, and whose nature is love.

True happiness consists in the knowledge of God, and in obedience to him. A man is not happy because he knows much; but because he receives much of the divine nature, and is, in all his conduct, conformed to the divine will.

The happiness of a genuine Christian lies far beyond the reach of earthly disturbances, and is not affected by the changes and chances to which mortal things are exposed. The martyrs were more happy in the flames than their persecutors could be on their beds of down.

God is the Centre to which all immortal spirits tend, and in connection with which alone they can find rest. Every thing separated from its centre is in a state of violence; and, if intelligent, cannot be happy. All human souls, while separated from God by sin, are in a state of violence, agitation, and misery. From God all spirits come; to him all must return, in order to be finally happy.

I knew a man who is distinguished among many for his writings, and who is still living, who thought that the saying of Christ, "Love your enemies," and the practice upon that saying, was the greatest insult that could be offered to human nature. "What!" said he, "rob men of those high feelings which are so common to them? No!" And then he blasphemed, and I shall not repeat his words. We may see whereabouts that man was; and we may be sure that, if a man be a Christian, he cannot hate another without being miserable while he feels it. GOD IS BENEVOLENCE, and he forbids men to entertain any feelings of malice or ill will toward others; because if they do they cannot be happy. If I could hate the devil himself—if I could wish him more penal fire, or greater inflictions of God's wrath—I could not at that moment love Jesus Christ.

COMMUNION OF SAINTS.

A SERIOUS public profession of the religion of Christ has, in all ages of the church, been considered not only highly becoming, but indispensably necessary to salvation. He who consistently confesses Christ before men shall be confessed by him before God and his angels. A Jew wore his phylacteries on his forehead, on his hands, and around his garments, that he might have reverence in the sight of the heathen; he gloried in his law, and he exulted that

Abraham was his father. Christian! with a zeal not less becoming, and more consistently supported, let the words of thy mouth, the acts of thy hands, and all thy goings show that thou belongest unto God; that thou hast taken his Spirit for the guide of thy heart, his Word for the rule of thy life, his people for thy companions, his heaven for thy inheritance, and himself for the portion of thy soul. And see that thou hold fast the truth, and that thou hold it in righteousness.

It is not merely sufficient to have the heart right before God; there must be a firm, manly, and public profession of Christ before men.

Be singular. Singularity, if in the right, can never be criminal. So completely disgraceful is the way of sin, that, if there were not a multitude walking in that way, who help to keep each other in countenance, every solitary sinner would be obliged to hide his head.

A religious profession, supported by a consistent walk, produces both reverence and respect even in the wicked. And even while they ridicule religion, they will put confidence in its professors, credit their words, and employ their services, in preference to all others. How forcible are right words! What a pity that all the professors of religion were not at all times faithful to their trust, and consistent in their conduct! How would infidelity and vice lose their glorying, and the faith and hope of the Gospel everywhere triumph! But alas! how few are clear in this matter! O God, mend thy church and thy ministers.

The genuine Christian is holy; — and happy, because holy: he not only lives an innocent life, but he lives a useful life — he labours for the welfare of society; and the peace of God keeps and rules his heart. He lives to grow wiser and better, and he misses not his aim. In affliction he is patient and submissive; in adversity his confidence in God is unshaken; in death he has no fears, because Christ dwells in his heart by faith: he overcomes his last enemy, and finally triumphs, Satan himself being beat down under his feet; and having overcome, he sits down with Christ on his throne, as he, having overcome, is sat down with the Father upon the Father's throne. Thus, then, his salvation on earth issues in an eternal weight of glory.

We may be said to give glory to God when we exhibit in the

clearest light, and in the most impressive manner we can, the various excellences of our God and Father; and when we do this so that by our example others are led to esteem, adore, and put their trust in him, we glorify him by showing forth the glory of his various attributes—telling forth how effectually he teaches, how powerfully he upholds, how mercifully he saves, and how kindly he supplies all our wants, succours us in distress, stands by us in difficulties, defends us in dangers, guides us by his counsel, and promises at last to receive us into his endless glory.

"Confess your faults one to another." This is a good general direction to Christians who endeavour to maintain among themselves the communion of saints. This social confession tends much to humble the soul, and to make it watchful. We naturally wish that our friends in general, and our religious friends in particular, should think well of us; and when we confess to them offences which, without this confession, they could never have known, we feel humbled, are kept from self-applause, and induced to watch unto prayer, that we may not increase our offences before God, or be obliged any more to undergo the painful humiliation of acknowledging our weakness, fickleness, or infidelity to our religious brethren.

It is not said, "Confess your faults to the elders that they may forgive them, or prescribe penance in order to forgive them." No; the members of the church were to confess their faults to each other; therefore auricular confession to a priest, such as is prescribed by the Romish Church, has no foundation in this passage. Indeed, had it any foundation here, it would prove more than they wish; for it would require the priest to confess his sins to the people, as well as the people to confess theirs to the priest.

"And pray one for another." There is no instance in auricular confession where the penitent and the priest pray together for pardon; but here the people are commanded to pray for each other, that they may be healed.

Without the communion of saints, who is likely to make a steady and consistent Christian, even though his conversion should have been the most sincere and the most remarkable?

He who frequents the company of bad or corrupt men will soon be as they are. He may be sound in the faith, and have the life and power of godliness, and at first frequent their company only for the sake of their pleasing conversation, or their literary accomplishments; and he may think his faith proof against their infidelity; but he will soon find, by means of their glozing speeches, his faith weakened; and when he once gets under the empire of doubt, unbelief will soon prevail; his bad company will corrupt his morals; and the two dry logs will soon burn up the green one.

FASTING.

IN all countries, and under all religions, fasting has not only been considered a duty, but also of extraordinary virtue to procure blessings, and to avert evils. Hence it has often been practised with extraordinary rigour, and abused to the most superstitious purposes.

Among the Hindoos there are twelve kinds of fasts.

Fasting is considered by the Mohammedans as an essential part of piety. Their orthodox divines term it "the gate of religion," With them it is of two kinds, voluntary and incumbent.

When a man fasts, suppose he do it through a religious motive, he should give the food of that day from which he abstains to the poor and hungry, who, in the course of Providence, are called to sustain many involuntary fasts, beside suffering general privations. Woe to him who saves a day's victuals by his religious fast! He should either give them or their value in money to the poor.

CONSCIENCE.

CONSCIENCE is defined by some, "that judgment which the rational soul passes on her own actions;" and is a faculty of the soul itself, and consequently natural to it. Others say, "It is a ray of the divine light." Milton calls it "God's umpire;" and Dr. Young seems to call it "a God in man." To me it appears to be no other than a faculty of the mind, capable of receiving light and information from the Spirit of God; and is the same to the soul in spiritual matters, as the eye is to the body in the things which concern vision. The eye is not light in itself, nor is it capable of discerning any object but by the instrumentality of natural or artificial light. But it has organs properly adapted to the reception of the rays of light, and the various images of the objects which they exhibit. When these are present to an eye, the structure of which is perfect, then there is discernment or perception of those objects which are within the sphere of vision: but when the light is absent there is no perception of the figure, dimensions, situation, or colour of any object, howsoever entire or perfect the optic nerves may be. In the same manner, comparing spiritual things with natural, the Spirit of God enlightens that eye of the soul which we call conscience; it penetrates it with its effulgence, and, speaking as human language will permit on the subject, it has organs properly adapted for the reception of the Spirit's emanations, which when received into the conscience exhibit a real view of the situation, state, &c., of the soul as it stands in reference to God and eternity. Thus the Scripture says, "The Spirit itself beareth witness with our spirits:" that is, it shines into the conscience, and reflects, throughout the soul, a conviction proportioned to the degree of light communicated, of condemnation, pardon, or acquittance, according to the end of its coming.

Conscience is sometimes said to be good,—bad,—tender,—seared; *good,* if it acquit or approve; *bad,* if it condemn or disapprove; *tender,* if alarmed at the least approach of evil, and is severe in scrutinizing the various operations of the mind and passions, as well as the actions of the body; and *seared,* if it no longer act thus, the Spirit of God being grieved that its light is no longer dispensed, and conscience no longer passes judgment on the actions of the man. These epithets can scarcely belong to it, if the common definition be admitted; but, on the general definition already given, these terms are easily understood, and are exceedingly proper; for instance, a good conscience is that to which the Spirit of God has brought intelligence of the pardon of all the sins of the soul, and its reconciliation to God through the blood of the covenant; and this good conscience, retained, implies God's continual approbation of such a person's conduct. A bad or evil conscience is that which records a charge of guilt brought against the soul by the Holy Spirit, on account of the transgression of God's holy law; the light of that Spirit showing the soul the nature of sin, and its own guilty conduct. A tender conscience is that which is fully irradiated by the light of the Holy Spirit, which enables the soul to view the good as good, the evil as evil, in every important respect; and, consequently, leads it to abominate the latter and cleave to the former; and, if at any time it act in the smallest measure opposite to those views, it is severe in self-reprehension, and bitter in its regrets. A darkened, seared, or hardened conscience is that which has little or none of this divine light; the soul having by repeated transgressions so grieved the Spirit of God, that it has withdrawn its light, in consequence of which, the man feels no remorse, but goes on in repeated acts of transgression, unaffected either by threatenings or promises; and careless about the destruction which awaits it; this is what the Scriptures mean by the "conscience being seared as with a hot iron;" that is, by repeated transgressions, and resisting of the Holy Ghost. The word *conscience* itself vindicates the above explanation: it is compounded of *con,* "together or with," and *scio,* "I know;" because it knows, or combines with, by or together with, the Spirit of God.

From the above, I think we may safely make the following inferences: —1. All men have what is commonly termed conscience, and conscience plainly supposes the influence of the divine Spirit in it, convincing of sin, righteousness, and judgment. 2. The Spirit of God is given to enlighten, convince, strengthen, and bring men back to God, and fit them for glory by purifying their hearts. 3. Therefore all men may be saved who attend to and coincide with the convictions and light communicated; for the God of the Christians does not give men his Spirit to enlighten, that is, merely to leave them without excuse; but that it may direct, strengthen, lead them to himself, that they may be finally saved. 4. That this Spirit comes from the grace of God, is demonstrable from hence: it is a good and perfect gift; and St. James says, "All such come from the Father of lights." Besides, it is such a grace as cannot be merited; for, as it is God's Spirit, it is of infinite value; yet it is given. That, then, which is not merited, and yet is given, must be of grace, not condemning or ineffectual grace, for no such principle comes from or resides in the Godhead.

Thus it appears that all men are partakers of the grace of God; for all acknowledge that conscience is common to all; and this implies, as I hope has been proved, the Spirit of grace given by Christ Jesus, not that the world might be hereby condemned, but that it might be saved. Nevertheless, multitudes who are partakers of this heavenly gift, sin against it, lose it, and perish everlastingly; not through any defect in the gift, but through the abuse of it.

It is dangerous to trifle with conscience, even when erroneous; it should be borne with and instructed; it must be won over, not taken by storm. Its feelings should be respected, because they ever refer to God, and have their foundation in his fear. He who sins against his conscience, in things which every one else knows to be indifferent, will soon do it in those things in which his salvation is most intimately concerned. It is a great blessing to have a well informed conscience; it is a blessing to have a tender conscience; and even a sore conscience is infinitely better than none.

Persons of an over tender and scrupulous conscience may be very troublesome in a Christian society; but as this excessive scrupulosity comes from want of more light, more experience; or more judgment, we should bear with them. Though such should often run into ridiculous extremes, yet we must take care that we do not attempt to cure them either with ridicule or wrath. Extremes generally beget extremes; and such persons require the most judicious treatment, else they will soon be stumbled and turned out of the way. We should be very careful lest, in using what is called Christian liberty, we occasion their fall; and for our own sake we must take heed that we do not denominate sinful indulgences "Christian liberties."

"We are verily guilty." How finely are the office and influence of conscience exemplified in these words (of Joseph's brethren!) It was about twenty-two years since they had sold their brother, and probably their conscience had been lulled asleep to the present hour. God combines and brings about those favourable circumstances which produce attention and reflection, and give weight to the expostulations of conscience. How necessary to hear its voice in time! for here it may be the instrument of salvation; but if not heard in this world, it must be heard in the next; and there, in association with the unquenchable fire, it will be the never dying worm. Reader, has not thy sin as yet found thee out? Pray to God to take away the veil from thy heart, and to give thee that deep sense of guilt which shall oblige thee to flee for refuge to the hope which is set before thee in the Gospel of Christ.

DANCING.

DANCING was to me a perverting influence, an unmixed

moral evil; for although, by the mercy of God, it led me not to depravity of manners, it greatly weakened the moral principle, drowned the voice of a well instructed conscience, and was the first cause of impelling me to seek my happiness in this life. Every thing yielded to the disposition it had produced, and every thing was absorbed by it. I have it justly in abhorrence for the moral injury it did me; and I can testify, (as far as my own observations have extended, and they have had a pretty wide range,) I have known it to produce the same evil in others that it produced in me. I consider it, therefore, as a branch of that worldly education which leads from heaven to earth, from things spiritual to things sensual, and from God to Satan. Let them plead for it who will; I know it to be evil and that only. They who bring up their children in this way, or send them to those schools where dancing is taught, are consecrating them to the service of Moloch, and cultivating the passions, so as to cause them to bring forth the weeds of a fallen nature, with an additional rankness, deep-rooted inveteracy, and inexhaustible fertility. *Nemo sobrius saltat,* "No man in his senses will dance," said Cicero, a heathen: shame on those Christians who advocate a cause by which many sons have become profligate, and many daughters have been ruined!

After so fatal an example of this, (the beheading of John the Baptist,) can we doubt whether balls are not snares for souls; destructive of chastity, modesty, and sometimes even of humanity itself; and a pernicious invention to excite the most criminal passions? How many on such occasions have sacrificed their chastity, and then, to hide their shame, have stifled the human being and the parent, and, by direct or indirect means, have put a period to the innocent offspring of their connections! "Unhappy mother who exposes her daughter to the same shipwreck herself has suffered, and makes her own child the instrument of her lust and revenge!" Behold here, ye professedly religious parents, the fruits of what was doubtless called in those times, "elegant breeding and accomplished dancing." "Fix your eyes on that vicious mother, that prostituted daughter, and especially on that murdered ambassador of God, and then send your children to genteel boarding schools, to learn the accomplishment of dancing."

DRESS.

IF St. Paul saw the manner in which Christian women now dress, and appear in the ordinances of religion, what would he think? What would he say? How could he ever distinguish the Christian from the infidel? And if they who are in Christ are new creatures, and the persons who ordinarily appear in religious assemblies are really new creatures (as they profess in general to be) in Christ, he might reasonably inquire: "If these are *new* creatures, what must have been their appearance when they were *old* creatures?" Do we dress to be seen? And do we go to the house of God to exhibit ourselves? Wretched is that man or woman who goes to the house of God to be seen by any but by God himself.

When either women or men spend much time, cost, and attention on decorating their persons, it affords a painful proof that *within* there is little excellence, and that they are endeavouring to supply the want of mind and moral good by the feeble and silly aids of dress and ornament. Were religion out of the question, common sense would say in all these things, "Be decent; but be moderate and modest."

The wife of Phocion, a celebrated Athenian general, receiving a visit from a lady who was elegantly adorned with gold and jewels, and her hair with pearls, took occasion to call the attention of her guest to the elegance and costliness of her dress, remarking at the same time, "My ornament is my husband, now for the twentieth year general of the Athenians." How few Christian women act this part! Women are in general at as much pains and cost in their dress as if by it they were to be recommended both to God and man. It is, however, in every case, the argument either of a shallow mind, or of a vain and corrupted heart.

Simplicity reigned in primitive times; natural ornaments alone were then in use. Trade and commerce brought in luxuries; and luxury brought pride, and all the excessive nonsense of dress. No female head ever looks so well as when adorned with its own hair alone. This is the ornament appointed by God. To cut it off, or to cover it, is an unnatural practice; and to exchange the hair which God has given for hair of some other colour, is an insult to the Creator. How the delicacy of the female character can stoop to the use of false hair, and especially when it is considered that the chief part of this kind of hair was once the natural property of some ruffian soldier who fell in battle by many a ghastly wound, is more than I can possibly comprehend.

It will rarely be found that women who are fond of dress, and extravagant in it, have any subjection to their husbands but what comes from mere necessity. Indeed, their dress, which they intend as an attractive to the eyes of others, is a sufficient proof that they have neither love nor respect for their own husbands. Let them who are concerned refute the charge.

Should not the garments of all those who minister in holy things still be emblematical of the things in which they minister? Should they not be for glory and beauty, expressive of the dignity of the Gospel ministry, and that beauty of holiness without which none can see the Lord? As the high priests' vestments, under the law, were emblematical of what was to come, should not the vestments of the ministers of the Gospel bear some resemblance of what is come? Is then the dismal black, now worn by almost all kinds of priests and ministers, for glory and for beauty? Is it emblematical of any thing that is good, glorious, or excellent? How unbecoming the glad tidings announced by Christian ministers, is a colour emblematical of nothing but mourning and woe, sin, desolation, and death! How inconsistent the habit and office of these men! Should it be said, "These are only shadows, and are useless because the substance is come:" I ask, "Why, then, is black almost universally worn? why is a particular colour preferred, if there be no signification in any? Is there not a danger that, in our zeal against shadows, we shall destroy or essentially change the substance itself?" Would not the same sort of argumentation exclude water in baptism, and bread and wine in the sacrament of the Lord's supper? The white surplice in the service of the church is almost the only thing that remains of those ancient and becoming vestments which God commanded to be made for glory and beauty. Clothing, emblematical of office, is of more consequence than is generally imagined. Were the great officers of the crown, and the great officers of justice, to clothe themselves like the common people when they appear in their public capacity, both their persons and their decisions would be soon held in little estimation.

DREAMS.

Dreams have been on one hand superstitiously regarded, and on the other, skeptically disregarded. That some are prophetic, there can be no doubt; that others are idle, none can hesitate to believe. Dreams may be divided into the six following kinds:—1. Those which are the mere nightly result of the mind's reflections and perplexities during the business of the day. 2. Those which spring from a diseased state of the body, occasioning startings, terrors, &c. 3. Those which spring from an impure state of the heart, mental repetitions of those acts or images of illicit pleasure, riot, and excess, which form the business of a profligate life. 4. Those which proceed from a diseased mind, occupied with schemes of pride, ambition, grandeur, &c. These, as forming a characteristic conduct of the life, are repeatedly reacted in the deep watches of the night, and strongly agitate the soul with illusive enjoyments and disappointments. 5. Those which come immediately from Satan, which instill thoughts and principles opposed to truth and righteousness, leaving strong impressions on the mind suited to its natural bent and turn, which, in the course of the day, by favouring circumstances, may be called into action. 6. Those which come from God, and which necessarily lead to him, whether prophetic of future good or evil, or impressing holy purposes and heavenly resolutions. Whatever leads away from God, truth, and righteousness, must be from the source of evil; whatever leads to obedience to God, and to acts of benevolence to man, must be from the Source of goodness and truth. Reader, there is often as much superstition in disregarding as in attending to dreams; and he who fears God will escape it in both.

GHOSTS.

The story of the disturbances at the parsonage-house in Epworth is not unique. I myself, and others of my particular acquaintances, were eye and ear witnesses of transactions of a similar kind, which could never be traced to any source of trick or imposture; and appeared to be the forerunners of two very tragical events in the disturbed family; after which no noise or disturbance ever took place.

A philosopher should not be satisfied with reasons advanced by Dr. Priestley. He who will maintain his creed in opposition to his senses, and the most undisguised testimony of the most respectable witnesses, had better at once, for his own credit's sake, throw the whole story in the region of doubt, where all such relations, no matter how authenticated,

> "Upwhirl'd aloft,
> Fly over the backside of the world far off,
> Into a limbus large and broad."

And instead of its being called "the paradise of fools," it may be styled "the limbus of philosophic materialists;" into which they hurry whatever they cannot comprehend, choose not to believe, or please to call superstitious and absurd. And they treat such matters so, because they quadrate not with principles unfounded on the divine testimony, feebly supported by true philosophy, and contradictory to the plain unbiased good common sense of nineteen-twentieths of all the inhabitants of the earth.[16]

TOBACCO.

EVERY medical man knows well that the saliva which is so copiously drained off by the infamous quid and the scandalous pipe is the first and greatest agent which nature employs in digesting the food.

But is the elegant snuff box as dangerous as the pipe and the quid? Let us hear evidence. "The least evil," says Mr. D. Bomare, "which you can expect it to produce, is to dry up the brain, emaciate the body, enfeeble the memory, and destroy, if not entirely, yet in a large measure, the delicate sense of smelling." This has been noticed and deplored in the case of many eminent men who have addicted themselves to this destructive practice.

The most delicate females have their complexion entirely ruined by it. Strange! that the snuff box should be deemed too great

---

[16] For many interesting particulars relative to the disturbances at Epworth, I must refer the reader to Dr. Clarke's "Memoirs of the Wesley Family." —S.D.

a sacrifice for that for which most people are ready to sacrifice every thing beside! Many cases have been observed where the appetite has been almost destroyed, and a consumption brought on, by the immoderate use of this powder.

I heartily wish the corporation of surgeons, and anatomists in general, would procure as many bodies of habitual smokers and snuff-takers as possible, that, being dissected, we might know how far that ever to be dreaded evil prevails, which J. Borrhi says happened to the brain of an immoderate smoker, which, on dissection, was found dried and shriveled up by his excessive use of the pipe.

A person of my acquaintance, who had been an immoderate snuff-taker for upward of forty years, was frequently afflicted with a sudden suppression of breathing, occasioned by a paralytic state of the muscles which serve for respiration. These affections grew more and more alarming, and seriously threatened her life. The only relief she got in such cases was from a cup of cold water poured down her throat. This became so necessary to her, that she could never venture to attend even a place of public worship without having a small vessel of water with her, and a friend at hand to administer it. At last she left off snuff: the muscles reacquired their proper tone; and, in a short time after, she was entirely cured of a disorder occasioned solely by her attachment to the snuff box, and to which she had nearly fallen a victim.

A single drop of the chemical oil of tobacco being put on the tongue of a cat, produced violent convulsions, and killed her in the space of one minute. A thread dipped in the same oil, and drawn through a wound made by a needle in an animal, killed it in the space of seven minutes. Indeed, the strong caustic oil and acrid salt which are contained in it, must produce evil effects beyond calculation.

That it is sinful to use it as most do, I have no doubt, if destroying the constitution, and vilely squandering away the time and money which God has given for other purposes, may be termed "sinful."

I have observed some whole families, and very poor ones too, who have used tobacco in all possible ways, and some of them for more than half a century. Now, supposing the whole family, consisting of four, five, or six, to have used but 1s. 6d. worth in a week, then, in the mere article of tobacco, nearly £200 sterling is totally and irrecoverably lost in the course of fifty years. Were all the expenses attending this business enumerated, probably five times the sum in several cases would not be too large an estimate; especially if strong drink, its general concomitant, neglect of business, and appropriate utensils be taken into the account. Can any who profess to call themselves Christians vindicate their conduct in this respect?

But the loss of time in this shameful work is a serious evil. I have known some who, strange to tell, have smoked three or four hours in the day, by their own confession; and others who have spent six hours in the same employment. How can such persons answer for this at the bar of God? "But it is prescribed to me by a physician." No man who values his character as a physician will ever prescribe it in this way.

I grant that a person who is brought under the dominion of the pipe or the snuffbox, may feel great uneasiness in attempting to leave it off, and get some medical man, through a false pity, or for money, to prescribe the continued use of it: but this does not vindicate it; and the person who prescribes thus is not to be trusted. He is either without principle or without skill.

The impiety manifested by several in the use of this herb merits the most cutting reproof. When many of the tobacco consumers get into trouble, or under any cross or affliction, instead of looking to God for support, the pipe, the snuff box, or the twist, is applied to with quadruple earnestness; so that four times (I might say in some cases ten times) the usual quantity is consumed on such occasions. What a comfort is this weed in time of sorrow! what a support in time of trouble! In a word, what a god!

Again: the interruption occasioned in places of public worship by the use of the snuff box, is a matter of serious concern to all those who are not guilty. When the most solemn and important matters relative to God and man, eternal glory and eternal ruin, form the subject of a preacher's discourse, whose very soul is in his work, it is no unusual thing to see the snuff box taken out, and officiously handed about to half a dozen of persons on the same seat.

To the great scandal of religious people, the abominable customs of snuff taking and chewing have made their way into many congregations, and are likely to be productive of great evil. Churches and chapels are most scandalously abused by the tobacco chewers who frequent them; and kneeling before the supreme Being, which is so becoming and necessary when sinners approach their Maker in prayer, is rendered in many seats impracticable, because of the large quantity of tobacco saliva which is ejected in all directions.

Some indeed have been so candid as to acknowledge that, "though they do not use it as such, yet they take it as a help to their devotions." O earth, earth, earth! "I cannot," says one, "hear to any advantage without it; it quickens my attention, and then I profit most by the sermon." I am inclined to think there is some truth in this; and such persons exactly resemble those who have habituated themselves to frequent doses of opium; who, from the well known effect of too free a use of this drug, are in a continual torpor, except for a short time after each dose. They are obliged to have constant recourse to a stimulant, which, in proportion to its use, increases the disease.

Such persons as these are unfit to appear in the house of God. This conduct sufficiently proves that they are wholly destitute of the spirit of piety, and of a sense of their spiritual wants, when they stand in need of such excitements to help their devotion. He can have no pity for the wretched who does not lift up his soul in prayer to God in behalf of such miserable people.

But are not many led into the practice of smoking by their pastors. I am sorry to have it to say, that this idle, disgraceful custom prevails much at present among ministers of most denominations. Can such persons preach against needless self-indulgence, destruction of time, or waste of money? These men greatly injure their own usefulness; they smoke away their ministerial importance in the families where they occasionally visit; the very children and maid servants pass their jokes on the piping parson; and should they unluckily succeed in bringing over the uninfected to their vile custom, the evil is doubled. I have known serious misunderstandings produced in certain families, where the example of the idle parson has influenced a husband or wife, against the consent of the other, to adopt the use of the pipe or the snuff box.

Some are brought so much under the power of this

disgraceful habit, that they must have their pipe immediately before they enter the pulpit. What a preparation for announcing the righteousness of God, and preaching the Gospel of our Lord Jesus! Did St. Paul do any thing like this? "No," you say, "for he had the inspiration of the Holy Spirit." Then you take it to supply the place of this inspiration! How can such persons smile at their own conduct? "Be ye followers of us as we are of Christ Jesus," can never proceed out of their mouths. On such characters as these pity would be misplaced; they deserve nothing but contempt.

Should all other arguments fail to produce a reformation in the conduct of tobacco consumers, there is one which is addressed to good breeding and benevolence, which, for the sake of politeness and humanity, should prevail. Consider how disagreeable your custom is to those who do not follow it. An atmosphere of tobacco effluvia surrounds you whithersoever you go. Every article about you smells of it; your apartments, your clothes, and even your very breath. Nor is there a smell in nature more disagreeable than that of stale tobacco, arising in warm exhalations from the human body, rendered still more offensive by passing through the pores, and becoming strongly impregnated with that noxious matter which was before insensibly perspired.

To those who are not yet incorporated with the fashionable company of tobacco consumers, I would say, "Never enter." To those who are entered, I would say, "Desist, first, for the sake of your health, which must be materially injured, if not destroyed, by it. Secondly. For the sake of your property, which, if you are a poor man, must be considerably impaired by it. But, supposing you can afford this extra expense; consider how acceptable the pence (to go no farther) which you spend in this idle, unnecessary employment would be to many, who are often destitute of bread, and to whom one penny would sometimes be as an angel of God! Thirdly. For the sake of your time, a large portion of which is irreparably lost, particularly in smoking. Have you any time to dispose of, to murder? Is there no need of prayer, reading, study? Fourthly. For the sake of your friends, who cannot fail to be pained in your company, for the reasons before assigned. Fifthly. For the sake of your voice, which a continuance in snuff-taking will infallibly ruin, as the nasal passages are almost entirely obliterated by it. Sixthly. For the sake of your memory, that it may be vigorous and retentive;

and for the sake of your judgment, that it may be clear and correct to the end. Lastly. For the sake of your soul. Do you not think that God will visit you for your loss of time, waste of money, and needless self-indulgence? Have you not seen that the use of tobacco leads to drunkenness? Do you not know that habitual smokers have the drinking vessel often at hand, and frequently apply to it? Nor is it any wonder; for the great quantity of necessary moisture which is drawn off from the mouth, &c., by these means, must be supplied by some other way. You tremble at the thought. Well you may; for you are in great danger. May God look upon and save you before it be too late!"

Some of the most disagreeable things relative to the practice against which I have been writing, are still behind the curtain; and designedly detained there; and it is THERE ALONE where I wish every persevering smoker to seek for a certain vessel, named the *spitting dish,* which, to the abuse of all good breeding, and the insult of all delicate feeling, is frequently introduced into public company. May they and their implements, while engaged in this abominable work, be ever kept OUT OF SIGHT!

WESLEY.

ON the return of Mr. Wesley and his brother Charles from America, being both fervent in spirit, they powerfully proclaimed repentance toward God, and faith in our Lord Jesus Christ; and strongly insisted on the necessity of being born again, and of having the witness of God's Spirit with theirs, that they were thus born of God. At first, all the churches in London were open to them; and the people flocked together to see and hear two weather-beaten missionaries, whose skin appeared as if tanned by their continual exposure to the suns and winds of summer and winter on the continent of America. God attended their preaching with the power and demonstration of the Holy Ghost. Multitudes were turned from darkness to light, and from the power of satan unto God; and many obtained that faith in Christ by which the guilt of sin was removed, and the fear of death taken away; and had the Spirit of God witnessing with theirs, that they were the sons and daughters of God Almighty. The crowds that attended the churches where they preached were so great, that the clergy thought it proper to refuse them any farther use of their pulpits; and hence, being turned out of these, they went to the highways and hedges to compel sinners to come to the marriage feast. For as they had sufficiently learned that nothing but the Gospel could be the power of God unto salvation to them that believe, they boldly and zealously proclaimed Christ crucified wherever they found a crowd of sinners; using extempore prayer, and preaching without notes. This seemed a new thing in the earth; and while many were awakened and turned to God, several, who did not think that such extraordinary exertions were necessary, ridiculed their zeal; and others, who imagined God could not give his approbation to any kind of spiritual service that was not performed within the walls of a church, became greatly offended: and it is a fact that not a few opposed and blasphemed.

METHODISM.

AN itinerant ministry established in these kingdoms for upward of fourscore years, teaching the pure unadulterated doctrines of the Gospel, with the propriety and necessity of obedience to the laws, has been the principal means, in the hand of God, of preserving these lands from those convulsions and revolutions that have ruined and nearly dissolved the European continent. The itinerant ministry to which this refers, is that which was established in these lands by the late truly reverend, highly learned and cultivated, deeply pious, and loyal JOHN WESLEY, A.M., formerly a fellow of Lincoln College, Oxford; whose followers are known by the name of METHODISTS; a people who are an honour to their country, and a blessing to the government of their most excellent and revered king, George III.; who, through a long reign, has been the patron of religion and learning, and the father of his people.

The following declaration was inserted in an album, by Dr. Clarke, during the last conference which he attended, exactly one month before his death:—

IN PERPETUAM REI MEMORIAM.

I HAVE lived more than threescore years and ten; I have

travelled a good deal, both by sea and land; I have conversed with and seen many people, in and from different countries; I have studied the principal religious systems in the world; I have read much, thought much, and reasoned much; and the result is, I am persuaded of the simple, unadulterated truth of no book but the Bible; and of the true excellence of no system of religion but that contained in the Holy Scriptures; and especially CHRISTIANITY, which is referred to in the Old Testament, and fully revealed in the New. And while I think well of, and wish well to, all religious sects and parties, and especially to all who love our Lord Jesus Christ in sincerity, yet, from a long and thorough knowledge of the subject, I am led, most conscientiously, to conclude that Christianity itself, as existing among those called Wesleyan Methodists, is the purest, the safest, that which is most to God's glory and the benefit of man; and *that,* both as to the creed there professed, form of discipline there established, and the consequent moral practice there vindicated. And I believe that among them is to be found the best form and body of divinity that has ever existed in the church of Christ, from the promulgation of Christianity to the present day. To him who would say, "Doctor Clarke, are you not a bigot?" without hesitation I would answer, "No, I am not; for, by the grace of God, I am a Methodist!" Amen.

ADAM CLARKE.

Liverpool, July 26th, 1832.

"London, May 15*th,* 1824.

"MY DEAR SAMMY,

"Our friends here have all agreed to hold the 'centenary of Mr. Wesley's ordination to the sacred ministry.' He was ordained by Bishop Potter, Sept. 19, 1725; so the centenary will be on Sept. 19, 1825, when you will have returned from Shetland to the Bristol conference. Two services will be on that day; and two papers will be prepared for each preacher to read after his sermon: that in the forenoon shall contain an abstract of Mr. Wesley's life, call to the ministry, and success in it: that in the evening, an epitome of our doctrines and discipline: after each service a collection to be made, in order to build what probably may be called, 'the Wesleyan Hall,' for the purpose of holding all our public meetings, accommodating the missionary committee, having rooms for a museum of foreign curiosities or antiquities sent home by the missionaries, and one for a public library, besides offices for the enrolment of our chapel deeds, registers of baptisms, &c., &c. This building, which we calculate on holding six or eight thousand persons, is to be erected as near the centre of the city as we can; and to be paid for by the money collected through all our circuits and stations at home and abroad, and by a previous subscription. The project arose from Mr. Butterworth; was proposed, considered, agreed on, and methodized in the missionary committee; then a select number of friends were invited to breakfast together at the morning chapel, by a note signed by Mr. Butterworth and myself. About one hundred came: the project was received with enthusiasm, and 2,400*l.* were almost instantly subscribed! I send you this as the principal news we now have.[17]

"Ever your affectionate brother,
"ADAM CLARKE."

---

[17] As the above project was not carried into execution, it is hoped that the year 1839, the centenary of the establishment of the Wesleyan Methodist Society, will not pass without services somewhat similar to those mentioned by the doctor. The collections, and the objects to which the moneys shall be applied, are but secondary considerations. —S.D.

SHETLAND.

QUESTIONS[18] RELATIVE TO THE SHETLAND ISLANDS.

I. — *Islands and their Productions.*

1. WHAT is their number? present names? original names, and the meaning of such in the Norse or Danish language?
2. What is the soil? clayey — gravelly — peat, &c. What its general depth?
3. What is the basis of each? Basalt rock — granite — clay, or marl?
4. Metals and minerals. — Any gold, silver, copper, or lead found in them? in what quantities? and how and where found? any quartz — fluor — chalcedony — arragonite — barytes — or any other? and which?

II. — *Grain, Seeds, &c.*

1. WHAT grain is cultivated? wheat, oats, barley, rye?
2. How do they cultivate their ground? What sort is their manure, and how applied to produce the different crops?

---

[18] What answers were given to these questions it is not necessary for the reader to know. The letter is inserted as a curiosity; and as likely to be of use to other missionaries in different parts of the world. The success of the mission to the islands may be learned from the letters and journals published in the Wesleyan Methodist Magazine since 1832. — S.D.

3. When do they sow their wheat, oats, rye, &c., and plant their potatoes?
4. Potatoes.—Of what kinds, colours, size, and quality? When do they plant, and when dig up? How much of each is sown or planted per acre, and what is the produce? that is, how many bushels per acre, to one sown or planted on the different soils?
5. Is there any flax or hemp sown? How are they prepared for the wheel and loom, and into what species of cloth are they manufactured?

III. – *Horticulture and Planting.*

1. GARDENS.—What pulse, beans, peas, the sorts, their time in the ground? carrots, parsnips, turnips? &c. What remarkable herbs and flowers?
2. Orchards.—What fruit? apples, pears, plums, gooseberries, currants? &c. What size and quality? What are their various kinds, and how used?
3. Plants.—What sorts? Are there any *peculiar* to the isles? meadow grass, of what sorts? clover, trefoil, lucerne, florin, &c.
4. Forest trees.—Fir, ash, elm, any plantations? Of what kinds, extent, and where?
5. What underwood, hazel, furs, or whins; juniper or other berries on the moors?

IV.—*Fish.*

1. SHELL-FISH.—Oysters, muscles, razor-fish, pearl oysters, crabs, lobsters, limpets, cockles? &c.
2. Fish in the seas.—Porpoise, whale, shark, dog-fish, cod, ling, salmon, herring, haddock, gurnet, conger, mackerel, sparling?
3. How are the fish cured for winter there, such as salmon, cod, ling, herring?
4. Shoals of fish.—Of what kinds? when do they appear, whence do they come, and whither do they go? &c.
5. Pearls from the oysters, or muscles.—Of what shape, colour, and size? How used, vended, or manufactured?

V. — *Fowls.*

1. WILD FOWL. — Geese, ducks, barnacles, gulls, grouse, pheasants, partridges, cuckoos, wrens, snipes, curlews, woodcocks, and birds of passage in general? Of what kinds? When do they usually appear and disappear?
2. Poultry. — Geese, ducks; hens, pigeons, turkeys? Of what size, and of what advantage to the inhabitants?

VI. — *Beasts.*

1. OF what sorts are the cattle? — Cows, what colour, size, what milk per diem, and how much butter from a given quantity of milk? Horses? size, colours, strength? &c. Shetland poney, describe.
2. Sheep. — What size; their wool, of what quality? Do they often bring forth twins? What is the time of shearing? How many pounds of wool off each?
3. Goats. — How used? Do they run at large, or are they tethered? Are they kept principally for breed or milk?
4. Dogs and cats. — Size, colour, propensities? any thing remarkable in their form or qualities?
5. Wild beasts. — Deer, foxes, badgers, pole cats, hares, rabbits, otters, weasels, squirrels? &c. 6. Winter provender for horses, cows, sheep, goats? &c.

VII. — *Inhabitants.*

1. INHABITANTS. — Size, colour, features, hair? Any thing peculiar in the formation of the head, mouth, nose, feet, and legs? Describe the general make both of the men and women.
2. Dispositions. — Phlegmatic or choleric, close or ingenuous?
3. Are there thefts? Of what kinds?
4. In their manners. — Are they cruel, morose, kind to strangers, litigious, apt to quarrel?

VIII. — *Food, &c.*

1. FOOD for the different seasons of the year. — What sorts, and how dressed? any thing peculiar in their mode of cooking? the usual time of their meals, and what the proportion of time allotted for sleep?
2. Beverage. — Ale, spirits, metheglin, or mead? Is there a great consumption of tea, ardent spirits, and tobacco?
3. Clothing. — Of what kinds? names and forms of their habits?
4. Fuel. — Coal, peat, or turf, dry sea-weed, wood, bog, fir? &c.

IX. — *Implements.*

1. AGRICULTURAL. — What sort of ploughs, harrows, spades, scythes, sickles? What the harness of the horses?
2. Carts or cars. — What sort of wheels? For what uses? Construction. — Is it good, light, or clumsy?
3. Domestic utensils. — Their names, figure, &c., of wood, tin, iron, brass, clay?
4. Houses. — How constructed? Of what materials, cabins, windows, chimneys, offices; or outhouses, stables, bouveries, or byars; sheep and pig cotes; separate or together?

X. — *Women and Children.*

1. WOMEN. — How are they treated? how employed? good housewives; cleanly? Do they often produce twins?
2. Children. — How are they nursed and educated? Does bastardy prevail?

XI. — *Trades, &c.*

1. TRADES, manufactures, and commerce. — What imported and exported, and with whom?
2. Domestic economy. — Spinning, knitting, sewing, weaving?
3. Day labourers. — What is their pay? How many hours do they work? servants, male and female? What their yearly wages? Are they active, slothful, faithful, cleanly? &c.

XII. – *Vices, Pastimes.*

1. WHAT vices are most prevalent among them?
2. Sports and pastimes. – What? when practised; their names, and how performed?
3. Traditions – Relative to their own origin, the exploits of their forefathers? tales; legends; what sorts? any of the tales of Ossian, Oscar, Ullin, Fin M'Cuol Odo, or any of the Scandinavian chiefs?
4. Weapons of defence. – Guns, swords, dirks, bows, targets; any old armour, or coins found in the isles?

XIII. – *Religion.*

1. RELIGION. – Generally prevalent? creed or notions, form of public worship?
2. Religious ordinances. – When, and how conducted? Lord's day well observed? family worship any, or general?
3. Ministers. – How supported? by tithes, stipends, free-will offerings? &c.
4. Schools. – Classical, commercial, or merely English; or the language of the place?
5. Are they naturally fond of learning? Can most of them read?
6. Are the families you visit well supplied with Bibles?
7. What are the books used in education generally? Of what sort of reading do they appear to be most fond?

XIV. – *Language and Polite Literature.*

1. WHAT is the prevalent language? What was the original tongue? Do any words of it still remain mixed with their present speech?
2. As the people were originally Scandinavians, or Norwegians, how came they to lose their native language? Where and how did the English language enter, and generally supplant the original tongue?
3. How are the winter evenings spent? While some work, do others tell tales, repeat legends? &c.
4. Are the people fond of poetry, music, dancing? &c.

5. What are their musical instruments?

XV. – *Popular Superstitions.*

1. HOLIDAYS.—Religious customs, or rites on midsummer, All Saints, or All Hallows even? Christmas, Candlemas, Easter?
2. Superstitions.—Charms, incantations, observations of the clouds, flight of birds, crowing of cocks at unusual times? about demons, fairies, brownies, wraiths, or appearances portending death; second sight; death watch; knockings? &c.

XVI. – *Population, Diseases, &c.*

1. LONGEVITY.—Do they live in general to a good old age? its general duration?
2. Proportion of males to females?
3. Diseases.—Of children; adults? What kinds prevail most? popular methods of cure? deaths, wakes, burials? &c., and attendant circumstances?

XVII. – *Laws, Courts of Justice, &c.*

1. ANY thing peculiar in their civil customs, laws, courts of justice, and punishments?
2. Lawyers, physicians, quack doctors? Are there many such in the islands?

XVIII. – *Phenomena.*

1. THE *aurora borealis,* or "northern lights."—When do they appear? in winter only? what time of the evening do they commence? Describe their appearance, and how long they last. Do they compensate for the shortness of the days?
2. What is the common opinion of their origin?
3. Tides.—Any thing remarkable in them? when greatest?
4. Seasons.—Winter, summer, autumn, spring? When do they begin, and how long continue?
5. Weather.—What are the signs of approaching good or bad? snow, rain, frost, winds, any remarkable sign in the heavens? and

from what do the country people draw their prognostications?
6. Does the magnetic needle suffer agitations, singular variations in its traversing, or in its dip, during the prevalence of the *aurora borealis*? Or does the atmosphere then show any peculiar signs of electricity?

XIX. — *Letting of Lands, Rents, Tenures, &c.*

1. How are lands let? What sort of tenures prevail? Have any of the farmers freeholds, copyholds, leases for a term of years, or for lives, or of a mixed nature?
2. How do they pay their rents? in money, in kind, by service? Are there any feudal services, or boons to the landlords?

XX. — *Taxation, Civil and Religious Contracts, &c.*

1. WHAT are the principal taxes and customs?
2. Are the people generally contented with their form of government? attached to the house of Brunswick or Stuart?
3. Does clanship prevail among them? Of what character are their chiefs? proud, haughty, kind, benevolent?
4. Marriages. — Dowries, wedding feasts, bringing home the bride, or in-fare? what the customs or ceremonies?
5. Christenings and weanings. — Any peculiar ceremonies or festivals on the occasion?

XXI. - *Miscellaneous Questions.*

1. ANY accounts of marine monsters, mermen, mermaids, craken, or kraken, sea snake?
2. Are there any remarkable ruins, temples, druidical monuments, churches, ancient fortresses? and in what form?
3. Any inscriptions, Runic, Oghams, Celtic? &c.

N.B. Answers of a certain kind to many of the preceding questions may be obtained from travellers, historians, &c. But these generally copy each other, and are not to be much regarded. I wish you therefore to see with your own eyes, and hear with your own ears; and to answer from knowledge and fact. Look at nature and practice as they lie before you: but when obliged to relate any thing from the testimony of others, see that the testimony be credible; and generally give the reasons upon which your own conviction is built?

Poor Shetland, I have worked hard for thee; many a quire, many a ream of paper have I written to describe thy wants, and to beg for supplies; and several thousands of miles have I travelled in order to raise those supplies which by letters I had solicited for thee. It is now "almost done, and almost over." May God raise thee up another friend, that will be, if possible, more earnest and faithful, and at the same time more successful! And now I may say, May the HOLY TRINITY be the incessant Friend, O my poor Shetland! Amen.

SUNDAY-SCHOOLS.

THE amazing success of Sunday schools has nearly annihilated the proverb, "A young saint, an old devil;" as we find in all directions both men and women, whether wives and husbands, or masters and servants, walking in all the ordinances and commandments of God unblamably, who were brought to an acquaintance with God, when little children, at such schools; whose piety never forsook them, but has carried them on through most of the troublesome and trying relations of life; till, now past their meridian, their sun is growing brighter and broader toward its setting, having before shone more and more to its perfect day. Nor do I know a Sunday school in the nation, under the direction of godly teachers, that has not been crowned with instances of this kind, and that has not had the satisfaction of registering the true Scriptural conversion and happy deaths of several of its pupils. When these results have been so numerous, and satisfactorily witnessed, we need not wonder that pious parents have been encouraged to cultivate their children's minds with more assiduity than formerly; looking to God to bless their endeavours, by pouring light upon the minds of their little ones, and peace and love into their hearts. Everywhere the most blessed fruits of such labour are seen; and we safely aver, that infant salvation is as frequent now as that of adults was a century ago; while the latter are in a tenfold ratio to what they have been, within the memory, at least, of the present generation. And it is not unfrequent that what formerly began at the greatest, and went down to the least, (at the parents, descending from them to their children,) now, in many cases, takes a contrary direction; as I have myself known many instances where little children at a pious Sunday school, having been brought to the true knowledge of salvation by faith, have become instruments in the hand of God of converting their parents. Some years ago the spirit of infidelity laboured hard to prevent all religious instruction to children. "Leave them to themselves," said this spirit of error; "do not prepossess their minds with religious notions and religious creeds! Bias them not; and when they come to age let them choose for themselves; and then we shall have religion without superstition." This has been tried, alas! in numerous cases; and the neglected child has found it more rational—that is, more according to the unfettered sinful bias of his own mind—to be a skeptic or an infidel than to believe with the orthodox; or, to perform an easy set of moral duties, with the careless and the unawakened, being at ease in Zion, and trusting in the mountains of their Samaria.

SCHISM.

SCHISM in religion is a dangerous thing, and should be carefully avoided by all who fear God. But this word should be well understood. In theology, it is generally allowed to signify "a rent in, or departure from the doctrine and practice of the apostles; especially among those who had been previously united in that doctrine and practice." A departure from human institutions in religion is no schism; for this reason, that the word of God alone is the sufficient rule of the faith and practice of Christians; and as to human institutions, forms, modes, &c., those of one party may be as good as those of another.

LUST OF POWER.

WHAT a truly diabolic thing is the lust of power! It destroys all the charities of life, and renders those who are under its influence the truest resemblants of the arch fiend.

POLITICAL PARTY-SPIRIT.

PARTY spirit, especially in political matters, is the great disgrace and curse of England. This spirit knows no friend; feels no obligation; is unacquainted with all dictates of honesty, charity and mercy; and leaves no stone unturned to ruin the object of its hate. We have elections by law no more than once in seven years; and the mischief that is then done to the moral character of the nation is scarcely repaired in the succeeding seven. All the charities of life are outraged and trampled under foot by it; common honesty is not heard, and lies and defamation go abroad by wholesale. The rascal *many* catch the evil reports which the opposed candidates and their committees spread of each other, and the characters of the best men in the land are wounded, and lie bleeding till slow-paced oblivion cancels the remembrance of the transactions which gave them birth.

FRIENDSHIP.

POOR friendship! it has been so kicked about in the world, that it has now become a complete cripple, and will go halting *usque ad Graecas Calendas*. However, in all its wanderings, it is always sure of a night's lodging with us; and seems quite at home under our roof; and declares, and I suppose with sincerity, that our house is one of the very few out of which it has never been turned, and where it can always confidently expect entertainment. It and myself have never had any misunderstanding; and having grown old together, we are resolved to keep on good terms. It has often interested itself on my behalf; and though it has frequently been unsuccessful, yet, knowing its sincerity, I have taken the good will for the successful deed, and have still kindly taken it in, with all those whom it has recommended. Some of these look well, and speak comfortably, and are full of good resolutions and professions; but a disposition to take offence so universally prevails, that several of them take themselves off without any previous warning; and others, after going out, linger a little at the door, and talk and look as usual: but every day I find them progressively farther off, till at last the distance is such that I cannot hear them, though they seem still to speak; and in time they get entirely out of sight! Nothing remains of them in our house but the name, with a scroll, in my own handwriting, under each: "Whenever thou art disposed to return, thou wilt find here the same welcome as formerly."

I can say I never formed a friendship which I broke. My list of friends has not a blot in it; some of them, it is true, have slunk away; some seem to have hurried off, and others stand at a great distance; but I have made no erasure in my list, and when they choose to return, it can never appear, by reinsertion that they have proved false to their friend, or have been careless about him.

Multitudes complain of the treachery of friends, betraying their secrets, &c., never considering that they themselves have been their first betrayers, in confiding to others what they pretend to wish should be a secret to the whole world! If a man never let his secret out of his own bosom, it is impossible that he should ever be betrayed.

FLATTERY.

MEN who praise you to your face are ever to be suspected. The Italians have a very expressive proverb on this subject: "He who caresses thee more than he was wont to do, has either deceived thee, or is about to do it." I have never known the sentiment in this proverb to fail.

SELF-INTEREST.

A MAN is to be suspected when he recommends those good works most from which he receives most advantage. Self-interest is a most decisive casuist, and removes abundance of scruples in a moment. It is always the first consulted, and the most readily obeyed. It is not sinful to hearken to it, but it must not govern nor determine by itself.

GOING TO LAW.

"DEBATE thy cause with thy neighbour." Take the advice of friends. Let both sides attend to their counsels: but do not tell the secret of thy business to any. After quandering your money away upon lawyers, both they and the judge will at last leave it to be settled by twelve of your fellow citizens! O the folly of going to law! O the blindness of men and the rapacity of lawyers!

One Christian sues another at law! This is almost as great a scandal as can exist in a Christian society. Those in a religious community who will not submit to a proper arbitration, made by persons among themselves, should be expelled from the church of God.

SURETYSHIP.

IF thou pledge thyself in behalf of another, thou takest the burden off him, and placest it on thy own shoulders. And when he knows that he has got one to stand betwixt him and the demands of law and justice, he will feel little responsibility; his spirit of exertion will become crippled, and listlessness as to the event will take place. His own character will suffer little; his property nothing,—for his friend bears all the burden: and perhaps the very person for whom he bore this burden treats him with neglect; and, lest the restoration of the pledge should be required, will avoid both the sight and presence of his friend. Give what thou canst; but, except in extreme cases, be surety for no man.

USURY.

"HE that by usury increaseth his substance."—By taking unlawful interest for his money; lending to a man in great distress money, for the use of which he requires an exorbitant sum. O that the names of all those unfeeling, hard-hearted, consummate villains in the nation, who thus take advantage of their neighbour's necessities to enrich themselves, were published at every market-cross; and then the delinquents all sent to their brother savages in New Zealand! It would be a happy riddance to the country.

SLAVERY.

"MEN stealers."—Slave dealers; whether those who carry on the traffic in human flesh and blood; or those who steal a person in order to sell him into bondage; or those who buy such stolen men or women, no matter of what colour or what country; or those who sow dissensions among barbarous tribes in order that they who are taken in war may be sold into slavery; or the nations who legalize or connive at such traffic: all these are men stealers, and God classes them with the most flagitious of mortals.

I here register my testimony against the unprincipled, inhuman, Antichristian, and diabolical slave trade, with all its authors, promoters, abettors, and sacrilegious gains; as well as against the great devil, the father of it and them.

PARABLE.

A PARABLE is a comparison or similitude, in which one thing is compared with another, especially spiritual things with natural, by which means these spiritual things are better understood, and make a deeper impression on an attentive mind.

MIRACLE.

I MEAN by miracle, something produced or known, that no power is capable of but that which is omnipotent, and no knowledge adequate to but that which is omniscient. The conversion of one rebellious soul is a greater miracle, and more to be admired, than all that can be wrought on inanimate creatures.

MILLENNIUM.

WHAT disappointment and confusion have been brought into the minds of many, by calculations relative to the termination of certain empires, Papal and Turkish; the beast and the false prophet; Christ's second coming to establish a universal empire, the laws of which are to be administered by his presence; corporeally manifested on earth; and also concerning the time of the final judgment, and the end of the world! When a fancy is pursued, the line of pursuit is only directed by a sort of telegraphic phantoms, unreal landmarks to unreal objects; and when the last *ignis fatuus* has terminated its uncertain dance by absorption in some other vapour by which it has been neutralized, we are left in sudden darkness, in the quagmire where all such mental aberrations must necessarily end; and thus prophecy is prostituted; faith and hope (improperly employed) are disappointed; and religion itself discredited.

It is truly an astonishing thing that men will prefer hope to enjoyment; and rather content themselves with blessings in prospect than in possession!

Thousands, in their affections, conversation, and conduct, are wandering after an undefined and indefinable period, commonly called a millennial glory, while expectation is paralyzed, and prayer and faith restrained in reference to present salvation: and yet none of these can tell what even a day may bring forth; for we now stand on the verge of eternity, and, because it is so, "now is the accepted time, and now is the day of salvation."

TIME.

BUY up those moments which others seem to throw away; steadily improve every present moment, that ye may, in some measure, regain the time ye have lost. Let time be your chief commodity; deal in that alone; buy it all up, and use every portion of it yourselves. Time is that on which eternity depends; in time ye are to get a preparation for the kingdom of God; if you get not this in time, your ruin is inevitable; therefore buy up the time.

THE END.

INDEX

A

Abbot, the Right Honorable Charles, 16
Abraham, tent of, 220 – prayer of, 227
Achan, punished for covetousness, 211
Adam, entailed corruption upon his descendants, 86
Adonai, explained, 56
Adoption, explained, 133 – a Roman custom, ibid.
Adoration, explained, 213
Adultery, forbidden, 206
Afflictions, all men subject to. 337 -- advantages of, 340
Album, lines written in an, 374, 400
Alphabetical characters, when invented, 197
America, North, savage tribes of, idolatrous, 199
Anarchy, explained, 272
Ancestors, our rude, the power of strength of the Divine Nature, the attribute principally contemplated by, 63
Angel of the Covenant, personal appearance of, 46
Angels, ministry of, 46, 326 – not made in the image of God, 77
Antediluvians, 89
Antinomianism, 131-132, 133
Apostasy, causes of, 349 – degrees of, 351 – every believer in danger of, 351 – consequences of, ibid.
A posteriori arguments to prove the being of God, 54
Apostolic uninterrupted succession, a fable, 290
A priori arguments to prove the being of God, 54
Archimedes, 378
Arminius, works of, 34
Aristocracy, explained, 271
Ascension of Christ, 110

Asia Minor, received the Gospel, 40-41
Assyrians, destitute of the knowledge of God, 86
Atonement of Christ, necessary, 104 – extent of, ib. 106
Attributes of God, 58 – perfect unity and harmony among the, 68
Audible voice, Revelation given by, 46
Augustine, Saint, a story of, 212
Augustine, Archbishop of Tarragon, the liberality of, 301
Autocracy, explained, 271
Ava, the followers of Budhoo, in, 199

B

Baal, adored by the Canaanites, 63 – pleaders for, 173
Babel-builders, 52
Backbiters, 207, 210, 322
Backsliding, see Apostasy.
Badcock, Mr. 147
Baptism, the mode of, 240 – proselytes to the Jewish religion received, 242, -- typical of the descent of the Holy Ghost, ib.
Barrow, Dr. Isaac, 34
Bates, Rev. Eli, 34
Baxter, "Saints' Everlasting Rest," of, 26
Bayley, Dr. C., Hebrew Grammar by, 29
Bell, Greek Grammar by, 30

Bellerophon, 63
Benevolence, 157, 159
Bennett, Mr. F., 5, 6
Benson, Rev. Joseph, 12
Bentley, Professor, 14
Bibliographical Dictionary, Dr. Clarke's, 14, 34
Bigots, 132, 163
Bill trade, the, 207
Blasphemy, forbidden, 199
Blood, circulation of, 378
Bodies of Divinity, 121 – danger of, 315
Bookseller, a, 265, 266
Boyd, II. S. Esq., Essay by, on the Greek article, 371
Boyle, the Hon. Robert, 286
Bradburn, Rev. Samuel, 12
Bradford, (Wilts.) Circuit, 7
Brainerd, David, Journal of, recommended, 26
British history, 30 – constitution, 274
Butterworth, Joseph, Esq., 10, 402
Bythner's Lyra Prophetica, 30

C

Caesars, the first, under them that the preaching of the Gospel took place, 44
Cain, defeat of, 215
Caley, John, Esq., 16
Cathedral windows, painting on, 215
Celibacy, a bad state, 252
Censoriousness, 164
Centenary of Mr. Wesley's

ordination, 401
Ceylon, the followers of Budhoo, in, 199
Chaldeans, destitute of the knowledge of God, 86
Chambers' Cyclopedia, 9
Chemist, a, 91, 265
Children, a spirit of inquiry, common to, 256 – should be early instructed, ib. – piety of, why formerly so rare, 256 – what they should be taught, 257 – business for, 265 – Christ loves, 266 – providential deliverances of, ib. – duties of, to their parents, 267
China, the visible heavens worshipped in, 199
Christ, a fountain of light and salvation, 44 – never wrote himself but once, ib. – begins where the law ends, 52 – the grand object of the whole sacrificial code, ib. – without him no human spirit can come into the presence of its Judge, 71 – divinity of, 96 – creation his work, ibid. – eternity of, 98 – omnipotence of, 98 – omnipresence of, 100 – omniscience of, ibid. – object of worship, ibid. – incarnation of, 100 – why a man, ibid. – offices of, 102 – a Philosopher, Moralist, and Divine, ibid. – shone on the world at the conclusion of the fourth millenary from the creation, 102-103 – compassion of, ibid. – atonement of, necessary, 104, 106 – his agony inexplicable if the atonement be denied, 105 – death of, 106 – his fear of death a widely different thing from what it is in man, ibid. – grace of, shines out upon all, 107-108 – resurrection of, 110 – ascension of, ib. – intercession of, ibid. – righteousness of, 129 – flock of, 132 – the Ambassador of the Father, 147 – the medium of prayer, 222
Christian, the genuine, 384
Christianity, rapid spread of, 41, 342 – differs from philosophic systems, 44 – from popular tradition, ibid. – from Pagan and Mahommedan revelations, ib. – made its appearance under the first Caesars, ib. – in Judea, ib. – challenges the Roman government, ibid.
Church, Christian, founded in Jerusalem, 40 – constitution of the, 237, 238 – the extension of the, 239 – officers of the, 286 – duties of the members of the, 316-317
Clarke, Dr. Adam, birth of, 1 – parents of, ib. – merciful recovery of, from the small-pox, 2 – education of, ib. – memory of, suddenly enlightened, ib. – the subject

of early religious impressions, ib. – reproved for disobedience to his mother, 3 – learns music and dancing, ib. – hears the Methodist preachers, ib. – conversion of, 4 – receives great intellectual enlargement, ib. – professions for which he was designed, 5 – is sent to Mr. F. Bennett, a linen-merchant, ib. – had two narrow escapes from sudden death, ib. – officiates at family worship, ib. – his relations become hearers of the Methodists, ib. – goes six miles to meet a class, ib. – begins to exhort in the surrounding villages, 6 – removes from Colerain, ib. – is urged by Mr Bredin to take a text, ib. – preaches his first sermon at New Buildings, ib. – directed by Mr. Wesley to come to Kingswood, 7 – the treatment he met with while there, ib. – is sent to the Bradford (Wilts.) Circuit, ib. – a circumstance which nearly proved ruinous to all his attainments in literature, 8 – ceases to drink tea or coffee, ib. – is appointed to the Norwich Circuit, ib. – to St. Austell, 8 – his character of Samuel Drew, 9 – his popularity, ibid. – is appointed to Plymouth-Dock, 9 – to the Norman isles, 10 – reads Walton's Polyglott Bible, ib. – has several remarkable deliverances, ib. – his marriage, 10 – is appointed to Bristol, 11 – to Dublin, ib. – forms the Stranger's Friend Society, 11 – is overwhelmed with grief on hearing of the death of Mr. Wesley, 12 – his opinion of Mr. Wesley, ib. – Mr. Wesley's opinion of, ib. – is appointed to Manchester, his health in a very declining state, ib. – goes to Buxton, and is completely restored, ib. – is appointed to Liverpool, ib. – Mrs. Pawson's opinion of, ib. – narrowly escapes assassination, 13 – commences authorship, ib. – his father's death, 14 – publishes Strum's Reflections, A Bibliographical Dictionary, A succinct Account of Polyglott Bibles, and of the principal Editions of the Greek Testament, 14 – is chosen President of the Liverpool and Manchester Philological Society, ib. – publishes Fleury's Manners of the ancient Israelites, and Baxter's Christian Directory, ib. – becomes a contributor to the Eclectic Review, ib. – is elected President of the

Conference, 15 – renders the British and Foreign Bible Society important assistance, ib. – publishes his Concise View of The Succession of Sacred Literature, ib. – is presented with the diplomas of A.M. and LL.D., ib. – is appointed sub-commissioner of the public records of the kingdom, 16 – becomes librarian of the Surrey Institution, ib. – publishes a short account of the last illness and death of the learned Porson, ib. – projects a new edition of the London Polyglott Bible, 17 – issues his Commentary, ib. – publishes a Missionary Address, ib. – removes to Millbrook ib. – makes a tour through part of Scotland and Ireland, ib. – takes charge of two high priests of Budhoo, 18 – becomes M.R.I.A., ib. – commences an acquaintance with the Duke of Sussex, 18 – chosen President of the Conference for the third time, 19 – takes great interest in Shettland Mission, 20 – visits the Isles, ib. – removes to Haydon Hall, ib. – establishes schools in Ireland, ib. – is present at the death of R. Scott, Esq., ib. – receives an invitation to visit America, 21 – attends the Conference in Liverpool, 23 – seized with cholera morbus, 24 – death of, 24 – personal appearance of, ib. – character of, ib. – Mr. Moore's testimony to, 26 – attachment to Methodism of, 27, 401 – mode of preparing for the pulpit, 30 – preaching of, ibid. – prayers of, 33 – writings of, 33 – literary honours of, 36 – letter from, on imputed righteousness, 131 – Memoirs of the Wesley family, by, 255 – prayer of, for his daughter, 264 – letter to a preacher, by 281

Clarke, Mrs., 1, 10, 20, 23
Clarke, Rev. J.B.B., 15
Coffee, never used by Dr. Clarke, 8
Collections, how to be made, 159
Commandments, the ten, 197
Communion of saints 383
Company, the danger of bad, 385
Confession of faults, 385
Confidence, the danger of self, 350
Conscience, definition of, 386 – plainly supposes the influence of the Divine Spirit, 388 – dangerous to trifle with, 389
Contentions, to be avoided, 164
Conversion, explained, 138
Copernicus, 378
Covetousness, forbidden, 211

D

Damascenus, Saint John, the means he employed to support the truth, 379
Dancing, the influence of, on Dr. Clarke, 3 – time spent in, 262, 389
David, introduced instruments of music into God's service, 234
Dawson, Greek lexicon by, 30
Death, sin the cause of, 355-356 – all men naturally fear, 356 – nearness of, ib. – death refines nothing, ib.
Decades, time divided into, by the French national assembly, 202
Deists never able to convert one soul, 286-287
Democracy, explained, 272
Demoniacal influence, a doctrine of the Bible, 328
Demons, can tempt no further than as permitted by God, 349
Des Cartes, 378
Despair, 165
Despotism, explained, 271
Detractors, 207-210
Devil, the, see Satan
Dii Majores, of the Heathens, 65
Dishonesty, forbidden, 206
Drawing, time spent in, 262
Dreams, revelation given in, 46 – six kinds of, 393
Dress, the folly and sin of gay and expensive, 391
Drew, Samuel, 9
Druggist, a, 265
Drunkenness, forbidden, 205
Duellists, all, are murderers, 205
Dunn, Samuel, letters to, 16, 17, 19, 20, 21, 28, 32, 35, 401

E

Earth, no disorders in, before the fall, 80 – now under the curse, 84
Education, defined, 255
Egyptians, destitute of the knowledge of God, 86
Eli, too indulgent to his sons, 261
Elohim, signification of the word, 72 – man the work of, 79
Emblematical appearances, revelation given by, 46
England, Sabbath broken in, 203
Enoch, character of, 187
Erasmus, how convinced of the doctrine of the Sacred Trinity, 74
Eternity of God, 60

F

Faith, definition of, 119, 126 – necessary to salvation, ib. – commanded by God, 120 – the act of, man's own, ib. – should be exercised the present moment, 121 –

encouragement to, ib. – unnecessary difficulties in the way of, ib. – little in action, 121 – one of the wiles of the devil to persuade man that the exercise of this grace is almost impossible without a miraculous power, ib. – the want of, strange and disgraceful, ib. – volunteers in, 122 – conveys the virtue of Christ into the soul, 123 – disregards apparent impossibilities, 123 – seems to put the power of God into the hands of men, ib. – many are looking for more without using that which they have, ib. – weak faith wishes for signs and miracles, ib. – Christ should be credited on his own word, ib. – degrees in, ib. – an increase of, ib. – why so rarely exercised, 124 – lives by love, ib. – produces godly living, ib. – will enter into eternal glory, 125 – objects of, in heaven, ib.
Faithfulness of God, 71
Farindon, Anthony, 34
Fasting, immoderate and superstitious, murder, 204 – the duty of, 386
Fear, filial, not cast out of the soul by perfect love, 162
Flattery, suspicious, 413
Fletcher, Rev. John, works of, recommended, 25
French, National Assembly of the, divided time into decades, 202 – Revolution of the, 12
Friendship, mentioned, 412
Foreigner, the saying of a, 204
Forgiveness of injuries recommended, 161, 163
Fornication, forbidden, 206
Fulness of God, explained, 180

G

Genesis, the most ancient record in the world, 43 – from which ancient philosophers, astronomers, chronologists, and historians, have taken their date, ib.
Geologists, the folly of many, 379
Geometry, no royal road to, 379
George III., an anecdote of, 400
Ghosts, 393
Glenbervie, Lord, 16
Gluttony, forbidden, 205
God, the sole Fountain of light and truth, 38 – observed a slow climax in bringing a knowledge of his will to mankind, 46 – the term God defined, 54, 57 – a general definition of, ib. – a living rational Essence, 55 – is underived, ib. – independent, ib., 57 – is distinguished from matter, 55 – is most excellent, 56 – perfect, ib. – unity of, 58 – spirituality of, ib. – eternity of, 55, 60 – omnipotence of,

59, 61 – omnipresence of, 63 – omniscience of, 56, 65 – benevolence of, 65, 75 – wills all men to be saved, 67 – will of, 67 – justice of, 68 – is represented in the Scriptures as dong what he only permits to be done, 69 – holiness of, 70 – faithfulness of, 71 – infinitely happy previous to the formation of man, 75 – perfections of, capable of being eternally manifested, 126 – no respecter of persons, 130

Good men, will not sell their consciences, 333

Going to law, condemned, 413

Gospel, by it is the cure of sin, 51, 183 – is God's method of saving a lost world, 52, 108 – makes no allowance for sin, 185

Grace of Christ, shines out upon all, 108

Greece, received the Gospel, 40-41 – government of, despotic, 49

Greeks, destitute of the knowledge of God, 86

Griesbach, Professor, 14

Grocer, a, 265, 266

Gynaeocracy, explained, 271

H

Hall, Rev. Robert, 36

Happiness, the seat of, 275 – source of, 381

Hearers, of the word, the duty of, to pray for their ministers, 316 – to support their ministers, 316 – directions to, 323

Heathen nations, ignorant, fierce, and cruel, 87

Heaven, in what the happiness of, consists, 366 – duration of the happiness of, 367

Hebrew MSS., examined by Dr. Clarke, 41 – contain nothing to strengthen any error in doctrine, or obliquity in moral practice, 42

Heliogabalus, a supper of, 232

Hell, made for the devil and his angels, 361 – no injustice in, ib. – causes of the torments in, 362-363 – degrees of punishment in, 363 – eternity of its torments, ib.

Hercules, adored by the Greeks and Romans, 63

Hiera Picra, the resemblance of the censorious to, 164

Hindostan, the devotees of Brahma and Siva in, 199

Holiness, of God, 70 – man created in holiness, 77, 78. See Sanctification.

Holy Ghost, the direct witness of the, the common privilege of believers, 140 – borne in the understanding, 141, 142 – makes intercession for us, 141, 153 – bears testimony to itself, 142 – necessary to assure a man of his salvation,

143 – the witness of, has nothing to do with final perseverance, 144-145 – professed to be received by Dr. Clarke, 146 – is God's seal, 147 – the Ambassador of Christ, 148 – every good man the temple of, 148, 150 – influences of, denied by many because they never felt them, 149 – is oft excluded from his own work, ib. – produces purity, ib. – represented under the similitude of fire, 150-151 – communion of, ib. – and Advocate, 152 – may be resisted, 153 – fruit of, 154

Hooker, an observation of, 172

Hope, will enter into heaven, 125 – objects of, in heaven, ib. – definition of, 126, 165 – a universal blessing, 165 – dead hope, 167 – living hope, 168 – the soul's anchor, 169

Hore, James, Esq., kindness of, 9

Hughes, Rev. Joseph, 35

Humility, 169, 192

Husbands, duty of, 250

I

Idleness, forbidden, 201, 202

Idolatry, prostration of, 41 – forbidden, 198

Image worship, forbidden, 198

Imagination, the evil, 90 – cannot long support a mental imposture, 145

Importunate widow, parable of 228

Impress service, 206

Imputed righteousness of Christ, not found in Rom. iv., 129 – as held by many, unscriptural, ib. – greatly abused, 130 – compounded of Pharisaism and Antinomianism, 131

Incarnation of Christ, a great mystery, 101

Infidels, rash and bold, have never read the Bible, 42 – confounded by God, 42 – sneers of, 45 – some eminent in arts and sciences, 91

Infirmities, explained, 188

Inspiration, direct, 46

Intellect, the human, cannot fathom the things of God, 38, 39

Intercession of Christ, 110

Irreverent use of the name of God, forbidden, 199

Italy, received the Gospel, 40

J

Java, the followers of Budhoo, in, 199

Jehovah, possessed of infinite perfections, 58

Job, 330

Joseph, history of, 44

Joy, religious, 164 – earthly, ib.

Judgment, general, awfulness and order of, 359

Justice of God, 68
Justification, explained, 128 – precedes sanctification ib. – is complete when it takes place, ib. – justification by faith, one of the grandest displays of the mercy of God, ib. – is plain, ib. –free, ib. – needed by all, ib. – is through the blood of Christ, and not by his obedience to the moral law, 129

K

Kennicott, Miss, kindness of, 9
King, Christ a, 103
Kingdom of Christ, 103
Knowledge, man created in, 77 – the importance of, 376

L

Language, confusion of every, but that of truth, 52 – in dead languages, the best authors should be selected, 315
Lavington, Bishop, 147
Law, signification of, 47 – a system of instruction, ibid. – aims at God's glory, ibid. – among the Romans was hung up in the most public places, 49 – called by the Greeks, nomos, 49 – by the law is the knowledge of sin, 51, 117 – not a system of external rites and ceremonies, 51 – a spiritual system, ibid. – it could not pardon, ibid. – it ends where Christ begins, 52 – what it serveth, 116 – should be preached, 117 – the giving of the, on Sinai, 197 – the folly of going to, 413
Learning, explained, 288
Lepers, ten could associate together, 92
Life, eternal, given in Christ, 132 – God the Fountain and Author of, 204 – life itself a wonder, 355
Light, the emblem of the purity, perfection, and goodness of God, 70
Literary merit, Dr. Clarke's notions of, 315
Littleton's Classical Dictionary, 3
Lives of the Saints, 45
Lord, signification of, 57 – Christ a, 102
Lord's Supper, instituted by Christ, 243 – unleavened bread should be used in the celebration of the, ib. – blessing and touching the bread mere Popish ceremonies, 244 – the bread should be broken, ibid. – a vile compound substituted for wine, condemned, ibid. – the design of, 245 – improper communicants, who, 246 – when and how it should be received, 247 – reasons for, 248
Love, God's love infinite, 63, 66

– love to God defined, 154 – spring of all our actions, 156 – counteracts the carnal mind, 156 – the image of God in the soul, 157 – preserves all the other graces, ibid. – indispensable, ibid. – the essence of religion, 158 – enemies should be the objects of, 162 – does not cast out every kind of fear, 162
Lust of power, is diabolical, 411
Luke, the facts he mentions iii, 1, 2, confirm the evangelical history, 44
Lying, forbidden, 210

M

Majesty of God, 70
Malevolence, none in God, 65, 68
Malice, forbidden, 205
Man, creation of, 75 – astonishing powers of, 76 – made in the image of God, 77 – made immortal, 78 – the work of Elohim, 79 – was adapted to his residence and occupation, ib. – had a law, 80, 81 – fall of, 82 – effects of the fall of, 83 – born in sin, 85 – without power, 86 – ungodly, 88 – a slave to his passions, 93 – redemption of, 104
Masters, duties of, 269
Materialism, the doctrine of, not apostolic, 357

Meekness, 169
Men without principle will sell themselves, 333
Methodism, Dr. Clarke's attachment to, 27, –- reason of the ruin of, in Scotland, 249 – effects of, 400
Methodist Preachers, lives of, 25
Methodists, the experience of, 149 – do not refer to Mr. Wesley, in proof of the doctrine of the witness of the Spirit, ib. – profess the doctrine of Christian perfection, 177-178
Milton, a passage from, 165 – what conscience is called by, 386
Millennium, the, explained, 415
Mining, the dangers of, 337
Ministers of the Gospel, the call of, 281, 285 – qualifications of, 282, 298 – the importance of the charge of, 284 – should not decry learning and science, 286-287 – should not preach for hire, 291, 292 – ought to be esteemed in love, and supplied with the conveniences and comforts of life, 292 – should not intermeddle with secular employments, 293 – should not be frequent in their visits to the rich, nor be lords over God's heritage, 294 – should preach the law, 296 – and avoid continually finding fault with the people, 297 –

nor conform to worldly fashions, ib. – should be continent of their tongues, 298 – should act with great caution, 299, 305 – must exercise discipline, 299 – how they should endeavour to avoid contagion in visiting the sick, 301 – trials and comforts of, 302 – should be diligent, 304 – should be men of prayer, 305 – should be judicious in their choice of texts, 307 – should guard against flowery preaching, ib., 313 – a hint to, by George III., 309 – their behavior in the pulpit, 310 – should not meddle with politics, 312 – should baptize in public, ib. – should administer the Lord's supper reverently, ibid. – evil reports against should be cautiously received, 316 – should be prayed for, ibid. – supported, 316 – are often neglected when aged and worn-out, 317
Miracle, explained, 415
Miracles, 40 – wrought by Christ, 99
Monarchy, explained, 271
Mohammedans, 221, 320, 386
Mosaic dispensation, 46
Moses, he alone gives a consistent and rational account of the creation, 39 – his works a general text book, 43 – prayer of, 219 – did not appoint musical instruments to be used in the Divine worship, 233
Murder, forbidden, 204
Music, the least of all the liberal arts, 26 – instruments of, in a place of worship, repugnant to the spirit of Christianity, 232, 234
Mythology, heathen, 3

N

Nachash, 82
Nadab and Abihu, 215
Napier, invention of the logarithims by, 378
Nature, delights in progression, 47 – the idol of infidels, 91
Newton, Rev. John, 34
Newton, Sir Isaac, 286, 378
Nichols, translation of Arminius's Works, by, 34

O

Oaths, false, forbidden, 198, 199, 200
Oligarchy, explained, 272
Omnipotence of God, 61
Omnipresence of God, 63
Omniscience of God, 65
Oracles, heathen, struck dumb, 41
Owen, Rev. John, 15
Oxen, God cares for, 203

P

Painting, time spent in, 262
Papists, a doctrine of the, 192 – God represented by, 198
Parable, explained, 415
Parents, should be thankful for children, 255 – duties of, 258, 259, 262 – admonition to indolent, 260 – should not strive to prevent their sons from becoming missionaries, 264 – should not make matches for their children, 266 – how far they should lay up money, 266
Parkhurst, Hebrew Lexicon by, 30
Party spirit, the effects of, in political matters, 412
Pascal, Blaise, 286
Passover, the, when and why celebrated, 244
Patriarchal dispensation, 46 – government, 271
Paul, St., his charge to the pastors of the church at Ephesus and Miletus, 286 – the learning of, 288 – call of, to the ministry, 289
Pawson, Mr. 12
Pawson, Mrs., her opinion of Dr. Clarke, 13
Peace, explained, 162 – to live in peace with others often difficult, ibid.
Perfection, Christian, opposed to all bad tempers, 132 – explained, 172, 173, 185 – objections to, answered, 175 – not disclaimed by St. Paul, Phil. iii. 12, 178. See Sanctification.
Perjury, forbidden, 210
Persecution, a proof of the wickedness of man's heart, 93 – should be expected by the righteous, 338 – should not be coveted, 339
Persians, destitute of the knowledge of God, 86
Pharaoh, the character of, 323, 341
Philanthropy, a character of God, 67
Philological Society, Liverpool and Manchester, 14
Philosophers, the most accurate of them, confirm the Mosaic account of the creation, 39, 43 – the Greek, opposed Christianity, 41 – were confounded, ibid. – the virtue of, 132, 221
Philosophy, every Christian should study, 444 – what, in its several stages, 183-184
Phocion, the wife of, 391
Physiognomist, an ancient, 183
Poets, Dr. Clarke's reading of, 26
Political party spirit, a disgrace to England, 412
Polyglot Bible, 10, 14, 17
Poor, duties of the, 276 – blessedness of the 278
Popes, the arrogance of, 198
Porrus, 14

Porson, Professor, 15
Power, lust of, 411
Praise, the duty of all, 229
Pratt, Rev. Josiah, 17
Prayer, irreverent, 199 – defined, 217 – parts of, ibid. – long prayers, ib. – technical prayers, ibid. – design of prayer, 218 – mental, 218 – closet, 220 – family, ibid. – the object of, 220 – posture in, 221 – watchfulness in, 214 – the Lord's prayer, 222 – faith in, ib. – the medium of, 223 – subjects of, ibid. – efficacy of, 225
Precepts, of the Bible, 39
Pride, absurd, 169, 192
Prideaux's History, 30
Priest, Christ a, 102
Priestley, Dr. 394
Prince of Peace, Christ the, 102
Principles, general, of the Christian religion, 370
Profession of religion necessary, 383
Promises, of Scripture, 40
Prophecies, fulfillment of, 40 – concerning Christ, 44
Prophet, Christ a, 102
Prophets, the, indebted to the books of Moses, 43
Proprietors of stage-coaches encouraged the breach of the Sabbath, 203
Protestants, a saying of certain, 192
Providence, universally energetic, 62, 343 – mysterious, 344
Psalms of David, versified by Dr. Clarke, 3
Purgatory, the doctrine of, baseless, 174, 192, 361, 362

Q

Qualifications for a Minister of Christ, 282
Quarles, lines from, 166-167

R

Rabbins, an opinion of the, 215
Rector of Manaccan, 147
Redemption by Christ, 106, 129
Regeneration, necessary, 137 – the effect of a Divine energy, ibid.
Reineccius, 14
Religion, what, 382 – profession of, 383
Repentance, defined, 112 – mistakes respecting, ibid. – confession of sin, 113 – restitution, 114 – instant repentance urged upon all, 115
Reprobation, 68, 120, 374
Resurrection of the dead, a work of God, 63 – revealed in the Scriptures, 359 – Christ's proved, 152
Review, Professor Bentley's opinion of what it should be, 14-15
Rich, dangers of the, 275 – duties of the, ib.

Righteousness, man created in, 77-78

Rings in the matrimonial service, why unadorned, 253

Rites and ceremonies, disputes about, 163

Robes, of the saints, explained, 133

Romans, ignorant of God, 86 – a maxim of the, 209

Rome, government of, 49 – church of, 199, 235, 236, 239, 298

Royal Irish Academy, 18

Rulers, what we owe to, 271

Rymer's Fœdera, 16

S

Sabbath, held on the first day of the week, 159 – profanation of, forbidden, 200 – explained, 200 – as a political regulation, wise and beneficent, ib. – why not insisted on by our Lord and his apostles, 201 – kept by the first Christians, ib. – a type of heaven, ib. – how it should be kept, 203

Sailors, constant peril of, 337

Salvation, effected by the power of God, 63 – the order of, 138-139

Sanctification, explained, 171 – entire, must be obtained in this world, ib., 175, 182 – opposition to, a proof that man is fallen from God, 173 – effected by the blood of Jesus, 175, 177 – professors of, 175, 178 – may be lost, 179 – God's holiness a reason for, 186 – felicity of those who possess, 190 – believers encouraged to seek, 192 – not to be sought gradatim, 194

Satan, God can destroy the power of, 62 – a speech of, 165 – brought sin into the world, 183 – all other evil spirits under the government of, 327 – fashionable to deny the existence of, 328 – deniers of, seldom pray, ib. – enmity between men and, 329 – temptations of, 329 – appalling representations probably made by, to Job, 330 – wicked men led captive by, ib. – the will of man cannot be forced by, 332

Schism, explained, 411

Schrevelius, 30

Science, first principles of every, implanted in the mind of Adam, 378

Scott, Robert, Esq. 20

Scriptures, the necessity of the, 38 – proofs that they are revelations from God, 38, 39 – the name generally give to, 39 – the oldest records among the Jews and Christians, mention the books both by number and name, of the Old Testament, 41 – biography of, impartial, 45 – how they have

been given, 46 – the use of, 39, 47, 49 – intended for all, 52, directions for the profitable reading of, 324
Self-interest, caution against, 413
Sellon, Rev. W., works of, recommended, 25
Servants, duties of, 269
Shetland Isles, mission to, 19, 20 – questions relating to, 403
Simeon ben Joachi, his description of the mystery in the word "Elohim," 72
Sin, the power of God can destroy, 62 – original, 85, 91 – universality of, ib. – effects of, 88-89 – infection of, 92 – tyranny of, 93 – besetting, 94 – the unpardonable, 95 – malignity of, 105 – cannot be destroyed by suffering, 116 – indwelling, cannot humble, 175 – no necessity of committing, 184-185
Sincerity, explained, 186
Singers, character of, 231, 232
Singing, the abuse of, 231, 232
Singularity, not always criminal, 384
Slander, forbidden, 210
Slavery, 414
Slothfulness, natural to man, 350
Socrates, the force of his philosophy, 184
Soldier, a drunken, converted, 10
Solomon, his opinion of matrimony, 252
Sonship, eternal, of Christ, 371
South, Dr., 34
Southey, Mr., a charitable hope of, 147
Space, not a part of God, 57
Spirit of God alone knows the mind of God, 39. See Holy Ghost
Spiritual slothfulness, reproved, 350
Spirituality of God, 59
Stars, paucity of large, 188
State of separate spirits, 357
Stealing, forbidden, 206
Sturm's Reflections, a translation of, 14
Subjects, duties of, 271
Suffering cannot destroy sin, 116
Suicide, forbidden, 204
Sunday-schools, the effects of, 410
Superstition, never produces settled peace, 145
Suretyship, evils of, 414
Sussex, His Royal Highness the Duke of, 18
Swearing, false, forbidden, 199
Sympathy, unaccountable, 160

T

Tale-bearing, forbidden, 210
Tea, never used by Dr. Clarke, 8
Temperance, recommended, 306
Temptation, the process of, 334 – a part of our Christian

warfare, ib. – what meant by entering into, ib. – no man exempted from, 335 – how to resist, 336
Theocracy, explained, 271
Theseus, 63
Time, improvement of, 416
Titus, epistle to, contains the duty of a Gospel minister, 286
Tobacco, the abuse of, 394
Trances, revelation given in, 46
Travellers, constant peril of, 337
Trial by Jury, a blessing, 274
Tribute, should be rendered to Caesar, 273
Trinity, the doctrine of the stated, 72, 370 – proofs from Scripture, 72, 73 – may be collected from appearances in nature, 73 – prayer to the, ib.
Truth, the language of, never confounded, 52. See Knowledge
Tuisco, adored by our ancestors, 63
Tyranny, explained, 271

U

Unbelief, inconsistency of, 119 – the damning sin, 122 – effects of, ib.
Union, among the followers of Christ, 158
Unity of God, 58
Unjust Judge, parable of, 228
Unregenerate men hate religion, 91
Usury, condemned, 414

V

Vales to servants, a disgrace to their masters, 269
Virgil, Eclogues and Georgics of, 2
Virgin Mary, worshipped by the Papists, 199
Visions, revelation given in, 46

W

Walpole, Sir Robert, 333
Walton, Polyglott Bible by, 10
War, 89, 204
Watchfulness, the necessity of, 350
Wesley, Rev. Charles, his character as a hymnologist, 235
Wesley, Rev. John, a letter of, on tea, 8 – ditto to Dr. Clarke, 11, a saying of, 26, 90 – the works of, recommended, 25, 36 – thought the Methodists once leaned too much towards Calvinism, 131 – not referred to by the Methodists in proof of the doctrine of the Witness of the Spirit, 149 – his opinion of preaching thrice on the same day, 310 – the preaching of, 399
Wesley, Rev. Samuel, jun., the visits of, to Lord Oxford, 269
Wesley, Mrs. Susanna,

professed to receive the knowledge of salvation, 147 – manner of training her children, 262 – did the work of an evangelist, 285

Westminster divines, an assertion of, 184

Whisperers, pests of society, 207, 209-210

Will, a free principle, 347, 373

Will of God, always good, 67

Wisdom. See Knowledge

Wives, duties of, 250

Works of charity should be performed with cheerfulness, 160, in private, if possible, ib.

World, the, ignorance of, 39 – wickedness of, 90

Worship, public, explained, 213 – the importance of, 215, reasons for, ib.

Y

Young, Dr., what conscience is called by, 386

Z

Zeal for God, recommended, 158

FINIS

www.ingramcontent.com/pod-product-compliance
Lightning Source LLC
Chambersburg PA
CBHW071645160426
43195CB00012B/1357